DIAGNOSIS AND CORRECTION IN READING INSTRUCTION

DIAGNOSIS AND CORRECTION IN READING INSTRUCTION

Dorothy Rubin

Trenton State College

Holt, Rinehart and Winston

New York   Chicago   San Francisco   Philadelphia
Montreal   Toronto   London   Sydney
Tokyo   Mexico City   Rio de Janiero   Madrid

With love to my understanding and supportive husband, Artie,
my delightful daughters, Carol and Sharon,
my precious grandchildren, Jennifer and Andrew,
and my dear brothers Herb and Jack.

Library of Congress Cataloging in Publication Data

Rubin, Dorothy.
  Diagnosis and correction in reading instruction.

  Includes bibliographies and index.
  1. Reading. 2. Reading—Ability testing. 3. Reading
—Remedial teaching. I. Title.
LB1050.2.R8   428.4′2   81-20227
                                            AACR2
ISBN 0-03-059292-5

2 3 4 5   016   9 8 7 6 5 4 3 2

CBS COLLEGE PUBLISHING
Holt, Rinehart and Winston
The Dryden Press
Saunders College Publishing

Preface

Diagnosis and Correction in Reading Instruction is based on the premise that diagnosis and correction are essential parts of reading instruction and that the two should be interwoven with instruction. If diagnosis and correction are practiced as an integral part of reading instruction on a daily basis, there should be less need for remediation. I have designed this book to help preservice and in-service teachers acquire the skills necessary to make diagnosis and correction integral parts of their daily reading program. To achieve this goal, *Diagnosis and Correction in Reading Instruction* combines theory, basic knowledge and skills, practical application, and hands-on materials.

This book starts with the role of the teacher in the diagnostic-reading and correction program because the teacher is the key person in the program. In a viable diagnostic-reading and correction program, teachers must be able to envision the totality of the reading program. They must have basic developmental reading skills at their fingertips, and they must recognize that reading is a thinking act. They must have knowledge of educational and noneducational factors that af-fect the reading act and be knowledgeable of diagnostic techniques, as well as the ability to administer and interpret them; and they must have knowledge of corrective techniques and be able to employ them. To help the teacher accomplish this kind of program, nothing should be taken for granted. In this book, nothing *is* taken for granted.

Part I sets the stage for a diagnostic-reading and correction program. I explain what a diagnostic-reading and correction program is and define special terms so that there will be no confusion when these terms are met later; then I present the teacher as the key person in the reading program, and his or her role in the program is explored. This part also presents an overview of those things a classroom teacher needs to know about tests, measurement, and evaluation. I introduce teachers to testing terminology and explain the differences between standardized and teacher-made tests, as well as differences between norm-referenced and criterion-referenced instruments. In Part II, I am concerned with the nature and interrelatedness of factors that affect reading performance.

Teachers need to know about the individual differences of children and about the educational and noneducational factors that can affect a child's ability to read if they are to provide proper instruction for their students. I explore the relationship of reading to language development, concept development, and listening; I also present a chapter on determining which students are underachieving in reading so that the teacher can identify those students who need further testing.

Part III presents instruments and techniques for the assessment and diagnosis of students' reading performance. In this part I explain and give examples of many kinds of diagnostic tests and techniques. I give special emphasis to the informal reading inventory and observation as diagnostic tools because these can be two of the classroom teacher's indispensable aids.

Part IV presents an analytical review of the basic developmental reading skills that teachers should have at their fingertips. In order to diagnose a reading problem effectively, teachers must know what skills students have and the various types of skills they should be acquiring. The chapters in Part IV also contain diagnostic tests and checklists. Chapter 13, in particular, has a special section on diagnosis and correction for selected interpretive comprehension skills.

Part V presents the diagnostic-reading and correction program in action. I present this part last because teachers need to have the background of information presented in the first four parts before they can effectively help children overcome their reading difficulties. In Chapter 15, I present scenarios about children with reading problems and show you step by step how the teacher helps each child. In Chapter 16, the emphasis is on special children and on mainstreaming. Chapter 17 is a vital chapter because it is concerned with helping you to get children to read. The last chapter highlights the importance of having parents as partners in any successful reading program and especially in a diagnostic-reading and correction program. Although it is placed last in the book, it is by no means last in importance.

To help the teacher further, a complete informal reading inventory is included in Appendix A. Instructions on how to administer it, as well as how to mark and score errors, are presented in Chapter 9. The Fry Readability Formula is also included in Appendix B as an additional aid to the teacher.

In *Diagnosis and Correction in Reading Instruction* I have tried to give principles in practical, comprehensible language as often as possible, for a book overburdened with esoteric terminology tends to obscure rather than to clarify concepts. Often, some explanations cannot be given without names, but whenever I use a technical term or one that is used in various ways, I define the term and then use it. I hope that readers will find that I have succeeded in cutting down on the number of terms to be learned and that they will benefit from a concentration on practical principles rather than one on terminology and theories.

Throughout this book the emphasis is on helping the classroom teacher incorporate diagnosis and correction as part of the ongoing developmental program on a daily basis. It is hoped that this book will help to raise the consciousness level of the teacher so that diagnosis and correction are interwoven with instruction.

Princeton, N.J.   D.R.

ACKNOWLEDGMENTS

I would like to thank David Boynton for being the personification of a perfect editor. His valuable suggestions, continuous support, intelligent insights, vast knowledge, and keen wit make working with him a pleasure, a delight, and a privilege. I would also like to thank Herman

Makler for being such a patient, kind, considerate, and extremely helpful production editor and for helping to give precision and polish to the manuscript. I enjoy working with him. In addition, I would like to express my appreciation to the administration of Trenton State College and particularly to Dean Phillip Ollio and Dr. Barbara Harned for their continued support. I would also like to express my gratitude to Dr. Ronald Johnson, University of Wisconsin—River Falls, for his scholarly suggestions and very helpful review of my manuscript. Also, I would like to thank my colleague Dr. Richard Shepherd for use of his extensive personal library. Finally, I would like to thank Dr. Edith Francis for allowing the photographs in this book to be taken in her school system, Ewing Township, and I would like to particularly thank James Foley for taking the appropriate photographs in a timely manner.

Contents

Scenario: The Profile of a First-Grade Failure   1

Part 1
SETTING THE STAGE FOR A DIAGNOSTIC-READING AND CORRECTION PROGRAM

CHAPTER 1
Introduction to a Diagnostic-Reading and Correction Program   5

Introduction   5

What Is a Diagnostic-Reading and Correction Program?   6

What Is Remedial Reading?   6

What Are the Advantages of a Diagnostic-Reading and Correction Program?   6

What Is a Developmental Reading Program?   6

Defining Reading   7

What Is Diagnosis?   10

Diagnosis and the Definition of Reading   11

Summary   12

Suggestions for Thought Questions and Activities   12

CHAPTER 2
The Teacher's Role in a Diagnostic-Reading and Correction Program   13

Introduction   13

The Teacher in a Diagnostic-Reading and Correction Program   14

The Teacher as the Key to a Good Reading Program   14

Some Important Characteristics of a Good Reading Teacher   15

Summary   18

Suggestions for Thought Questions and Activities   19

CHAPTER 3
What a Teacher Should Know About Tests, Measurement, and Evaluation   20

Introduction   20

Assessment for Diagnosis and Evaluation   21

Standardized Tests   23

Teacher-Made Tests 25

Criterion-Referenced Tests 25

Group and Individual Tests 26

Reading Tests 28

Summary 28

Suggestions for Thought Questions and Activities 29

Part II
THE NATURE AND INTERRELATEDNESS OF FACTORS THAT AFFECT READING PERFORMANCE

CHAPTER 4
Concept Development and Its Relationship to Language and Reading

Concept Development and Its Relationship to Language and Reading 33

Introduction 33

Language Development, Concept Development, and Reading 34

What Is a Concept? 35

Piaget and Concept Development 36

Semantic Mapping 38

Concept Development in Primary Grades K–3 39

Concept Development and the Educationally Disadvantaged Child 44

Summary 44

Suggestions for Thought Questions and Activities 44

CHAPTER 5
Some of the Factors That Affect Reading Performance

Some of the Factors That Affect Reading Performance 46

Introduction 46

Differentiating Between Noneducational and Educational Factors 47

Home Environment 48

Dialect and Language Differences 49

Intelligence and Reading 50

Sex Differences 51

Perceptual Factors 54

Physical Health 57

Educational Factors 58

Summary 58

Suggestions for Thought Questions and Activities 59

CHAPTER 6
Listening and Reading

Listening and Reading 61

Introduction 61

Listening as Decoding 62

Auditory Discrimination and Memory Span 62

Different Levels of Listening 64

Listening and Reading 66

The Development of Listening 68

Nonstandard English and Listening 69

Nonstandard English and Its Implications for Instruction 70

Classroom Teachers' Assessment of Listening Comprehension Skills 72

Standardized Listening Tests 73

Oral Directions Test 74

Diagnostic Checklist for Listening 77

Summary 79

Suggestions for Thought Questions and Activities 79

CHAPTER 7
Who Is Underachieving in Reading?

Who Is Underachieving in Reading? 81

Introduction 81

A Diagnostic Pattern 81

Who Is a Disabled Reader? 82

Intelligence 82

Differences Between Individual and Group Intelligence (Aptitude) Tests 84

Individual Intelligence (Aptitude) Tests 84

Group-Administered Measures of Intelligence (Aptitude) 86

Mental Age Span in the Regular Classroom 87

Reading Expectancy Formulas 89

Who Is a Candidate for Further Testing? 93

Listening Capacity Test 94

Summary 95

Suggestions for Thought Questions and Activities 95

Part III
INSTRUMENTS AND TECHNIQUES FOR THE ASSESSMENT AND DIAGNOSIS OF READING PERFORMANCE

CHAPTER 8
Standardized Reading Achievement Tests: Survey Type 99

Introduction 99

Standardized Achievement Tests and Standardized Survey Reading Tests 100

Reading Readiness Tests 103

Summary 106

Suggestions for Thought Questions and Activities 106

CHAPTER 9
Diagnostic Reading Tests and Techniques I: An Emphasis on the Informal Reading Inventory 108

Introduction 108

What Are Diagnostic Reading Tests? 109

Oral Reading 110

What Are the Purposes of an Informal Reading Inventory? 110

An Overview of the Informal Reading Inventory 111

Determining Reading Levels 112

Constructing Your Own Informal Reading Inventory 114

Diagnostic Checklist for Oral and Silent Reading 120

Administering the IRI 121

Published (Commercially Produced) IRIs Versus Teacher-Made IRIs 130

Who Should Be Given an IRI? 130

Modified IRI Approaches: A Caution 135

Miscue Analysis 137

Points of Caution Concerning IRIs 138

Summary 141

Suggestions for Thought Questions and Activities 142

CHAPTER 10
Diagnostic Reading Tests and Techniques II 144

Introduction 144

Standardized Diagnostic Oral Reading Tests 145

Standardized Diagnostic Reading Tests 146

Standardized Criterion-Referenced Reading Tests 149

Teacher-Made (Informal) Diagnostic Reading Tests 151

Teacher-Made Criterion-Referenced Tests 157

Behavioral Objectives 157

Cloze Procedure 159

Knowledge of Results and Cloze Procedure 163

Summary 163

Suggestions for Thought Questions and Activities 163

CHAPTER 11
Observation and Other Child Study Procedures as Diagnostic Techniques 165

Introduction 165

The Uses of Observation 166

Anecdotal Records 166

Checklists 168

Diagnostic Checklist of Speech Problems 169

Other Helpful Child Study Techniques 170

Summary 177

Suggestions for Thought Questions and Activities 177

Part IV
A REVIEW OF WORD RECOGNITION, COMPREHENSION, VOCABULARY EXPANSION, AND STUDY SKILLS, INCLUDING DIAGNOSTIC TESTS, CHECKLISTS, AND CORRECTIVE TECHNIQUES

CHAPTER 12
Word Recognition Skills 181

Introduction 181

Word Recognition Strategies for Pronunciation 182

Word Recognition Strategies for Word Meaning 184

Word Recognition Strategies: Some Further Remarks 186

The Importance of Decoding in Reading 186

Defining Phonics 186

Learning Phonic Skills 186

A Developmental Sequence of Phonic Instruction 187

Diagnostic Checklist for Word Recognition Skills 202

Summary 204

Suggestions for Thought Questions and Activities 204

CHAPTER 13
Reading Comprehension and Vocabulary Expansion: An Emphasis on Diagnosis and Correction 206

Introduction 206

Reading Comprehension Skills 207

Categorizing Reading Comprehension 208

Time Spent in Comprehension Instruction 209

Helping Children Acquire Comprehension Skills 209

Questioning as a Diagnostic Technique 211

Some Important Comprehension Skills: A Diagnostic and Corrective Approach 212

Completing Analogies (Word Relationships) 244

Diagnosis and Correction in Content Areas 249

Vocabulary Expansion 249

Diagnostic Checklist for Selected Reading Comprehension Skills 250

Vocabulary Expansion in Content Areas 256

Diagnostic Checklist for Vocabulary Development (Primary Grades) 256

Diagnostic Checklist for Vocabulary Development (Intermediate Grades) 258

Summary 260

Suggestions for Thought Questions and Activities 260

CHAPTER 14
Reading and Study Skills 263

Introduction 263

What Are Some Good Study Procedures? 264

How to Study 265

Concentration 267

Following Directions 269

Skimming 271

Outlining 271

Summaries 274

Knowing Your Textbook 274

Asking Questions 275

Notetaking for Studying 276

Test-Taking 277

The School Library and Library Skills 278

Diagnostic Checklist for Reading and Study Skills 280

Summary 286

Suggestions for Thought Questions and Activities 286

Part V
THE DIAGNOSTIC-READING AND CORRECTION PROGRAM IN ACTION

CHAPTER 15
Helping Children Overcome Reading Difficulties 291

Introduction 291

Student Involvement 292

Scenario 1 292

Record Keeping 293

Scenario 2 294

Scenario 3 296

Scenario 4 298

Scenario 5 299

Individualized Instruction 300

Learning Centers in the Classroom 301

Computer-Aided Instruction and Reading in a Diagnostic-Reading and Correction Program 303

Reading Management Systems 304

Peer Instruction 305

Summary 306

Suggestions for Thought Questions and Activities 306

CHAPTER 16
Helping Special Children 307

Introduction 307

The "Average" Child 308

The Borderline Child or the "Slow Learner" 308

Reading for the Borderline Child 309

Gifted Children 310

Reading for the Gifted Child 311

Mainstreaming 312

Who Are the Exceptional Children? 313

Identification Biases of Children Labeled "Educable Mentally Retarded" 314

Learning Disabilities 315

Summary 315

Suggestions for Thought Questions and Activities 315

CHAPTER 17
Getting Children to Like Books 317

Introduction 317

What Is Reading for Appreciation? 318

The Importance of Providing Time for a Reading for Appreciation Program 319

Setting the Environment for the Enjoyment of Reading in the Classroom 320

Whetting Children's Interest in Books 320

Children's Interests and Book Selection 322

Child Development Characteristics and Book Selection 322

Sex Differences in Book Selection 322

Children's Literature and Culturally Different Children 332

The Black Child and Books: A Special Look 333

Bibliotherapy 334

Readability and Interest Levels in Choosing Books 338

Television and Reading for Appreciation 340

Diagnostic Checklist for Getting
Children to Like Books 341

Summary 342

Suggestions for Thought Questions and
Activities 343

CHAPTER 18
Teachers and Parents as Partners in
the Diagnostic-Reading and Correction
Program 346

Introduction 346

Parental Involvement in the Schools 347

What Is Title I? 348

What Is the Role of Parents in Title I
Programs? 349

Parental Involvement in Preschool
Programs 350

Parental Involvement in Regular School
Reading Programs 351

Grandparents Should Be Involved Too 355

Parent-Teacher Conferences 356

Summary 357

Suggestions for Thought Questions and
Activities 357

GLOSSARY 359

APPENDIX A   Informal Reading
Inventory 367

APPENDIX B   The Fry Readability
Formula 409

Index 411

SCENARIO: THE PROFILE OF A FIRST-GRADE FAILURE

Larry is a blond, blue-eyed little boy, who comes from an upper-middle-class home. He has parents who care for him and who are highly educated. Larry, according to the statistics, should be doing well in school. He is not, though, and there are many others just like him. Why? If children like Larry have problems, what hope is there for those who don't have Larry's social and economic advantages?

Larry's parents had spoken to me about their little boy and told me how unhappy they were with his situation. They told me that Larry had been left back in the first grade because he couldn't read. His first-grade teacher and the principal had recommended that Larry repeat the first grade, and they, the parents, had not objected. They were told that by repeating the first grade, Larry would be happier and would do much better. Well, he was not happy, and he was not doing much better. Larry hated school. His personality was changing. He felt that he was dumb, and he didn't like himself very much. His parents spoke to the teacher, who said that Larry was having difficulty with the reading program, but it was the only program the school was allowed to use. She was sure that Larry would soon adjust to it. The parents, not so sure, went to see the principal. The principal told them that he and his staff knew what was good for Larry. After all, they were the professionals. Also, the principal told the parents that they were justified in retaining Larry because on the group IQ test he had scored in a range that put him in the category of borderline intelligence. He told the parents not to worry, that he and his staff knew what they were doing,

that Larry would have to continue in the same program, and that the same method of instruction would be used.

Larry's parents were confused and bitter. They did worry. The private schools would not accept Larry because the school term had already begun, and their son was becoming unhappier and unhappier. Larry didn't want to go to school. The parents, who had thought that their son was a bright boy, were beginning to wonder whether the IQ test score was correct and whether their son was a slow learner.

Larry's parents decided to go to outside sources for help. They asked me to test Larry, and I consented. When I met him, he said to me, "I'm the biggest one in my class because I was left back. Everyone knows that I was left back. I hate school." We talked for a little while, and I tried to learn about some of the things he liked to do. I discovered that he enjoyed looking through *National Geographic,* that he loved sports, that he went fishing and camping with his father and brother, and that he loved animals.

Even though Larry was only in the first grade, I decided to give him an informal reading inventory. When I asked him to state the words in the word recognition list, he picked up the sheet with the words and put it so close to his face that the paper was actually touching his nose. I asked Larry if he wore glasses. He said, "No." Larry had difficulty recognizing the words in isolation. I had him start at the lowest level in oral reading. Even at the preprimer level, he had trouble decoding words. His decoding problems were so pronounced that I decided to give Larry a listening capacity test because I felt his decoding problems would probably hinder his comprehension. I read aloud the passages to Larry and then asked him questions about them. Larry was able to answer the comprehension questions almost perfectly up to the seventh-grade level. He was able to tell me what a nocturnal bird was, as well as answer some very difficult and involved questions.

Larry is a highly able boy; he certainly is not "dumb." A crime has been perpetrated against him. Who is to blame? When Larry was retained, no one had given him any diagnostic reading tests or an individual IQ test. To give a child who is having decoding problems a group IQ test and then to use that test to assert that the child is of borderline intelligence is ludicrous. The parents should have noticed from Larry's behavior that he had some kind of eye problem. When the parents were asked about it they claimed that the school nurse had tested Larry's eyes and that no eye problem had been noticed. From Larry's behavior, the teacher also should have noticed that Larry appeared to have some kind of eye problem and should have recommended that the parents have his eyes checked by an eye doctor, since the school nurse only tests for nearsightedness and farsightedness. Based on my suggestion, Larry was taken to an ophthalmologist. The eye specialist found that Larry had very severe astigmatism, which probably would account for his decoding problems. Larry had difficulty focusing on words. This does not excuse the school for insisting that Larry adjust to the program rather than adjusting the program to suit Larry. Regardless of who is to blame, Larry sees himself as a failure. At seven years of age, he can't wait to leave school. Damage has been done to Larry, and he is still suffering from it.

This profile of Larry, which is based on fact, was not written to show the school personnel as being the devils and the author as being the angel. It has been written to raise the consciousness level of teachers to the importance of diagnosis.

It would be foolish and presumptuous of me to say that one book in diagnostic-reading and correction will be able to do away with all the reading problems that teachers will encounter in their classrooms. However, it will help teachers gain an insight into the dynamics of a diagnostic-reading and correction program, as well as the skills necessary to implement it.

Part I

SETTING THE STAGE FOR A DIAGNOSTIC-READING AND CORRECTION PROGRAM

CHAPTER 1

Introduction to a Diagnostic-Reading and Correction Program

INTRODUCTION

"And only *one* for birthday presents, you know. There's glory for you!"

"I don't know what you mean by 'glory,'" Alice said.

Humpty Dumpty smiled contemptuously. "Of course you don't—till I tell you. I meant 'there's a nice knockdown argument for you.'"

"But 'glory' doesn't mean 'a nice knockdown argument,'" Alice objected.

"When *I* use a word," Humpty Dumpty said in rather a scornful tone, "it means just what I choose it to mean—neither more nor less."

"The question is," said Alice, "whether you *can* make words mean so many different things."

"The question is," said Humpty Dumpty, "which is to be master—that's all."[1]

Communication cannot take place unless there is a consensus of meaning. In the field of

reading, similar terms are used many times to convey different meanings, and this often leads to confusion. This chapter will define a number of terms that are used in this book and discuss the relationship of diagnosis to the ongoing reading program. After you finish reading this chapter, you should be able to answer the following questions:

1. What is a diagnostic-reading and correction program?

2. What is remedial reading?

3. What is a developmental reading program?

4. How is reading defined in this book?

5. What is a total integrative reading program?

6. How does a definition of reading influence the diagnostic-reading program?

7. What are some principles of a good diagnostic-reading and correction program?

[1]Lewis Carroll, *Through the Looking Glass* (New York: Grosset & Dunlap, 1963), pp. 216–17.

WHAT IS A DIAGNOSTIC-READING AND CORRECTION PROGRAM?

A diagnostic-reading and correction program (DRCP) consists of reading instruction interwoven with diagnosis and correction. This program is based on the premise that diagnosis and correction are an integral part of the daily developmental reading program and that teachers can and should be able to implement such a program if they have the necessary skills.

WHAT IS REMEDIAL READING?

Corrective reading programs take place in the regular classroom. Remedial reading programs usually take place outside the regular classroom and are handled by special personnel such as a special reading teacher, a therapist, or a clinician. The special reading teacher usually works with students who have severe reading problems that cannot be handled in the regular classroom. The students are usually referred for help by the regular classroom teacher.

WHAT ARE THE ADVANTAGES OF A DIAGNOSTIC-READING AND CORRECTION PROGRAM?

A diagnostic-reading and correction program is superior to remedial reading programs because it focuses on potential reading problems or those related to reading and tries to head them off. It is part of the ongoing reading program, and it takes place in the regular classroom under the leadership of the classroom teacher. The sooner an astute teacher recognizes a problem, the sooner the problem is diagnosed; and the sooner steps are taken to correct the problem, the less need there will be for later remediation.

A diagnostic-reading and correction program could help to stop the "failure cycle." For example, if a child continually has reading difficulties, he begins to see himself as a failure; his self-concept is destroyed. The more he perceives himself as a failure, the more he fails. And so the cycle continues.

A diagnostic-reading and correction program will not make the jobs of special reading personnel obsolete, but it will make their load lighter and easier. It would be foolhardy to presume that the initiation of a diagnostic-reading and correction program would eliminate all reading problems. It will not. However, its implementation would free special reading personnel so that they could spend more time with those students who have severe reading problems, and it would give reading therapists more time to act as consultants to the regular classroom teachers.

WHAT IS A DEVELOPMENTAL READING PROGRAM

Ask three different reading authorities to give you a definition of *developmental reading,* and the chances are high that you will receive three different definitions. (This is, of course, not limited to merely *developmental reading* or a few terms but seems to be the general rule in the field of reading.) The difficulty with such terms is that they are so commonly used that many persons assume that they are using them in the same manner. This can be an erroneous assumption and lead to confusion. For example, some reading authorities differentiate among developmental reading, functional reading, and recreational reading. For these persons, *developmental reading* refers to those activities "in which the main purpose of the teacher is to bring about an improvement in reading skills—activities in which learning to read is the main goal.

Functional reading includes all reading in which the primary aim is to obtain information. . . . *Recreational reading* consists of reading activities that have enjoyment, entertainment, and appreciation as major purposes.''[2] Some reading authorities differentiate among the developmental reading program, the corrective reading program, and the remedial reading program; whereas some others look upon the developmental reading program as encompassing the corrective and remedial program. For example, some well-known reading authorities define the developmental reading program as emphasizing ''reading instruction that is designed to develop systematically the skills and abilities considered essential at each level of reading advancement.''[3] For these persons, developmental reading instruction, corrective reading instruction, and remedial reading instruction all come under the umbrella of the developmental reading program, and developmental reading encompasses functional and recreational reading as well as all those skills that are needed to learn to read.

Developmental reading, in this book, refers to all those reading skills that are systematically and sequentially developed to help students become effective readers throughout their schooling. ''All those reading skills'' refers to learning-to-read skills as well as reading-to-learn skills and reading for appreciation. Developmental reading is the major reading program, and the diagnostic-corrective program that takes place in the regular classroom is part of the developmental reading program; all other programs are adjuncts to the developmental program, but they are also developmental in nature. For example, the remedial reading program that takes place outside the regular classroom has as its prime purpose the task of helping students attain those developmental skills that they lack. This program, which usually employs different strategies and techniques, is not a replacement for the student's classroom developmental instruction in reading; it is reading instruction that is given in *addition* to the reading instruction in the regular classroom, and therefore it must be related to or considered part of the developmental program. This is imperative because studies show that there is a consistent negative relationship between the time students spend in ''pull-out'' classes and reading.[4] Many times the ''pull-out'' program becomes the complete reading program for severely retarded readers, and rather than spending more time, the students spend less time in reading. Also, if the remedial program is looked on as separate from the developmental reading program, there is usually a lack of coordination between the teaching of the regular classroom teacher and that of the remedial reading teacher.

DEFINING READING

The relationship of reading to diagnosis is important in a diagnostic-reading and correction program. To fully understand this relationship it is first essential to define reading. The definition that we choose will not only influence the instructional component of the program but also the diagnostic component. (See ''Diagnosis and the Definition of Reading'' in this chapter.)

John is able to decode correctly all the words in a passage; however, he cannot answer any

[2]Albert J. Harris and Edward R. Sipay, *How to Increase Reading Ability,* 7th ed. (New York: Longman, 1980), p. 73.
[3]Emerald V. Dechant and Henry P. Smith, *Psychology in Teaching Reading,* 2nd ed. (Englewood Cliffs, N.J.: Prentice-Hall, 1977), p. 393.

[4]G. V. Glass and M. L. Smith, *Pull-Out in Compensatory Education,* paper prepared for Office of the Commissioner, U.S. Office of Education, 1977.

questions about it. Is John reading? Susie makes a number of errors in decoding words, but the errors she makes do not seem to prevent her from answering any of the questions on the passage. Is Susie reading? Maria reads a passage on something about which she has very strong feelings; she has difficulty answering the questions based on the passage because of her attitudes. Is she reading? José can decode the words in the passage, and he thinks that he knows the meaning of all the words; however, José cannot answer the questions. Is José reading?

To answer these questions, we would have to state: They depend on our definition of reading. A definition of reading is necessary because it will influence what goals will be set in the development of the reading program. A teacher who sees reading as a one-way process, consisting simply of the decoding of symbols or the relating of sounds to symbols, will develop a different type of program from that of a teacher who looks on reading as getting meaning from the printed page.

There is no single, set definition of reading. As a result, it is difficult to define it simply. A broad definition, which has been greatly used, is that reading is the bringing to and the getting of meaning from the printed page. This implies that readers bring their backgrounds, their experiences, as well as their emotions, into play. Students who are upset or physically ill will bring these feelings into the act of reading, and this will influence their interpretative processes. A person well versed in reading matter will gain more from the material than someone less knowledgeable. A student who is a good critical thinker will gain more from a critical passage than one who is not. A student who has strong dislikes will come away with different feelings and understandings from those of a pupil with strong likings.

By defining reading as the bringing to and getting of meaning from the printed page, Susie is actually the only child who is reading, because she is the only one who *understands* what she is reading. Although John can verbalize the words, he has no comprehension of them. Maria can also decode the words, but her strong feelings about the topic have prevented her from getting the message that the writer is conveying. José can decode the words and knows the meanings of the individual words, but either he is not able to get the sense of the whole passage or he does not know the meaning of the words in another context.

Reading as a Total Integrative Process

By using a broad or global definition of reading, we see reading as a total integrative process that includes the following domains: (1) the *affective,* (2) the *perceptual,* and (3) the *cognitive.*

The Affective Domain

The affective domain includes our feelings and emotions. The way we feel influences greatly the way we look at stimuli on a field. It may distort our perception. For example, if we are hungry and we see the word *fool,* we would very likely read it as *food.* If we have adverse feelings about certain things, these feelings will probably influence how we interpret what we read. Our feelings will also influence what we decide to read. Obviously, attitudes exert a directive and dynamic influence on our readiness to respond.

The Perceptual Domain

In the perceptual domain, perception can be defined as giving meaning to sensations or the ability to organize stimuli on a field. How we organize stimuli depends largely on our background of experiences and on our sensory receptors. If, for example, our eyes are organically defective, those perceptions involving sight would be distorted. In the act of reading, visual perception is a most important factor. Children need to control their eyes so they move from left to right across the page. Eye movements influence what the reader perceives.

Although what we observe is never in exact accord with the physical situation,[5] readers must be able to accurately decode the graphemic (written) representation. If, however, readers have learned incorrect associations, it will affect their ability to read. For example, if a child reads the word *gip* for *pig* and is not corrected, this may become part of his or her perceptions. Whether children perceive the word as a whole, in parts, or as individual letters will also determine whether they will be good or poor readers. The more mature readers are able to perceive more complex and extensive graphemic patterns as units. They are also able to give meaning to mutilated words such as

Perception is a cumulative process which is based on an individual's background of experiences. The perceptual process is influenced by physiological factors as well as affective ones. As already stated, a person who is hungry may read the word *fool* as *food*. Similarly, a person with a biased view toward a topic may delete, add, or distort what is being read.

Betts presents a number of factors on which the perceptual process of decoding writing into speech is dependent. Here are most of them:[6]

1. Motivation, for example, the attitudinal factor *need* to identify the unknown part or parts of a particular word.

2. Attention as a powerful selector of stimulus information to be processed and as a constant feature of perceptual activity.

3. Set, a determiner of perception, which, among other things, causes the pupil to regard reading as a poverty-stricken word-calling process or as a thinking process.

4. Grouping of stimuli into recognizable syllables, phonograms, and other patterns for making optimum use of a limited span of attention.

5. Meaning, both structural and referential, needed for the closure of perception.

6. Contrast, such as the contrastive letter patterns which represent contrastive sound patterns.

7. Feedback, a circular process, from the examination of letter groupings of the written word to the sounds of the spoken word; for example, the *application* of word perception skills to the written word during silent reading.

8. Closure, as in the identification of the word *noise* after the usual sound represented by *oi* is recalled.

The Cognitive Domain

The cognitive domain includes the areas involving thinking. Under this umbrella we would place all the comprehension skills (see Chapter 13). Persons who have difficulty in thinking (the manipulation of symbolic representations) would obviously have difficulty in reading. Although the cognitive domain goes beyond the perceptual domain, it builds and depends on a firm perceptual base. That is, if readers have faulty perceptions, they will also have faulty

[5]Julian E. Hochberg, *Perception* (Englewood Cliffs, N.J.: Prentice-Hall, 1964), p. 3.

[6]Emmett A. Betts, "Linguistics and Reading," *Education* 86 (April 1966): 457–58.

concepts. (See Chapter 4 for a discussion of concept development.)

Recent research about the human brain and cognition is providing new and interesting information which may affect our teaching practices. The human brain is actively involved in selecting, transforming, organizing, and remembering information;[7] in many ways, it is analogous to a computer's information-processing system. However, the human brain, unlike the computer, is constantly reprograming itself, generating new strategies, and learning new knowledge. The better strategies a learner has for processing information, the better able the learner is to retain and retrieve the information. Recent studies on the brain are looking at the kinds of strategies that people use to organize, encode, and store information. The researchers are also interested in how individuals differ in their information-processing strategies; that is, researchers are interested in the cognitive styles that the individuals use.

Research on the brain and cognitive processes have implications for teaching and instruction. By looking at the brain as an active consumer of information, able to interpret information and draw inferences from it as well as ignore some information and selectively attend to other information, the learner is "given a new, more important active role and responsibility in learning from instruction and teaching."[8] Readers as active consumers of information relate what they are reading to their past experiences; they interpret information, draw inferences from it, ignore some information, and attend to other information. Good readers are good thinkers.

[7]Merlin C. Wittrock, "Education and the Cognitive Processes of the Brain," *The National Society for the Study of Education Seventy-seventh Yearbook,* Part II (1978): 64.
[8]Ibid., p. 101.

WHAT IS DIAGNOSIS?

Some educators are disturbed by the term *diagnosis* because it seems to connote illness or disease, and they do not like the analogies that are often made between medicine and education. *Diagnosis* is a term that has been borrowed from medicine. For example, the first definition in *Webster's Third International Dictionary* is as follows: "the act or art of identifying a disease from its signs and symptoms. . . ." The third definition given for *diagnosis* is, however, a more general one: "investigation or analysis of the cause or nature of a condition, situation, or problem. . . ." Reread the first definition, and replace the term *disease* with the phrase *reading difficulties and strengths.* Now reread the first and third definitions. You should have the following: Diagnosis is the act or art of identifying reading difficulties and strengths from their signs and symptoms, and diagnosis involves the investigation or analysis of the cause(s) or nature of a condition, situation, or problem. This definition does describe diagnosis as it is used in reading. It seems obvious that we should not be concerned with where the term comes from, that is, from which field it has been borrowed, but rather whether the definition that we use is valid for our purposes.

Let us analyze the definition further.

1. The first step in diagnosis is the identification of strengths and weaknesses by observing certain signs or symptoms. Some examples of these signs or symptoms would be a child's inability or ability to read fluently, a child's inability or ability to decode words; or a child's ability or inability to answer questions on comprehension.

2. The second step is to determine the cause or causes of the difficulty by analyzing the

kinds of difficulties the child is having. This is done through a careful investigation of the strategies and techniques the child uses in reading. It may include looking for some of the underlying factors, noneducative or educative, that could be causing the reading problem.

Note that in the first step, we look for both reading difficulties and strengths; knowledge of what a child can do is helpful many times in giving us an insight into a child's reading problem. In the second step, we generally find that a reading problem is due to a number of factors rather than to just one. (See Chapter 7 for information on a diagnostic pattern.)

DIAGNOSIS AND THE DEFINITION OF READING

As has already been stated, the definition that is chosen for reading also influences the diagnostic program. If we see reading as a total integrative process, diagnosis should also be seen as a total integrative process. If a global definition is chosen, then the diagnostic program will be a broad one. Under a global definition, when one makes a diagnosis, it is recognized that a reading problem is usually caused by many different factors. Therefore, a diagnosis of a reading problem would include considerations of ecological (environmental), personal, and intellectual factors. Educative factors, as well as noneducative ones, are scrutinized. It is recognized that learning takes place in some kind of relationship; that is, not all children respond in the same way, and not all children respond to the same person. An atmosphere conducive to growth is recognized as important, as well as the maxim that success breeds success. Diagnosis is looked on as continuous, as underlying prevention as well as remediation, and as interwoven

with instruction.[9] The emphasis in diagnosis is on determining the child's reading problems and the conditions causing them. Here is a list of some principles of diagnosis:

The Principles of Diagnosis

1. Diagnosis underlies prevention.
2. Early diagnosis is essential.
3. Diagnosis is continuous.
4. Diagnosis and instruction are interwoven.
5. Diagnosis is a *means* to correction.
6. Diagnosis is not an end in itself.
7. Teacher-made as well as published instruments are used in diagnosis.
8. Noneducative as well as educative factors are diagnosed.
9. Diagnosis identifies strengths as well as deficiencies.
10. Diagnosis is an individual process; that is, in diagnosis the teacher focuses on the individual child. (Diagnostic information can be obtained from working in a one-to-one relationship with a child, from observing a child in a group, or from observing a child doing seatwork.)
11. The diagnostician looks for a number of causes of reading difficulty rather than just one.
12. The diagnostician is able to establish rapport with the student.
13. The diagnostician avoids labeling students.
14. The diagnostician treats each student as an individual worthy of respect.

[9]Ruth Strang, *Diagnostic Teaching of Reading* (New York: McGraw-Hill, 1969), pp. 23–24.

SUMMARY

Chapter 1 is an introduction to a diagnostic-reading and correction program. Such a program consists of reading instruction interwoven with diagnosis and correction. Since the definition that is chosen for reading will influence the diagnostic program, reading is defined in a global manner: Reading is the bringing to and getting of meaning from the printed page. By using a broad definition, we look on reading as a total integrative process. Under a global definition when one makes a diagnosis, it is recognized that a reading problem is usually caused by many different factors.

SUGGESTIONS FOR THOUGHT QUESTIONS AND ACTIVITIES

1. You have been assigned to a special committee to develop a reading program in your school that would help stem the number of reading problems that now exist. You have decided to advocate the implementation of a diagnostic-reading and correction program. Give your rationale for doing so. How would you go about implementing such a program?

2. Make a study of the ways that persons in a school district are defining *developmental reading*.

3. Make a study in your school district to see whether remedial reading is a "pull-out program" that is or is not integrated with the developmental reading program.

4. Ask a number of teachers how they define reading. Observe their classes and try to discern whether their reading program reflects their definition of reading.

SELECTED BIBLIOGRAPHY

Clymer, Theodore. "Research in Corrective Reading: Findings, Problems, and Observations." In *Corrective Reading in the Elementary Classroom,* eds. Marjorie S. Johnson and Roy A. Kress. Newark, Del.: International Reading Association, 1967.

Dechant, Emerald V., and Henry P. Smith. *Psychology in Teaching Reading,* 2nd ed. Englewood Cliffs, N.J.: Prentice-Hall, 1977.

Harris, Albert J., and Edward R. Sipay. *How to Increase Reading Ability,* 7th ed. New York: Longman, 1980.

Rubin, Dorothy. *A Practical Approach to Teaching Reading.* New York: Holt, Rinehart and Winston, 1982.

Smith, Frank. *Understanding Reading,* 2nd ed. New York: Holt, Rinehart and Winston, 1978.

Spache, George D. *Diagnosing and Correcting Reading Disabilities,* 2nd ed. Boston: Allyn and Bacon, 1981.

Strange, Michael, and Richard L. Allington. "Use the Diagnostic Prescriptive Model Knowledgeably." *The Reading Teacher* 31 (December 1977): 290–93.

Wittrock, Merlin C., "Learning and the Brain." In *The Brain and Psychology,* ed. Merlin C. Wittrock. New York: Academic Press, 1980.

CHAPTER 2

The Teacher's Role in a Diagnostic-Reading and Correction Program

INTRODUCTION

David is a quiet boy with an endearing smile. He is small in stature and not well dressed; he is determined to learn to read. Although he is in the fourth grade, David cannot read. "I want to read," he told his teacher. "My father bring one big book when he came home at night. He say it for me to read. I read. You see." David has hope, so he comes to school each day. But how much longer will he do so? Will he succeed in entering and mastering the land of books filled with those magic symbols called words? Will he unlock these symbols and discover the wonders of far-off places? David is waiting. Will we, as teachers, be able to help him?

The answer depends on how well we as teachers are equipped to diagnose the reading problems of the Davids in our classrooms and on our skill in developing a corrective program that helps them to read.

The significance of children's early years in reading achievement has been amply documented; however, this should not be used as an excuse for not helping children when they come to school. Rather than putting blame on social, political, and economic factors, over which teachers and children have little control, more should be done in the schools.

The importance of learning to read in the early grades cannot be overstated. The longer children remain nonreaders, the less likely are their chances to get up to their grade levels or their ability levels, even with the best remedial help. Underachievers in reading tend to have many emotional and social problems, and these are compounded as the child goes through school. Studies have shown that severe underachievement in reading appears to follow the individual all through life.[1]

Teachers want to help children to learn—that is their intent. Those teachers who cannot help students soon lose confidence in themselves,

[1]Diane Haines, *The Long-Term Consequences of Childhood Underachievement in Reading,* Doctoral Dissertation (Ann Arbor, Mich.: University Microfilms International, 1979).

and their own self-concept is impaired. This feeling eventually gets picked up by their students.

This book has been written to help you to acquire the skills necessary for you to help children who are having reading problems, to spot potential problems, and to develop corrective measures to overcome them.

This chapter focuses on you, the classroom teacher, as a teacher of reading in a dynamic diagnostic-reading and correction program. After you finish reading this chapter you should be able to answer the following questions:

1. What is the role of the teacher in a diagnostic-reading and correction program?

2. What skills are needed to implement a diagnostic-reading and correction program?

3. Why is the teacher considered the key person in a diagnostic-reading and correction program?

4. What are some important characteristics of a good reading teacher?

5. What is "self-fulfilling prophecy"?

6. What should a teacher know about planning and instructional time?

7. What should the teacher know about classroom management and organization?

THE TEACHER IN A DIAGNOSTIC-READING AND CORRECTION PROGRAM

The role of a teacher in a diagnostic-reading and correction program is broad. The teacher must observe individual children, understand individual differences and the factors that influence them, build readiness for reading at various reading levels, identify those children who are having reading difficulties, combine diagnosis and correction with everyday reading, and help children gain an appreciation of reading. Teachers must have knowledge of the various word recognition and comprehension skills at their fingertips and be able to teach these effectively. They must know the techniques of observation and be aware of the factors that influence children's reading behavior. Teachers must be able to administer and interpret such diagnostic techniques as the informal reading inventory and word analysis tests. If teachers cannot construct their own informal diagnostic tests, they should be aware of those that are commercially available. Obviously, teachers in a diagnostic-reading and correction program must be well prepared and well informed.

THE TEACHER AS THE KEY TO A GOOD READING PROGRAM

Although a school may have the best equipment, the most advanced school plant, a superior curriculum, and children who want to learn, it must have "good teachers" so that the desired kind of learning can take place. With today's emphasis on accountability, the spotlight is even more sharply focused on the teacher. Although there is no definitive agreement on how to evaluate teachers, researchers and educators do agree that teachers influence students' behavior and learning.

Studies show that it is difficult to compare different methods or sets of materials in researches and that students seem to learn to read from a variety of materials and methods.[2] More importantly, researchers of these and other

[2]Guy L. Bond and Robert Dykstra, "The Cooperative Research Program in First-Grade Reading Instruction," *Reading Research Quarterly* 2 (Summer 1967): 1–142. Albert J. Harris and Coleman Morrison, "The CRAFT Project: A Final Report," *The Reading Teacher* 22 (January 1969): 335–40.

studies point to the *teacher as the key* to improving reading instruction. Here are some of their statements:

> To improve reading instruction, it is necessary to train better teachers of reading rather than to expect a panacea in the form of materials.[3]
>
> The results of the study have indicated that the teacher is far more important than the method. Costly procedures such as smaller classes and provision of auxiliary personnel may continue to give disappointing results if teaching skills are not improved.[4]
>
> The main lesson, it seems to me, is that the teacher is of tremendous importance in preventing and treating children's reading and learning disabilities . . . good teaching is probably the best way to help children.[5]

Although most persons agree that the teacher is the key to improved instruction, there is no unanimity on what factors affect teaching performance and student learning or on the objective criteria for evaluating teacher performance. It is beyond the scope of this book to try to answer or resolve the teacher-evaluation controversy. We will concern ourselves with possible descriptions and means for evaluating those characteristics, traits, and competencies that teachers in a diagnostic-reading and correction program should possess.

SOME IMPORTANT CHARACTERISTICS OF A GOOD READING TEACHER

Although unanimity does not exist among educators as to which characteristics are the

most salient in producing good teachers, most would agree that verbal ability, good educational background including such knowledge as the content of reading, ability to read with skill oneself, good planning and organizing ability, and positive teacher expectations and attitudes would be ones that reading teachers should possess.

Studies have shown that teachers who have a good educational background and verbal ability are usually better teachers than those who do not.[6] This information makes good sense and should come as no surprise. What is surprising is that there are some teachers who themselves lack necessary reading skills. A four-and-one-half-year study measuring the reading skills of almost 350 teachers found "many of the teachers tested demonstrated a wide range of deficiencies or discrepancies in their reading abilities."[7] Although researchers stated that care should be taken not to generalize from these results, it is clear that teacher deficiencies in reading ability should warrant concern. Another study found that teachers scored low on tests of study skills intended for children completing elementary or junior high school.[8] Obviously, if a teacher feels insecure about a subject, that teacher will tend to avoid teaching it, and when it is taught, concepts and skills may be taught erroneously. If teachers lack a broad vocabulary, are unable to read critically, and

[3]Bond and Dykstra, op. cit., p. 123.
[4]Harris and Morrison, op. cit., p. 339.
[5]Jeanne Chall, "A Decade of Research on Reading and Learning Disabilities," *What Research Has to Say About Reading Instruction* (Newark, Del.: International Reading Association, 1978), pp. 39, 40.

[6]Charles E. Bidwell and John D. Kasarda, "School District Organization and Student Achievement," *American Sociological Review* 40 (February 1975): 55–70. Eric Hanushek, "The Production of Education, Teacher Quality and Efficiency," paper presented at the Bureau of Educational Personnel Development Conference: "How Do Teachers Make a Difference?" Washington, D.C.
[7]Lance M. Gentile and Merna McMillan, "Some of Our Students' Teachers Can't Read Either," *Journal of Reading* 21 (November 1977): 146.
[8]Eunice N. Askov, et al., "Study Skill Mastery Among Elementary School Teachers," *The Reading Teacher* 30 (February 1977): 485–88.

have not mastered study skills, their students will suffer. How can teachers construct questions that challenge students' higher levels of thinking if the teachers lack the ability to read at high levels of comprehension? They can't. How can teachers diagnose students' problems if they do not know what skills the students are supposed to have? They can't. How can teachers instill a love for books in students if they themselves are not reading? They can't. Obviously, if teachers are seen by students as not placing a high value on reading, students may begin to feel likewise. (Chapters 12 to 14 present those reading skills that teachers should have at their fingertips, and Chapter 17 helps teachers learn how to interest their students in books.)

Teachers' Expectations

The more teachers know about their students, the better able they are to plan for them. However, teachers must be cautioned about the self-fulfilling prophecy—where teachers' assumptions about children become true, at least in part, because of the attitude of the teachers, which in turn becomes part of the children's self-concept. Studies have shown that teachers' expectations about students' abilities to learn will influence students' learning.[9] For example, if a child comes from an environment not conducive to learning, the teacher may assume that this child cannot learn beyond a certain level and thus treat this child accordingly. If this happens, the teacher's assumptions could become part of the child's own self-concept, further reinforcing the teacher's original expectations.

Teachers who are aware of the effect that their expectations have on the learning behavior

of students can use this to help their students. For example, teachers should assume that *all* their students are capable of learning to read; they should avoid labeling their students; and they should use positive reinforcement whenever feasible to help students become motivated.

Teacher Planning and Instructional Time

Teachers in a diagnostic-reading and correction program must also be good planners. Planning helps guide teachers in making choices about instruction; it helps them to clarify their thinking about objectives, students' needs, interests, and readiness levels, as well as to determine what motivating techniques to use.

The teacher in a diagnostic-reading and correction program bases instruction on continuous analysis of students' strengths and weaknesses. The teacher is flexible and is always alert to student feedback to determine whether to proceed with instruction, to slow down instruction, or to stop and correct or clarify some misconception.

The teacher in a diagnostic-reading and correction program must wisely plan time allotments for reading. Reading helps reading; that is, the more time that one spends in reading, the better reader one will be. Confusion exists, however, as to whether the time spent must consist of direct instruction or if it also includes reading independently. Both are probably important.

From the studies it appears that direct instructional time is related to reading achievement at the lower grades; however, at the upper grades direct instructional time seems to be more necessary for those of low rather than high socioeconomic status. The researchers hypothesize that the reason may be "that middle-class children tend to spend substantial amounts of time reading outside of school, increasing their total reading practice and reducing the sig-

[9]Robert Rosenthal and Lenore Jacobson, *Pygmalion in the Classroom* (New York: Holt, Rinehart and Winston, 1968). Douglas A. Pidgeon, *Expectation and Pupil Performance* (London: National Foundation for Educational Research, in England and Wales, 1970).

nificance of differences in amount of instructional reading time in school, while low socio-economic children are less likely to do so."[10]

Time spent in reading seems to be an important variable for success in reading, whether it is direct instructional time or independent reading. However, teachers cannot assume that students will read outside of school because of the many other enjoyable activities that compete for their time; therefore teachers must plan for students to have time to read as well as direct instruction in reading. (See "Time Spent in Comprehension Instruction" in Chapter 13, and see also Chapter 17.)

The Teacher As a Good Organizer and Classroom Manager

Teachers in a diagnostic-reading and correction program must be good organizers and classroom managers. It is simply not practical, and it probably is not possible, to provide a completely individualized reading program for each student. Teachers must be able to work with large groups, small groups, the whole class, and individual students. Usually the basis for selection in reading groups is the achievement level of students. During the first few weeks of the term, teachers collect data concerning the achievement levels of each of the students in their classes through observation, teacher-made

[10]Albert J. Harris, "The Effective Teacher of Reading, Revisited," *The Reading Teacher* 33 (November 1979): 136.

tests, and standardized tests. After evaluating the collected data, tentative groups are organized. The number of groups in a skill area depends on the amount of variability within the class. For some areas, there may be three or four groups; for some, there may only be two groups; for some, the teacher may decide to work with the whole class as a unit; and for some areas, the teacher may have a number of children working individually. The grouping pattern is a flexible one, and the groups themselves are recognized as flexible units; children can easily flow from one group to another.

The teacher as a good classroom manager is able to deal with more than one situation at a time. A teacher working with a group should be aware of what is going on not only in that group but also with the other children in the class. A teacher cannot "dismiss" the rest of the class because he or she is working with a particular group. Even though the children have been given challenging work based on their individual needs, the teacher must be alert to what is happening. A teacher who ignores the rest of the class while working with one group will probably have a number of discipline problems. The following scenario presents an example of a good classroom manager. Notice especially how Ms. Mills is able to manage a number of ongoing activities at the same time. Notice how she is always aware of what is going on in her class, and notice how she prevents problems from arising.

SCENARIO

One teacher and six children are seated at a round table engaged in reading. The rest of the class is involved in a variety of activities: A number of children are working individually at their seats or at learning centers; one child, sitting in a rocking chair, is reading; two children are working together; and a group of children are working together in the rear of the room.

The teacher says to her group at the round table, "We've talked about what inference means, and we've given examples of it. Who can tell us what we mean by inference?" A few children raise their hands.

Ms. Mills calls on one, and he gives an explanation of inference. "Good," says Ms. Mills. "Now, I'd like you to read the paragraph about Mr. Brown and then tell us what inferences you can make about Mr. Brown. Be prepared to support your inferences with evidence from the paragraph."

Ms. Mills looks at each of the children as they are reading. She then glances around the room. She says, "Judy, may I see you for a moment?" Judy comes to Ms. Mills. The teacher asks Judy in a very quiet tone if she can help her. She says, "Judy, you look confused. What's wrong?" Judy says that she is having trouble figuring out a question. Ms. Mills tells Judy to work on something else for about ten minutes, and that then she will help her. As Judy goes back to her seat, Ms. Mills again quickly glances around the room. As her eyes catch some of the children's, she smiles at them. Ms. Mills then looks at the children in her group. She sees that they are ready and asks them what inferences they can make about Mr. Brown. All the children raise their hands. Ms. Mills calls on one of the children, who makes an inference about Mr. Brown. Ms. Mills asks the rest of the group if they agree with the inference. Two students say that they do not agree. Ms. Mills asks all the students to skim the paragraph to find clues that would support their position. Ms. Mills again looks around the room. A child approaches and asks her a question. She answers the question and then goes back to the group. After a while Ms. Mills and the group discuss whether they have accomplished what they were supposed to. They then discuss, for a moment, what they will be doing next time. They all go back to their seats. Before Ms. Mills calls another group, she checks off in her plan book the objectives that have been accomplished by the group. She also makes some remarks in her record book about the individual children in the group. Ms. Mills puts down her book and walks around the room to check on what the students are doing. She smiles to a number of the students, says "good" to some others, helps Judy with her problem, and listens in on the group that has been working together on a special project. Ms. Mills asks the group how they are doing and how much more time they will need before they will be ready to report their progress to her and the class. Ms. Mills then goes back to the reading table and calls the next group.

SUMMARY

Chapter 2 focuses on the teacher as the key person in a diagnostic-reading and correction program. The teacher is seen as that person who should help children when they come to school regardless of their backgrounds. The role of a teacher in a diagnostic-reading and correction program is viewed as broad, so a teacher must be well prepared and well informed. A discussion of a number of studies shows that teachers influence students' behavior and learning and that the teacher is more important than the method of instruction or the materials used. Chapter 2 also discusses what characteristics a good teacher of reading should have: verbal ability, a good educational background including such knowledge as the content of reading, an ability to read, and positive expectations and attitudes.

SUGGESTIONS FOR THOUGHT QUESTIONS AND ACTIVITIES

1. Make a list of all those characteristics you think a good teacher of reading should have in a diagnostic-reading and correction program.

2. Think of one of the best teachers you have ever had. Write those characteristics of the teacher you remember best.

3. Think of the worst teacher you have ever had. Write those characteristics that you feel made him or her your worst teacher.

4. Observe a teacher during a reading lesson. Check off all those characteristics he or she exhibits that you listed in number 2.

5. Make a videotape recording of yourself teaching a reading lesson. Check off all those characteristics you exhibited that were in your list in number 2.

6. You have been assigned to a special committee that is concerned with teacher accountability. What are your views concerning teacher accountability? What suggestions would you have for the committee?

SELECTED BIBLIOGRAPHY

Ashton-Warner, Sylvia. *Teacher.* New York: Simon & Schuster, 1963.

Bagford, Jack. "Evaluating Teachers on Reading Instruction." *The Reading Teacher* 34 (January 1981): 400–404.

Brophy, Jere E., and Carolyn M. Evertson. *Student Characteristics and Teaching.* New York: Longman, 1981.

Brown, Linda A., and Rita J. Sherbenou. "A Comparison of Teacher Perceptions of Student Reading Ability, Reading Performance, and Classroom Behavior." *The Reading Teacher* 34 (February 1981): 557–60.

Buike, Sandra, and Gerald G. Duffy. "Do Teacher Conceptions of Reading Influence Instructional Practice?" Paper presented at the American Educational Research Association Convention, San Francisco, April 1979.

Do Teachers Make a Difference? Department of Health, Education and Welfare Report No. OE 58042. Washington, D.C.: U.S. Government Printing Office, 1970.

Guthrie, John T. "Time in Reading Programs." *The Reading Teacher* 33 (January 1980): 500–502.

Harris, Albert J. "The Effective Teacher of Reading, Revisited." *The Reading Teacher* 33 (November 1979): 135–40.

Kounin, Jacob S. *Discipline and Group Management.* New York: Holt, Rinehart and Winston, 1970.

McNeil, John D. *Toward Accountable Teachers: Their Appraisal and Improvement.* New York: Holt, Rinehart and Winston, 1971.

Pidgeon, Douglas A. *Expectation and Pupil Performance.* London: National Foundation for Educational Research, in England and Wales, 1970.

Rosenthal, Robert, and Lenore Jacobson. *Pygmalion in the Classroom.* New York: Holt, Rinehart and Winston, 1968.

Silberman, Charles E. *Crisis in the Classroom.* New York: Random House, 1970.

Strang, Ruth. *Diagnostic Teaching of Reading.* New York: McGraw-Hill, 1969, Chap. 2.

Taylor, Gail Cohen. "Findings from Research on Teacher Effectiveness." *The Reading Teacher* 34 (March 1981): 726–30.

CHAPTER 3

What a Teacher Should Know About Tests, Measurement, and Evaluation

INTRODUCTION

Ms. Smith is a new teacher. She's excited about having a position and wants to be the best teacher possible; however, she's a little over-awed and confused. At the orientation meeting at the beginning of the school term, the principal talked about the school district's testing program, and then the reading specialist talked about the various kinds of reading tests that the teachers were expected to give. They talked about norm-referenced tests, informal tests, and criterion-referenced tests. They also talked about group and individual tests. Ms. Smith regretted that she had never had a course in tests and measurements, but rather than lamenting this fact, she decided to gain as much background information as possible in this area.

She agrees with the principal and reading specialist that a good teacher must be able to administer and interpret various types of tests, not only for evaluation but also for diagnostic purposes. At the meeting, knowledge of different types of diagnostic techniques was especially emphasized since the school is committed to a diagnostic-reading and correction program.

This chapter should help Ms. Smith and others like her to gain background information on the various types of tests. After you finish reading this chapter, you should be able to answer the following questions:

1. What is the difference between measurement and evaluation?
2. What are the values of measurement?
3. What are some of the criteria of good tests?
4. What are standardized tests?
5. What are some differences between group and individual tests?
6. What are criterion-referenced tests?
7. What are some of the different kinds of reading tests available?

THE CONCEPT OF EVALUATION

The word *evaluation* seems to bring shudders to most people. Although some individuals may look on evaluation as necessary, it is often considered an intrusion on privacy and is avoided for as long as possible. The following remarks were overheard in one school. Do they sound familiar to you?

> PERSON A: "Shh, everyone be alert! Keep the kids quiet! We're being evaluated!"
> PERSON B: "Oh no! Don't tell me we're being evaluated again. We just finished testing our students."

To some, evaluation and testing are synonymous. But they are not.

"'Evaluation' designates a process of appraisal which involves the acceptance of specific values and the use of a variety of instruments of observation, including measurement, as the bases for value judgments."[1] Good evaluation occurs at the beginning, during, and end of the educative process; is based on an adequate collection of data; and is made in terms of desired objectives and standards. Evaluation involves making value judgments, and it is therefore larger in scope than measurement, which is limited to quantitative descriptions. Since evaluation is a process carried on by humans, good evaluators avoid emotional bias in their judgments by using measurement techniques and other assessment instruments.

ASSESSMENT FOR DIAGNOSIS AND EVALUATION

Examinations are formidable, even to the best prepared, for the greatest fool may ask more than the wisest man can answer.

C. C. COLTON

[1]Ralph W. Tyler, "The Functions of Measurement in Improving Instruction," *Educational Measurement,* E. F. Lindquist, ed. (Washington, D.C.: American Council on Education, 1951), p. 48.

The positive values of measurement outweigh the negative connotations associated with assessment. Measurement is useful for diagnostic, review, and predictive purposes. It can be used as a motivating technique for students, as well as a basis for grades and promotion. Through student assessment, teachers are also able to reevaluate their own teaching methods.

In order for measurement to be an effective part of the evaluative process, teachers must master varied techniques and be able to administer and interpret them. Such measurements include standardized tests and teacher-made tests. Direct observation of student behavior is also necessary in order to collect data for valid evaluations.

Criteria for a Good Test

Whatever tests teachers choose for assessment, they should meet all these criteria:

1. *Objectivity:* The same score must result regardless of who marks the test. Since essay questions do not lend themselves to a high degree of objectivity, the users of such tests should give specific directions for scoring and should make the essay question as explicit as possible.

2. *Validity:* The appraisal instrument should measure what it claims to measure. There are different kinds of validity, but reading teachers will be concerned primarily with the content of a test. In order to determine content validity the test should be compared with course content.

3. *Reliability:* The test is reliable if it consistently produces similar results when repeated measurements are taken of the same students under the same conditions.

4. *Suitability:* In selecting or preparing a test, the teacher must determine not only whether it will yield the type of data desired but also whether the test is suitable for the age and type of students and for the locality in which they reside.

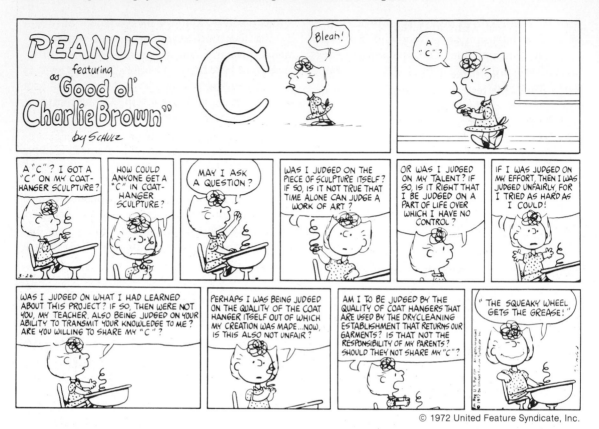

The Validity and Reliability of Tests

Validity and reliability are two especially important criteria of tests. Validity is concerned with the concept of truthfulness; it determines whether a test measures what it is supposed to measure. Reliability is concerned with consistency; it determines whether we get similar results between two measures of the same thing. Any test that is valid must be reliable, but reliability is not a sufficient condition for validity. It is possible to get a consistent measure of something, but it does not mean that the measure is correct.

"Validity is a matter of degree, and a test has many validities, each dependent upon the spe-cific purposes for which the test is used."[2] As stated earlier, for our purposes content validity of achievement tests is the most important type. Content validity is concerned with how adequately the test items represent what is being tested so that inferences can be made concerning a student's degree of attainment of the subject matter.

Reliability tells us that a student's score will remain consistent, even if conditions under which the test are taken change slightly, even if different scorers are used, or even if similar but

[2]William A. Mehrens and Irvin J. Lehmann, *Standardized Tests in Education,* 3rd ed. (New York: Holt, Rinehart and Winston, 1980), p. 79.

not identical test items are used. There are a number of reasons why a student's test score could vary: The test may not be testing what it is supposed to; the student does not have good rapport with the tester; the student may not be motivated; the student may be ill; or the student may be tired. Another reason may be that the student has good or bad luck in guessing.[3]

STANDARDIZED TESTS[4]

Standardized tests are published tests which generally have been constructed by experts in the field and are available from publishers. They are usually developed in a very precise fashion and they should be precisely administered. Standardized tests contain exact instructions on how to administer them, and these instructions are supposed to be followed by all testers.

Confusion may exist concerning the definition of standardized tests because of changes in the way the term is currently being used in comparison with how it has been used in the past and is still being used by many, especially in the reading field. *Good's Dictionary of Education,* the *Dictionary of Psychology,* the *Dictionary of Behavioral Sciences,* and the *International Dictionary* all include *norm-referenced* as one of the criteria for a standardized test; however, today the definition does not necessarily include that criterion. Today, a standardized test may or may not be a norm-referenced test. A test is considered to be a standardized test if it is a published test with specific instructions for administration and scoring.[5] Michael Zieky, a senior examiner at Educational Testing Service, defines a standardized test "as any published test in which rules exist such that the test is administered to all examinees under the same conditions.[6] In this text, a test that has been published by experts in the field and has precise instructions for administration and scoring will be considered a standardized test.

Although not all standardized tests have norms, most usually do. Norms are average scores for a given group of students, which allow comparisons to be made for different students or groups of individuals. The norms are derived from a random sampling of a cross-section of a large population of individuals. The use of a large representative sample of students for research is obviously not possible with a teacher-made test. (See "Teacher-Made Tests" in this chapter.)

Norm-referenced tests are used to help teachers learn where their own students stand in relation to others in the class, school system, city, state, or nation. Although a child may be doing average work in a particular class, the child may be above average when compared to other norms. Similarly, it is possible for a child to be doing above-average work in a third-grade class but to be below average for all third-graders in the nation.

Teachers must be cautious in their analysis of test results. They should not be intimidated by standardized tests, and they must recognize the limitations of these tests. Teachers must determine whether a test is appropriate for their students. If the class has not covered the work in the standardized test, the test obviously would

---

[3]Ibid., p. 44.

[4]Oscar K. Buros's *Mental Measurements Yearbooks* are an important source on standardized tests. A teacher can use these reference yearbooks to obtain information about specific tests or to locate tests in specific areas.

[5]J. Stanley Ahmann and Marvin Glock, *Evaluating Student Progress: Principles of Tests and Measurements,* 6th ed. (Boston: Allyn and Bacon, 1981), p. 285.

[6]Michael Zieky, senior examiner, Educational Testing Service (ETS), Princeton, N.J.

not be valid. Differences in student populations must also be taken into account in interpreting test results.

Another important factor concerns the students themselves. Students who are overly anxious or upset by a test, who are tired or hungry, or who lack motivation, will not perform as well as others not burdened in this manner. Such factors will adversely affect test performance. Read Dick Gregory's disturbing words:[7]

> The teacher thought I was stupid. Couldn't spell, couldn't read, couldn't do arithmetic. Just stupid. Teachers were never interested in finding out that you couldn't concentrate because you were so hungry, because you hadn't had any breakfast. All you could think about was noontime, would it ever come? Maybe you could sneak into the cloakroom and steal a bite of some kid's lunch out of a coat pocket. A bite of something. Paste. You can't really make a meal of paste, or put it on bread for a sandwich, but sometimes I'd scoop a few spoonfuls out of the big paste jar in the back of the room. Pregnant people get strange tastes. I was pregnant with poverty.

Classification of Standardized Tests

Standardized tests may be classified in a number of ways, one of which is according to the *way* they are administered. For example, some tests are group administered and some are individually administered, so these tests would be called group or individual tests. Some persons classify tests according to whether they have oral instructions or written instructions. Usually, tests are classified according to *what* is measured. Based on this, standardized tests are

generally divided into the following categories: aptitude (intelligence) tests; achievement tests, which include diagnostic, single subject-matter, and survey batteries; and interest, personality, and attitude inventories.[8]

Special Note

Survey batteries consist of a group of tests in different content areas. These tests have been standardized on the same population so that the results of the various components may be meaningfully compared.[9] Standardized achievement tests that yield a general score are usually called survey tests. They may be part of a survey battery, or they may be single-subject tests (see Chapter 8).

Selection of Standardized Tests by Teachers

Many times teachers are not involved in the selection of standardized tests. This is a mistake. The more teachers know about standardized tests, the better able they will be to use the results. The problem is that there are so many standardized tests on the market, and many of them are considered worthless. Read the following statements made by Oscar Buros, the compiler of the *Mental Measurements Yearbooks:*[10]

> Unfortunately, the rank and file of test users do not appear to be particularly alarmed that so many tests are either severely criticized or described as

---

[7]Dick Gregory, *Nigger: An Autobiography* (New York: E. P. Dutton, 1964), p. 44.

[8]William A. Mehrens and Irvin J. Lehmann, *Measurement and Evaluation in Education and Psychology,* 2nd ed. (New York: Holt, Rinehart and Winston, 1975), p. 390.

[9]Mehrens and Lehmann, *Standardized Tests in Education,* p. 161.

[10]Oscar Buros, ed., *The Sixth Mental Measurements Yearbook* (Highland Park, N.J.: Gryphon Press, 1965), pp. xxiii-xxiv.

having no validity. Although most test users would probably agree that many tests are either worthless or misused, they continue to have the utmost faith in their own particular choice and use of tests regardless of the absence of supporting research or even of the presence of negating research. When I initiated this test reviewing service in 1938, I was confident that frankly critical reviews by competent specialists representing a wide variety of viewpoints would make it unprofitable to publish tests of unknown or questionable validity. Now 27 years and five Mental Measurements Yearbooks later, I realize that I was too optimistic.

Buros in his *Seventh* and in his *Eighth Mental Measurements Yearbooks* reiterates the same thoughts: "At least half of the tests currently on the market should never have been published."[11]

Buros's *Mental Measurements Yearbooks* and his companion book, *Reading: Tests and Reviews,* are excellent resources for the teacher intent on choosing a standardized reading test that best suits his or her purposes. The books help acquaint teachers with new tests in the field as well as with old ones. Frank critical evaluations of tests are written by authorities in the field. Test users are also warned about the dangers of standardized tests and are told of their values. An essential contribution that the books make is to "impress test users with the desirability of suspecting all standardized tests—even though prepared by well-known authorities—unaccompanied by detailed data on their construction, validity, uses, and limitations."[12]

TEACHER-MADE TESTS

Teacher-made tests are also called either classroom or informal tests. These are prepared by the classroom teacher for a particular class and given under conditions of his or her own choosing.[13] Usually, teacher-made tests are the primary basis for evaluating students' school progress. Teachers can get quick feedback on learning behaviors by constructing appropriate classroom tests. The tests with which you are probably the most familiar are those used to determine students' grades; these tests are generally classified into essay and objective tests and are mostly group tests.

In the field of reading, classroom tests are generally used to help diagnose a student's reading problem or to learn more about a student's weaknesses and strengths. Many of the teacher-made tests used for diagnosis are individually administered. The informal reading inventory, which may be commercially produced or teacher-made, can be one of the teacher's most valuable aids in diagnosing reading problems (see Chapter 9).

CRITERION-REFERENCED TESTS

Criterion-referenced tests are based on an extensive inventory of learning objectives in a specific curriculum. The objectives are presented in behavioral terms. (See "Behavioral Objectives" in Chapter 10.)

Criterion-referenced tests are designed to diagnose specific behaviors of individual students. They are used to gain more information about the students' various skill levels, and the

[11]Oscar Buros, ed., *The Eighth Mental Measurements Yearbook* (Highland Park, N.J.: Gryphon Press, 1978), p. xxxi.
[12]Oscar Buros, ed., *Reading: Tests and Reviews* (Highland Park, N.J.: Gryphon Press, 1968), p. xvi.

[13]William A. Mehrens and Irvin J. Lehmann, *Measurement and Evaluation in Education and Psychology,* p. 14.

information is used to either reinforce, supplement, or remediate the skill-development area being tested. The test results help the instructor plan specific learning sequences to help the students master the objective they missed.

Criterion-referenced tests are not norm-based; that is, they do not provide a means for comparing students to a standardization sample or a norm group. Criterion-referenced tests are concerned primarily with mastery of behavioral objectives, which are based on classroom curriculum. On criterion-referenced tests an individual competes only with him- or herself. There is very little difference in appearance between a norm-referenced test and a criterion-referenced test; however, differences do exist, as has already been noted, in the purposes for the tests. An example of a question from a criterion-referenced test and the specific pupil behavioral objective to which the test question correlates follow:

> *General area:* reading comprehension (interpretation)
> *Specific area:* drawing references
> *Behavioral objective:* The student will draw inferences about the personality of the main character based on the content of reading material.

The child is asked to read a short story carefully. After the child has finished reading, the child is asked to answer questions based on the story. An example of a question based on the given behavioral objective follows:

> What can you infer about the personality of Dennis?

The child is then asked to choose the best answer from the given statements. (Note that in criterion-referenced testing *every* test item is related to a corresponding behavioral objective.)

Criterion-referenced tests can be standardized tests or teacher-made, and they can be administered individually or to a group. (A criterion-referenced test is considered standardized if it is a published test that has been prepared by experts in the field and has precise instructions for administration and scoring. See Figure 3.1, p. 27.) Many criterion-referenced tests are used in individualized programs. (See Chapter 10 for more on criterion-referenced tests.)

Before we proceed to a general discussion of reading tests, we should differentiate between group and individual tests.

GROUP AND INDIVIDUAL TESTS

It seems evident that group tests are administered to a group of persons, whereas individual tests are administered to one person at a time. It also should be obvious that it would be more time-consuming to give an individual rather than a group test. What may not be as obvious are the reasons for administering an individual test. Individual tests in reading are usually given when the teacher feels that some inconsistency exists between the student's classroom behavior or his or her reading potential and his or her test score on a group-administered standardized reading achievement test (see Chapters 9 and 10). Individual tests are administered when teachers wish to learn more about a student's specific behavior, such as oral reading, and the only way to do so would be through an individual test. An individual test may also be given if the teacher suspects that a child has difficulty following directions. On an individual test the tester can determine whether the student understands a question and whether the student is tired, hungry, or not feeling well.

Group tests are more limited in their format than individual tests because they must be administered by the reading of simple directions

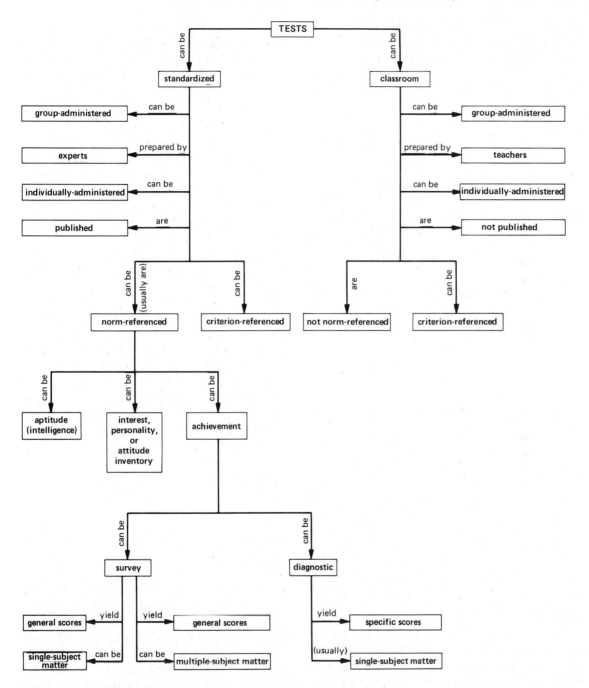

Figure 3.1. A tree diagram of the various types of tests. This diagram is a simplification, showing the relationship of the tests.

and answered by some kind of mark on an answer sheet. Group tests are usually given by the classroom teacher, and there are as many different types of group tests as there are individual tests. For example, there are group and individual aptitude tests, group and individual achievement tests, group and individual personality inventories, group and individual attitude inventories, and so on. There are some individual tests, such as individual IQ tests, that must be administered by a specially trained clinician or psychologist; and there are some, such as individual diagnostic tests, that can be administered by the regular classroom teacher. Whether a teacher or a specially trained person administers an individual test, it is not given as often as a group test because it is more costly and more time-consuming. However, individual tests are generally more reliable than group tests; they are more useful with students who have reading difficulties because they usually require less reading than group tests; more can be learned about a student in a clinical-test one-to-one situation than in a class; and they are usually more valid for those students who have difficulty taking tests in a group.

READING TESTS

There are a number of different kinds of standardized and teacher-made reading tests; some measure study skills, vocabulary, comprehension, speed in reading, oral reading, and so on. No single test or single score can tell all there is to know about a student's reading behavior. The purpose for the test should determine the type of test that is used.

Teachers in a diagnostic-reading and correction program must be knowledgeable of the many different types of reading tests that exist so that a wise selection of tests can be made. Tests used to identify a problem are different

from those used to uncover specifics about the problem. For example, it is one thing to discover that a child is reading below his or her ability level, and it is another to determine *why*.

Choosing the proper standardized test for a specific purpose is difficult in reading because the name of the test may not be descriptive of it; that is, the name may be misleading. There are a number of tests measuring the same type of skills that have different names, and there are a number of tests measuring different types of skills that have the same name. Because of this, teachers must be very cautious in choosing a standardized test and make sure that they read the examiner's manual or a description of the test in publishers' catalogs.

Teachers should not depend solely on standardized tests to help them learn more about the reading behavior of their students. As stated earlier in this chapter, a teacher can get quick feedback from a classroom test. It is possible that the skill that teachers would like to learn more about may not be covered in a standardized test, or it may be easier to make up a test than to hunt one down that will reveal needed information. (See Part III for detailed information on reading tests.)

SUMMARY

Chapter 3 has presented general information about what teachers should know concerning tests, measurement, and evaluation. It was stated that good evaluators use measurement techniques and other assessment instruments to avoid bias in their judgments. A discussion concerned the criteria that all good tests should have: objectivity, validity, reliability, and suitability. Because there is confusion concerning the term *standardized,* it was defined according to the way that it is presently being used in the field. A standardized test is a published test with specific instructions for administration and scoring. It may or may not be a norm-referenced test. The terms *norm-referenced* and *criterion-referenced* were also defined, and the ways that standardized tests may be classified were explored. Because there are so many standardized tests on the market, teachers need help in determining which ones to use. Buros's *Mental Measurements Yearbooks* were given as excellent sources. Teacher-made tests, which are also called classroom or informal tests, were discussed too. In this chapter, teachers were introduced to reading tests and the fact that many different kinds exist. It was emphasized that teachers in a diagnostic-reading and correction program must be knowledgeable of the various kinds of tests so that a wise selection can be made for the proper purpose.

SUGGESTIONS FOR THOUGHT QUESTIONS AND ACTIVITIES

1. Your school is interested in using criterion-referenced tests. You have been appointed to explain the differences between criterion-referenced and norm-referenced tests. What will you say?

2. Many teachers in your school are confused about the many different types of tests that exist. You can help them by drawing a tree diagram showing the relationships among tests.

3. Discuss some of the important criteria that good tests must have.

4. Explain some of the differences between teacher-made tests and published or commercially produced tests.

SELECTED BIBLIOGRAPHY

Ahmann, Stanley, and Marvin Glock. *Evaluating Student Progress: Principles of Tests and Measurements,* 6th ed. Boston: Allyn and Bacon, 1981.

Calfee, Robert C., Priscilla A. Drum, and Richard D. Arnold. ''What Research Can Tell the Reading Teacher About Assessment.'' In *What Research Has to Say About Reading Instruction,* pp. 135–62. S. Jay Samuels, ed. Newark, Del.: International Reading Association, 1978.

Gronlund, Norman E. *Measurement and Evaluation in Teaching.* New York: Macmillan, 1981.

Mehrens, William A., and Irvin J. Lehmann. *Measurement and Evaluation in Education and Psychology,* 2nd ed. New York: Holt, Rinehart and Winston, 1975.

———. *Standardized Tests in Education,* 3rd ed. New York: Holt, Rinehart and Winston, 1980.

Part II

THE NATURE AND INTERRELATEDNESS OF FACTORS THAT AFFECT READING PERFORMANCE

CHAPTER 4

Concept Development and Its Relationship to Language and Reading

INTRODUCTION

Figure 4.1.

© 1974 King Features Syndicate, Inc.

The cartoon on page 33 illustrates the interrelationships among language, concepts, and cognitive development. Since Punkin Head did not know what a hare or tortoise is, he could not understand the story told to him by Tiger. Punkin Head must be able to differentiate these animals from others which may have some similar characteristics. At a higher cognitive level, he must also be able to conceptualize why the tortoise beat the hare in the race, and thereby comprehend the meaning of the adage "Slow and steady wins the race."

Concept development is closely related to language development. Unless children attain the necessary concepts, they will be limited in reading as well as in all other aspects of the language arts (listening, speaking, and writing). A special chapter on concept development is being presented in this book because of its importance in the reading process; reading is a thinking act. Knowledge of how children attain concepts and what they are is especially essential in a diagnostic-reading and correction program; teachers in such a program must recognize *early* when a child is lacking certain concepts and help that child to attain them. Teachers must help children all through the grades with both learning to read and reading to learn. This chapter is concerned with helping you better understand concept development and its interrelatedness with other vital areas. After you finish reading this chapter you will be able to answer the following questions:

1. How are language development, concept development, and reading related?

2. What is a concept?

3. What is *assimilation* according to Jean Piaget?

4. What is *accommodation* according to Jean Piaget?

5. What is *equilibrium* according to Jean Piaget?

6. How do children develop concepts?

7. What is semantic mapping?

8. What are examples of concepts that primary-grade children should have?

9. What are some informal techniques for measuring concept development?

LANGUAGE DEVELOPMENT, CONCEPT DEVELOPMENT, AND READING

The quality of language development depends on the interrelationships of such factors as intelligence, home environment, sex differences, cultural differences, and family makeup. The factors that influence language development also influence concept development. As a result, children who are more advanced in language development are also usually more advanced in concept development, and these children tend to be better readers than those who are not as advanced.[1]

Studies show that high-achieving readers come from homes with enriched verbal environments, whereas low-achieving readers come from homes in which little conversation takes place with the parents.[2] David Ausubel claims that "it is in the area of language development, and particularly with respect to the abstract dimension of verbal functioning that the culturally deprived child manifests the greatest degree of intellectual retardation."[3]

This report on the language ability of "disad-

[1]Walter D. Loban, *Language Development: Kindergarten through Grade Twelve,* Research Report No. 18 (Urbana, Ill.: National Council of Teachers of English, 1976).

[2]Esther Milner, "A Study of the Relationship between Reading Readiness in Grade One School Children and Patterns of Parent-Child Interaction," *Child Development* (June 22, 1951), 95–112.

[3]David P. Ausubel, "How Reversible Are the Cognitive and Motivational Effects of Cultural Deprivation? Implications for Teaching the Culturally Deprived Child," *Urban Education* 1 (Summer 1964): 23.

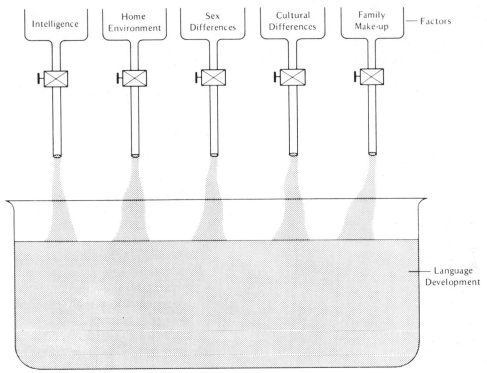

Figure 4.2. Factors affecting the language and concept development of the child.

vantaged children'' comes from an English writer:[4]

Twenty-four children of one-and-a-half to two years old, living in an orphanage, were divided into two groups, matched for "measured intelligence"—as far as it could be measured at that age: what is clear is that both groups showed *low* ability. Each of the twelve in one group was sent to be looked after by an adolescent girl living in a mental home: the other group was left at the orphanage. After two years the group that had been living with the girls showed extraordinary increases in measured intelligence (well over twenty points), while those in the orphanage showed a *decrease* of similar proportions. What is more astounding still is that after *twenty-one years,* the experimenter

was able to trace the children and discovered that the average of the final school achievement of the group looked after in infancy by the girls was twelfth grade (work normal for seventeen-to-eighteen-year-olds) whereas the average for the other group was fourth grade (work normal for nine-to-ten-year-olds).

WHAT IS A CONCEPT?

A group of stimuli with common characteristics is a concept. These stimuli may be objects, events, or persons. Concepts are usually designated by their names, such as book, war, man, woman, animal, teacher, and so forth. All these concepts refer to classes (or categories) of stimuli. Some stimuli do not refer to concepts;

[4]James Britton, *Language and Learning* (Middlesex, Eng.: Penguin, 1970), pp. 94–95.

FIGMENTS   **By Dale Hale**

Figure 4.3.   Language development and concept development are closely related. Not understanding one meaning of the word *toast*, the boy incorrectly interprets adult speech.

Miss Dawn, the hairdresser, Hemingway's "The Killers," World War II, and the Super Bowl are examples. These are particular (not classes of) stimuli, persons, or events.[5]

Concepts are needed to reduce the complexity of the world. When children learn that their shaggy pets are called dogs, they tend to label all other similar four-footed animals as "dogs." Young children overgeneralize, tending to group all animals together, and have not yet perceived the differences between and among various animals. Unless children learn to discern differences, the class of words that they deal with will become exceptionally unwieldy and unmanageable. However, if children group each object in a class by itself, this too will bring about difficulties in coping with environmental stimuli because it will also be such an unwieldy method.

PIAGET AND CONCEPT DEVELOPMENT

Concept development is closely related to cognitive (thinking) development. Jean Piaget,

a renowned Swiss psychologist, has written on children's cognitive development in terms of their ability to organize (which requires conceptualization), classify, and adapt to their environments.

According to Piaget,[6] the mind is capable of intellectual exercise because of its ability to categorize incoming stimuli adequately. Schemata (structured designs) are the cognitive arrangements by which this categorization takes place. As children develop and take in more and more information, it is necessary to have some way to categorize all the new information. As children develop, their ability to categorize, by means of schemata, grows too. That is, children should be able to differentiate, to become less dependent on sensory stimuli, and to gain more and more complex schemata. Children should be able to categorize a cat as distinct from a mouse or a rabbit. They should be able to group cat, dog, and cow together as animals. Piaget calls the processes which bring about these changes in children's thinking *assimilation* and *accommodation.*

Assimilation does not change an individual's concept but allows it to grow. It is a continuous

[5]John P. DeCecco, *The Psychology of Learning and Instruction: Educational Psychology,* 2nd ed. (Englewood Cliffs, N.J.: Prentice-Hall, 1974), p. 288.

[6]Jean Piaget, *The Origins of Intelligence in Children* (New York: International Universities Press, 1952).

process which helps the individual to integrate new, incoming stimuli into existing schemata or concepts. For example, when children tend to label all similar four-footed animals as dogs, the children are assimilating. They have assimilated all four-footed animals into their existing schemata.

If the child meets stimuli which cannot fit into the existing schema, then the alternative is either to construct a new category or to change the existing one. When a new schema or concept is developed, or when an existing schema is changed, it is called accommodation.

Although both assimilation and accommodation are important processes that the child must attain in order to develop adequate cognition, a balance between the two processes is necessary. If children overassimilate, they will have categories that are too large to handle and, similarly, if they overaccommodate, they will have too many categories, as we have already seen. Piaget calls the balance between the two *equilibrium.* A person having equilibrium would be able to see similarities between stimuli and thus properly assimilate them, and would also be able to determine when new schemata are needed for adequate accommodation of a surplus of categories.

As children develop cognitively they proceed from more global (generalized) schemata to more particular ones. For the child there are usually no right or wrong placements but only better or more effective ones. That is what good education is all about.

Instructional Implications

Concepts are necessary to help students acquire increasing amounts of knowledge. For example, as one proceeds through the grades in school, learning becomes more abstract and is expressed in words, using verbal stimuli as labels for concepts. Many teachers take for granted that those spoken concept labels are understood by their students, but this is not always so. Many times these concepts are learned either incompletely or incorrectly. This example illustrates incomplete concepts for *tourist* and *immigrant.*[7]

All the tourists may be obviously American whereas all the immigrants may be obviously Mexican. The tourists may be well dressed, the immigrants poorly dressed, and so on. If the natural environment is like a grand concept-formation experiment, it may take the child a long time to attain the concepts *tourist* and *immigrant;* indeed, the environment may not be as informative as the usual experimenter since the child may not always be informed, or reliably informed, as to the correctness of his guesses. No wonder a child might form the concept that a tourist is a well-dressed person who drives a station wagon with out-of-state license plates!

When children come to school the teacher must assess their concept-development level, then help them to add the attributes necessary and relevant for the development of particular concepts, while helping them to delete all those concepts that are faulty or irrelevant.

Studies on learning have shown that persons will retain information over an extended period of time if they are able to make generalizations about the information and if they can see relationships between what they are presently learning and material that they have already learned. Obviously, persons who have strategies for processing information will be in a better position to retain and transfer learning than those persons who do not. Good thinkers have strategies for processing information; they are able to assimilate and accommodate information; they

[7]John B. Carroll, "Words, Meanings and Concepts," in *Thought & Language: Language and Reading,* Maryanne Wolf et al., eds. (Cambridge, Mass.: Harvard Educational Review, 1980), p. 42.

are active consumers of information. Readers as active consumers of information must give structure or order to what they are reading. They must relate new experiences to what they already know.[8] No one can do this for the reader; however, the teacher is the facilitator for helping the reader gain skill in higher cognitive operations. Teachers can give the students practice in many activities that help them to develop their categorizing abilities, and they can ask questions that challenge them to seek relationships and to make comparisons. If children are exposed to these activities, they will be better prepared to do this kind of thinking when they are reading alone. (See Chapter 13 for more on categorizing.)

SEMANTIC MAPPING

Semantic mapping is "a graphic representation used to illustrate concepts and relationships among concepts such as classes, properties, and examples."[9] Semantic mapping is a technique for organizing information; it helps to give structure or order. It helps persons to see the relationships among concepts and it shows the various ways that information can be organized or categorized in more general or more specific categories. Using semantic maps to help us to see the relationships between and among ideas is not new; it is an offshoot of diagraming, and it is closely related to outlining. Figure 4.4 is an example of a simplified semantic map of the concept *living organism* going from the most general to more specific. Although a specialized vocabulary exists for semantic mapping, teachers do not really need it in order to help students see how concepts are related and that the more

[8]Frank Smith, *Comprehension and Learning* (New York: Holt, Rinehart and Winston, 1975), p. 10.

[9]David P. Pearson and Dale D. Johnson, *Teaching Reading Comprehension* (New York: Holt, Rinehart and Winston, 1980), p. 232.

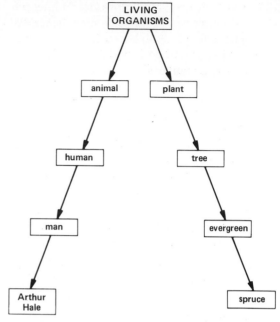

Figure 4.4.

general a category is the more abstract it is, and the more specific a category is the more concrete it is.

Rather than using semantic maps to help students see the relationships among categories, teachers can use sets (see "Sets and Outlining" in Chapter 14), for example:

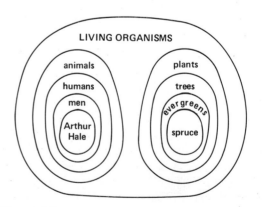

Figure 4.5.

Teachers can also use outlines (see "Outlining" in Chapter 14) to help students see relationships, for example:

I. Living Organisms
   A. Plants
      1. Trees
         a. Evergreens
            (1) Spruce
   B. Animals
      1. Humans
         a. Men
            (1) Arthur Hale

CONCEPT DEVELOPMENT IN PRIMARY GRADES K–3

Preschool children learn concepts, for the most part, from direct experience. Unless young children have had direct sensory experiences, they will have difficulty in concept development.

When children enter kindergarten they may know the following concepts: above and below, on top of, underneath, next to, the middle one, start, stop, go, come, sit, stand, and so on. They may not know this type of concept: the one before, the next one, double, like, and unlike, nor are they likely to recognize grapheme-phoneme (letter-sound) correspondences or number names for quantities.[10] It is important to state, however, that individual differences exist among children entering kindergarten, and some young children entering kindergarten can read and have some number names for quantities.

Kindergarten children are learning to group many objects. Different kinds of apples—such as Delicious, McIntosh, Cortland, and Greening—would all go under the class *apples*. Also, pears, apples, bananas, plums, and so forth would go under the class *fruit*.

In primary grades children are learning simple concepts such as over and under, big and little. The pupils learn to classify things such as dogs and animals, days and weeks, pennies and money, and so on, proceeding from a concrete to a more abstract level. For example, a child can name his or her dog "Champ," who is a pet, and as a pet it is also in the class of animals. Teachers can use semantic maps and sets to help children see relationships between and among various concepts. (See the previous section and Chapter 13 for more on categorizing.)

As children grow in their use of listening, speaking, and reading skills, their concept development continues. They learn that some words designate different levels of things and feelings. They put on their *coats*. They put *coats* of paint on the toy. These two uses illustrate a

[10]Robert M. Gagné, *Conditions of Learning* (New York: Holt, Rinehart and Winston, 1965).

Figure 4.6.

homograph. The children learn about different kinds of elevators, forms, cities. They develop the relational concepts of afraid, brave, proud, faraway, and so on. They learn about associations and how some words are associated with certain ideas and objects. For example, they would associate *farmer, barn, cows, pigs, chickens,* and so on with farm. They learn the meaning of figures of speech, such as, "The trees trembled in the night" or "The wind roared its disapproval." The students should also learn the concepts of *synonyms* (words that mean the same or nearly the same) and *antonyms* (words that mean the opposite) in isolation and in context. As children gain skill in working with such concepts as classification, synonyms, antonyms, and word associations, they are gaining the ability to recognize and work with word relationships (analogies).

An informal inventory test of concepts in the primary grades, such as the one given below, could be developed and easily administered to the whole class as a paper-and-pencil test, or it can be given orally to individual students, whichever is more convenient in the classroom.

Another method to determine whether children have the concept of opposites is for the teacher to ask each child to give some opposites for the following words:

no	good	fat
boy	mommy	go
happy		

In order to determine whether the children understand the concepts of left and right, the teacher could play the game "Simon Says" with the children and use directions with the words *left* and *right*. The teacher could also observe whether children understand the concept of *first* and *last* by asking children to name who is first or who is last in line. The teacher can learn much about the concept development of students by using such informal techniques.

EXAMPLE OF AN INFORMAL INVENTORY TEST OF CONCEPTS FOR PRIMARY-GRADE STUDENTS

For each concept the teacher will orally state the tested term in the context of a sentence. The children will show they understand the concept by correctly checking or putting a circle around the picture that best describes the concept. Before beginning, the teacher should make sure that all children understand the symbol for a check (✓) and that they can draw a circle around an object.

1. Concept *over.* Concept in sentence: The check (✓) is over the ball.

Directions

Put a circle around the picture that shows a ✓ is over a ball. (Again, the teacher should put a ✓ on the board to make sure children understand this term. The teacher should make a circle on the board to make sure children understand this concept as well.)

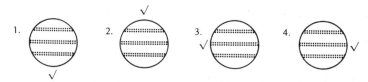

2. Concept of *under.* Concept in sentence: The check (✓) is under the ball.

Directions

Put a circle around the picture that shows a ✓ is under a ball.

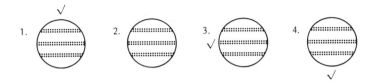

3. Concept of *square.* Sentence: Which picture shows a square?

Directions

Put a check in the square.

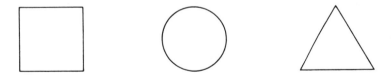

4. Concept of *triangle.* Sentence: Which picture shows a triangle?

Directions

Put a check in the triangle.

5. Concept of *most.* Sentence: Which box has the most balls?

Directions

Draw a circle around the box that has the most balls.

1.    2. 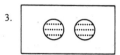   3.

6. Concept of *least.* Sentence: Which box has the least number of balls?

Directions

Draw a circle around the box that has the least number of balls.

1. 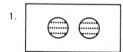   2. 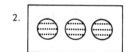   3.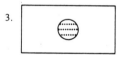

7. Concept of *smallest.* Sentence: Which ball is the smallest?

Directions

Draw a circle around the smallest ball.

1.   2.   3.   4.

8. Concept of *largest*. Sentence: Which ball is the largest?

Directions

Draw a circle around the largest ball.

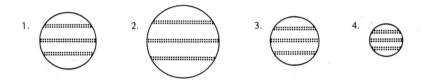

9. Concept of *opposites.*

Directions

Draw a circle around the picture that is the opposite of the word that I am going to say. (For example, the teacher says, "What is the opposite of girl?")

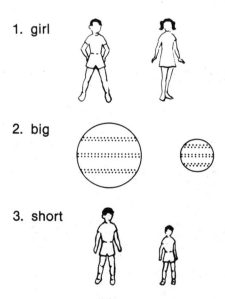

1. girl

2. big

3. short

CONCEPT DEVELOPMENT AND THE EDUCATIONALLY DISADVANTAGED CHILD[11]

In the case of educationally disadvantaged children teachers cannot assume that certain concepts have already been attained. For example, most teachers would take for granted that the term *pet* is a concrete, clear-cut name that all children could easily learn. However, this may not be so. Many children from a low socioeconomic area in Washington, D.C., did not know the word *pet*. To the children living in this area *pet* was an abstraction, because a child living in an overcrowded apartment does not usually have a pet. In order to have a dog one must obtain a license, feed the pet, give it medical attention, have a place for it to stay, and so on. Although children who live in low socioeconomic environments may have rich, expressive vocabularies of their own, they will not be the same vocabulary that is predominantly used in middle-class schools and curriculums.[12]

In helping educationally disadvantaged children to develop concepts, the teacher must help them to attain the concepts that are of greatest concern, interest, and use to them. It is claimed by some authorities that these children use adjectives better than verbs, that they are able to express themselves better in spontaneous or unstructured situations than in formal ones, that they understand more language than they use, and that they have the verbal ability to fantasize.[13]

---

[11]The term *disadvantaged* is applied to those students who come from a low socioeconomic class. These children are disadvantaged in school because they may lack the concept-development experiences and the vocabulary that is needed in order to achieve.

[12]Edgar Dale, "Vocabulary Development of the Underprivileged Child," *Elementary English* 42 (November 1965): 778–86.

[13]Frank Riessman, *The Culturally Deprived Child* (New York: Harper & Row, 1962).

Using these descriptive factors as a guide, the teacher could create a program to help such children attain the concepts necessary for developing cognitive processes and reading.

SUMMARY

Chapter 4 emphasizes the interrelatedness of language development, concept development, and reading. It is shown how a child with a problem in language will also have problems in acquiring concepts, and how this will affect a child's reading performance because reading is a thinking act. All of the individual factors which are discussed in the following chapter affect a child's language and concept development. The area of language development is the one in which educationally disadvantaged children are in need of help. A special section is presented on concept development because of its importance in the reading process. Knowledge of how children attain concepts and what they are is especially essential in a diagnostic-reading and correction program because teachers in such a program must recognize *early* when a child is lacking certain concepts and help that child attain them. Some informal techniques to assess a child's concept development are presented, as well as a discussion of semantic mapping.

SUGGESTIONS FOR THOUGHT QUESTIONS AND ACTIVITIES

1. Explain *assimilation* and *accommodation* as used by Piaget.
2. What are some of the concepts that primary-grade level children should possess?
3. Develop an informal technique to assess whether young children possess certain concepts. Use the one in the text as an example.

4. Why is *equilibrium* necessary in concept development?

5. Reread the cartoon presented on page 36. Give some other humorous examples similar to the one in the cartoon.

6. What should the teacher know concerning the relationship of language development, concept development, and reading?

SELECTED BIBLIOGRAPHY

Britton, James. *Language and Learning.* Middlesex, Eng.: Penguin, 1970.

Carroll, John B. "Words, Meanings and Concepts." In *Thought & Language: Language and Reading,* pp. 26–50. Maryanne Wolf et al., eds. Cambridge, Mass.: Harvard Educational Review, 1980.

Dale, Philip S. *Language Development.* Hinsdale, Ill.: Dryden, 1972.

Hardy, William G. *Communication and the Disadvantaged Child.* Baltimore, Md.: Williams and Wilkins, 1970.

Lindfors, Judith. *Children's Language and Learning.* Englewood Cliffs, N.J.: Prentice-Hall, 1980.

Loban, Walter D. *Language Development: Kindergarten through Grade Twelve,* Research Report No. 18. Urbana, Ill.: National Council of Teachers of English, 1976.

Pearson, David P. and Dale D. Johnson. *Teaching Reading Comprehension.* New York: Holt, Rinehart and Winston, 1980.

Piaget, Jean. *The Language and Thought of the Child.* New York: Harcourt, 1926.

Rawson, Hildred. "Cognition and Reading: An Approach to Instruction." In *Reading Research: Advances in Theory and Practice.* T. Gary Waller and G. E. Mackinnon, eds. New York: Academic Press, 1979.

Rubin, Dorothy. *Teaching Elementary Language Arts,* 2nd ed. New York: Holt, Rinehart and Winston, 1980.

Rupley, William H. "Language Development and Beginning Reading Instruction." *Elementary English* 52 (March 1975): 403–407.

Smith, Nila Banton. "Early Language Development: Foundation of Reading." *Elementary English* 52 (March 1975): 399–402; 418.

Some of the Factors That Affect Reading Performance

INTRODUCTION

Here are composites of two children. Which child would you predict will succeed in school? Why?

SUSAN X
First born

Middle-class socioeconomic status

College-educated parents

English is dominant language

Parents read to Susan

Many books are available for Susan

Parents read for pleasure

Television viewing is supervised

Parents discuss books and television shows with Susan

JIM Y
Third born of five children

Low-class socioeconomic status

Parents have seventh-grade education

Nonstandard English is spoken

No one reads to Jim

Hardly any books are available for Jim

Parents do not read for pleasure

Television viewing is unsupervised

Parents do not discuss television shows with Jim

You probably answered "Susan," and if you did, you would probably be correct. You are also probably saying that the deck has been stacked in Susan's favor. It has been; however, many children have backgrounds similar to those of Jim and Susan. The Susans do well in school because they have had the preschool background and experiences that seem to correlate well with school success.

This chapter will present a number of those factors which determine in part the reading success of children. It is important that teachers recognize how many of these individual factors affect reading success, even though there are a number—such as home environment, family makeup, and cultural differences—that educators can do nothing about. However, if educators are aware that some students come from backgrounds that are not conducive to school learning, they will try to provide those experiences that these children need to be successful readers. It is to be hoped that teachers will also recognize how important their role is in helping these children and not, as was discussed in Chapter 2, invoke the self-fulfilling prophecy, which will guarantee the children's failure.

After you finish reading this chapter, you should be able to answer the following questions:

1. What are some factors that influence a child's reading performance?

2. How are some factors that influence a child's reading performance interrelated?

3. How does a child's home environment influence his or her reading ability?

4. What is the relationship of language to reading?

5. What is the relationship of intelligence to reading?

6. What is the relationship of sex differences to reading?

7. What is the relationship of birth order to language development?

8. What is the relationship of language and dialect to the development of standard English?

9. How can perceptual factors interfere with reading success?

10. What should a teacher know about laterality and reading?

DIFFERENTIATING BETWEEN NONEDUCATIONAL AND EDUCATIONAL FACTORS

Before we proceed to some of the various noneducational and educational factors that can affect a child's reading performance, it is necessary to differentiate between *noneducational* and *educational* factors. When persons talk about educational factors, they generally are referring to those factors that come under the domain or control of the educational system and influence learning. Under educational factors, we would usually include the various methods and materials that the child has been exposed to, the teacher, the instructional time, the school environment, the school district, and so on. Under noneducational factors, we generally would include physical health (general), vision, hearing, intelligence, personality, and sex differences. Noneducational factors are supposedly those that do not come under the domain or control of the educational system and cannot be influenced by it. However, if we were to scrutinize these factors, we would see that some, such as sex differences, can be learned and influenced by the schools. Intelligence is another factor that is influenced by school and learning. Obviously, for some of the factors, overlapping exists. A case could even be made for general physical health as being influenced by educational practices. For example, children who are doing poorly in school may wish to avoid school to such an extent that they become ill every morning. The children's emotional health has influenced their physical health so that they actually get ill; that is, they may get a stomachache, headache, or throw up. Their emotional state may so affect them that they cannot eat or sleep. The physical symptoms are real, even though the cause may not be a virus or bacterium.

A child's personality can also be affected by what takes place in school. For example, the little boy Larry, who was presented in a scenario at the beginning of the book, had an undetected eye problem, and he was subjected to methods and materials in school that were not helping him learn to read. Larry soon changed from a happy, outgoing, and helpful young boy to a sullen, irritable, unhappy child who didn't like himself or anyone else.

It is imperative that teachers be aware of the interrelatedness of the various factors, regardless of whether they are educational or noneducational. A child who has difficulty learning to read usually has concommitantly many emotional and social problems, and these are compounded as the child goes through school if he or she is not helped as soon as a problem is detected or suspected.

HOME ENVIRONMENT

Socioeconomic class, parents' education, and the neighborhhood in which children live are some of the factors which shape children's home environments. Studies have shown that the higher the socioeconomic status, the better the verbal ability of the child.[1] Children who have good adult language models and are spoken to and encouraged to speak will have an advantage in the development of language and intelligence. Parents who behave in a warm, democratic manner and provide their children with stimulating educationally oriented activities, challenge their children to think, encourage independence, and reinforce their children are preparing them very well for school.

Children who come from homes where parents have only an elementary-school education, where many people live in a few rooms, and where unemployment among the adults in the home is common will usually be at a disadvantage in learning language.

Teachers should also be aware of the adult composition of the child's home environment. Whether a child is reared by both parents, a single parent, a servant, grandparents, or foster parents will affect the child's attitudes and behavior. A child who is reared by a female single parent may behave differently from one reared by a male single parent, for instance. The death of one parent or of another family member will usually cause emotional stress in the child. Divorce can also be a traumatic experience for children. Teachers who are aware of the home environment and are sensitive to sudden changes in this important area are in a better position to understand and help such students.

How many children are born into a family and the order in which these children are born affect the achievement levels of individuals, at least to some degree. Research is still being done on these factors, but it has been hypothesized that firstborn children do better both in school and in life than other children in the family. A child without siblings has been shown to be more articulate for the most part than a child who is a product of a multiple birth (like twins or triplets) or a singleton (one child born at a time) who has other brothers and sisters.[2]

Studies have shown that the only child, who is more often in the company of adults, has more chances of being spoken to by the grown-ups around him or her than is the case when there are many children in the family. Then, too, twins seem to have less need to communicate with others because they have a close relationship.

Singletons with siblings also have "interpreters" near at hand, that is, older siblings who can often understand a younger child's messages so well that the younger child need not attempt to express him- or herself more effectively.

All these factors form part of the learning climate in the home and influence the degree and amount of learning the child will do in school.

---

[1]Walter D. Loban, *Language Development: Kindergarten through Grade Twelve,* Research Report No. 18 (Urbana, Ill.: National Council of Teachers of English, 1976).

[2]Mildred A. Dawson and Miriam Zollinger, *Guilding Language Learning* (New York: Harcourt, 1957), pp. 36–37. Didi Moore, "The Only-Child Phenomenon," *The New York Times Magazine,* January 18, 1981, pp. 26–27, 45–48.

DIALECT AND LANGUAGE DIFFERENCES

Standard English is defined in *Webster's New Collegiate Dictionary* as "the English that with respect to spelling, grammar, pronunciation, and vocabulary is substantially uniform though not devoid of regional differences, that is well established by usage in the formal and informal speech and writing of the educated, and that is widely recognized as acceptable wherever English is spoken and understood."

Children who speak a variation or dialect of English or another language are not inferior to children speaking standard English, nor is their language inferior. Research by linguists (persons who study language) has shown that many variations of English are highly structured systems and not accumulations of errors in standard English. Children speaking in a dialect of English have no difficulty communicating with one another. However, any dialect which differs from standard English structure and usage will usually cause communication problems for children in school and in society at large. Many expressions used by children who speak a variation of English may be foreign to teachers, and many expressions used by teachers may have different connotations for the students. The similarities between the dialects of English and standard English can also cause misunderstandings between the students and teachers because both groups may feel they "understand" what the others are saying when, in actuality, they do not. (In this book nonstandard English refers to English dialects that vary from standard English.)

Children who come from homes where a language other than English is the dominant one may also have language difficulties when they enter school unless they are truly bilingual. The dictionary definition of *bilingual* states that one must be "capable of using two languages.[3]

However, many schoolchildren who speak a language other than standard English at home are not bilingual. These children may hear only "noises" when they first enter school because the English sounds have little or no meaning for them. They will often confuse the language spoken at home with their newly acquired English and vice-versa. It is not a question of one language being better than or preferred over another, but rather one of helping children to get along in the dominant social, economic, and political culture and to become a part of it. Unless students learn to communicate in standard English as well as in a dialect or another language, they will have difficulty in succeeding in the economy.

Children Who Speak Nonstandard English

Children who speak nonstandard English may have more problems than children who come from homes in which a foreign language is spoken because more prestige and status are generally attributed to a foreign language. It is reported in a large-scale Educational Testing Service study of Title I reading programs that teachers do hold negative attitudes toward nonstandard language.[4] Other studies with similar findings have also reported that the negative attitudes have influenced teacher practices. For example, "teachers tend to rate black English speaking students as lower class, less intelligent, and less able to do well academically than standard English speaking students."[5] In 1979 a United States district court judge ruled on a case concerning the Ann Arbor school system. Judge Charles W. Joiner wrote that "a language barrier develops when teachers, in

---

[3]*Webster's New Twentieth Century Dictionary,* Unabridged, 2nd ed. (Cleveland, Ohio: World, 1970), p. 182.

[4]Mary K. Monteith, "Black English, Teacher Attitudes, and Reading," *Language Arts* 57 (November/December 1980): 910.

[5]Ibid.

helping the child switch from the home [black English] language to standard English, refuse to admit the existence of a language that is the acceptable way of talking in his local community."[6]

The rejection of the child's language "may more deeply upset him than rejection of the color of his skin. The latter is only an insult, the former strikes at his ability to communicate and express his needs, feelings—his self."[7] The language of children who do not speak standard English has been an effective means of communication for them until they come to school. If such children are made to feel inferior because of their language by a teacher who constantly attacks their speech as incorrect, they may not attempt to learn standard English.

INTELLIGENCE AND READING

Since reading is a thinking process, it seems reasonable to assume that highly able persons, who have the ability to think at high levels of abstraction and the ability to learn, should be good readers. To a degree this is so, and many gifted children do learn to read before they come to school. However, studies have shown that not all highly able children become good readers, which suggests that there are factors besides intelligence that contribute to success in reading and consequently to achievement in school.

Studies have shown that the correlation between intelligence and reading achievement seems to increase as children go through the grades.[8] It has been suggested that "mental age actually is a more basic determinant of reading success when children have reached the stage at which they *read to learn* than it is when they are *learning to read.*"[9] Singer, an educational psychologist, has done research on *learning how to read* and on *reading to learn* or *reading to gain information.* Even though he claims that there is no way the two functions of reading can be completely separated, he does differentiate between the two; *reading for information* "depends not only on *learning how to read,* but also on increments in experience, conceptual development, vocabulary ability, general cognitive development, plus desire to know and understand."[10] Many basal reader series in the 1980s emphasize the teaching of both word recognition skills and comprehension in the primary grades, and the comprehension skills include those that were usually reserved for the higher grades (see Chapter 13). With the emphasis on reading and thinking skills in the early grades, it will be interesting to see if there will be as great a change in the relationship between intelligence and reading achievement as the children go through the grades.

Most intelligence tests are highly verbal, and persons who do well on vocabulary tests also seem to do well on intelligence tests. Studies have also shown that there is a positive correlation between reading achievement test scores and intelligence test scores. These findings seem to suggest that reading achievement tests and in-

[6]Reginald Stuart, *The New York Times,* July 13, 1979, p. 8.
[7]E. Brooks Smith, Kenneth S. Goodman, and Robert Meredith, *Language and Thinking in the Elementary School* (New York: Holt, Rinehart and Winston, 1976), pp. 46–47.

[8]Alice Cohen and Gerald G. Glass, "Lateral Dominance and Reading Ability," *The Reading Teacher* 21 (January 1968): 343–48. Dolores Durkin, *Children Who Read Early* (New York: Teachers College Press, 1966), pp. 20–21.
[9]Emerald V. Dechant and Henry P. Smith, *Psychology in Teaching Reading* (Englewood Cliffs, N.J.: Prentice-Hall, 1977), pp. 94–95.
[10]Harry Singer, "Measurement of Early Reading," *Contemporary Education* 48 (Spring 1977): 146.

telligence tests may be measuring some similar factors. It seems reasonable to assume that a major factor both kinds of tests have in common is verbal ability. Obviously, reading as a thinking process hinges on the continuous development of higher levels of verbal ability (see "Language Development, Concept Development, and Reading" in Chapter 4, and Chapter 7 for more on intelligence).

Special Note

Some educators talk about *learning to read* and *reading to learn* as two different processes taking place at different times. *Learning to read* is usually associated with the primary grades, whereas *reading to learn* is usually associated with the intermediate and upper grades. *Learning to read* and *reading to learn* are not two mutually exclusive processes; they can and do take place together. Teachers should bear in mind that children in the lower grades as well as in the higher grades should be involved in both.

SEX DIFFERENCES

Are females really the weaker sex? Why are there more male underachievers in elementary-school grades? Why are there more remedial readers among boys than girls? Why do males usually receive poorer grades in school than females? Since there are more adult males in important positions in society, does this mean that males are smarter than females?

There are vast differences between males and females besides the obvious physical ones. Females seem to have a biological precocity evident from birth onward.[11] The skeletal develop-

ment of girls is superior to that of boys at birth, and this physical superiority continues until maturity.[12] Males, however, give off more carbon dioxide than females,[13] which means that boys need to take in more food and consequently produce more energy. Even though the male matures later than the female, his oxygen intake is greater and continues so throughout life.[14] It has been hypothesized that sex differences in behavior may be due to these differences in metabolism.

These factors may affect the readiness levels of children in listening, speaking, reading, and writing—the language arts. Teachers must realize that some primary-grade boys may not be as mature as some girls of the same chronological age. They should not be expected to do equally well on tasks using specific hand muscles—such as handwriting. Similarly, teachers should not expect these more immature male students to be able to sit still as long as some more mature female students or to have a comparable attention span. Teachers should know that although studies reveal no significant differences between males and females in general intelligence,[15] there are differences in specific aptitudes. For example, males in general, according to the studies, are superior in mathematical ability and in science, but in rote

---

[11]Amram Scheinfeld, *Women and Men* (New York: Harcourt, 1944), pp. 58–71.

[12]J. M. Tanner, "Physical Growth," in *Carmichael's Manual of Child Psychology,* 3rd ed., Paul H. Mussen, ed. (New York: Wiley, 1970), p. 109.

[13]Stanley M. Garn and Leland C. Clark, Jr., "The Sex Difference in the Basal Metabolic Rate," *Child Development* 24 (September–December 1953): 215–24.

[14]Ibid., p. 222.

[15]Scottish Council for Research in Education, *The Intelligence of a Representative Group of Scottish Children* (London: University of London Press, 1939). Scottish Council for Research in Education, *The Trend of Scottish Intelligence* (London: University of London Press, 1949).

memory females are usually superior.[16] It also has been consistently shown that girls usually surpass boys in verbal ability. From infancy to adulthood, females usually express themselves in words more readily and skillfully than males. Researches show that in general girls seem to learn to talk a little earlier; are usually somewhat superior during the preschool years in articulation, intelligibility, and correctness of speech sounds; and learn grammar and spelling more readily and are less likely to be stutterers.[17] It is important to note that the studies in this area are not definitive. More recent studies show that for "large unselected populations the situation seems to be one of very little sex difference in verbal skills from about 3 to 11, with a new phase of differentiation occurring at adolescence."[18] Comparisons of males and females on a variety of tests have made it clear that girls and women do not have larger vocabularies than boys and men.

Sex Differences and Reading

Innumerable studies have found that boys usually outnumber girls in remedial reading classes,[19] and reading disabilities are "from three to ten times more common for boys, depending on how the disability is defined and what population is studied."[20] Researchers have also found "greater variability in reading scores among boys from grades 2 through 7 . . . and

boys outnumbered girls among the lowest scores by about 2 to 1 in the lower grades, with the ratio decreasing thereafter."[21]

Many causes have been suggested as reasons for the sex differences. A number of researchers have hypothesized that the female superiority in reading in the United States may be caused by cultural factors, and therefore a number of cross-cultural studies have been made. A much quoted one is Preston's study comparing the reading achievement of German and American boys and girls. He found that the German boys excelled over the German girls in all reading areas tested except that of speed, and his results for the American children were similar to those of previous researchers; that is, "the incidence of 'retardation' and of 'severe retardation' was greater among the American boys than among the American girls—significantly so in almost all instances."[22] His study supported culture as a major factor influencing sex differences in reading. A review of some of the cross-cultural studies found conflicting results; that is, many studies confirm the superiority of girls in reading in countries other than the United States, whereas some studies support the Preston findings.[23]

Some researchers have claimed that the differences in reading achievement in the early grades are the result of the greater educational readiness of girls for formal reading when they

[16]Leona E. Tyler, *The Psychology of Human Differences* (New York: Appleton-Century-Crofts, 1965), pp. 244–45.

[17]Ibid., pp. 243–44.

[18]Eleanor E. Maccoby and Carol M. Jacklin, *The Psychology of Sex Differences* (Stanford, Cal.: Stanford University Press, 1974), p. 85.

[19]Norma Naiden, "Ratio of Boys to Girls Among Disabled Readers," *The Reading Teacher* 29 (February 1976): 439–42.

[20]Maccoby and Jacklin, op. cit., p. 119.

[21]Ibid.

[22]Ralph C. Preston, "Reading Achievement of German and American Children," *School and Society* 90 (October 1962): 352.

[23]Howard A. Klein, "Cross-Cultural Studies: What Do They Tell About Sex Differences in Reading?" *The Reading Teacher* 30 (May 1977): 880–85. Dale D. Johnson, "Sex Differences in Reading Across Cultures," *Reading Research Quarterly* 9 (1973–1974): 67–85. Alice Dzen Gross, "Sex-Role Standards and Reading Achievement: A Study of an Israeli Kibbutz System," *The Reading Teacher* 32 (November 1978): 149–56.

come to school.[24] Both cultural and biological or maturational factors have been put forth as reasons for girls' superior readiness for formal reading. A perusal of the literature seems to lend support to theories suggesting that the sex differences in reading may be caused by a combination of both maturational and environmental factors.

Let's look at the environmental or cultural evidence a little more closely to see how this factor may affect children's readiness to read. Since language learning is closely related to reading success, and since girls usually surpass boys in verbal ability, it would appear that girls have an advantage over boys when they come to school. The question is why girls have this superior ability. It has been hypothesized, and the evidence is mounting, that the language differences observed between the sexes in the early years may also be due to cultural factors. For example, mothers might spend more time with young females during the day than with young males, since it would be "sissy stuff" for boys to help Mommy clean the house. As a result, there would be more verbal interaction between the mother and daughter.

Also, studies made of sex-role standards have shown that American boys look upon reading as "feminine" and not in accord with a masculine role. It has been suggested that this factor may influence greatly how males will achieve in reading. For example, in a study made in an Israeli kibbutz, where the boys perceive reading as a desirable masculine skill appropriate for their sex, boys achieve at equally high levels, and boys and girls exhibit an equal amount of reading disability.[25] Preston suggests that the

apparent reading superiority of German boys to German girls may be caused by the masculinization of the German schools. In German culture, reading and learning are considered to be more in the male than the female domain, and the teachers in Germany are predominantly males even in the elementary school.[26]

The *teacher* also has been put forth as a possible cause for boys' depressed reading achievement. Some researchers claim that American teachers *expect* their girls to read better than their boys, and that this influences sex differences.[27] Other investigators suggest that sex differences in reading achievement are the result of classroom teachers' *treatment* of boys and girls; that is, "classroom teachers treat boys and girls differently and this difference in treatment is associated with differences in early reading achievement."[28] The studies in this area are also confusing because different studies seem to find different results. For example, a review of the research comparing male and female elementary-school teachers did not find any significant differences between male and female teachers' perception or treatment of boys and girls.[29]

Although it has not been shown that either sex has a preference for vision or hearing to gain information, Maccoby and Jacklin, two noted authorities in the psychology of sex differences, put forth an intriguing possibility. It is that "modality preferences during the early school years might feed into the development of dif-

---

[24]Irving H. Balow, "Sex Differences in First Grade Reading," *Elementary English* 40 (March 1963): 306. Guy L. Bond and Robert Dykstra, "The Cooperative Research Program in First-Grade Reading Instruction," *Reading Research Quarterly* 2 (Summer 1967): 122.

[25]Gross, op. cit., pp. 149–56.

[26]Preston, op. cit., p. 353. Also, Ralph C. Preston, "Letters," *The Reading Teacher* 31 (December 1977): 318–19.

[27]Johnson, op. cit., p. 85.

[28]John D. McNeil, "Programed Instruction Versus Usual Classroom Procedures in Teaching Boys to Read," *American Educational Research Journal* 1 (March 1964): 113.

[29]Henriette M. Lahaderne, "Feminized Schools—Unpromising Myth to Explain Boys' Reading Problems," *The Reading Teacher* 29 (May 1976): 776–86.

ferent subject-matter skills at a later time."[30] This theory is based on a study by a researcher who identified individual differences among first- and second-grade children in how they took in information. The study discussed by Maccoby and Jacklin found that the "visual" children do better in reading, and the "auditory" children do better in arithmetic. The researcher of the study, however, does not report whether there are sex differences in the perceptual orientations he has identified.[31]

PERCEPTUAL FACTORS

In Chapter 1 the importance of perception (giving meaning to sensations) as part of the process of reading was discussed. It was stated that a child who has problems in the perceptual domain will most assuredly encounter difficulty in concept development and consequently in reading. The area of perception will be pursued further in this chapter as a significant factor affecting reading achievement. (Chapter 6 will discuss auditory perception.)

Throughout this book it is stressed that reading is a complex process and that a reading difficulty is usually due to multiple causes rather than a single one. In learning to read children need auditory and visual perceptual skills and such sensory-motor skills as eye-movement control for scanning the pages and finger control for turning them,[32] as well as the skills in language and concept development. For example, a child would have difficulty decoding if he or she has not achieved such skills as "discrimination, retention and recall of sounds and letters, sequential ordering of phonemes and

grapheres, and the ability to interrelate one with the other.[33] (See Chapter 6 for information on listening.)

Visual Perception

Since reading requires the sense of sight, it seems almost absurd to say that a visual deficit will influence a child's ability to read. However, a visual problem is not always obvious and, as a result, is not always detected. Most schools have some kind of visual screening that each child must undergo. The screening is generally done by the school nurse and usually makes use of the Snellen chart. This chart uses line figures for young children and letters for those who can read letters; it tests acuity (keenness of vision). The test making use of the Snellen chart requires that the child stand twenty feet away from the chart with one eye covered. The child must identify letters of various sizes with each eye. A score of 20/20 is considered normal. A score of 20/40 or 20/60 means that a child has defective vision because the child with normal vision can see the letters at a distance of forty or sixty feet, whereas the child with defective vision can only see these letters at a distance of twenty feet.

The accuracy of the scores obtained from the Snellen chart has been questioned because the test does not "detect moderate degrees of far-sightedness or astigmatism and fails completely to detect even severe cases of poor fusion and eye-muscle imbalance. The one defect it readily discloses is nearsightedness."[34]

Although better instruments, such as the *Keystone Visual Survey Tests* and the *Ortho-*

---

[30]Maccoby and Jacklin, op. cit., p. 35.

[31]Ibid.

[32]Marianne Frostig, "Visual Modality—Research and Practice," in *Perception and Reading,* Vol. 12, Helen K. Smith, ed. (Newark, Del.: International Reading Association, 1966–1967).

[33]Joseph M. Wepman, "The Modality Concept—Including a Statement of the Perceptual and Conceptual Levels of Learning," in *Perception and Reading,* Vol. 12, Helen K. Smith, ed. (Newark, Del.: International Reading Association, 1966–1967).

[34]Albert J. Harris and Edward R. Sipay. *How to Increase Reading Ability,* 7th ed. (New York: Longman, 1980), p. 301.

Figure 5.1.

Rater, could be used as a preliminary screening for eye defects, most schools do not own such instruments.

Since the emphasis in this book is on the teacher's ability to detect a possible vision problem, here is a listing of some symptoms that teachers should look for:

1. The child complains of constant headaches.
2. The child's eyes show some of the following: red rims, swollen lids, crusted lids, red eyes, frequent sties, watering eyes.
3. The child squints while reading.
4. The child asks to sit closer to the chalkboard.
5. The child can't seem to sit still while doing close work.
6. The child holds the book very close to his or her face while reading.
7. The child skips lots of words or sentences while reading.
8. The child makes many reversals while reading.
9. The child confuses letters.
10. The child avoids reading.
11. The child mouths the words or lip reads.
12. The child confuses similar words.
13. The child makes many repetitions while reading.
14. The child skips lines while reading.
15. The child has difficulty remembering what he or she just read silently.

If a teacher notices some of these symptoms, he or she should speak to the child's parents or refer the child to the school nurse. It is important to state, however, that the presence of one or more of the listed symptoms does not mean a child has an eye problem, nor does it mean that it is the cause of the child's reading problem if one exists.

Visual Discrimination

Visual discrimination is the ability to distinguish between written symbols. If pupils have difficulty discriminating between and among letters, they will not be able to read. In learning to read children need to be able to make fine discrimination, and therefore need activities involving letters rather than geometric figures or pictures. Also, transfer of learning is greater if the written symbols children work with are similar to those they will meet in reading.

A visual discrimination test such as the following is excellent for discovering if a child has some reversal problem:

Directions: Put a circle around the letters that are the same as the first in the line. (Read aloud the directions for children who cannot read.)

b   d b b d p b

p   d b d p b p

© 1979 United Features Syndicate, Inc.

Figure 5.2.

Directions: Put a circle around the numbers that are the same as the first in the line. (Read aloud the directions for children who cannot read.)

7   6 9 4 7 9 7

9   7 8 9 7 6 9

Directions: Put a circle around the words that are the same as the first in the line. (Read aloud the directions to children who cannot read.)

saw   was saw saw was won now

won   now won won now not won

Most reading readiness tests have a subtest on visual discrimination. (See Chapters 10 and 12 for examples of more visual discrimination tests.)

Laterality and Reading

Human perceptual-motor activity is usually initiated from the one dominant side of the body, even though humans are bilateral, or two-sided. By the time children enter school they usually show a fairly consistent preference for their right or left hand, as well as preferences in the use of eyes and feet. Such preferences concern laterality or sidedness. People are said to have a dominant side if their hand, eye, and foot preferences are similar. When people have a dominant hand on one side and a dominant eye on the other, they are said to have crossed domi-

nance. Individuals who do not have a consistent preference for an eye, hand, or foot are said to have mixed dominance. It has been hypothesized that children who have crossed or mixed dominance may tend to have reversal difficulties in reading and writing, but studies made in this area have not been definitive. Children with crossed dominance can perhaps shift from a left-handed orientation to a right-handed one in writing, but this might cause difficulties for them.

No substantial evidence exists concerning cognitive deficits of left-handers;[35] however, a number of left-handers do have orientation problems in reading and writing. To better understand the left-handed child's problem in reading and writing we must refer to proximo-distal development—development from the midpoint of the body to the extremities. Right-handed children move their right hands from left to right naturally. Left-handed children find moving their left hand from left to right against their natural inclination.

Try this simple experiment to illustrate the point: Bring both hands to the center of your body. Now, move both hands out away from your body. The right hand will follow a left to right path corresponding to the English pattern of writing; the left hand follows a right to left path. Ask some left-handed persons to write a *t*.

[35]Merlin C. Wittrock, "Education and the Cognitive Processes of the Brain," *The National Society for the Study of Education 77th Yearbook,* Part II, 1978, p. 85.

Observe carefully how they make the horizontal line. Most of them, unless they have been well conditioned, will draw the line from right to left.

Teaching reading is a complex task, and one of the things that the child learns is to read from left to right. This follows natural development for right-handed people. However, teachers must recognize that reading from left to right is not natural for left-handed children and must be alert for possible reversal problems.

A teacher can easily test whether a child has crossed or mixed dominance. To determine hand dominance, a teacher can observe which hand the child uses to throw a ball, write, or open a door. The teacher can tell which eye is dominant by observing which eye the child uses to look through a microscope, telescope, or an open cylinder formed by a roll of paper. Foot dominance can be easily determined by observing which foot the child uses to kick a ball or stamp on the floor with.

Teachers should be cautioned that crossed or mixed dominance in a child does not mean that the child will have a problem, although the possibility exists. The teacher should give special attention to those children who are having reversal problems by emphasizing left-to-right orientation for reading and writing.

The teacher should also try to determine whether the child's reversal problem was caused by not *overlearning*[36] the word or letter being reversed. Many times if the letters *b* and *d* are presented together or taught one after the other, a child who has not sufficiently learned the first letter will confuse it with the next one. Traditionally, it is recommended that teachers should not teach letters such as *b* and *d,* or numbers such as *6* and *9,* together or one after the other. However, some research has found that confusable letters such as *b/d* and *m/n* should be

taught together to help students notice the slight differences between them.[37] If teachers decide to teach confusable letters together, they should stress the fine detail that differentiates one letter from another rather than just having students notice that the letters are different.

PHYSICAL HEALTH

A child who is ill is not able to do well in school. This is obvious; however, it may not be obvious that a child is ill. A teacher should be alert for certain symptoms that may suggest a child is not well or not getting enough sleep. For example, a child who is listless, whose eyes are glazed, who seems sleepy, and who actually does fall asleep in class may need a physical checkup. The teacher should speak to the school nurse about such a child and also discuss the child's behavior with his or her parents.

The reason a child who is ill does not usually do well in school is not necessarily because of the child's illness but because the child is out of school so often. Children who have illnesses that keep recurring are generally absent from school a lot. Moreover, the illnesses may be as mundane as the simple omnipresent cold. Such children should be seen by their doctor for a complete physical checkup to determine why they are so susceptible to colds. It may be that they are run-down or not eating the proper food.

The effects of nutrition, and particularly malnutrition, on learning are not new. Many studies have shown that children who are hungry and malnourished have difficulty learning because they cannot concentrate on the task at hand; they also lack drive. Some studies have suggested that severe malnutrition in infancy

---

[36]*Overlearning,* unlike overcooking, is not bad. The additional practice you engage in after you think you have mastered the material is called *overlearning.*

[37]Robert L. Hillerich, *Reading Fundamentals for Preschool and Primary Children* (Columbus, Ohio: Charles Merrill, 1977), pp. 57–58.

may lower children's IQ scores.[38] A number of researchers have found that the lack of protein in an infant's diet may adversely affect the child's ability to learn.[39] More recent studies have found that food additives may be a deterrent to learning for certain children.[40]

Special Note

A teacher should be cautious about making any diagnosis about a child's physical health. The teacher should also not make any inferences about a student's behavior unless she or he has sufficient evidence to warrant it. For example, if a child keeps putting his head on the desk, it may mean that he is frustrated or bored rather than ill or sleepy (see Chapter 11).

EDUCATIONAL FACTORS

Educational factors in learning, as stated earlier in this chapter, come under the domain or control of the educational system. Examples are approaches to instruction, methods and materials of instruction, instructional time, teachers, school environment, and so on. If a child is having a reading problem, it's generally a good idea for the teacher to check his or her school record to see if there is any information that might shed light on the child's problem. From the records, the teacher may be able to learn about the methods and materials the child has been exposed to in previous terms. It may be

that these were not effective, and something different should be tried.

Educational factors extend beyond the individual school to the entire school district and the community. The values of the community will affect the kind of education that will take place in the schools. For a diagnostic-reading and correction program to be effective, teachers need the support of their principals and other administrative and supervisory staff, as well as the support of the community and parents (see Chapter 18).

Only a short section is being devoted to this area here for a number of reasons. First, it would be prohibitive in a book such as this to present in detail all the methods and materials used to teach reading and the reading approaches; these can be found in reading method books. Also, throughout this book, there are sections that do discuss educational factors. For example, in Chapter 2, the teacher as the key to a good reading program is discussed as well as instructional time. Chapters 12, 13, and 14 present a review of many important reading skills, and the chapters in the last part of the book also present important educational factors.

SUMMARY

This chapter has presented a variety of educational and noneducational factors that may affect a child's reading performance. Many of these individual differences, such as home environment, family makeup, and culture, teachers can do nothing about. However, if teachers are aware that some of their children come from environments not conducive to learning, they will try to provide experiences in school to help these children become successful readers. Since reading is a thinking act, and since intelligence measures a person's ability to reason abstractly, it seems logical that the more intelligent an in-

---

[38]Merlin C. Wittrock, "Learning and the Brain," in Merlin C. Wittrock, ed., *The Brain and Psychology* (New York: Academic Press, 1980), pp. 376–77.

[39]Nevin S. Scrimshaw, "Infant Malnutrition and Adult Learning," *Saturday Review,* March 16, 1968, pp. 64–66, 84.

[40]Eleanor Chernick, "Effects of the Feingold Diet on Reading Achievement and Classroom Behavior," *The Reading Teacher* 34 (November 1980): 171–73.

dividual is, the better reader he or she should be. However, studies show that not all highly able students become good readers, which means that there are other factors besides intelligence that affect a student's ability to read. This chapter explores many of these other factors, one of which is sex differences. Many studies have found that there are more boys in remedial reading classes than girls. A number of reasons have been put forth for this phenomenon, one of the most greatly researched being cultural factors; another is biological or maturational factors. This chapter also explores some of the perceptual factors that could affect the child's reading performance. Practical information is given for classroom teachers about how they could detect the presence of a possible vision problem. The subject of laterality and its possible influence on reading is also discussed, and simple tests are provided which can help a teacher detect whether a child has crossed dominance. Educational factors, which are defined as those factors that come under the domain or control of the school, include instructional time, the teacher, methods of instruction, materials of instruction, and so on. It is shown how noneducational factors can be influenced by educational ones and that there are a number of factors that overlap.

SUGGESTIONS FOR THOUGHT QUESTIONS AND ACTIVITIES

1. Explain why cultural factors have been suggested as an explanation for why there are more boys in remedial reading classes or with reading disabilities than girls.

2. How have researchers tried to refute the "cultural factors theory" about why there are more boys with reading problems?

3. You have been asked to give a talk to your colleagues about why there are more read-ing disabilities among boys than among girls in the United States. What will you say?

4. What is the relationship of intelligence to reading?

5. State five symptoms suggesting that a child has a vision problem.

6. Explain crossed dominance.

7. Why may children who speak nonstandard English have more problems in school than children who speak a foreign language such as French or German?

8. Why would the community be considered an educational factor that could affect children's reading?

9. Construct some visual discrimination activities.

10. How can the physical health of a child affect his or her work at school?

SELECTED BIBLIOGRAPHY

Allen, Virginia G. "The Non-English Speaking Child in Your Classroom." *The Reading Teacher* 30 (February 1977): 504–508.

Anastasi, Anne. *Individual Differences.* New York: Wiley, 1965.

Cohen, Alice, and Gerald G. Glass. "Lateral Dominance and Reading Ability." *The Reading Teacher* 21 (January 1968): 343–48.

Deutsch, M., I. Katz, and A. R. Jensen, eds. *Social Class, Race, and Psychological Development.* New York: Holt, Rinehart and Winston, 1968.

Dillard, Joey L. *Black English.* New York: Random House, 1972.

Labov, W. *The Study of Non-Standard English.* Urbana, Ill.: National Council of Teachers of English, 1970.

Leong, Che Kan. "Laterality and Reading Proficiency." *Reading Research Quarterly* 15 (1980): 185–202.

Loban, Walter D. *Langauge Development: Kinder-*

garten through Grade Twelve, Research Report No. 18. Urbana, Ill.: National Council of Teachers of English, 1976.

Lugo, James O., and Gerald L. Hershey. *A Multidisciplinary Approach to Psychology of Individual Growth.* New York: Macmillan, 1974.

Maccoby, Eleanor E., ed. *The Development of Sex Differences.* Stanford, Cal.: Stanford University Press, 1966.

Maccoby, Eleanor E., and Carol M. Jacklin. *The Psychology of Sex Differences.* Stanford, Cal.: Stanford University Press, 1974.

McLaughlin, Barry. *Second Language Acquisition in Childhood.* New York: Halsted Press, 1978.

Monteith, Mary K. "Black English, Teacher Attitudes, and Reading." *Language Arts* 57 (November/December 1980): 908–12.

Moore, Didi. "The Only-Child Phenomenon." *New York Times Magazine,* Section 6, January 18, 1981, pp. 26–27, 45–48.

Schell, Leo M., and Paul C. Burns. *Remedial Reading: An Anthology of Sources.* Part Two, "Causal and Associated Factors," pp. 29–111. Boston: Allyn and Bacon, 1968.

Schubert, Delwyn G., and Howard N. Walton. "Visual Screening—A New Breakthrough." *The Reading Teacher* 34 (November 1980): pp. 175–77.

Spache, George D. *Diagnosing and Correcting Reading Disabilities,* 2nd ed. Chapter 2, "Diagnosis: Vision and Visual Perception," pp. 17–48. Boston: Allyn and Bacon, 1981.

Tyler, Leona E. *Individual Differences: Abilities and Motivational Directions.* Englewood Cliffs, N.J.: Prentice-Hall, 1974.

CHAPTER 6

Listening and Reading

INTRODUCTION

For a number of reasons a special chapter on listening is warranted in a book concerned with diagnosing reading difficulties. One reason involves the interrelatedness of the language arts (listening, speaking, reading, and writing). This fundamental relatedness can be deduced from the observations of children's development of oral and written expression, which follows the sequence listening, speaking, reading, and writing. Because of this sequence, a problem encountered in one segment of the language arts will usually carry over to another, and proficiency in one segment usually facilitates the acquisition of another area. Another reason involves diagnostic tests. The informal reading inventory (see Chapter 9) includes a listening capacity test, which is often used to determine a child's reading "potential."

In Chapter 2 a reference is made to David, a fourth-grader, who cannot read. David's case aptly emphasizes the interrelatedness of the language arts and how difficulty in one facet will generally carry the problem over to another. If we ask why David, in the fourth grade, is not reading, his teacher claims that he was tested the year before and was found to have impaired hearing. Digging into the problem further, we find that David had been "tested" by another teacher in the school, who knew little about the study of hearing. When David's teacher is asked if referrals had been made for more professional opinions and testing, we are told that it doesn't really pay to bother because all special personnel from the psychologist to the remedial reading teachers are overloaded, and the teacher would only be wasting his time.

By pinning the label "hearing impairment problem" on David the teacher is psychologically relieved of his responsibility. But David has not yet lost his determination to learn to read. He does not have a hearing problem. He has a language problem, which might be mistaken for a hearing impairment difficulty in the third or fourth grade. David comes from a bilingual home where Spanish is the dominant language. He has trouble discriminating between sounds in English; therefore he needs help in auditory discrimination. If David does not hear English words correctly, how can he be expected to say them correctly, or for that matter, read or write them? To David, many of the words in English are mere noises because the words are not in his listening vocabulary. David needs help in learning the English language.

This chapter will help you gain a better understanding of the relationship of listening to reading and of the role of listening in the diagnostic-reading and correction program. After you finish reading this chapter, you should be able to answer the following questions:

1. What is listening?
2. How is listening related to reading?
3. What are the levels of listening?
4. What factors influence the various listening levels?
5. What is the relationship of auditory discrimination to reading?
6. What does listening capacity mean?
7. What is a listening capacity test?
8. How is listening capacity measured?
9. When is a listening capacity test given?
10. What is the relationship of nonstandard English to listening?

LISTENING AS DECODING

Listening is the intake of language. The listener is involved in decoding a message from the speaker. The listener hears sound symbols which are called *phonemes*. These are analogous to the Morse code, for the listener must be able to decode the various sounds which stand for symbols. In order to decode, listeners must be able to hear differences between and among the various sounds of their language. If you were to ask a salesperson about the price of an item and were told fifty cents a pound, how could you be sure that the salesperson didn't say ninety cents a pound or five dollars a pound? You might say, "Because with my ears I heard that person say fifty cents rather than ninety cents. Fifty cents sounds *different* from ninety cents."

However, the buyer-listener might think he or she heard fifteen rather than fifty cents because of the similarity of the sounds. The emotional bias toward wanting to hear the lower price could also influence the listener.

Phonemes have no meaning in themselves except as they are combined into a specific pattern to form a *morpheme,* which is the smallest word unit. Morphemes are combined into an arrangement which gives the sentence its unique meaning. The listener must be able to assimilate the flow of sound symbols into meaningful concepts or no communication can occur. If a listener heard the sentence: "I blibed the blob," the sounds cannot be assimilated into meaningful concepts because *blibed* and *blob* are nonsense words. Similarly, if listeners heard the delightful poem "Jabberwocky" recited by Alice in *Through the Looking-Glass,* they would be as perplexed as Alice was about its meaning. Read one stanza and see if you agree.

> 'Twas brillig, and the slithy toves
> Did gyre and gimble in the wabe:
> All mimsy were the borogoves,
> And the mome raths outgrabe.

AUDITORY DISCRIMINATION AND MEMORY SPAN

Auditory discrimination, which is the ability to distinguish between sounds, is essential for the acquisition of language and for learning to read. The essence of what speech clinicians have learned about auditory discrimination is summarized as follows:

1. There is evidence that the more nearly alike two phonemes are in phonetic (relating to speech sounds) structure, the more likely they are to be misinterpreted.

2. Individuals differ in their ability to discriminate among sounds.

3. The ability to discriminate frequently matures as late as the end of the child's eighth year. A few individuals never develop this capacity to any great degree.

4. There is a strong positive relation between slow development of auditory discrimination and inaccurate pronunciation.

5. There is a positive relationship between poor discrimination and poor reading.

6. Although poor discrimination may be at the root of both speech and reading difficulties, it often affects only reading or speaking.

7. There is little if any relationship between the development of auditory discrimination and intelligence, as measured by most intelligence tests.[1]

For children who speak a nonstandard dialect of English or for whom English is a second language, it is well to bear in mind that the acquisition of speech sounds for any given dialect is learned very early in life and is usually established by the time the child starts school. These children especially need help in auditory discrimination if they are to learn standard English.

Auditory memory span is essential for individuals who must judge whether two or more sounds are similar or different. In order to make such comparisons, the sounds must be kept in memory and retrieved for comparison. Auditory memory span is defined as "the number of discrete elements grasped in a given moment of attention and organized into a unity for purposes of immediate reproduction or immediate use."[2] A deficiency in memory span will hinder effective listening. (See Chapter 14 for a digit-span scale for determining how well children are doing in memory span.)

The *Wepman Auditory Discrimination Test,* which was developed by Joseph M. Wepman and published by Language Research Associates, is a norm-referenced test that teachers use to discern whether students have auditory discrimination problems. (This test is similar to the first test item of the informal auditory discrimination test presented in Chapter 10.) The teacher asks the student to turn around so that he or she cannot lip-read; then the teacher very distinctly pronounces each pair of words. The student must determine if the words are the same or different. There are two forms of the test, each one consisting of forty pairs of words.

Many of the reading diagnostic tests presented in Chapter 10, and many of the reading readiness tests presented in Chapter 8, have subtests which test a child's auditory discrimination.

Individual intelligence tests, such as the *Stanford-Binet* and the *Wechsler,* have subtests which measure an individual's memory span. These tests are called *Digits Forward* and *Digits Backward.* The individual is told to listen carefully, and then the examiner says some numbers at the rate of one per second. After the entire series of numbers has been given, the individual must repeat them in the exact order. For the *Digits Backward,* the individual must repeat the digits in reverse order after the examiner has stopped (see Chapters 10 and 14).

[1] Joseph M. Wepman, "Auditory Discrimination, Speech and Reading," *Elementary School Journal* 60 (1960): 326.

[2] Virgil A. Anderson, "Auditory Memory Span as Tested by Speech Sounds," *American Journal of Psychology* 52 (1939): 95.

DIFFERENT LEVELS OF LISTENING[3]

In order to have a better understanding of the hierarchical and cumulative nature of listening, a discussion of the various levels of listening is necessary. *Hearing,* the lowest level in the hierarchy, refers to sound waves being received and modified by the ear. Someone in the process of hearing physically perceives the presence of sounds but would not be able to make out what the sounds are; they would merely be noise. Hearing, being a purely physical phenomenon, cannot be taught.

Listening is in the middle of the hierarchy of listening,[4] in which individuals become aware of sound sequences. They are able to identify and recognize the sound sequences as known words, if the words are in their listening capacity.

Auding is at the highest level of the hierarchy and involves not only giving meaning to the sounds but assimilating and integrating the oral message. An individual at the auding level would be able to gather the main idea of a spoken passage, discern analogies and inferences, and perform all the other high-level comprehension skills that are usually associated with reading. Creative problem-solving as well as critical listening are also skills included in this level. Although we are looking at each level as a separate entity, the act of listening is not divided into parts but functions as a whole.

Factors Influencing Hearing—The Lowest Level

Auditory Acuity

Auditory acuity is concerned with the physical response of the ear to sound vibrations.

If individuals have organic ear damage, they will not be able to hear properly, if at all, depending on the extent of the damage. Auditory acuity is the ability to respond to various frequencies (tones) at various intensities (levels of loudness).

Human speech comprises frequencies ranging from 125 to 8,000 Hertz (Hz).[5] The intensity or loudness level found in everyday speech will range typically from 55 decibels (faint speech) to 85 decibels (loud conversation). When hearing is tested, a person's ability to hear is checked across the entire speech-frequency range. If persons require more than the normal amount of volume (d.b. level) to hear sounds at certain frequencies, they are most probably exhibiting a hearing loss. The most critical frequencies for listening to speech lie in the frequency range between 1,000 and 2,500 Hertz because the majority of word cues are within this range. Frequencies above 2,500 Hertz contribute to the fineness with which we hear such sounds as /b, d, f, g, s, t, v, sh, th, zh/ (Webster's symbols).

An audiometer is used by audiologists for precise measurement of hearing loss. But teachers can make a lot of informal measurements on their own. Teachers can observe if any of the following behavior is present:

Does the child appear to be straining to push himself or herself closer to the speaker?
Does the child speak either very softly or very loudly?
Does the child have difficulty following simple directions?
Does the child turn up the sound of the record player or tape recorder?
Does the child have difficulty pronouncing words?
Does the child seem confused?

[3]Stanford E. Taylor, *Listening: What Research Says to the Teacher* (Washington, D.C.: National Education Association, 1969).
[4]The term *listening* is usually used to refer to both listening, the middle level, and auding, the highest level of the hierarchy.

[5]*Hertz* is the accepted international scientific word for cycles per second, named after the great nineteenth-century German physicist who proved the existence of electromagnetic waves.

Although these questions could be posed for a number of other problems, a teacher should have the student checked for possible hearing loss if one or more of these symptoms are manifested.

Auditory Fatigue

This is a temporary hearing loss caused by continuous or repeated exposure to sounds of certain frequencies. A monotonous tone or droning voice will have the effect of causing auditory fatigue. It has been shown that exposure to continuous loud noises over an extended period of time could be permanently harmful to an individual's hearing ability. Listening to music at a very high volume or being constantly exposed to cars and trucks rumbling through highway tunnels can have deleterious effects.

Binaural Considerations

When individuals are in the presence of two or more conversations, they must be able to direct their attention to only one of the speakers in order to be able to get the essence of what is being said. The more readily listeners are able to separate the sound sources, the more they will be able to grasp messages correctly. *Binaurality* thus refers to the ability of listeners to increase their reception sensitivity by directing both ears to the same sound.

Masking

Masking occurs when other sounds interfere with the message being spoken. Background noises drowning out a speaker or noisy classrooms or simultaneous group discussions will retard hearing ability.

Factors Influencing Listening—The Middle Level

Listening involves the way in which one identifies and recognizes sounds. Unless people are attentive to sounds, they will not understand their meaning, and meaning of sounds is an important part of listening. Sustained attention is concentration. If individuals are physically or mentally unwell, their chances for attending, and thus listening, are slim. Speakers play an important role in maintaining sustained attention. If they are boring, disliked, or unenthusiastic, they will not be as readily listened to as speakers who are interesting, liked, enthusiastic, and who use motivating techniques. Similarly, the physical environment of the classroom plays an important role in maintaining sustained attention. If the room is too hot or cold, if the chairs are uncomfortable, if there are provisions for writing, if the lighting is adequate and free of glare, if the acoustics are good, and if there are visual distractions—all these play a part in whether listening occurs.

Factors Influencing Auding—The Highest Level

Auding is the highest level of listening, as we have seen. It is not only the ability to discriminate between one word and another, or one syllable and another, but it also involves the individual's ability to assimilate the spoken message using the individual's total experience. The thinking skills used during auding are quite similar to those used during speaking, reading, and writing. Since the average speaking rate is 150 words per minute, the individual has time to formulate thoughts about what is being said, if what is being said is in the experience of the auditor. If the words are not in the listener's listening capacity, or if the topic is beyond the scope of his or her experiences, the listener will not understand what is being said. An individual who knows nothing about linguistics will have trouble comprehending an advanced lecture on this topic. A person with a background in linguistics may also have difficulty with the lecture if the words being used by the speaker are not familiar.

Figure 6.1[6] depicts the three stages of hearing, listening, and auding.

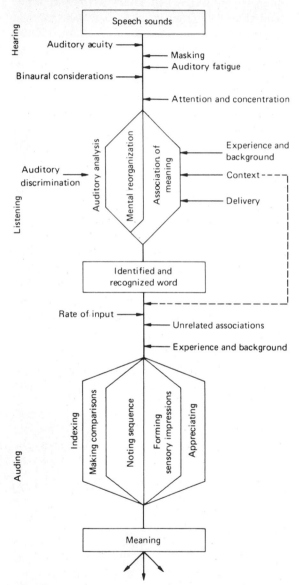

Figure 6.1   The total act of receiving auditory communication.

[6]Taylor, op. cit., p. 5.

LISTENING AND READING

To be able to recognize expressions in print, students must have heard these phrases correctly in the past; they must be in the reader's listening capacity. Reading comprehension depends on comprehension of the spoken language. Students who are sensitive to the arrangement of words in oral language are more sensitive to the same idea in written language. Listening helps to enlarge a student's vocabulary. It is through listening that pupils learn many expressions they will eventually see in print. Listening takes place all the time. Teachers orally explain word meanings and what the text says. Students listen to other children read orally, talk about books, and explain their contents.

In the elementary grades, when children are learning to read, students of low and average achievement usually prefer to listen rather than to read independently. These children gain more comprehension and retention from listening because of the important added cues they receive from the speaker, such as stress given to words or phrases, facial expressions, and so on.[7] Children who are very able and who have had success in reading achievement prefer to read because these children can set their own rate of reading for maximum comprehension and retention. They don't wish to be constrained by the fixed oral rate of the teacher.

The case in which students can understand a passage when it is orally read to them, but cannot understand it when they read it themselves, indicates that the words are in the students' listening capacity but that they have not gained the skills necessary for decoding words from their written forms.

It may be that some words are in the children's listening capacity (for example, they know the meaning of the individual words when they are said aloud), but they still might not be

[7]Robert Ruddell, "Oral Language and the Development of Other Language Skills," *Elementary English* 43 (May 1966): 489–98.

ship between reading and listening found that practice in listening for detail will produce a significant gain in reading for the same purpose.[10] More recent studies have also found that training in listening comprehension skills will produce significant gains in reading comprehension[11] and that reading and listening have similar thinking skills.[12]

Although there are many common factors involved in the decoding of reading and listening—which would account for the relationship between the two areas—listening and reading are, nonetheless, separated by unique factors. The most obvious is that listening calls for *hearing,* whereas reading calls for *seeing.* As has already been stated, in the area of listening, the speakers are doing much of the interpretation for the listeners by their expressions, inflections, stresses, and pauses. Similarly, the listeners do not have to make the proper grapheme (letter)-phoneme (sound) correspondences because these have already been done for them by the speakers. It is possible for students to achieve excellent listening comprehension but not to achieve as well in reading.

Readers must first make the proper grapheme–phoneme correspondences and must then organize these into the proper units to gain meaning from the words. Readers must also be able to determine the shades of meaning implied by the words, to recognize any special figures of speech, and finally to synthesize the unique ideas expressed by the passage.

able to assimilate the words into a meaningful concept. The instructor will have to help these children in concept development and in gaining the necessary reading comprehension and listening skills. A person who does not do well in listening comprehension skills will usually not do well in reading comprehension skills. Help in one area usually enhances the other because both listening and reading contain some important similar skills,[8] and researchers going as far back as the 1930s seem to support this view. For example, an investigation made in 1936 found that children who did poorly in comprehension through listening were also poor in reading comprehension.[9] Research in 1955 on the relation-

[8]Thomas Jolly, "Listen My Children and You Shall Read," *Language Arts* 57 (February 1980): 214–17.

[9]William E. Young, "The Relation of Reading Comprehension and Retention to Hearing Comprehension and Retention," *Journal of Experimental Education* 5 (September 1936): 30–39.

[10]Annette P. Kelty, "An Experimental Study to Determine the Effect of Listening for Certain Purposes Upon Achievement in Reading for Those Purposes," *Abstracts of Field Studies for the Degree of Doctor of Education* 15 (Greeley: Colorado State College of Education, 1955): 82–95.

[11]Sybil M. Hoffman, "The Effect of a Listening Skills Program on the Reading Comprehension of Fourth Grade Students," Ph.D. Dissertation, Walden University, 1978.

[12]Thomas Sticht et al., *Auding and Reading: A Developmental Model* (Alexandria, Va.: Human Resources Research Organization, 1974). Walter Kintsch and Ely Kozminsky, "Summarizing Stories After Reading and Listening," *Journal of Educational Psychology* 69 (1977): 491–99.

The relationship between listening and reading ability is succinctly summarized by these four rules:

1. When auding[13] ability is low, reading ability more often tends to be low.
2. When auding ability is high, reading ability is not predictable.
3. When reading ability is low, auding ability is not predictable.
4. When reading ability is high, auding ability is, to a very small extent, predictable—and likely to be high.[14]

THE DEVELOPMENT OF LISTENING

"Listen! Listen to me!" Children want to be heard. Whether their parents spend time listening to them, and whether they encourage them to express themselves, will affect the kind of listening the children are able to do, as well as influence their oral expression.

By the time children come to school they have emerged from an egocentric view of the world, where everything they do and say concerns *me, my,* or *I.* In this egocentric world, children speak in parallel, in a collective monologue. They are not in the role of listeners, and so there is no communication. According to Piaget, the eminent Swiss psychologist, not until children need to be social do they need to become logical in their speaking.

Read the following noncommunicative egocentric speech of a preschooler:

> Mlle. L. tells a group of children that owls cannot see by day.

LEV: Well, I know quite well that it can't."

LEV (at a table where a group is at work): "I've already done 'moon' so I'll have to change it."

Lev picks up some barley-sugar crumbs: "I say, I've got a lovely pile of eyeglasses."

LEV: "I say, I've got a gun to kill him with. I say, I am the captain on horseback. I say, I've got a horse and a gun as well."[15]

If children are to learn effectively in school, they must first learn to listen. Since they have spent their early childhood years in egocentric thought, they have not developed this skill adequately. When children come to school they participate in dialogue, which is a giving and receiving of ideas between two persons. Though they must listen, children still need someone to listen to them.

When Lev emerged from egocentric speech, he was able to engage in a communicative conversation with other children of his age:

> PIE: (6.5) "Now you shan't have it [the pencil] because you asked for it."
> HEI: (6.0) "Yes I will, because it's mine . . ."
> PIE: "Course it isn't yours. It belongs to everybody, to all the children."
> LEV: (6.0) "Yes, it belongs to Mlle. L. and all the children, to Ai and to My too."
> PIE: "It belongs to Mlle. L. because she bought it, and it belongs to all the children as well."[16]

Dialogue between children and their classmates and between teachers and children is very important to children's development of listening skills and in making their thinking more objective. Teachers should listen to children; observe them at play and work; introduce new materials and ideas to them; add information; raise questions; allow opportunities for children to raise questions as well; and *talk* with children about what they see, think, and feel. It is essen-

---

[13]*Auding* refers to the highest level of listening. It is defined as listening plus comprehension. The term *listening* is many times used to mean auding.

[14]John Caffrey, "The Establishment of Auding-age Norms," *School and Society* 70 (November 12, 1949): 310.

[15]Jean Piaget, *The Language and Thought of the Child* (London: Routledge & Kegan Paul, 1959), pp. 18–19.

[16]Ibid., p. 71.

tial that teachers show they respect their pupils' ideas and act as models of "good listeners" for them. Children must have sufficient practice or "play" in the intake and outgo of language. Unless children are given ample opportunities to engage in listening and being listened to, they may not develop their listening ability adequately.

NONSTANDARD ENGLISH AND LISTENING

The teaching of standard English as a second language to children who speak other languages or dialects is a complex process involving all the language arts, but it begins with listening, which is basic to any constructive learning.

When children who speak nonstandard English come to school they may face special difficulties since they may have trouble both in understanding what other people say to them and in being understood by these people. Since listening and the whole range of aural and oral communications are so important to success in school—and so important to the development of good skills in reading, thinking, and problem-solving—it is imperative that attention be given immediately to improving the listening skills of such pupils. These children must be helped with the basic listening skills and with setting the purpose of the listening they do. The sooner these children get help, the greater their chances for later success will be.

Language is acquired from the utterances of the adults who surround the child. Therefore, the listening process determines the child's output, namely, speech. As a result, children who hear standard English would learn to speak standard English, whereas culturally different children, who hear another dialect or language, would learn to speak what they hear. Although we must recognize that differences exist in language and help children to learn standard English, at the same time we must maintain their dignity and self-respect and be careful not to extend value judgments preferring one language or dialect over another.

It is probably true that facility in standard English is necessary for academic success and for admission into the higher economic community of the culture, but that does not mean that nonstandard English is "bad," nor that the persons who speak it are not worthy. There must be no implication that one language or dialect is inferior to another; learning standard English should be looked on as a useful added skill.

Since it is very important for the teacher to help all children to be able to listen to and discriminate among speech sounds which may be strange or foreign to them, it would help teachers to have a better understanding of the difficulties involved if they recognized some language differences. Teachers who know the phonological and syntactic features of nonstandard English will be better able to appreciate the differences between the listening environment of the standard English speaker and that of the child who speaks a nonstandard dialect. For example, read the following dialogue between a second-grade student and his teacher. The child asks his teacher to spell the word *rat*. The teacher replies, *r-a-t*. The child says, "No, ma'am. I don't mean rat mouse. I mean right now."[17]

The child who speaks nonstandard English uses many more homonyms than standard English has, and this may cause confusion. Here are illustrations of some of them:

Vowel variations may produce a set of homonyms; for example, pin = pen and beer = bear. Simplification of final consonant clusters can produce another set of homonyms; for example, guest = guess, past = pass, and walked = walk. The weakening of final consonants

---

[17]Diane N. Bryant et al., *Variant English* (Columbus, Ohio: Charles Merrill, 1978), p. 207.

creates yet another set of homonyms; for example, road = row and seat = sea.

Children who omit the *r* before vowels, as well as consonants, may produce another set of homonyms; for example, Carol = Cal, Paris = Pas, and guard = god. Those students who omit the *l* from a word may also be forming another set of homonyms; for example, toll = toe, help = hep, fault = fought, and tool = too. It can be seen that students who hear "toe" for "toll" will certainly have difficulty in spelling or reading "toll."[18]

The teacher with an understanding of dialects will be able to comprehend the child's message and will be more accepting of the child; such a teacher will also be better prepared to plan listening training lessons for this child.

Since there are many dialects of English, and since a student could have grown up with an entirely different language, no attempt will be made to summarize the differences in language here. The important thing to be stressed is attitude. Teachers must demonstrate by their attitudes that one language is as good as another, that it is just as useful for people to learn someone else's language as it is for children who speak nonstandard English to learn standard English. Everyone in the classroom can learn from everyone else. Unless the complete classroom environment—physical, emotional, social, and intellectual—reinforces this attitude, very valuable learning opportunities will be lost and actual damage to some students might occur.

The teacher must lead the way. Find out what kinds of language differences exist in the community; check with other professionals who know such communities for information about the varieties of nonstandard English likely to be encountered. Find people who can tutor these languages or dialects, read books and articles on

them, listen to recordings, or develop other learning tools. You will find a bibliography of some available materials at the end of this chapter, but that is only a starting point. New materials are being produced almost daily. The process of teaching and learning is continuous and serious. If it is not, that attitude cannot help but be communicated to the entire classroom.

NONSTANDARD ENGLISH AND ITS IMPLICATIONS FOR INSTRUCTION

So that children can learn standard English, they must first feel a need to do so. To be successful they must be able to hear differences between sounds. If they only hear nonstandard English at home, from their peers, and in the school, they will not have a need to learn, nor will they hear the differences necessary for learning. Children should be encouraged to express themselves as often as possible early in their school careers, in kindergarten or in preschool organized activities. Children should not be criticized. They should not be told, "No, that's wrong. Say it this way." The teacher should repeat the children's sentences in standard English so that they can hear the sentence in a standard structural pattern. When a child says, "Her a good girl," the teacher might say, "Yes, she is a good girl." Unless children learn to hear differences in both the patterns of speech and in the phonemes, they will not be able to reproduce them in standard English. Similarly, unless they learn to hear the sounds and patterns of standard English, they will usually have difficulty in reading and writing.

Schools seem to have had very little effect on teaching the patterns of standard English speech to speakers of nonstandard English, as evidenced by the fact that many students leave school knowing only the same speech patterns with which they entered. If a new pattern is to be learned, the process must begin as soon as the children enter school. Such children must have

[18]William Labov, *The Study of Nonstandard English* (Champaign, Ill.: National Council of Teachers of English, 1970), pp. 65-67.

instructors who speak standard English exceptionally well.

In order to help children who speak nonstandard English develop sound differentiations, auditory discrimination exercises among initial consonants, final consonants, and phonograms or graphemic bases (successions of graphemes that occur with the same phoenetic value in a number of words, such as *ight, ake, at, et,* and so on) should be emphasized. Here are some examples:

Auditory Discrimination Activities

"Listen carefully! I am going to say some words that begin like *b*aby and *b*all. Listen and try to pick out all those words that start just like *b*aby and *b*all." Say such lists of three words as

*b*ook	cake	*b*ox
*b*ang	*B*obby	hat
*b*anana	candy	*b*icycle
*b*aseball	apple	dog

"Now listen carefully; I may be tricky. Does everyone know what tricky means? Yes, it means to fool someone. Well, I may try to fool you. I am going to state a group of words and you will have to pick out all those words which begin like book. Now here's the tricky part. There may be some groups of words that have no words starting like book—cookie, dog, chicken. Are there any words that start like book in that list? No. That's correct. Good! Let's begin."

farm	cow	bear
box	land	school
girl	drum	letter
boy	Tom	bait
cracker	train	drum

"Now, listen carefully as I say some words. Which ones sound alike?"

man   can   tan   book

"Yes, man, can, and tan sound alike. Good. Now listen again."

look   book   cook   man

"Yes, look, book, cook sound alike. Good! Now listen again."

cake   bake   lake   boy

"Listen carefully. I have a riddle for you."

The word I am thinking of rhymes with lake.
It also rhymes with bake.
When mother makes it, I love to eat it.
Who knows what it is?

"Very good! It's cake. Listen again."

The word I am thinking of rhymes with man.
It also rhymes with can and tan.
When I am very hot I use it.
Who knows what it is?

"Yes. Very good! It's a fan. Listen again."

The word I am thinking of rhymes with mat.
It also rhymes with hat and fat.
It likes to drink milk and says, "Meow."
Who knows what it is?

Other activities could involve the taping of standard and nonstandard English sentences which children are asked to group to determine whether they can discriminate between them:

Nonstandard pattern: "She didn't have no money."
Standard pattern: "She didn't have any money."

It is essential that the objective of the lesson is made clear to the children at the start and that only one pattern is introduced at a time.

In order to give them practice, for overlearning purposes, a good motivating technique is to make this activity into a game. The pupils can be divided into two, three, or four groups. The tape recorder plays four or five sentences in a nonstandard pattern and then four or five similar sentences in standard English. The children on the first team have to differentiate between them and then state all the sentences in the standard pattern. The same procedure is followed for teams two, three, and four. Different sentences are used for each team.

The teacher can also tape children's conversations. Before playback, the teacher can ask the children to listen for their voices. Next, he or she can have them all say a number of simple sentences in standard English, which would also be taped. The teacher then can play these back so that the children can listen to themselves speaking standard English.

The Effect of a Rich Oral Program in Developing Reading Skills

A number of studies[19] have found that children who speak nonstandard English make significant gains toward standard English when they are involved in a rich oral program, one that stresses the reading aloud of stories and the active involvement of the children in related oral activities. Teachers, beginning with kindergartners, should plan a program for linguistically different children which should include regular and continuous listening to storybooks based on their students' interest and concept development levels. Speech-stimulating activities such as choral speaking, creative dramatics, discussion, storytelling, and so on should follow the story so that the children can have an opportunity to express themselves.

A rich oral program is a necessary first step to prevent reading failure because it helps prepare the children for reading. The closer the children's language is to the written symbols encountered in reading, the greater their chance of success. Hearing standard English in the context of something meaningful with which they can identify helps the children to gain "facility in listening, attention span, narrative sense, recall of stretches of verbalization, and the recognition of new words as they appear in other contexts."[20] (See Chapters 13 and 16.)

CLASSROOM TEACHERS' ASSESSMENT OF LISTENING COMPREHENSION SKILLS

The informal assessment is not concerned with determining organic ear malfunctions. If a teacher feels that a student is having difficulty which might be physiological, he or she should go through the proper referral procedures and inform the principal, school nurse, and parents so that the child can be properly diagnosed by professionally trained personnel. Many times a child is diagnosed as having a "hearing impairment" problem and perceptual learning problems when the difficulty is not due to physiological factors but to experiential ones.

In order to determine the student's level of listening at the auding level, the teacher could easily develop a diagnostic instrument by choosing paragraphs based on the student's concentration and vocabulary ability according to grade levels. The selections can vary in length from grades one to six. A grade-one selection would be approximately 50 words, whereas a grade-six selection would be approximately

[19]Dorothy Strickland, "A Program for Linguistically Different Black Children," Eric # ED 049 355, April 22, 1971. Bernice E. Cullinan, Angela M. Jagger, and Dorothy Strickland, "Language Expansion for Black Children in the Primary Grades: A Research Report," *Young Children* 29 (January 1974): 98–112.

[20]Dorothy H. Cohen, "The Effect of Language on Vocabulary and Reading Achievement," *Elementary English* 45 (February 1968):217.

150 words. The number of comprehension questions asked would depend on the specific grade level or ability levels of students. For the first grade the teacher could ask three or four questions, whereas in sixth grade, six or seven questions could be asked. The questions asked should include interpretive and critical comprehension questions as well as literal ones. From these tests the teacher can determine whether there is a listening problem common to all students or just to a few. (See Chapter 9 for a discussion of listening capacity and listening capacity tests.)

STANDARDIZED LISTENING TESTS

There are many different kinds of standardized tests that have listening subtests. For example, the *PRI Reading Systems,* published by CTB/McGraw-Hill, is a criterion-referenced test, which has an oral comprehension test at Level A (prekindergarten to first grade) and at Level B (first to second grade). The tests measure literal and inferred meaning. The third edition of the *Sequential Tests of Educational Progress* (STEP III), which is published by ETS/Addison-Wesley Testing Service, is a norm-referenced achievement battery that includes listening subtests in its four CIRCUS Levels (A to D) for the preprimary and early primary grades. The *Durrell Analysis of Reading Difficulties,* 3rd ed., published by the Psychological Corporation, is a diagnostic reading test that includes both a listening comprehension subtest and a listening vocabulary subtest. "The purpose of this test is to provide an estimate of the child's reading capacity as indicated by his or her ability to understand paragraphs that are read aloud by the examiner."[21] The purpose of the listening

vocabulary test is "to assess the child's listening vocabulary as a second index . . . of the child's reading capacity."[22] The *Durrell Listening–Reading Series,* which is also published by the Psychological Corporation, is a comprehension test "designed to provide a comparison of children's reading and listening abilities. Its purposes are to identify children with reading disability, and to measure the degree of retardation in reading as compared to listening."[23]

The series, which consists of both reading and listening tests, has three levels: primary (grades 1 to 3.5), intermediate (grades 3.5 to 6), and advanced (grades 7 to 9). The tests at each level include vocabulary comprehension; the tests at the primary level consist of sentence comprehension, whereas those at the intermediate and advanced levels consist of paragraph comprehension. (The *Durrell Listening–Reading Series* may not be reprinted.)

There are very few tests available that measure only listening skills. One such test is the *Brown-Carlsen Listening Comprehension Test.* (Note, however, that it is a test for older students.) Here is a description of it:

Brown-Carlsen Listening Comprehension Test by James I. Brown, G. Robert Carlsen; c1953, 1955; Grades 9–13 and Adults; The Psychological Corporation.

The test measures five important listening skills: Immediate Recall, Following Directions, Recognizing Transitions, Recognizing Word Meanings, and Lecture Comprehension.

The *Detroit Tests of Learning Aptitude,* which are published by the Bobbs-Merrill Company, have an oral direction test that measures

[21]Donald D. Durrell and Jane Catterson, *Durrell Analysis of Reading Difficulty Manual of Directions* (New York: The Psychological Corporation, 1980), p. 22.

[22]Ibid., p. 26.

[23]Donald D. Durrell and Mary B. Brassard, *Durrell Listening–Reading Series Manual for Listening and Reading Tests; Intermediate Level Form DE* (New York: The Psychological Corporation, 1970). p. 3.

auditory attentive ability, practical judgment, motor ability, and visual attentive ability. You can use this test as a diagnostic procedure to determine your students' concentration ability. The procedures for administering the test, the listening sheet, the scoring scale, and the norms for the test follow.

ORAL DIRECTIONS TEST

General Directions[24]

Place the sheet before the subject. Give the directions for each set *slowly* and *very clearly* without special emphasis on any word or phrase. Be sure that the subject waits until the directions for a given set are *completed* before he or she is permitted to start. Say: "You see this page. I am going to tell you some things to do with what you see on this page. Now, listen carefully, and each time, after I get through, you do just exactly what I have said to do. Be sure to wait each time until I finish and say, 'Do it now.' Look at Number 1. It has three drawings." [Point to all three drawings on the pupil's sheet. Pause.]

Give directions for each set as indicated below. Say, "Stop" at the end of each time allowance. Any set must be entirely correct for credit.

It is best to call attention to the next set by saying, "Look at Number 2," "Look at Number 3," and so on throughout the test. Continue through three successive failures.

Instructions

Time allowance is 10 seconds each for Numbers 1–6 inclusive.

[24]*Detroit Tests of Learning Aptitude—Oral Directions* (Indianapolis, Ind.: Bobbs-Merrill, 1967).

1. Put a one in the circle and a cross in the square box. Do it now!

2. Draw a line from the thimble to the star that will go down under the comb and up over the hammer. Do it now!

3. Be sure to wait until I get all through. Draw a line from the rabbit to the ball that will go up over the fish, and put a cross on the fish. Do it now!

4. See the three circles. Put a number two in the first circle, a cross in the second circle, and draw a line under the third circle. Do it now!

5. Draw a line from the bottom of the first circle to the top of the second and put a cross in the second circle. Do it now!

6. Put a three in the part that is in the large box only and a cross in the part that is in both boxes. Do it now!

Time allowance is 15 seconds each for Numbers 7, 8, and 9.

7. This drawing is divided into parts. Put a number one in the biggest part, a number two in the smallest part, and a three in the last part. Do it now!

8. Draw a circle around the pig, a line under the apple, and make a cross on the cow. Do it now!

9. Draw a line under the letter *F.* Cross out the letter *K,* and draw a line above *O.* Do it now!

Time allowance is 20 seconds each for Numbers 10, 11, and 12.

10. Cross out the number that is three times five, cross out every number that is in the thirties, and cross out the largest number. Do it now!

11. Put the first letter of the first word in the first circle, the second letter of the first word in the second circle, the last letter of the first word

in the fourth circle, and the last letter of the last word in the last circle. Do it now!

12. Put a cross in the big square, a letter *F* in the triangle, a number four in the little square, and a letter *H* in the first circle. Do it now!

Time allowance is 30 seconds each for Numbers 13–17 inclusive.

13. Cross out a number that is eight times eight, the number one less than one hundred, the number that is five times five, the number in the fifties, and the fourth number in the line. Do it now!

14. Put the last letter of the second word in the third circle, the first letter of the third word in the fifth circle, and the second letter of the first word in the last circle. Do it now!

15. Draw a line under the letter after *S*, cross out *J* and *V*, and draw a line over the first letter before *O*. Do it now!

16. Put the third letter of the alphabet in the third figure, a six in the diamond, the letter *L* in the first circle, a number four in the triangle, and the first letter of the alphabet in the last figure. Do it now!

17. Cross out the even number in a square, the odd number in the second triangle, the number in the third circle, the biggest number that is in a square, and the number in a circle before twelve. Do it now!

Scoring Scale*

Items 1–6, 1 point each
Items 7–9, 2 points each
Items 10–13, 3 points each
Items 14–17, 4 points each
Maximum score: 40 points

*To receive credit, the student must have *everything* in the set correct.

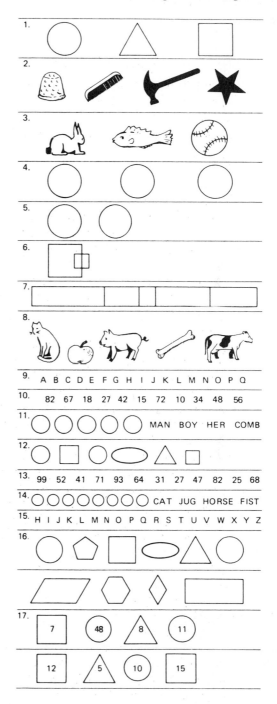

Norms

M.A. (MENTAL AGE)	ORAL DIRECTIONS	M.A. (MENTAL AGE)	ORAL DIRECTIONS
5-0		13-6	16
5-3		13-9	16
5-6			
5-9		14-0	17
		14-3	18
6-0		14-6	19
6-3		14-9	20
6-6	1		
6-9	2	15-0	21
		15-3	22
7-0	2	15-6	23
7-3	3	15-9	24
7-6	3		
7-9	4	16-0	25
		16-3	26
8-0	4	16-6	27
8-3	5	16-9	28
8-6	5		
8-9	6	17-0	29
		17-3	30
9-0	6	17-6	31
9-3	7	17-9	32
9-6	7		
9-9	8	18-0	33
		18-3	34
10-0	8	18-6	35-36
10-3	9	18-9	37-38
10-6	9		
10-9	10	19-0	39-40
11-0	10		
11-3	11		
11-6	11		
11-9	12		
12-0	12		
12-3	13		
12-6	13		
12-9	14		
13-0	14		
13-3	15		

Special Note

A listening comprehension test helps estimate a student's reading potential; however, if the student has some hearing problem, the test would not be an accurate estimate of that student's reading potential. Obviously, any hearing impairment would invalidate any type of listening test given to assess comprehension or concentration.

Student's Name:_____

Grade:_____

Teacher:_____

Diagnostic Checklist for Listening

Part One: Listening (Organic)

Symptoms	Observation Dates				
The child					
1. is absent due to ear infection.					
2. speaks very softly.					
3. speaks very loudly.					
4. speaks in a monotone.					
5. complains of noises in head.					
6. turns head to one side to hear.					
7. reads lips while listening.					
8. asks to have things repeated.					
9. cups hand behind ear to listen.					

Part Two: Auditory Discrimination

Symptoms	Yes	No
The child		
1. can state whether sets of words are similar or different.		
2. can state whether words begin with the same initial sound.		
3. can state whether words end with the same sound.		
4. can state whether words rhyme.		
5. can give the letter that stands for the first sound heard in presented words.		
6. can give the two letters that stand for the first two sounds heard in presented words.		
7. can give the two letters that stand for the first sound heard in presented words.		
8. can give the letter that stands for the last sound heard in presented words.		

Part Three: Listening Concentration

Symptoms	Yes	No
The child		
1. is able to repeat sets of digits forward.		
2. is able to repeat sets of digits backward.		
3. is able to follow orally presented sets of directions.		

Student's Name:_____

Grade:_____

Teacher:_____

Diagnostic Checklist for Listening (Cont.)

Part Four: Listening Comprehension*

	Yes	No
1. Literal listening. The child, after listening to a passage, can answer questions that relate to information explicitly stated in the passage.		

2. Interpretive listening. The child, after listening to a passage, can answer questions dealing with

	Yes	No
a. finding the main idea.		
b. generalization.		
c. "reading between the lines."		
d. conclusions.		
e. cause–effect relationships.		
f. multiple meanings.		

3. Critical listening. The child, after listening to a passage, can answer questions dealing with

	Yes	No
a. propaganda.		
b. fact or opinion.		
c. fantasy or reality.		
d. objectivity or subjectivity.		

	Yes	No
4. Creative listening. The child, after listening to a passage, can answer questions dealing with divergent thinking.		

Part Five: Listening for Appreciation

Auditory Discrimination	Yes	No
The child voluntarily chooses to listen to records, tapes, and so on.		

*The length and difficulty of the selection used are determined by the grade level and the readiness of the individual child. Also, this is not an inclusive list of listening comprehension skills.

SUMMARY

Chapter 6 is concerned with the relationship of listening to reading. Since the language arts (listening, speaking, reading, and writing) are interrelated, a problem in one area will usually carry over to another. Listening is the foundation of the language arts and closely related to reading; therefore it deserves special attention. Auditory discrimination, which is the ability to distinguish between sounds, is essential for the acquisition of language and for learning to read. Auditory memory span is important for individuals to make comparisons of sounds. In order to make such comparisons, the sounds must be kept in memory and retrieved for comparison. Tests to assess these abilities were discussed. The hierarchical nature of listening, which includes hearing, listening, and auding, was presented as well as the factors that influence each level. In order to be able to recognize expressions in print, students must have heard these phrases correctly before; they must be in the reader's listening capacity. Reading comprehension depends on comprehension of the spoken language. Children need to be involved in dialogue so that they can develop their listening skills. A special section was presented on nonstandard English and listening because the teaching of standard English as a second language is a complex process involving all the language arts—but it begins with listening. Examples of classroom teacher assessments of listening comprehension were presented, as well as examples of standardized listening tests and a diagnostic checklist.

SUGGESTIONS FOR THOUGHT QUESTIONS AND ACTIVITIES

1. Develop a listening comprehension test suitable for primary-grade children.

2. Construct a listening comprehension test suitable for intermediate-grade students.

3. You have been asked to present a talk on the listening program in your school. Develop a talk for a hypothetical school. Present what you think a good listening program should have, and give reasons why.

4. Explain how a teacher can provide an environment conducive to listening.

5. You have been put on a committee to assess the listening program in your school. What are some of the things you would suggest to look at?

6. Explain how listening is related to reading.

SELECTED BIBLIOGRAPHY

Anastasiow, Nicholas. *Oral Language: Expression of Thought,* updated ed. Newark, Del.: International Reading Association, 1979.

Duker, Sam. *Listening: Readings.* Metuchen, N.J.: Scarecrow Press, 1966.

————. *Teaching Listening in the Elementary School: Readings.* Metuchen, N.J.: Scarecrow Press, 1971.

Fletcher, David B. "Oral Language and the Language Arts Teacher." *Language Arts* 58 (February 1981): 219–24.

Hall, Edward T. "Listening Behavior: Some Cultural Differences." *Phi Delta Kappan* 50 (1969): 379–80.

Jolly, Thomas. "Listen My Children and You Shall Read." *Language Arts* 57 (February 1980): 214–17.

Labov, William. *The Study of Nonstandard English.* Champaign, Ill.: National Council of Teachers of English, 1970.

Lundsteen, Sara W. *Listening: Its Impact at All Levels of Reading and the Other Language Arts,* rev. ed. Urbana, Ill.: National Council of Teachers of English, 1979.

Rubin, Dorothy. "Developing Listening Skills." In *The Intermediate-Grade Teacher's Language*

Arts Handbook. New York: Holt, Rinehart and Winston, 1980.

_____. "Developing Listening Skills." In *The Primary-Grade Teacher's Language Arts Handbook.* New York: Holt, Rinehart and Winston, 1980.

_____. *Teaching Elementary Language Arts,* 2nd ed. New York: Holt, Rinehart and Winston, 1980.

Shepherd, Richard. "Oral Language Performance and Reading Instruction." *Elementary English* 51 (April 1974): 544–46, 560.

Stewart, W.A., ed. *Nonstandard Speech and the Teaching of English.* Washington, D.C.: Center for Applied Linguistics, 1964.

Taylor, Stanford E. *Listening: What Research Says to the Teacher.* Washington, D.C.: National Education Association, 1969.

CHAPTER 7

Who Is Underachieving in Reading?

INTRODUCTION

Read the following conversation between two teachers in the teachers' lounge:

MR. BROWN: I have some questions about two different students in my class. Jim scored two grade levels below his present grade level on a standardized reading achievement test. How do I determine whether he's underachieving or not since he is a slow learner? Also, David is supposed to be gifted according to a group IQ test, but he's only reading at grade level. Isn't he underachieving? Maybe there's something wrong with the tests.

MS. GRANT: Good questions. I know that there are supposed to be formulas to help you to figure out which child is underachieving, but are they really any good? I never know which students need further testing.

Many teachers have questions and concerns similar to Mr. Brown's and Ms. Grant's. After you finish reading this chapter, you will be able to help Mr. Brown and Ms. Grant answer their questions, as well as the following ones:

1. What does underachievement in reading mean?
2. Who is a disabled reader?
3. What is intelligence?
4. How is intelligence measured?
5. What are the major differences between individual and group intelligence tests?
6. What is a diagnostic pattern?
7. What are reading expectancy formulas?
8. What is listening capacity?
9. What is appraisal?

A DIAGNOSTIC PATTERN

Throughout this book it is emphasized that appropriate instruction stems from and is interwoven with accurate and pertinent diagnostic information for each child in the regular classroom. It is also stressed that diagnosis is ongoing and is necessary for prevention as well as for correction and remediation. In a diagnostic-reading and correction program the teacher is interested in determining the student's reading strengths and weaknesses, as well as the conditions causing them, as soon as possible so that any emerging reading difficulty can be nipped in the bud. To do this the teacher must first *identify* the student's present level of performance in word recognition and comprehension by using both standardized reading achievement tests and classroom tests for screening purposes. (See Chapter 8.) The teacher must then *appraise* the student's present level of reading performance in relation to his or her potential. This is done to determine if there is a discrepancy between the student's present reading performance and the student's reading potential, which is calculated by a reading expectancy formula. (See "Who Is a Disabled Reader?" in this chapter.) After appraisal, if a discrepancy exists between a student's present reading status and his or her reading expectancy, the teacher does extensive and intensive *diagnosis*. Step 3 is done to determine in detail the student's specific strengths and weaknesses, as well as to discover the specific conditions and abilities that underlie the student's performance in a particular reading area. Then the teacher must help that student to set attainable goals in the area. Identification, appraisal, and diagnosis are the three steps in a diagnostic pattern.[1] This chapter is concerned with step 2—that of appraisal. Step 2 helps the teacher to determine which children are underachieving in reading.

WHO IS A DISABLED READER?

It is not inconceivable to have a sixth-grade class with a span of reading levels ranging from third grade to eighth grade or above. The teacher in such a class must determine who the

[1]The terms are adapted from Ruth Strang, *Diagnostic Teaching of Reading,* 2nd ed. (New York: McGraw-Hill, 1969).

disabled readers are. Not all students working below grade level are underachievers. A child reading at a third-grade level in a sixth-grade class may be reading at his or her ability level, whereas another child may not be. Similarly, children reading at their grade levels may be reading far below their ability levels. A teacher may be pleased that a pupil is working on grade level, but gifted children working on grade level are *not* working up to their ability levels. A gifted child working on grade level is "underachieving." However, a child with a 70 IQ in the third grade working at the second-grade level would be achieving at his or her reading expectancy level. The reading expectancy scores presented in Table 7.2 for the Bond and Tinker formula on page 90 are "idealized" ones; that is, there are many other variables that affect ability to read than just the intelligence of an individual. Usually a child with a 70 IQ on an individual IQ test would be working more than one year below grade level. Since a child with a 70 IQ would usually not be able to work in the abstract, that child would have difficulty in doing reading skills involving inferences, analogies, and so on. (See Chapter 16 for information on borderline or slow-learning children.)

From this discussion, it can be seen that a disabled reader may be any student who is reading below his or her ability level; a disabled reader is one who is underachieving.

INTELLIGENCE

Since most reading expectancy formulas are based on intelligence quotients, it is important to know what intelligence is and what intelligence tests measure.

It is difficult to pick up a newspaper, journal, or magazine without finding some reference to achievement or intelligence. Usually when intelligence—specifically an intelligence test—is brought up, the atmosphere becomes highly charged. Hardly anyone seems to regard IQ objectively.

Intelligence refers to the ability to reason abstractly or to solve problems. Since intelligence is a construct—that is, it is something which cannot be directly observed or directly measured—testing and research have necessitated an operational definition. Such a definition coined in the early part of the century is still much quoted: "Intelligence is what the intelligence test measures."[2] There are a variety of tests designed to measure intelligence, yet no test exists which actually does. In other words, intelligence tests cannot adequately determine an individual's absolute limits or the potential of the intelligence. Yet many persons, both lay and professional, actually behave as if the intelligence test will tell all.

This state of affairs may be due to the nature–nurture controversy. Advocates of the nature side believe that heredity is the sole determiner of intelligence, and that no amount of education or the quality of the environment can alter it. Those who believe in the nurture side claim that intelligence is determined in great part by the environment. For them, intelligence can be affected if the child is exposed to different environments and education. Most professionals take an in-between position, saying that intelligence may be determined by an interaction between heredity and environment. "Heredity deals the cards and environment plays them."[3] Yet the heredity theory dies hard.

The majority position, which believes that intelligence is determined by some combination of heredity and environment, brings up the question as to *which* factor is more important. Conflicting studies attribute different percentages to each factor. The controversy continues to rage, as does the confusion surrounding what intelligence tests are measuring.

Most intelligence tests are highly verbal, and studies have shown that persons who do well on vocabulary tests also seem to do well on intelligence tests.[4] If a child has language problems—or if a dialect of English or a language other than English is spoken at home—the child could easily have difficulty in performing well in school. IQ tests are valid mainly for a middle-class standard English curriculum, and they predict the ability of an individual to do well in such environments. The positive correlation or agreement between individuals' IQs and their ability to work in school is neither very high nor low. There are factors other than IQ which determine an individual's success in school. One very important factor for school success is *motivation*—the desire, drive, and sustained interest to do the work.

The IQ test is an imperfect tool which helps teachers and parents to understand the abilities of children better. If students are doing very well in school, and if, according to their IQ scores, they are only supposed to be doing average work, one would be misusing the IQ test by thinking, "Stop, you're not supposed to be doing well."

The IQ test also helps show teachers the wide range of levels of ability in their classes. If teachers are aware of the wide span of mental age of their students, they can design programs based especially on individual needs.

However, teachers are cautioned not to see the IQ test as a perfect predictor of a child's ability to work well in school, for there are other factors, discussed in previous chapters, which influence school achievement. (See Chapter 5 for a discussion of intelligence and reading.)

[2]E. G. Boring, "Intelligence as the Tests Test It," *New Republic* 35 (1925):35–37.
[3]Lee J. Cronbach, *Educational Psychology* (New York: Harcourt, 1954), p. 204.
[4]Leona Tyler, *The Psychology of Human Differences* (New York: Appleton-Century-Crofts, 1965), p. 80.

DIFFERENCES BETWEEN INDIVIDUAL AND GROUP INTELLIGENCE (APTITUDE) TESTS

Teachers should recognize that differences exist between individual and group IQ tests. The most obvious difference is that an individual test is given to one person at a time, whereas a group test is given to a number of persons at one time. (See the section on individual and group tests in Chapter 3.) Although it is not difficult to administer group tests, and a person can be trained rather quickly to administer a group IQ test, there are some problems associated with these tests which teachers should be aware of. One involves administering the test to young children, who may have difficulty following directions and also paying attention long enough to finish the test. On an individual IQ test this is not a problem because the examiner can adjust the test to suit the individual needs of the child.

Individual IQ tests require persons who are specially trained to give them, and scoring tends to be more subjective than on group tests. On tests such as the *Stanford-Binet,* the examiner must on many occasions use his or her discretion to determine whether a response is correct or not. The authors of the *Stanford-Binet* are so concerned about the role of the examiner that they state the following in their *Examiner's Manual:*[5]

> The most essential requirement for determining a valid test score on the *Stanford-Binet Scale* is an examiner who knows his instrument and who is sensitive to the needs of the subject whom he is testing.

The authors of the *Stanford-Binet* also caution the examiners about "halo effect." Examiners are told to judge each response on its own merits, without regard to the student's successes or failures, and to guard against allowing the scoring to be influenced by any general impression he or she has formed of the subject's ability. The authors of the *Stanford-Binet* feel that there is a natural tendency to overestimate the ability of a sprightly, self-confident, talkative child.[6]

Individual tests usually yield more valid results for persons who have physical, emotional, or reading problems. They are generally given when a teacher suspects that the group IQ test results are not valid.

Special Note

The teacher should recognize that group tests emphasize reading ability more than individual tests, and they must be careful not to interpret a low score on a group intelligence test to mean a lack of native ability, when it may actually be a lack of reading achievement.[7]

INDIVIDUAL INTELLIGENCE (APTITUDE) TESTS

Wechsler Intelligence Scale for Children, Revised (WISC-R)

The Wechsler Intelligence Scale for Children, Revised (WISC-R) is an individual test that is most often used with children who have reading difficulties. It was first published in 1949 and revised (WISC-R) in 1974. The original WISC was standardized for children ages 5 to 15; WISC-R was restandardized for ages 6-0 to 16-11. In the restandardization, substantial portions of the original 1949 WISC were retained, but items judged culturally biased or found

[5]Lewis M. Terman and Maud A. Merrill, *Stanford-Binet Intelligence Scale,* 1972 Norms Edition (Boston: Riverside Publishing Co., 1973), p. 46.

[6]Ibid., p. 55.

[7]J. Stanley Ahman and Marvin Glock, *Evaluating Student Progress: Principles of Tests and Measurements,* 6th ed. (Boston, Mass.: Allyn and Bacon, 1981), p. 319.

unacceptable on psychometric grounds were replaced.

WISC-R, as in the 1949 WISC, has ten tests (with two alternates available if needed)[8] and these yield an IQ based on scaled scores for each age level—not on a mental age. An IQ score can be derived also from either the verbal or the performance scale alone. The verbal subtests consist of the following: Information, Similarities, Arithmetic, Vocabulary, Comprehension, and Digit Span (optional). The performance subtests consist of the following: Picture Completion, Picture Arrangements, Block Design, Object Assembly, Coding, and Mazes (optional).[9]

The Digit Span and the Mazes subtests have been retained in the WISC-R and are considered supplementary tests. They are added when time permits, or they are used as alternate tests when some other test is not appropriate or is invalidated.

The performance tests make the WISC-R more suitable for students who have verbal difficulties. The *Stanford-Binet,* which is another most widely used individual intelligence test, correlates well with the verbal scale of the WISC-R, but poor readers do not do as well on the *Stanford-Binet* because it does not have a separate performance scale. Poor readers usually do better on the performance scale of the WISC-R because these tests do not depend on school learning, whereas the tests in the verbal scale do.

The WISC-R, as well as the 1949 WISC, is a highly regarded testing instrument. One reviewer states the following: "The more accurate standardization sample, the up-dated norms, and the many item changes make the WISC-R an even more valuable tool than its highly praised and well-used predecessor."[10]

Stanford-Binet Intelligence Scale

The present *Stanford-Binet Intelligence Scale* is an outgrowth of the 1916 scale, which attempted to provide standards of intellectual performance for average American-born children from age three to young adulthood—which was assumed on the basis of available information for purposes of the scale to be age 16. Tests are arranged in order of difficulty by age levels. The intellectual ability of an individual, determined by his or her performance on the scale, was judged by comparison with the standards of performance for normal children of different ages.

Intelligence ratings were expressed as mental age scores. One of Binet's basic assumptions of the original scale was that persons are thought of as normal if they can do the things a person of their age normally can do, retarded if their test performance corresponds to the performance of persons younger than themselves, and accelerated if their performance exceeds that of persons their age.[11]

In 1937 there was a second revision, in which the age level was extended downward to age two, and in 1960 there was a third revision. In 1972 a new set of norms was published to be used with the 1960 revision. In the 1960 revision the IQ tables were extended to include ages 17 and 18. This was done because retest findings showed that mental age, as measured by the *Stanford-Binet,* extends beyond age 16.[12]

Here are some examples of the items that are tested at various years:

---

[8]Obviously, with the alternate tests, the WISC-R contains twelve tests. There are, however, only ten main tests.

[9]David Wechsler, *Wechsler Intelligence Scale for Children (WISC) Manual* (New York: The Psychological Corporation, 1974), p. 8.

[10]Oscar K. Buros, ed., *The Eighth Mental Measurements Yearbook,* Vol. 1 (Highland Park, N.J.: Gryphon Press, 1978), p. 355.

[11]Terman and Merrill, op. cit., p. 5.

[12]Ibid., pp. 26–27.

Year II (Year 2)

1. Three-hole form board
2. Delayed response
3. Identifying parts of the body
4. Block building
5. Picture vocabulary
6. Word combinations

Year V (Year 5)

1. Picture completion: Man
2. Paper folding: Triangle
3. Definitions
4. Copying a square
5. Pictorial similarities and differences II
6. Patience: Rectangles

Year IX (Year 9)

1. Paper cutting
2. Verbal absurdities II
3. Memory for designs I
4. Rhymes: New form
5. Making change
6. Repeating four digits reversed

Year XII (Year 12)

1. Vocabulary
2. Verbal absurdities II
3. Picture absurdities II
4. Repeating five digits reversed
5. Abstract words I
6. Minkus completion I

The examiner is also supposed to note the following factors that affect performance: attention, reactions during test performance, emotional independence, problem-solving behavior, independence of examiner's support, and whether it was hard to establish a positive relationship with the person taking the test.

GROUP-ADMINISTERED MEASURES OF INTELLIGENCE (APTITUDE)

Group intelligence tests are those that are generally administered by the regular classroom teacher in the regular classroom. There are a great number of group intelligence tests on the market today. The list that follows contains examples of some that are more generally used and that are favorably reviewed in Buros's *Mental Measurements Yearbooks*.

California Short-Form Test of Mental Maturity, 1963 S-Form, Level 1H by Elizabeth T. Sullivan, Willis W. Clark, Ernest W. Tiegs; c1962-64;[13] Grades 3-4; CTB/McGraw-Hill.

> Subscores are: Opposites, Similarities, Analogies, Numerical Values, Number Problems, Verbal Comprehension, Delayed Recall. The test assesses four factors: Logical Reasoning, Numerical Reasoning, Verbal Concepts, Memory.

Cognitive Abilities Test, Multi-Level Edition, Levels A-H by Robert L. Thorndike; c1971; Grades 3-13; The Riverside Publishing Company.

> Subscores are: Verbal (Vocabulary, Sentence Completion, Verbal Analogies, Verbal Classification); Quantitative (Number Series, Quantitative Relations, Equation Building); Nonverbal (Figure Analogies, Figure Classification, Form Synthesis).

Cognitive Abilities Test: Multi-Level Edition, Form 3, Robert L. Thorndike, Elizabeth Hagen; c1978; Grades 3-12; The Riverside Publishing Company.

---

[13]A dash in a copyright citation (1962–64) means that pieces of tests have been published over a number of years. A comma in a copyright citation (1962, 1964) means that the complete test has two different copyright dates.

Subscores: Verbal (Vocabulary, Sentence Completion, Verbal Classification, Verbal Analogies); Quantitative (Quantitative Relations, Number Series, Equation Building); Nonverbal (Figure Classification, Figure Analogies, Figure Synthesis).

Henmon-Nelson Tests of Mental Ability: 1973 Revision, Form 1 by Martin J. Nelson, Tom A. Lamke, revised by Joseph L. French; c1973; Grades 3-12; The Riverside Publishing Company.

Designed to measure those aspects of mental ability which are important for academic success. Available in three overlapping levels covering grades 3-6, 6-9, and 9-12.

Kuhlmann-Anderson Intelligence Test, Seventh Edition by Rose G. Anderson; c1927-67; Grades K-12; Scholastic Testing Service, Inc.

Subscores are for the following: G (Grades 7-9), H (Grades 9-12) Levels only: Verbal, Quantitative.

Lorge-Thorndike Intelligence Tests, Multi-Level Edition (Levels A-H) by Irving Lorge, Robert L. Thorndike, Elizabeth P. Hagen; c1954-66; Grades 3-13; The Riverside Publishing Company.

Designed to assess abstract intelligence. Subscores are: Verbal (Word Knowledge, Sentence Completion, Arithmetic Reasoning, Verbal Classification, Verbal Analogies); Nonverbal (Figure Classification, Number Series, Figure Analogies).

Lorge-Thorndike Intelligence Tests, Separate Level Edition, Nonverbal Battery by I. Lorge, R. L. Thorndike; c1954; Grades 4-13; The Riverside Publishing Company.

Subscores are: Pictorial Classification, Pictorial Analogy, Numerical Relationships.

Otis-Lennon Mental Ability Test, Elementary II Level by Arthur S. Otis, Roger T. Lennon; c1967; Grades 4-6; The Psychological Corporation.

Is designed to provide a measure of scholastic aptitude with emphasis being placed upon facility in reasoning and in dealing abstractly with verbal, symbolic, and figural test content.

MENTAL AGE SPAN IN THE REGULAR CLASSROOM

The teacher in a regular classroom usually has students with a mental age span of five years. It can be more. Mental age (MA) refers to a child's present level of development; it helps to indicate the child's present readiness. As children progress through the grades the span between the borderline (slow-learning), average, and gifted child gets wider.

Children enter school based on chronological age rather than mental age; however, instruction needs to be geared to their mental ages rather than their chronological ages. For example, a child of six with an IQ ($\frac{MA}{CA} \times 100 = IQ$) of 75[14] has a mental age of 4.5, and a child of six with an IQ of 130 has a mental age of 7.8 (see Table 7.1). Obviously, these children need extremely different programs, even though both are chronologically the same age. Note that students with similar mental ages and different chronological ages also do not have similar mental abilities. For example, a child with a chronological age of ten and a mental age of six has an IQ of 60. A child with an IQ of 60 will not progress in reading as a child of five with a mental age of six and a half, who has an IQ of 130.

Even teachers who believe in individual differences and who attempt to develop an individualized instructional program for each child in their classes will not be able to build a mean-

[14]Teachers may have children with IQs as low as 68 in their regular classrooms because borderline children's IQs range from approximately 68 to 85.

9-63000

THE HENMON-NELSON TESTS OF MENTAL ABILITY

Grades 3-6   Form 1

Tom A. Lamke, Ph.D., and M. J. Nelson, Ph.D.
Revised by Joseph L. French, Ed.D.
Pennsylvania State University

HOUGHTON MIFFLIN COMPANY • Boston
Atlanta • Dallas • Geneva, Illinois • Hopewell, N.J. • Palo Alto

Name_____

Grade_____Date of Test_____
                                            Yr.   Mon.   Day

School_____Date of Birth_____
                                            Yr.   Mon.   Day

Teacher_____Age_____

SCORE_____

IQ_____

PR_____

STA-9_____

● The three practice exercises below are given so that you may see how to do the test.

Practice 1. **Boys like to:**

(1) run   (2) hat   (3) lost   (4) red   (5) same .... ☒ ② ③ ④ ⑤

Which word tells what boys like to do? Yes, *run* is the right answer. What is the
number of the word *run?* The number is *1.* Answer space number 1 has been marked
to show that word number 1, *run,* is the right answer. You are to mark your answers
in the same way.

Practice 2. **I saw a .... tree.** A word for the blank is:

(1) quite   (2) care   (3) big   (4) so   (5) and .... ① ② ③ ④ ⑤

Mark the answer space that you think is right. Your mark should be in the answer
space numbered 3.

Practice 3. ▢ **is to** ▢ **as** △ **is to:**

(1) ◯   (2) ▯   (3) ○   (4) ▭   (5) △ ...... ① ② ③ ④ ⑤

What is the number of the right answer? The answer, of course, is number *5,* since
a *square* is to a *smaller square* as a *triangle* is to a *smaller triangle.* Mark the answer
space numbered 5.

● During the test, if you find that you have made a mistake and marked in the wrong
answer box, do not erase your mark, but draw a circle around it and then mark in the
right answer box.

ingful program for their students unless they know the cognitive styles that children at different intellectual levels possess (see Chapter 16).

READING EXPECTANCY FORMULAS

Reading expectancy formulas help teachers determine who needs special help. A child's

Table 7.1

Comparison of Mental Ages

Grade	CA	75 IQ MA	85 IQ MA	100 IQ MA	115 IQ MA	130 IQ MA
K	5.6	4.2	4.8	5.6	6.4	7.3
1	6.0	4.5	5.1	6.0	6.9	7.8
	6.6	5.0	5.6	6.6	7.6	8.6
2	7.0	5.3	6.0	7.0	8.1	9.1
	7.6	5.7	6.5	7.6	8.7	9.9
3	8.0	6.0	6.8	8.0	9.2	10.4
	8.6	6.5	7.3	8.6	9.9	11.2
4	9.0	6.8	7.7	9.0	10.4	11.7
	9.6	7.2	8.2	9.6	11.0	12.5
5	10.0	7.5	8.5	10.0	11.5	13.0
	10.6	8.0	9.0	10.6	12.2	13.8
6	11.0	8.3	9.4	11.0	12.7	14.3
	11.6	8.7	9.9	11.6	13.3	15.1
7	12.0	9.0	10.2	12.0	13.8	15.6
	12.6	9.5	10.7	12.6	14.5	16.4
8	13.0	9.8	11.1	13.0	15.0	16.9
	13.6	10.2	11.6	13.6	15.6	17.7

Example: An eight-year-old child with an IQ of 115 has a mental age of 9.2.

$$IQ = \frac{MA}{CA} \times 100$$

$$115 = \frac{x}{8} \times 100$$

$$x = 1.15 \times 8$$

$$x = 9.2$$

Chronological age (CA) is given in years and tenths rather than in years and months so that mengal age (MA) is also expressed in years and tenths.

reading expectancy, calculated by a reading expectancy formula, is compared to his or her reading achievement level, measured by a reading achievement test score. If the child's expectancy level is significantly higher than his or her reading achievement score, further diagnosis should be undertaken. (See "Who Is a Candidate for Further Testing?" in this chapter for a discussion of the term *significantly*.)

Bond and Tinker Reading Expectancy Formula

This formula is used often because of its simplicity, but as stated earlier in this chapter, it is rather idealized for the child with a low IQ and underestimates the reading expectancy of a child with a high IQ. Also, many children are starting to learn to read in kindergarten, but the Bond and Tinker formula does not take this factor into account.

Harris and Sipay Reading Expectancy Formula

This formula, as does the Bond and Tinker formula, stresses intelligence—which makes sense since reading is a thinking act. The more intelligent a person is, the better thinker he or she should be; the better the person is in thinking, the better reader he or she should be.

$$\text{Reading Expectancy Age (R Exp A)} = \frac{2\,MA + CA}{3}$$

(MA and CA should be expressed in years and tenths so that R Exp A may also be expressed in years and tenths. Table 7.3 helps you to do this.)

The Harris and Sipay formula, unlike the Bond and Tinker, gives a child's reading expectancy in age rather than in grade levels. The concept of using age is a sound one and would tend to give a more realistic reading expectancy

Table 7.2

Bond and Tinker Formula for Estimating Reading Expectancy* for IQs 70 and 120 (Grades 1–6)*

Years in School times $\dfrac{IQ}{100}$ plus 1 =	Expected Reading Achievement at End of School Year
(1 × .70) + 1	= 1.7 at end of 1st grade
(2 × .70) + 1	= 2.4 at end of 2nd grade
(3 × .70) + 1	= 3.1 at end of 3rd grade
(4 × .70) + 1	= 3.8 at end of 4th grade
(5 × .70) + 1	= 4.5 at end of 5th grade
(6 × .70) + 1	= 5.2 at end of 6th grade
(1 × 1.20) + 1	= 2.2 at end of 1st grade
(2 × 1.20) + 1	= 3.4 at end of 2nd grade
(3 × 1.20) + 1	= 4.6 at end of 3rd grade
(4 × 1.20) + 1	= 5.8 at end of 4th grade
(5 × 1.20) + 1	= 7.0 at end of 5th grade
(6 × 1.20) + 1	= 8.2 at end of 6th grade

*The Bond and Tinker formula begins at grade one; that is, at the end of grade one the child is considered to have been in school one year.

because children's entrance into school varies. Some children, because of their birthdays, may not enter school until almost a year later than some other children. Harris and Sipay's formula takes this into account. The use of age levels can, however, be confusing for teachers because they are used to working with either grade levels or with reading levels, which are easily converted to grade equivalent levels. To make the Harris and Sipay formula more useful to the teacher, it would help to convert the reading expectancy age to grade equivalent levels. This is easily done by subtracting 5 from the reading expectancy age to obtain the grade equivalent level (see Table 7.4).

Table 7.3

Conversion of Age Months to Decimal Tenths

Age	
Months	Decimal-Tenths (of Year)
0	0
1	1
2	2
3	3
4	3
5	4
6	5
7	6
8	7
9	8
10	8
11	9

To convert age months to decimal years, look in the table for months desired and read the decimal tenths next to it. For example, 5 months is approximately equal to 0.4 years. If you have 7 years 5 months to convert to tenths, it would be approximately 7.4 in tenths of a year.

Special Note

For those students who are mathematically minded, here is the formula for calculating

months to decimal tenths. Take the number of months divided by 12 and round the result to the nearest tenth. For example, 4 months converted to tenths of years = $\frac{4}{12}$ = .33, and rounded to the nearest tenth equals .3 years. With modern hand calculators, the conversion is very easy to do.

Table 7.4

Reading Grade Level	Reading Age (RA)
1.0	6.0
2.0	7.0
3.0	8.0
4.0	9.0
5.0	10.0
6.0	11.0
7.0	12.0
8.0	13.0
9.0	14.0
10.0	15.0
11.0	16.0
12.0	17.0

For reading grade level scores between the listed grade levels, add the decimal fraction to corresponding pairs of Reading Grade Level and Reading Age numbers in the conversion table. For example, if someone has a reading grade level score of 3.4, his or her reading age would be 8.4. Or, more simply, add 5.0 to the reading grade level to obtain the reading age.

Special Note

A grade year equals only ten months, so a reading age level in *tenths* is directly convertible to a reading grade level in months.

Examples Using the Expectancy Formulas

This example uses the Harris and Sipay Formula for a student 9.0 years of age with an IQ of

100. From looking at Table 7.1, we can see that a student with an IQ of 100 who is 9.0 years of age would have a mental age of 9.0. This student, according to the Harris and Sipay formula should be reading at a reading expectancy of age 9.0. From Table 7.4, we can see that a 9.0 year old should be reading at approximately the beginning of fourth grade.

$$R \ Exp \ A = \frac{2(MA) + CA}{3}$$
$$= \frac{2(9) + 9}{3} = \frac{27}{3} = 9$$

Special Note

From looking at the formula, it can be seen that any child with an IQ of 100 should be reading at his or her grade level.

Let's look at two more examples. The first is a student who is 9.0 years of age with an IQ of 75, and the second is a student who is also 9.0 years of age but has an IQ of 130.

First we must determine the mental age for each student. From looking at Table 7.1, we can see that a student who is 9.0 years old with an IQ of 75 would have a mental age of 6.8, and a student who is 9.0 years old with an IQ of 130 would have a mental age of 11.7. Now, let's apply the Harris and Sipay formula to determine these students' reading expectancy age.

Student with 75 IQ, 9.0 years of age, 6.8 MA, fourth grade (beginning)

$$R \ Exp \ A = \frac{2MA + CA}{3}$$
$$= \frac{2(6.8) + 9}{3} = \frac{13.6 + 9}{3}$$
$$= \frac{22.6}{3} = 7.5$$

Age 7.5 is equivalent to the midpoint (or fifth month) of second grade (see Table 7.4).

Student with 130 IQ, 9.0 years of age, 11.7 MA, fourth grade (beginning)

$$R \ Exp \ A = \frac{2MA + CA}{3}$$
$$= \frac{2(11.7) + 9}{3} = \frac{23.4 + 9}{3}$$
$$= \frac{32.4}{3} = 10.8$$

Age 10.8 is equivalent to the eighth month of fifth grade.

These children, according to the Bond and Tinker formula, should be reading at the following levels:

Student with 75 IQ, 9.0 years of age, 4th grade (beginning)

$3 \times .75 + 1 = 3.25$ (close to the third month of third grade)

Student with 130 IQ, 9.0 years of age, fourth grade (beginning)

$3 \times 1.30 + 1 = 4.90$ (the ninth month of fourth grade)

In comparing the Harris and Sipay and Bond and Tinker formulas, we can see that the former is more complicated than the latter; however, it is also more realistic for the slow learner and the highly able student. Teachers must remember, if they are using the Harris and Sipay formula, that R Exp A yields an age level, not a grade level. If they want or need a grade level equivalent, the age level can easily be converted to one (see Table 7.4).

Harris and Sipay suggest another formula should be used for children who are younger than eight years of age because it will give a closer approximation than their own. The formula they suggest is the Horn formula, which was developed for use in the Los Angeles schools. Teachers are also aptly cautioned that any formula used to determine the reading expectancy of children under eight years of age is to be regarded with skepticism.[15] This makes sense since reading expectancy formulas are based on intelligence quotients, and the younger a child is, the more difficult it is to obtain a reliable intelligence test score.

Horn-L.A. formula for R Exp A $= \dfrac{MA + CA}{2}$
(used with children below eight years of age)

WHO IS A CANDIDATE FOR FURTHER TESTING?

Teachers must be cautioned about using reading expectancy formulas as absolute determinants of reading potential. They are not; they are merely indicators of possible reading potential. Most reading expectancy formulas are based on intelligence quotients, which may not be valid for the child, especially if a group IQ test was used and the child has word recognition problems. (See the case of Larry, which was presented at the beginning of this book.) It may be that the child should actually be reading at a much higher level than is indicated by the reading expectancy formula. Therefore, teachers may want to administer diagnostic reading tests to children for whom there may not be any discrepancy between their present reading achievement level and their reading potential, but who exhibit behavior in class that seems to indicate that they should be reading at a higher level.

Teachers should also recognize that there really is no set rule for determining when or which child should be a candidate for further testing. Each case is different. Although some educators state that a child should be tested further or is a candidate for an informal reading inventory if a child's reading achievement score is approximately one year or more below his or her reading potential, this guideline is not very helpful or realistic. For example, a three-month underachievement in reading in first grade is probably significant and should be looked into by the teacher, whereas a three-month underachievement in sixth grade would probably not be as significant. In the former case, because we are dealing with small numbers in the first one-year period in school, small underachievements may be significant. Also, since this book is based on the premise that early diagnosis is more helpful than later remediation, it is better to err on the safe side with overzealous diagnosis in the early grades than to let the gap get too large in the later grades, which would then require extensive remediation. The adage "an ounce of prevention is worth a pound of cure" is an apt one in the field of diagnosis and reading. (See "Who Should Be Given an IRI?" in Chapter 9.)

Harris and Sipay provide a formula not only for reading expectancy age but also for comparing a student's present level of reading with his or her reading potential.[16] This formula is actually one of appraisal because it attempts to determine which student is in need of further testing and special help.

Reading Expectancy Quotient (R Exp Q)
$$= \frac{RA \times 100}{R \; Exp \; A}$$
(RA = Reading Age)
(R Exp A = Reading Expectancy Age)

Let's see how this formula works:

Student *Y* has a R Exp A of 10.0 (he is in fifth grade) and an IQ of 100. He has scored at the 5.0 grade level on a standardized reading achievement test in early fall, which is equal to a RA of 10 (see Table 7.4).

$$R \; Exp \; Q = \frac{RA \times 100}{R \; Exp \; A} = \frac{10 \times 100}{10}$$
$$= \frac{1000}{10} = 100$$

---

[15] Albert J. Harris and Edward R. Sipay, *How to Increase Reading Ability,* 7th ed. (New York: Longman, 1980), pp. 154–55.

[16] Ibid., p. 155.

According to Harris and Sipay, if a person scores between 90 and 100, he or she is within a normal range; this child does not need any further testing. A score below 90 would indicate that some reading disability exists. The greater the score falls below 90, the greater the reading disability. Obviously, you did not need any formula to determine that a child with an IQ of 100, who is 10 years of age and in fifth grade and is reading at a fifth-grade level, is reading according to his ability, assuming, of course, that the IQ score is an accurate measure of his or her ability. The formula would come in handy to uncover less obvious cases. Here is an example:

Student *Z* has a R Exp A of 12.0 (he is in fifth grade) and an IQ of 130. He has scored at the 5.0 grade level on a standardized reading achievement test in early fall. This is equal to a RA of 10.0 (see Table 7.4).

$$R \text{ Exp } Q = \frac{RA \times 100}{R \text{ Exp } A} = \frac{10 \times 100}{12}$$
$$= \frac{1000}{12} = 83.3$$

This student is a candidate for further testing and special help.

The standardized reading achievement test gives a score that is usually expressed in grade levels in tenths of a grade. (Some standardized norm-referenced achievement tests give the age equivalents for grade levels, but not all do.) To use the Harris and Sipay formula to determine who is a disabled reader, you must convert the reading grade level to a reading age (RA). Table 7.4 helps you to do this.

Special Note

Teachers who are in school systems that do not administer intelligence tests to their students will, obviously, not be able to use reading expectancy formulas that depend on a measure of intelligence. These teachers will have to rely on astute observations (see Chapter 11) and listening capacity tests. (See Chapter 6 for information on standardized listening tests and on the construction of informal listening comprehension tests.) Chapter 9 also discusses which children would be candidates for further testing when the teacher does not have information about a student's intelligence as measured by an intelligence test.

LISTENING CAPACITY TEST

In Chapter 6, you learned about listening comprehension tests, which are used to assess a student's reading potential, and in Chapter 9 you will learn more about these tests. Because this chapter is concerned with helping teachers determine the reading potential of students, it is necessary to mention listening comprehension or listening capacity tests here also.

The purpose of the listening capacity test is to determine the child's "potential" for reading. A child may have excellent comprehension ability, but it may be masked because of word recognition problems. Because of this, reading ability is not predictable when auding ability is high (see "Listening and Reading" in Chapter 6).

A child's word recognition difficulties could also interfere with the assessment of intelligence if a group IQ test were used rather than an individual test. Some test constructors feel that "listening comprehension may be used as the most satisfactory measure of 'potential' for reading"[17] and that listening comprehension is more directly related to reading than are most tests of intelligence. Therefore, a listening capacity test is useful also to determine reading potential if no IQ score is available for a child.

[17]Donald D. Durrell and Mary B. Brassard, *Manual for Listening and Reading Tests* (New York: Harcourt, 1970), p. 11.

SUMMARY

Chapter 7 provides information that teachers need to determine which child is underachieving in reading. Teachers must recognize that a child can be reading on grade level yet be underachieving because the child is not reading according to his or her ability level. Conversely, a child can be reading below grade level but not be underachieving because he or she is reading according to his or her ability level. To help teachers determine the reading potential or reading expectancy of their students, reading expectancy formulas are presented and explained. Since these formulas are based on information about a student's intelligence as measured by an intelligence test, a special section is presented on intelligence and intelligence tests. Differences between individual and group IQ tests are discussed and examples of each type are given. Individual IQ tests usually require a person specially trained to administer them, whereas group IQ tests are generally given by the classroom teacher in the regular classroom.

To determine who is underachieving in reading, the teacher must compare a student's reading potential as determined by a reading expectancy formula with his or her present level of reading achievement as determined by a reading achievement test. The comparison between the present status of a child in reading with his or her reading potential is called *appraisal*, which is the second step in a diagnostic pattern. Teachers are cautioned about using reading expectancy formulas as absolute determinants of a student's reading potential. One of the reasons given for this caution is that the child's IQ score may not be a valid one for the child. It is also stressed that there is no set rule for determining which child should be a candidate for further testing. It is better to err on the safe side with overzealous diagnosis in the early grades than to let the gap get too large in the later grades. Information is also given about what a teacher can do to determine a student's reading potential if there is no IQ test score available.

SUGGESTIONS FOR THOUGHT QUESTIONS AND ACTIVITIES

1. Choose a few students for whom intelligence test scores are available, and using the Bond and Tinker formula for computing reading expectancy, determine the students' reading expectancy.

2. Compute the reading expectancy for the same students by using the Harris and Sipay formula.

3. Compare the students' reading expectancy with their present reading achievement as measured by a standardized reading achievement test. Determine which students should receive further diagnostic testing.

4. Choose three group intelligence tests and look up reviews about them in Buros's *Mental Measurements Yearbooks*.

5. You have been asked to address this month's meeting of the Parent/Teacher Organization in your school. You have been asked to speak about intelligence and intelligence tests. There has been a lot of controversy concerning this topic in your community. What will you say? Write the address.

6. Look up reviews about the *Stanford-Binet Intelligence Scale* and the *Wechsler Intelligence Scale for Children* in Buros's *Mental Measurements Yearbooks*. Which would you choose to use with a child who is having reading problems if you were specially trained to give these tests?

7. Explain why a listening capacity test would be useful for determining a child's reading

potential if an IQ score is not available for the child or if you feel that the child's IQ score is not valid for the child.

SELECTED BIBLIOGRAPHY

Bond, Guy L., Miles Tinker, and Barbara Wasson. *Reading Difficulties: Their Diagnosis and Correction,* Chapter 3, "Description of Disabled Readers," pp. 53–69. Englewood Cliffs, N.J.: Prentice-Hall, 1979.

Boring, E.G. "Intelligence as the Tests Test It." *New Republic* 35 (1925):35–37.

Dechant, Emerald. *Diagnosis and Remediation of Reading Disabilities,* Chapter 1, "The Screening Process," pp. 3–31. Englewood Cliffs, N.J.: Prentice-Hall, 1981.

Harris, Albert, and Edward R. Sipay. *How to Increase Reading Ability,* 7th ed., Chapter 7, "Reading Disability, Dyslexia, and Learning Disability," pp. 140–62. New York: Longman, 1980.

Hunt, McVicker, ed. *Human Intelligence.* New Brunswick, N.J.: E. P. Dutton, 1972.

Jensen, Arthur R. *Environment, Heredity, and Intelligence.* Compiled from the *Harvard Educational Review.* Cambridge, Mass.: President and Fellows of Harvard College, 1969.

Monroe, Marion. *Children Who Cannot Read.* Chicago: The University of Chicago Press, 1932.

Strang, Ruth. *Diagnostic Teaching of Reading,* 2nd ed. New York: McGraw-Hill, 1969.

Part III

INSTRUMENTS AND TECHNIQUES FOR THE ASSESSMENT AND DIAGNOSIS OF READING PERFORMANCE

CHAPTER 8

Standardized Reading Achievement Tests: Survey Type

INTRODUCTION

In schools across the nation, you always know when it's that ominous time of the year—time for the dreaded standardized achievement tests. A hush seems to envelop the school; it's as if everyone is walking on tiptoe. Doors are closed, and anxious students and teachers are captives within. Everyone waits with bated breath for the results. Will they be an embarrassment to the school district, or will the students score substantially above the national norms? It's a tense time for all involved. A few school districts have decided to solve the problem by eliminating the use of standardized norm-referenced achievement tests in their schools. This seems rather drastic and is analogous to "throwing the baby out with the bath water." These tests do have value if properly used.

Tests should be used for more than comparative purposes; all tests that are administered should have instructional implications. This chapter will concentrate on standardized norm-referenced reading achievement tests that yield a general score, not because these are the most popular tests administered in schools, but because they play an important role in the diagnostic-reading and correction program. After you finish reading this chapter, you should be able to answer the following questions:

1. Are there major differences between a survey reading test and a reading achievement subtest of an achievement test battery? Explain.

2. What are some uses of standardized norm-referenced reading achievement or survey tests?

3. How can survey tests be used in a positive manner?

4. What are some examples of survey reading tests?

5. What are some examples of test batteries that have a reading achievement subtest?

6. When should standardized achievement tests be given?

7. What are reading readiness tests?

8. What have studies found about the predictive validity of reading readiness tests?

9. What subtests on a reading readiness test have been found to be the most effective in predicting reading success?

10. Why are reading readiness tests still used?

11. What are some examples of reading readiness tests?

STANDARDIZED ACHIEVEMENT TESTS AND STANDARDIZED SURVEY READING TESTS

Some persons differentiate between survey reading tests such as the *Iowa Silent Reading Tests* and the reading subtest of an achievement test battery such as the *California Achievement Tests*. Actually, the survey reading test and the reading subtest of an achievement test battery are quite similar and serve the same purposes. Both measure a student's overall reading achievement. The major difference between the two types of tests is that a standardized survey reading test, such as the *Iowa Silent Reading Tests,* only measures reading, whereas the reading achievement subtest of an achievement test, such as the *California Achievement Tests,* is part of a battery of achievement tests; that is, the reading achievement test is one of many tests that measure different curricula. For example, the *California Achievement Tests* are designed for measuring achievement in the basic curricular areas of reading, spelling, language, mathematics, and reference skills. As already stated, the reading component of the test battery yields very similar information to a survey reading test. Both survey reading tests and reading achievement tests from test batteries yield a general or overall score and were not developed to be used as diagnostic instruments; however,

they play an essential role in any diagnostic program. (See Special Note on pages 24–25 in Chapter 3.) These are group tests that are usually very easy to administer in a relatively short period of time, and they are useful for screening or identification which is the first step in a diagnostic pattern (see "Diagnostic Pattern" in Chapter 7). Standardized norm-referenced reading achievement or survey tests are used to assess the students' present achievement status. The results of these kinds of tests are used for a number of purposes. One use is usually to make comparisons among other schools in the district, state, or nation. Another use is to tell us which child is doing well and which is doing poorly; it helps to identify that child who may need help. If the teacher uses the survey test as a means for identifying those children who may need help, the instrument is being used in a positive manner.

You are probably the most familiar with standardized achievement tests such as the *Metropolitan Achievement Tests,* the *Stanford Achievement Tests,* and the *California Achievement Tests* because most schools employ these kind of tests. They are generally given either at the beginning or the end of the school year by the classroom teacher. It's usually a good idea to give the test at the same time that the test was given to the students who determined the norms for the test. For example, if you wish to give an achievement test in the fall to help you determine how to group for instruction, you should choose a test in which the norms were gathered in the fall. Standardized achievement tests that are given in the fall are usually used for instructional purposes and screening, whereas standardized achievement tests that are given at the end of the year are generally used for comparison purposes.

Before giving any tests you should study the test manual that accompanies each one. The manual usually contains information about the test, such as how norms were gathered, instructions on how to administer and score the test, and what the test measures. If teachers know that their students have not had any instruction in a specific area, the teachers would be subjecting their students to a very frustrating experience by giving them an achievement test in that area; it would be a misuse of a test instrument. The teachers do not need a test to confirm what they already know.

Examples of Standardized Survey Reading Tests

The *Iowa Silent Reading Tests* (ISRT) are group survey reading tests that come in two forms and consist of the following three levels: grades 6 to 9, grades 9 to 14, and grades 11 to 16. The tests in Level 1 are Vocabulary; Reading Comprehension; Directed Reading, which assesses a student's work-study skills; and Reading Efficiency, which uses a modified cloze technique to assess a student's speed and accuracy. Roger Farr is the coordinating editor, and it is presently published by The Psychological Corporation.

The *Gates-MacGinitie Reading Tests,* 2nd ed., are also group survey tests that have been greatly used for screening. The tests consist of seven levels, and each level, except the Basic R level, yields a vocabulary, comprehension, and total score. The levels begin at a readiness level (Basic R, Grade 1) and proceed through the twelfth grade. After the readiness level, there is another level for grade one (Level A), grade 2 (Level B), and grade three (Level C). The intermediate grades (4, 5, and 6) are combined in Level D; grades 7, 8, and 9 are combined in Level E; and grades 10, 11, and 12 are combined in Level F. Arthur I. Gates (deceased) and Walter H. MacGinitie are the developers of the test batteries, and it is published by The Riverside Publishing Company.

Examples of Standardized Achievement Tests[1]

According to Educational Testing Service (ETS) in Princeton, N.J., the following test batteries are those about which the most frequent inquiries are made.

California Achievement Tests. c1970 and 1978 (both editions available). CTB/McGraw-Hill. Grades K–12.9

> This battery of overlapping tests measures achievement growth in order to improve instruction. Norm scores and criterion-referenced information are available in curricular areas: Reading, Language, Mathematics, Spelling, and Reference Skills.

Comprehensive Tests of Basic Skills. c1975, 1981. CTB/McGraw-Hill. Grades K–12.9.

> Assesses level of attainment of skills required for academic study and out-of-school needs. Covers the following areas: Reading, Language, Mathematics, Reference Skills, Science, Social Studies.

Iowa Tests of Basic Skills, Multilevel Edition, Forms 7 and 8; c1978; The Riverside Publishing Company.[2] Grades 3–9.

> Designed to provide for measurement of achievement in fundamental skills. There are eleven subtests that cover the following areas: Reading, Language Skills, Work Study Skills, Mathematics.

Metropolitan Achievement Tests; c1970 and 1978 (both editions available); The Psychological Corporation; Grades K–12.9.

> This instructional test series consists of

---

[1]Adapted from Educational Testing Service, Test Collection Bibliography.
[2]All tests formerly published by Houghton Mifflin are now available only from their subsidiary, The Riverside Publishing Company.

criterion-referenced information and norm-referenced measures in Reading, Mathematics, and Language designed for use in assessing competence for curriculum planning purposes.

SRA Achievement Series; c1978; Science Research Associates; Grades K–12.

This series covers the following areas: Reading, Mathematics, Language Arts, Reference Materials, Social Studies, Science.

Sequential Tests of Educational Progress Series III; c1969, 1979 (both editions available); ETS/Addison Wesley Publishing Company; Grades 3.5–12.9.

This series has the following subscores: Reading, Vocabulary, Writing Skills, Mathematics Computation, Mathematics Basic Concepts, Study Skills/Listening, Social Studies, Science. Two parallel forms and out-of-level norms are available for the first five subtests.

Stanford Achievement Test; c1973; The Psychological Corporation; Grades 1.5–9.9.

This test has the following subscores: Reading Comprehension, Language Skills, Mathematics Skills, Science Tests, Social Science Tests, Auditory Skills.

Special Note

A number of the standardized norm-refer enced tests are reporting criterion-referenced *information.* Do not get confused. The standardized achievement test batteries are not criterion-referenced tests; they are norm-referenced tests, which are also reporting or giving a form of criterion-referenced information. John Stewart explains why standardized norm-referenced achievement tests are including criterion-referenced information. He says that "publishers are moving in this direction because it is believed that if testing does not contribute to the instruc-

tional process, then it has no valid reason for existing. The criterion-referenced information is making testing a valid classroom exercise."[3]

Locator Tests

Many of the achievement batteries supply a locator test, which is used to determine at what level a student should begin testing, when testing out-of-level because the U.S. Office of Education for Title I testing recommends functional level testing. Locator tests are becoming increasingly widespread among test-makers because of the need to provide students with tests to which they can relate well. Students in sixth grade reading at a fourth-grade level will not relate well to a sixth-grade reading test. The locator test is used to determine the approximate functional level of these students, and it is recommended that those students who test out-of-level on the locator test be given the achievement test at the approximate functional level at which they tested on the locator test. Therefore, the sixth-grade students who score at the fourth-grade level on the locator test would be tested with a fourth-grade level test.

Practice Tests

Some tests, such as the *California Achievement Tests,* provide a practice test. These tests, which were utilized during the standardization of CAT Forms C and D at Levels 10 through 16, are designed to ensure that students know how to mark an answer *before* they take the test. The practice tests are supposed to ensure that the test measures what students know and not their previous familiarity with test-taking procedures.

Student Previews

Some tests such as the *Sequential Tests of Educational Progress* (STEP) provide a student

---

[3]John Stewart, senior product manager, CTB/McGraw-Hill, 1981.

preview, which is supposed to be given to students one day before the first testing session and carefully reviewed with them. It is suggested that children in the lower grades, who may have reading difficulties, should have the previews—which describe all the STEP tests—read to them.

READING READINESS TESTS

Reading readiness tests are usually the first type of standardized achievement test a child encounters in his or her life at school. These tests, which are designed to predict those children who are ready to read, are a direct result of the readiness movement, which believed that children are not *ready* to read until they have reached a mental age of six and a half. Even though most educators have discarded the "waiting" theory of readiness, reading readiness tests are alive and going strong. Studies show that administrators rank them as the number one criterion for determining when a child should begin formal reading instruction.[4] Because the chances are high that your school will use a reading readiness test, you should have some understanding of the kinds of tasks included and how good they are at predicting future reading success. (Note that most achievement test batteries have readiness tests.)

First, it is important to state that all reading readiness tests are not the same. They vary as to purpose, number and kinds of subtests, and administration time. They also vary in when they are given. For example, the *Gates-MacGinitie Readiness Skills Test* consists of eight subtests and takes approximately 120 minutes to administer, whereas the *Metropolitan Readiness Tests, Level I* has six subtests and an administra-

tion time of 80 to 90 minutes, and the *Murphy-Durrell Reading Readiness Analysis* takes about 60 minutes to administer and has only three subtests. Studies have shown that the predictive validity of reading readiness tests is not very high, that they could not predict with accuracy how well nonreaders would learn to read, and that teachers' ratings were as accurate in predicting reading success as were the tests.[5]

It has been stated that "a great saving in testing time could well stem from using only the letters and numbers subtests or, perhaps, by not testing readiness at all. In either case, the sacrifice in information would be minimal."[6] Despite many such statements, test makers continue to produce reading readiness tests, and as has already been stated, most school systems use them. It must be that educators feel more secure with the results of commercially produced tests than with teachers' judgments, even though evidence weighs against such security. Also, most reading readiness tests are administered at the end of kindergarten or at the beginning of first grade. In most kindergartens children are involved in a beginning reading readiness program, which used to be reserved for the beginning of first grade. When a reading readiness test is given now, it seems more likely that it is a measurement of the childrens' beginning reading readiness achievement than a test to predict future success in reading.

Why is a test needed to predict future reading success? We already know from voluminous research that high-achieving readers usually come from homes with enriched verbal environments, whereas low-achieving readers usually come from homes in which little conversation takes place with the parents. We also know that

---

[4]Robert L. Hillerich, *Reading Fundamentals for Preschool and Primary Children* (Columbus, Ohio: Charles Merrill, 1977), p. 25.

[5]Max Coltheart, "When Can Children Learn to Read—And When Should They Be Taught?" in *Reading Research: Advances in Theory and Practice,* Vol. I, T. Gary Waller and G.E. MacKinnon, eds. (New York: Academic Press, 1979), p. 15.

[6]Hillerich, op. cit., p. 25.

a rich verbal environment is more likely to be found among middle- and upper-socioeconomic classes than in lower classes.

Unfortunately, there are some dangers attached to reading readiness tests if they are misused. One danger is a self-fulfilling prophecy. If a child does poorly on a reading readiness test, the teacher may feel that the child cannot benefit from reading instruction; the child is not expected to be able to learn to read, and as a result, the teacher defers instruction in reading. Eventually, the teacher's feelings concerning the inability of the child to read become part of the child's own self-concept (see "Teachers' Expectations" in Chapter 2).

Here are some suggestions on how to choose and use reading readiness tests if they are required in your school system:

1. Use a reading readiness test that can provide diagnostic information, that is, one that will give a child's beginning reading-readiness skills'[7] profile.

2. Check the subtests to determine how directly the tasks required are related to reading. For example, some tests require children to match pictures and geometric figures rather than letters. Those children who do well in matching pictures and geometric figures may not do well in matching letters. To use the reading readiness test for diagnostic purposes, check to see if the subtests are similar to the activities presented in the beginning reading readiness program.

3. Check the administration time of the test. Make sure that it is suited to the attention span of your students.

[7]*Beginning reading readiness* is defined as "those activities designed to teach prerequisite skills that are *directly* related to the skills that will be necessary in the formal reading program." See Dorothy Rubin, *A Practical Approach to Teaching Reading* (New York: Holt, Rinehart and Winston, 1982).

4. Make sure children understand the terminology used on the test and understand the directions.

5. Do not use the results of the test to delay a child from beginning to read. Remember, our purpose is to diagnose rather than to determine whether a child is *ready* for reading. Unfortunately, as stated earlier, reading readiness tests often are used to test when a child is *ready* to learn to read. A child who does poorly on the test is often delayed from beginning to read, and he or she is put into programs that do not provide direct instruction in reading. This is ironic because the child who does poorly on a reading readiness test that involves the use of letters probably needs more exposure to letters and the sounds they represent than a child who does well. Delaying a child's entrance into the formal reading program is assuring failure for that child rather than success.

6. Do not use the reading readiness test as an end in itself; also use informal assessments and a teacher's judgment to make decisions concerning the child's readiness.

Special Note

As stated earlier in this chapter, a number of achievement test batteries have a preinstructional or readiness test as part of their battery. For example, the *California Achievement Tests* (CAT) and the *Comprehensive Tests of Basic Skills* (CTBS) have readiness tests. The CAT Form C Level 10 and the CTBS Level A are readiness tests for children in kindergarten or those children in first grade who have not attended kindergarten. Both readiness tests consist of the following subtests: letter forms, letter names, listening for information, letter sounds, visual discrimination, and sound matching. The CTBS also has a subtest on language.

Because most achievement test batteries have overlapping age levels and take into account whether a child has had instruction in kindergarten or not, these tests may be more helpful than many of the regular reading readiness tests.

Here are some examples of reading readiness tests adapted from the Test Collection compiled by the Educational Testing Service:

CIRCUS; c1972, 1974; Level A (Preschool–K.5); ETS/Addison-Wesley Publishing Company.

Assesses children's skills in a variety of cognitive and social areas including the following: mathematics, listening, problem solving, general information, productive language, visual discrimination, visual memory, perceptual-motor coordination, letter and number recognition, divergent production, auditory discrimination, functional language, receptive vocabulary, recognizing common sounds. An Activities Inventory, an Educational Environment Questionnaire, and a CIRCUS Behavior Inventory are also included. (Two basic assessments—mathematics and listening; all others are supplementary assessments.)

Clymer-Barrett Prereading Battery by Theodore Clymer, Thomas C. Barrett; c1966-68; Grade 1; Ginn and Company.

The battery includes a Prereading Rating Scale which covers facility in oral language, concept and vocabulary, listening ability, skills in critical and creative thinking, social skills, emotional development, attitude toward and interest in reading, and work habits. Subscores are: Visual Discrimination (Letter Recognition, Word Matching); Auditory Discrimination (Beginning Sounds, Ending Sounds); Visual-Motor Coordination (Shape Completion, Copy-A-Sentence).

Gates-MacGinitie Reading Tests: Readiness Skills by Arthur I. Gates, Walter H. MacGinitie;

c1966-68; Grades Kindergarten–Grade 1; The Riverside Press.

Yields a total score and eight subscores. The subscores are for the following: Listening Comprehension, Auditory Discrimination, Visual Discrimination, Following Directions, Letter Recognition, Visual-Motor Coordination, Auditory Blending, and Word Recognition.

Metropolitan Readiness Tests: 1976 Edition, Level I by Joanne R. Nurss, Mary E. McGauvran; c1974-76; Kindergarten; The Psychological Corporation.

Designed to assess basic prereading skills. Subtests are as follows: Auditory Memory, Rhyming, Letter Recognition, Visual Matching, School Language and Listening, and Quantitative Language. A Copying subtest is optional.

Metropolitan Readiness Tests: 1976 Edition, Level II by Joanne R. Nurss, Mary E. McGauvran; c1974-76; Grades: End Kindergarten-Beginning Grade 1; The Psychological Corporation.

Designed to assess skills important in beginning reading and mathematics. Subtests are as follows: Beginning Consonants, Sound-Letter Correspondence, Visual Matching, Finding Patterns, School Language, Listening, Quantitative Concepts, Quantitative Operations. A Copying subtest is optional.

Murphy-Durrell Reading Readiness Analysis by Helen A. Murphy, Donald D. Durrell; c1964-65; Grades K.8–1.5; The Psychological Corporation.

A group administered test of abilities considered essential for success in beginning reading. The child is asked to identify separate sounds in spoken words, to identify capital and lower-case letters named by the examiner, and to recognize sight words one hour after they have been taught. Subscores are for the following areas: Phonemes Test, Letter Names Test, Learning Rate Test.

SUMMARY

Chapter 8 discusses reading achievement tests that yield a general score. It is emphasized that survey reading tests such as the *Iowa Silent Reading Tests,* which measure only reading, and the *California Achievement Tests,* which have a reading test as one of their subtests, are similar and serve the same purpose. They both measure a student's overall reading achievement. Both survey reading tests and reading subtests from achievement test batteries yield a general or overall score and were not developed to be used as diagnostic instruments. They do, however, play an essential role in the diagnostic program. They are group tests that are easy to administer in a relatively short period of time, and they are useful for screening, that is, as an aid in identifying those students who may need help. Reading achievement tests that yield an overall score are generally used for comparison purposes. Various types of reading achievement tests that yield an overall or general score are discussed, and examples of some are presented.

Reading readiness tests are usually the first type of standardized achievement test that a child encounters in his or her life at school. They are designed to predict those children who are ready to read. A discussion of the usefulness of these tests, as well as suggestions on how to choose and use them, is given.

SUGGESTIONS FOR THOUGHT QUESTIONS AND ACTIVITIES

1. You have been appointed to a schoolwide committee which is interested in evaluating the testing procedures and the kinds of tests that are given during the school year. You are supposed to help committee members evaluate their use of reading readiness tests. Your suggestions will help them decide whether or not to use such tests. How will you go about helping them to make their decision? What factors should you take into consideration? What are your views concerning reading readiness tests? What does research say about them?

2. People in your school are confused about survey reading tests and reading achievement subtests of achievement test batteries. You have been asked to give examples of each and to explain their purposes.

3. Choose three standardized achievement tests and look them up in Buros's *Mental Measurements Yearbooks.*

4. Choose one survey reading test, such as the *Iowa Silent Reading Tests,* and look it up in Buros's *Mental Measurements Yearbooks.*

5. Choose three reading readiness tests and look them up in Buros's *Mental Measurements Yearbooks.*

SELECTED BIBLIOGRAPHY

Ahmann, Stanley, and Marvin Glock. *Evaluating Student Progress: Principles of Tests and Measurements,* 6th ed. Boston, Mass.: Allyn and Bacon, 1981.

Blanton, William E., Roger Farr, and J. Joap Tuinman. *Measuring Reading Performance.* Newark, Del.: International Reading Association, 1974.

Brown, Clair G., Jr., and Jane H. Root. "Evaluation in the Elementary School: Corrective Reading Instruction." In *Corrective Reading in the Elementary Classroom,* Marjorie S. Johnson and Roy A. Kress, eds. Newark, Del.: International Reading Association, 1967.

Buros, Oscar, ed. *The Eighth Mental Measurements Yearbook.* Highland Park, N.J.: Gryphon Press, 1978.

———. *Reading: Tests and Reviews.* Highland Park, N.J.: Gryphon Press, 1968.

Farr, Roger, and Nicholas Anastasiow. *Tests of Read-*

ing Readiness and Achievement: A Review and Evaluation. Newark, Del.: International Reading Association, 1969.

Mehrens, William A., and Irvin J. Lehmann. *Measurement and Evaluation in Education and Psychology,* 2nd ed. New York: Holt, Rinehart and Winston, 1975.

_____. *Standardized Tests in Education,* 3rd ed. New York: Holt, Rinehart and Winston, 1980.

Pumfrey, Peter D. *Measuring Reading Abilities: Concepts, Sources, and Applications.* London: Hodder and Stoughton, 1977.

Schreiner, Robert, ed. *Reading Tests and Teachers: A Practical Guide.* Newark, Del.: International Reading Association, 1979.

Smith, William E., and Michael D. Beck. "Determining Instructional Reading Level with the 1978 Metropolitan Achievement Tests," *The Reading Teacher* 34 (December 1980): 313–19.

Tierney, Robert J., and Diane Lapp. *National Assessment of Educational Progress in Reading.* Newark, Del.: International Reading Association, 1979.

Tuinman, J. Joap. "Criterion Referenced Measurement in a Norm Referenced Context." In *What Research Has to Say about Reading Instruction,* S. Jay Samuels, ed., pp. 165–73. Newark, Del.: International Reading Association, 1978.

CHAPTER 9

Diagnostic Reading Tests and Techniques I: An Emphasis on the Informal Reading Inventory

INTRODUCTION

TEACHER: You read that passage aloud very well. Now, let's see how well you do answering questions about it.

STUDENT: Oh, I can't answer any questions on it because I wasn't listening to what I was reading.

How many times has this happened? Probably often, but why? Obviously, the child was so intent on pronouncing the words correctly that he or she was not paying any attention to the meaning of what was read. Since reading *is* meaning, we couldn't say that this child was reading. He or she was merely reciting without thinking.

Although a number of students may not do as well comprehending material that they read orally rather than silently, oral reading does have value. It is especially useful for diagnostic purposes. In this chapter and in the next, you will encounter a number of diagnostic instruments that test a student's oral reading ability,

as well as other reading abilities. You will learn how to gain detailed information about a pupil's reading behavior. This chapter will emphasize the informal reading inventory, which can be an indispensable tool for the classroom teacher if it is properly used. After you read this chapter you should be able to answer the following questions:

1. What are diagnostic reading tests?

2. What is the place of oral reading in diagnosis?

3. What is an informal reading inventory?

4. How does a teacher administer an informal reading inventory?

5. When does a teacher administer an informal reading inventory?

6. To whom does a teacher administer an informal reading inventory?

7. How can a teacher construct his or her own informal reading inventory?

8. How do published informal reading inventories compare with teacher-made ones?

9. How are reading levels determined on an informal reading inventory?

10. What are some controversial issues concerning informal reading inventories?

11. How are oral reading errors scored?

12. What are some of the problems concerning the scoring of oral reading errors?

13. What is miscue analysis?

14. What is a word recognition formula for computing percent correct and percent wrong in oral reading?

15. What is a listening capacity test?

16. When is a listening capacity test given?

17. What are word lists used for?

18. What is a modified informal reading inventory approach?

19. What criteria should you look for if you are interested in using a published informal reading inventory?

20. What are some points of caution concerning informal reading inventories?

WHAT ARE DIAGNOSTIC READING TESTS?

A diagnostic reading test is designed to break down a complex skill into its component parts to help teachers gain information about a student's specific reading weaknesses and strengths. It is generally given after a group standardized survey reading test has screened those children who seem to be reading below their ability.

Diagnostic reading tests can be standardized or teacher-made tests. Most reading diagnostic tests are individually administered and given by a special reading teacher rather than by the regular classroom teacher. However, many of these diagnostic tests can be given by the regular classroom teacher, and in a diagnostic-reading and correction program, many should be. Informal reading inventories are examples of diagnostic tools that are indispensable to the classroom teacher.

Although agreement does not exist on how to define a diagnostic reading test and what tests to include under the umbrella of diagnostic tests, it seems clear that a test on a test battery that provides subscores discrete enough so that specific information about a student's reading behavior can be attained and used for instructional purposes should be included in this category. A reading diagnostic test or test battery may consist of oral reading, silent reading, comprehension, phonic analysis, structural analysis, sight vocabulary, visual and auditory discrimination, reading and study skills, or rate of reading.

The diagnostic test that is chosen should fulfill the criteria for all tests; that is, it should be valid, reliable, easy to administer in a reasonable period of time, and easy to score. Most importantly, the test should be one that will help the teacher diagnose a student's specific problem. Teachers should check the diagnostic test carefully before administering it to make sure that it does indeed diagnose the specific skill that the teacher wishes to have diagnosed.

Most of the standardized diagnostic tests are very helpful in diagnosing word recognition difficulties, but they are not very effective in diagnosing comprehension problems. The questions that are asked on most standardized norm-referenced diagnostic reading tests seem to be concerned primarily with recall; they do not probe into higher comprehension skills. As a result, teacher-made diagnostic measures and published or teacher-made criterion-referenced tests are usually more helpful in probing for an individual's specific comprehension problem (see Chapter 15).

ORAL READING

The child read aloud, of course: throughout antiquity, until the late Empire, silent reading was exceptional. People read aloud to themselves, or, if they could, got a servant to read to them.[1]

Closely associated with reading was recitation: the selected passages were not only read aloud but also learnt by heart, and it seems that beginners at least used to recite in a sing song manner, syllable by syllable: "Com-ing through, ray by ray, A-pol-lo, the mor-ning sun. . ."[2]

The above excerpts help shed light on why reading was taught in a recitation manner until the beginning of the twentieth century and silent reading was ignored: It's difficult to break with tradition. As a matter of fact, in some classes today you can still find remnants of the oral tradition in reading—some teachers still have their students read in a round-robin rote fashion. Fortunately, however, this practice is not as common as in the past. Fortunately, also, the misuses and overuses of oral reading did not culminate in its complete banishment, even though there was a movement for a time to ban oral reading in the classroom.

Oral reading has a place in the reading program if properly used, and it can be an essential diagnostic tool, which helps teachers learn about the word recognition skills of their students.

Oral Reading as a Diagnostic Tool

Astute teachers can gain a great deal of information about a student's word recognition skill by listening to the student read aloud. A teacher can determine the reading level of the child and avoid having the child read silently at a frustration level. Oral reading helps a teacher gain insight into a student's reading difficulty, if he or she has one, as well as a student's strengths.

There are many opportunities for children to read orally during their day at school. Even though a choral reading or the reading of a book report or poem is not planned as a diagnostic testing session, knowledgeable teachers use these opportunities to study their students. Much important information is gained from informal diagnostic techniques if teachers know what to look for. The key, of course, is to know what to look for. (See Chapter 11 for a discussion on the use of observation as a diagnostic technique.)

Many standardized diagnostic reading tests test oral reading ability. Some test *only* oral reading ability, whereas others may have a subtest of this (see Chapter 10). All informal reading inventories test oral reading ability. This chapter and the next will present a number of tests that diagnose oral reading ability.

WHAT ARE THE PURPOSES OF AN INFORMAL READING INVENTORY?

An informal reading inventory (IRI) is probably one of the most valuable diagnostic aids because of the amount of information it can convey to a perceptive teacher who knows how to use it to its best advantages.

An essential function of an IRI is to help the teacher determine the child's levels of independence, instruction, frustration, and capacity. These are needed to make a proper match between the child and the books he or she reads.

Another important job of an IRI is to help a teacher learn about a student's reading strengths and weaknesses so that he or she can develop a proper reading program for the stu-

[1]H. I. Marrou, *A History of Education in Antiquity* (New York: The New American Library of World Literature, 1956), p. 214.
[2]Ibid., p. 215.

dent. For example, if on giving a child an IRI the teacher learns that the child has difficulty answering comprehension questions that call for interpretation or inference, the teacher can develop a program for the child to help him or her gain skill in this area (see Chapters 13 and 15). From listening to the student reading orally, the teacher can learn whether the student has word recognition problems that may be interfering with comprehension when the child is reading silently.

From listening to a child's oral reading, the teacher can hypothesize possible skill deficiencies that may be limiting the student's performance. If the teacher sees that a student has a word recognition problem, he or she would probably want to administer other informal skills tests (see Chapter 10) for more specific diagnosis because there are generally not enough opportunities to observe any given skill in great depth in a relatively short passage. For example, how many initial blends are there in a selection? From listening to the child read, the teacher can determine whether the child reads with expression and observes punctuation marks or whether the student reads hurriedly without any concern for punctuation signals.

Yet another function of the IRI is to give the student feedback on his or her reading behavior. As the student reads passages at graduated levels of difficulty, he or she becomes aware of the reading level that is appropriate for him or her. It helps the student recognize his or her word recognition and comprehension strengths and weaknesses. Student awareness of a problem is a vital factor in helping the student overcome the difficulty or difficulties.

It must again be stressed that the IRI is an excellent instrument for estimating students' reading levels and for diagnosing their strengths and weaknesses, but the IRI is only as good as the person administering it and interpreting its results.

Special Note

The term *informal* implies that the inventory is teacher-made; however, many informal reading inventories are published (commercially produced) ones. In this chapter, information will be provided on how to construct an informal reading inventory, if a teacher wishes to do so, based on the basal reader series in use in the class (see "Constructing Your Own Informal Reading Inventory").

AN OVERVIEW OF THE INFORMAL READING INVENTORY[3]

This section will give you an overview of an informal reading inventory. The sections that follow will go into detail on many of the points presented here. It is good to see the whole before discussing its parts so that you can better determine the relationship of the parts to their whole.

An IRI is individually administered and usually consists of oral and silent reading passages selected from basal readers from the preprimer to the sixth- or eighth-grade levels (some exist up to the twelfth grade). Usually each selection has the following kinds of comprehension questions: factual, inferential, and word meanings. (A few may contain evaluative questions.)

Graded word lists, which usually are also taken from basal readers and generally consist of twenty or twenty-five words from each reader level, are used to determine at what grade level the student should begin reading the oral passages. The student usually begins the word list at two levels below his or her present grade level. The highest grade level at which the student has no errors on the graded word list is the grade level at which he or she begins reading the oral

---

[3]An informal reading inventory may also be referred to as an individual reading inventory.

passage. The student reads aloud the oral passage, and the teacher records any omission, substitution, insertion, pronunciation, repetition, and hesitation errors. If the student reads the oral passage at the independent or instructional level, the student is asked the comprehension questions; he or she then proceeds to read the silent passage at the same grade level and is asked the questions to the silent passage. The student then goes to the next reading grade level, continuing until he or she reaches his or her frustration level. If the student makes so many word recognition errors in oral reading that he or she is reading at or close to his or her frustration level, the teacher begins to read the passages aloud to the student to determine his or

her comprehension ability. This is called a listening capacity test.

DETERMINING READING LEVELS

The IRI, which originated from the work of Emmett A. Betts and his doctoral student Patsy A. Killgallon, is used to determine three reading levels and a capacity or listening capacity level. The criteria for reading levels on the IRI were determined by Betts, and many informal reading inventories still use the same levels or modifications of them. The levels as determined by Betts and his percentages that designate the levels follow:

Betts Reading Levels

Independent Level*	Children read on their own without any difficulty.	Word Recognition—99% or above Comprehension—90% or above
Instructional Level	Teaching level.	Word Recognition—95% or above Comprehension—75% or above
Frustration Level	This level is to be avoided. It is the lowest level of readability.	Word Recognition—90% or less Comprehension—50% or less
Listening Capacity Level*	Highest level at which a pupil can comprehend when someone reads to him or her.	Comprehension—75% or above

*Betts also called the *independent level* the *basal level,* and the *listening capacity level* was called the *capacity level.*

In designating these levels Betts not only gave percentage determinants, he also gave other criteria that the teacher should look for at each level.[4]

Independent Level

This level "is the highest level at which an individual can read and satisfy all the criteria for

[4]Adapted from Emmett A. Betts, *Foundations of Reading Instruction* (New York: American Book Co., 1946), pp. 445–54.

desirable reading behavior in silent- and oral-reading situations."[5] At the independent level the child can read successfully on his or her own without any assistance. When the student is reading orally or silently at this level, he or she should be able to achieve a minimum comprehension score on literal and interpretive questions of at least 90 percent. The pupil should also be free from such observable evidence of tension as frowning, movements of

[5]Ibid., p. 445.

feet and hands, finger pointing, and holding the book too close or too far.

For oral reading the student should have good rhythm with proper phrasing and attention to punctuation. The student's voice should be free from tension, and he or she should have an accurate pronunciation of 99 percent or more of the words. The student's silent reading should be free from lip movement or subvocalizing.

The independent level is an important one for the child, teacher, parents, and librarian. It is at this level that the child will read library or trade books in school and at home. The reference books that children choose to read for a special project or assignment should also be at their independent level because they will be reading these on their own. If they choose books to read independently that are too hard for them, that will deter them from reading. One of the ways that teachers can determine whether they have done a good job in teaching reading is to observe whether students voluntarily choose books to read during the school day (see Chapter 17).

Instructional Level

The instructional level is the one at which teaching is done. This level must not be so challenging that it frustrates the student nor so easy that the student becomes bored. At this level there should be a minimum comprehension score of at least 75 percent for both oral and silent reading on literal and interpretive questions, and in the oral reading there should be accurate pronunciation of at least 95 percent of the running words. As on the independent level, there should be no observable tensions or undue movements of feet and hands. There should be freedom from finger pointing, lip movements, and head movements; and there should be acceptable posture. Oral reading should be rhythmical with proper phrasing; there should be

proper attention paid to punctuation; and the child's voice should be free from tension.

Frustration Level

This is the level to be avoided; however, for diagnostic purposes, it is helpful for teachers to know what this level is so that they can avoid giving students reading material at this level. The fact that a child has reached his or her frustration level is evidenced by the child's attaining a comprehension score of 50 percent or less on literal and interpretive questions for oral and silent reading, and the child's inability to pronounce 10 percent of the words on the oral reading passage.

At the frustration level, the child has difficulty anticipating meanings and is not familiar with the facts presented in the selection. The child shows his or her frustration by frowning, constantly moving in a nervous fashion, finger pointing, blinking, or faulty breathing. The child may also be unwilling to read, and he or she may cry.

At this level, when the child reads silently, he or she reads at a slow rate, uses lip movements, and makes low vocal utterances. During oral reading, the child does not observe punctuation, reads in a high-pitched voice, and reads with a lack of rhythm or word by word. The child's reading is further characterized by irregular breathing, meaningless word substitution, insertion of words, repetition of words, partial and complete word reversals, omission of words, almost no eye-voice span, and an increased tendency to stutter.

Listening Capacity Level

The listening capacity level, as first determined by Betts, is the "highest level of readability of material which the learner can comprehend when the material is read to him.''[6] Betts also established the minimum comprehension score of at least 75 percent, based on both factual and inferential questions for listening capacity, and he designated that the term "*level* refers to the grade level at which the material was prepared for use; for example, preprimer, primer, first reader, second reader, and so on.''[7]

Special Note

Teacher judgment plays an important role in determining whether to continue testing or not. For example, it is possible to stop testing, even though a child has not reached his or her frustration level because the child is nervous or upset. Also, even though minimum criteria are usually given for estimating the various reading levels of IRIs, these are actually general standards because of teacher judgment. "The powers of observation and the standards of judgment of the examiner are the final determinants of the adequacy of the information gained."[8]

The Buffer Zone of the IRI

The *buffer zone* of the IRI is that area that falls between the instructional and frustration levels. For word recognition it is 94 percent to 91 percent, and for comprehension it is 74 percent to 51 percent (Betts's criteria). When a child's score falls in the buffer zone, the teacher must decide whether to continue testing or not, even though the child has not yet reached the frustration level. If the child appears interested in continuing, testing should continue. If, on the other hand, the child exhibits symptoms of frustration, testing should be stopped. Even though the

decision of whether to continue testing or not is a subjective one, there are some factors that the teacher could take into consideration; for example, the types of errors the child has made, the personality of the student, the student's prior reading record, the health of the child, whether the child speaks another language at home, whether the child speaks nonstandard English, and so on.

CONSTRUCTING YOUR OWN INFORMAL READING INVENTORY

Although it is time-consuming to construct your own IRI, there are some teachers who would like to do so. This section will present more specific information on the parts of an IRI as well as information on how to construct and score one.

Usually an IRI, as stated earlier in this chapter, consists of word lists at varying levels which have been selected from a basal reader series; passages which are based on graduated levels of difficulty that have also been selected from a basal reader series for oral and silent reading; and comprehension questions for both the oral and silent reading passages.

Graded Word Lists

The graded word lists usually consist of twenty or twenty-five words. There is a word list for every level of the basal series. The list usually starts at the preprimer level and proceeds to the highest level book available. If the IRI begins at the preprimer level and ends at the eighth-grade level, there would be a word list for each level up to the eighth. (Some basal reader series have two levels for certain grades.)

The words for the word lists are selected from those introduced in the basal reader for each book level. (At the back of each basal reader

[6]Ibid., p. 452.
[7]Ibid., p. 439.
[8]Marjorie S. Johnson and Roy A. Kress, *Informal Reading Inventories* (Newark, Del.: International Reading Association, 1965), p. 22.

there is usually a list of words that have been introduced in the book.) Words for the word lists are based on a random sampling, so that each word introduced at a particular level has an equal and independent chance of being chosen.

If you are constructing your own IRI, an easy way to get a random sampling of the words for the word lists, if there are fewer than 100 words, is to put each word on a slip of paper and put the slips in a small box or hat. (Make sure the slips of paper are well mixed.) Pull 20 words from the hat. (If there are only 20 words that have been introduced at a particular reader level, you obviously would use all the words.) However, at the upper-grade levels, where there are more than a 100 words presented at each level, you need a method different from the cumbersome "old hat" random sampling method. You need a formula to help you determine the number of random samples of the required sample size for a given word list. The formula for this is as follows:

$$\frac{\text{Word List}}{\text{Sample Size}} = \text{Number of Samples}$$

The number of words you want on your word list is your sample size, and the word list is the total number of words. For example, if you want to select 20 words from a 100-word list, first apply the formula

$$N = \frac{100}{20} = 5.$$

Since the number of samples is 5, number the total number of words sequentially up to 5, that is, 1, 2, 3, 4, 5. (Choose which number you will use by any method you wish, and then choose all words that have that number.) To get the 20 words from the 100-word list, select all those words that are numbered either 1, 2, 3, 4, or 5. This will give you a sample of 20 words from the 100-word list covering the entire alphabetical range, if the words are presented alphabetically.

Graded Oral and Silent Reading Passages

To randomly draw sample passages for your IRI, note the number of pages in each basal reader, and then choose any one of the numbers. For example, if there are 200 pages, choose any number from 1 to 200. Open the book to the number you have chosen. Choose a selection on that page that can be easily excerpted; that is, it can stand alone and make sense. The first sentence of the selection should not have any pronouns that have antecedents in the previous paragraph. If there are no paragraphs on that page that can be easily excerpted, go to the previous page. It may be that you will have to go to the beginning of the story to get a selection that can stand alone.

The sample selections should contain approximately the following sample sizes:

Preprimer level, approximately 40 to 70 words

Primer level, approximately 50 to 85

First-grade level, approximately 70 to 100

Second-grade level, approximately 100 to 150

Third-grade level, approximately 125 to 175

Fourth-grade level, approximately 150 to 225

Fifth-grade level, approximately 175 to 250

Sixth-grade level and up, approximately 175 to 300

The paragraphs that are chosen to comprise your IRI should be representative of the readability level of the basal reader from which they were taken. There are times when this is not so; it's a good idea to double-check the chosen paragraphs with a readability formula (see Appendix B for the Fry Readability Formula). If your selection does not pass the readability formula criterion, repeat the process to choose a different passage. Each selection chosen for the IRI should have a short statement telling something about it.

Special Note

Publishers may use more complicated methods for randomizing word and passage selection than the sampling techniques just described.

The Comprehension Questions

Both the oral and the silent reading passages must have questions based on each passage. These are usually literal comprehension questions, interpretive questions, and word meaning questions. (Some IRIs may contain critical reading questions.) (See Chapter 13 for an in-depth discussion of literal, interpretive, and critical reading skills.) Examples of the types of questions that can be asked to assess selected comprehension skills at each level follow.

Literal Comprehension Questions

Literal questions are the easiest to construct, and they are generally the ones most often asked. The answers for literal questions are directly stated in the selection. Here is an example of a selection and some literal comprehension questions based on it.

Sharon and Carol are sisters.

They like to play together.

They play lots of games.

Their favorite game is Monopoly.

Literal Questions:

1. Who are sisters? (story detail)
2. What do the sisters like to do? (story detail)
3. What do the sisters play? (story detail)
4. What is their favorite game? (story detail)

Interpretive Questions

Interpretive questions are more difficult to answer because the answers are not directly stated in the selection; they are implied. Interpretive questions are also usually more difficult to construct and are usually not asked as often as literal comprehension questions. Here is an example of a selection and some interpretive questions based on it.

Do you ever think of the right thing to say too late? I always do, but my friend George always has the right words and answers at the snap of your fingers. Whenever you see George, there's always a crowd around him, and they are always laughing at his jokes. He is never serious about anything. I'm always serious about everything. There's an old saying that definitely explains our friendship.

Interpretive questions:

1. What is the main idea of the selection? (main idea)
2. What can you infer about the speaker in the selection? (inference or "reading between the lines")
3. State the old saying that explains the friendship between the two persons in the selection and then tell why it explains their relationship. (figurative language; making comparisons)
4. Choose the row with ideas from the story that belong together. (association)
    a. George, unfriendly, crowds
    b. George's friend, friendly, witty
    c. George, witty, people
    d. George's friend, serious, witty
5. Choose the word that best completes this analogy: George's friend is to somber as George is to _____ (analogy)
    a. people.
    b. happiness.
    c. grave.
    d. cheerful.

Critical Reading Questions

Critical reading questions are those that in-volve evaluation, which is the making of a personal judgment on the accuracy, value, and truthfulness of what is read. Questions that require critical thinking answers are usually more difficult to answer. Here is an example of a selection and some critical reading questions based on it.

Fortunately, the school election will be over soon. I don't think that I can stand another week such as the last one. First, there was John, who told me that I was the only one not voting for his candidate, ''True-Blue Tim.'' Then there was Mary, who told me that if I were a student with lots of school spirit, I'd be out campaigning for her candidate, "Clever Jane." Mary says that the majority of students are supporting her candidate. She says that even the famous local star thinks that Jane is the best person. Personally, I think that both their candidates are creeps, and I don't intend to vote for either one. I'm going to vote for Jennifer because she is so democratic and fair.

Critical Comprehension Questions:

1. State at least five propaganda techniques that are used in the selection, and give examples of them. (propaganda techniques)
2. Determine whether each of the following statements are facts or opinions. (fact or opinion)
   a. The speaker in the selection doesn't think much of the candidates.
   b. Jennifer is democratic and fair.
   c. Mary supports Jane.
   d. Jane is the best candidate.

Special Note

An IRI is presented in Appendix A for your use. This IRI is adapted from the *Placement Inventory* of the latest Holt *Basic Reading* series. The directions for administration are those presented in this chapter.

Code for Marking Oral Reading Errors

Before you can administer any IRI, you must be proficient in marking oral reading errors. A number of different codes exist for this purpose. The one that you choose should be easy to use, and it should incorporate all the types of errors that are counted in the scoring scale. *Consistency* is important; that is, once you find a code that works for you, use it, rather than continuously changing. When you are listening to a child read, you must have overlearned the code so that you can quickly record the errors. Remember, the code is merely a shorthand method you are using to record information quickly; it is an aid. Table 9.1. presents a marking code that you can use to administer the IRI in Appendix A. Most of the *terms* that are used to describe the errors and the symbols that represent them are used in many published IRIs, oral reading tests, and other diagnostic tests that have an oral reading subtest.

Scoring Oral Reading Errors

The scoring scale, which is to be used with the IRI in Appendix A, is based on the philosophy that most good oral readers make some errors when they read. The counting of repetitions, hesitations of less than five seconds, and self-corrected words as errors would yield too low a score for the student. In the scoring scale of errors, multiple errors on the same word will only count as one error; mispronunciations due to dialect differences will not count as an error; mispronunciations of difficult proper nouns will not count as errors; hesitations of less than five seconds and repetitions will not count as errors, and an immediate self-correction will not count as an error. All other errors that are made will count one point (see Special Note). (The examiner should note all the errors, even those that do not count as errors.)

The teacher should keep a record of the errors

Table 9.1

Code for Marking and Scoring Errors

Type of Error	Rule for Marking	Examples	Error Count
Omissions—leaves out a word, part of a word, or consecutive words	Put circle around omitted word or part of word.	She went in(to) the store. The (big) black dog is here.	1 1
Substitutions—substitutes a whole word	Put line through substituted word, and insert word above.	home She went into the ~~house.~~ along. She went ~~alone.~~	1 1
Insertions—adds a word, part of a word, or consecutive words	Put caret to show where word or word part was inserted, and write in inserted part of word or word(s).	big The∧dog is black. very big The∧dog is black.	1 1
Mispronunciations—mispronounces a word to produce a nonsense word (unlike substitution where an actual word is substituted)	Put line through word that was mispronounced, and insert phonetically the word if possible	harse A ~~horse~~ went into the barn. kar rot′ It weighed a ~~caret.~~	1 1
Words pronounced by examiner after a five second pause by child	Put P over word or words pronounced by tester	P The anecdote was funny.	1
Hesitations—a pause of less than five seconds	Put an H above the word on which the hesitation occurs	H She reiterated that she wouldn't go.	0
Repetitions—a word, part of a word, or a group of words repeated	Draw a wavy line under the part of word or word(s) repeated	She mumbled her acceptance. We were reluctant to go. His probation would be up soon.	0 0 0
Reversals—word order is changed	Enclose words in a horizontal S	The big black cat drinks milk.	1
Self-corrections—error is spontaneously corrected	Enclose incorrect word in parentheses	(brought) He bought something.	0

made so that he or she can determine what kinds of strategies the student is using in figuring out words. The teacher should try to determine whether a pattern exists among the errors made and whether the student relies on graphic, semantic, or syntactic clues. The Summary Sheets on pages 127–128 and 132–133 have a checklist of possible errors, which should be helpful in recording a student's specific errors. (See "How Should Oral Reading Errors Be Scored?" in this chapter.)

Special Note

If a child meets the same word a few times in a selection and makes either a substitution, omission, or mispronunciation error on it each time, it would count as *one error* the first time, and as *one-half error* each subsequent time. After the third time, the teacher should pronounce the word for the child.

Sample Marking of an Oral IRI Passage

H polet
"What is making the lake polluted?" asked Jill.
      s
"It could be a lot of things," said Mr. Brown.
"Let's go down to the lake and look at it."
                                    big
Mr. Brown and the children went to the lake. They looked into the water. It wasn't clean. They
      about   was
walked around the lake. Then they saw why it wasn't clean.

The error on *making* is actually a mispronunciation error. The omission symbol is used because it illustrates best what the child did.

Total Error Count = 7
Polluted counts for one error only.

The error on *saw* is shown as a substitution error, even though it actually is a reversal error.

To simplify the marking, only inverted word order is shown as a reversal error (see Table 9.1) because it is easier to show this than to show letter reversals. When marking errors, it is easier to assume substitution errors than reversals because a reversal error requires analysis. However, after the testing, the teacher should review all substitution errors to determine whether they have been caused by possible reversal problems. Of course, as already stated, all errors should be analyzed to determine whether a pattern exists among the errors. It is possible, also, that mispronunciation errors are caused by reversal problems.

Word Recognition Formula for Percent Correct

Here is a formula to help you to figure out the percent correct for word recognition:

$$\frac{\text{Number of words in passage} - \text{number of errors}}{\text{number of words in passage}} \times 100\% = \text{percent correct}$$

Example: 150 words in passage
7 errors

$$\frac{150 - 7}{150} \times 100\% = 95\%$$

(This is at the instructional level using Betts's criteria.)

Word Recognition Formula for Percent Wrong

It is often easier to work with the number wrong rather than with the number correct because there are fewer errors than correct readings. In working with the number wrong, you are dealing with smaller numbers. Here is the formula for allowable errors for each level:

Independent level: allowable errors
   = .01 × number of words in a passage

Instructional level: allowable errors
= .05 × number of words in a passage
Frustration level: allowable errors
= .10 × number of words in a passage
Examples: 150 words in passage

Level	Allowable Errors
Independent	1.5 = 2.0 rounded to nearest whole word
Instructional	7.5 = 8 rounded to nearest whole word
Frustration	15

From the above, you can see that a child who makes 7 errors in a 150-word passage would be at the instructional level using Betts's criteria.

Diagnostic Checklist for Oral and Silent Reading

Coding is necessary if you are analyzing error patterns to determine a student's word recognition difficulties. If, however, you are only interested in quickly determining a student's reading level, you can simply check (✔) errors, because all you need is an error count. Diagnostic checklists are useful in recording errors, especially if you are only interested in an error count.

Here is one you can use. Note that this checklist is helpful in recording a student's manner of reading, as well as his or her word recognition errors.

Diagnostic Checklist for Oral and Silent Reading

Oral Reading	Yes	No	Specific Errors
1. Word recognition errors. The teacher listens to the child while he or she is reading orally and records whether the child makes any of the following errors:			
a. omissions			
b. insertions			
c. substitutions			
d. repetitions			
e. hesitations			
f. mispronunciations			
g. reversals.			
2. Manner of reading. The teacher observes the child while he or she is reading aloud and records whether the child exhibits any of the following behaviors:			
a. word-by-word phrasing			
b. finger pointing			
c. head movement			
d. fidgeting			
e. voice characteristics high-pitched loud soft monotonous			
f. other.			

Oral Reading (Cont.)	Yes	No	Specific Errors
3. Comprehension. *(See* Comprehension Diagnostic Checklist in Chapter 13.)			

Silent Reading	Yes	No
1. Comprenhension. (See Comprehension Diagnostic Checklist in Chapter 13.) 2. Manner of reading. The teacher observes the child while he or she is reading silently and records whether the child exhibits any of the following behaviors: a. lip movement b. reads aloud c. head movement d. continually looks up e. finger pointing f. other.		

ADMINISTERING THE IRI

Step 1: Establishing Rapport

Establishing rapport with the child who is to be tested is the first step. Since you are the child's teacher, you should know this child quite well and should be able to allay any fears or apprehensions that the child may have about taking the test. You should help the child recognize that the IRI is not a test that will give him or her a grade; it is a test to help you and the student to learn more about his or her reading. The IRI will give both of you more information so that the two of you can work together to help him or her overcome the reading problem.

Step 2: The Word Recognition Inventory

The Word Recognition Inventory (WRI), which is composed of the word lists selected from the basal readers series, is used to determine at what level to begin the oral reading passages of the IRI. It evaluates a student's ability to recognize (call) words in isolation and is administered to one student at a time.

Preparation

1. The WRI begins two grade levels below the student's grade level.

2. Duplicate the word lists for at least three grade levels above and below the grade level at which you will begin. (Note that the WRI in Appendix A has more than one reader level for each grade level up to grade 4.)

3. Decide how you will flash the words to the student and prepare the necessary materials. Here are two possible methods. Both require index cards.

   a . Cut out a rectangle no more than ⅜ inch by 1½ inches in the center of an index card. Expose the words being tested, one at a time, through the rectangular opening.

   b. Use one index card to cover any printed matter that appears above the word the student is being asked to recall. Use a second index card to cover all matter below the card. Continue this procedure for each word on the list.

Administration

1. Because you will be working with students on an individual basis, try to use a relatively isolated part of the classroom when administering the WRI.

2. Keep the word lists covered as you explain the method of presentation to the student.

3. Begin the WRI with a flash exposure of the first word. Be sure that the word is clearly and completely shown. The student should respond immediately.

   a . If the student's response is correct, place a check (✓) beside the word and proceed to the next word.

   b. If an initial response is incorrect but the student makes an immediate, independent correction, place a check with a plus sign (✓ +) beside the word and proceed to the next word.

4. When the student's response is incorrect and is not independently corrected, re-expose the word. Allow a reasonable length of time for the student to study the word and to apply, without assistance, any word analysis skills he or she may have.

   a. If this untimed response is correct, place

a check with a minus sign (✓ −) beside the word and proceed to the next word.

   b. If the student is unable to decode the word correctly after an untimed exposure, record a zero (0) and proceed to the next word. For later reference, you may want to record the error made, for example, *run* for *ran*. To avoid confusion or the inaccurate reporting of results, it is important to record the responses immediately.

5. After the student has responded to all the list words for a particular level, record the total number of correct responses, including flash recognitions, independently corrected recognitions, and untimed recognitions. This total is the student's WRI score for that level.

6. Continue administering the WRI until the student misses four or more words at any level. Start the oral reading at the highest level at which the child has made 0 errors.

Examples[9]

1. Student: John X, fifth grade (the beginning)

   Begin WRI at third-grade reader level (beginning)

Results

Level*	No. of Errors
3¹	4
2²	2
2¹	1
First	0

*Refers to the grade level at which the material was prepared for use.

[9]Examples are based on the WRI presented in Appendix A.

Interpretation of results: Begin oral reading passages at first reader level

2. Student: Jane Y, fifth grade (middle)
   Begin WRI at third-grade reader level (middle)

Results

Level	No. of Errors
3^2	0
4	0
5	1
6	4

Interpretation of results: Begin oral reading passages at fourth-grade reader level

3. Student: George Z, fourth grade (beginning)
   Begin WRI at second-grade reader level (beginning)

Results

Level	No. of Errors
2^1	0
2^2	0
3^1	1
3^2	0
4	2
5	5

Interpretation of results: Begin oral reading passages at third-grade reader level (middle)

Note that each student is administered the WRI until he or she has made four or more errors so that you can see a pattern of the types of errors that the student has made.

Step 3: Oral and Silent Reading Passages

The student begins to read the oral passage at sight at the highest reader level at which he or she has made zero errors on the Word Recognition Inventory (see examples given in step 2). The teacher introduces the child to the passage and tells the child that he or she will read aloud the passage and then will be asked questions on what was read. The child is asked to read aloud the passage without first looking at it.

While the child is reading aloud, the teacher records any oral reading errors the child makes (see Table 9.1). If the child's word recognition in oral reading is at the independent or instructional levels, the child is asked the comprehension questions. If the child's response is correct, the teacher puts a check (✓) next to the question. If the answer is not correct, the teacher records the student's response. The child is then asked to read the silent passage. Again, the student is not given an opportunity to look over the passage before reading it. After the student finishes reading the silent passage, he or she is asked the comprehension questions. If the child's response is correct, a check (✓) is put next to the response. If the answer is incorrect, the student's response is recorded next to the question.

The student goes to the oral passage at the next reader level. The same procedure continues until the child reaches his or her frustration level.

If the student makes many word recognition errors while reading aloud, and the errors are those that the teacher feels will interfere with the child's ability to answer the comprehension questions, the teacher usually does not have the child read the silent reading passage at the same reader level. The teacher administers a listening capacity test to the child; that is, the teacher reads aloud to the child and then asks the comprehension questions.

The Listening Capacity Test[10]

Listening capacity is the ability to understand a word that is spoken because the word has been met before, and the child has acquired its meaning. Obviously, if a child hears a word that he or she has not met before, the child will not know its meaning unless he or she can figure it out from the context of the sentence. A listening capacity test is given to determine a child's comprehension through listening. The teacher is interested in determining a child's ability to comprehend material that is read aloud so that he or she can gauge the child's ability to listen to instruction and oral reports. Also, a listening capacity test can help to identify those students who seem to gain information better through listening than through reading. This knowledge is important in planning proper modes of instruction for the child. (See Chapters 6 and 7 for more on listening capacity tests and for a discussion on how listening capacity tests help provide an estimate of a child's reading potential.)

The passages from the IRI are generally used to determine a child's listening capacity. The passages are evaluated in the same way that the oral and silent reading passages are evaluated except that the teacher reads aloud the selections to the child. If the passages that are to be read aloud have already been read by the child, alternate ones should be used. Some commercially produced IRIs have a separate set of selections

for the listening capacity test. It is a good idea to have a separate set of selections for the listening capacity test. The IRI in Appendix A does not have this because of space limitations.

When Is a Listening Capacity Test Given?

A listening capacity test is usually given when a child has reached or is rapidly approaching the frustration level in word recognition on the oral reading part of the IRI. If a child has difficulty decoding a large number of words in oral reading, this will probably interfere with his or her ability to answer comprehension questions. Also, if a child has difficulty with a large number of words at a certain reader level, the child is usually not asked to read the silent passage at the same level because the decoding problems would probably interfere with the child's ability to answer comprehension questions. (See Example 1 below.) If a child does not

Examples[1]

1. Student Jim X, fifth grade (beginning).
Begin Word Recognition Inventory at 3^1 level.

Level	No. of Errors
3^1	2
2^2	0
3^2	4

---

[10]A listening capacity test may also be referred to as a hearing capacity test, a listening comprehension test, or a capacity test.

[11]Examples are based on the IRI presented in Appendix A.

| Level | Oral Reading | | | Silent Reading Comprehension | | Listening Capacity | |
| | Word Recognition | Comprehension | | | | | |
	No. Errors/ Total No. Words	% Errors	% Correct	% Errors	% Correct	% Errors	% Correct
2^2	4/148	0	100	0	100		
3^1	8/212	0	100	0	100		
3^2	14/181	20	80	25	75		

have any extensive word recognition problems, the listening capacity test is usually given when the child is approaching or has reached his or her frustration level in silent reading on the IRI. (See Example 2 beginning on p. 129.) (Although the student had reached zero errors at the 2^2 level [see chart, bottom of page 124], the WRI was continued until he reached four errors so that a pattern of the errors could better be seen.)

Jim begins oral reading at 2^2 level. The chart above shows his reading behavior.

At the 3^2 level the teacher must decide whether to let Jim read silently or whether to give him a listening capacity test. His word recognition errors may be interfering with his ability to answer the comprehension questions. The teacher decides to let him read silently, even though he is in the "buffer" zone, which is between the instructional and frustration levels because she wants to see how well he uses context clues. Even though Jim has a word recognition problem, he seems to do quite well in comprehension. He scores 25 percent errors. The teacher has Jim read at the next level because he does not appear to be frustrated. At the next level, however, he makes 23 errors, and he has difficulty answering the comprehension questions. The teacher decides to give him a listening capacity test. She starts to read aloud the silent reading passage at the fourth-grade reader level. Then she continues to read aloud one passage

Listening Capacity

Level	% Errors	% Correct
4	0	100
5	0	100
6	0	100
7	20	80
8	40	60

from each level. The chart above shows Jim's listening capacity scores. (It doesn't make any difference whether the passage is chosen from the oral or silent reading selections.) From the listening capacity test the teacher sees that Jim has excellent comprehension but his word recognition is hindering him from working at his ability level. The teacher had decided to give Jim an IRI because his verbal behavior in class belied his reading achievement test scores. The teacher continues administering the oral reading part of the IRI to determine Jim's independent oral reading level and to gain some more insight into the types of errors that he makes in word recognition so that she can develop a program to help him. (Jim reads the oral passage at the 2^2

level. He makes one error out of 99 words. This is his independent oral reading level.) She will probably also give Jim another word analysis diagnostic test. Here is a summary sheet, showing a complete record of Jim's reading behavior on the IRI.

Summary Sheet*

Name _____ *Jim X* _____   Age _____ *10* _____

Grade _____ *5* _____   Teacher _____ *Mrs. Smith* _____

Level	Word Recognition in Isolation (No. of Errors)	Oral Reading W.R. No. of Errors/ Total No. Wds.†	Oral Reading Comp. % Errors	Oral Reading Comp. % Correct	Silent Reading Comp. % Errors	Silent Reading Comp. % Correct	Listening Capacity % Errors	Listening Capacity % Correct
Preprimer								
Primer								
First								
2^1		1/99						
2^2	0	4/148	0	100	0	100		
3^1	2	8/212	0	100	0	100		
3^2	4	14/181	20	80	25	75		
4		23/232	40	60			0	100
5							0	100
6							0	100
7							20	80
8							40	60

Level at which WRI was begun _____ 3^1

Level at which oral reading was begun _____ 2^2

*For use with the IRI in Appendix A.

† Percentages can be easily calculated using the word recognition formula on page 119, or see the IRI in Appendix A for corresponding reading levels, that is, independent, instructional, or frustration levels.

Oral reading—word recognition

    Independent level 2^1

    Instructional level 2^2–3^1 (range)

    Frustration level   4

Oral reading—comprehension

    Independent level 3^1

    Instructional level 3^2

    Frustration level

Silent reading—comprehension

    Independent level 3^1

    Instructional level 3^2

    Frustration level

Listening capacity level   7

Word analysis

    Consonants—single

      initial

      medial

      final

    Consonants—double

      blends

      digraphs   ch, sh, ph

    Consonants—silent

    Vowels—single

      short   ă, ĕ

      long

    Vowels—double

      digraphs   oa, ea

      diphthongs   ou in bough

    Effect of final *e* on vowel

    Vowel controlled by *r*

Structural analysis
  prefixes   _____
  suffixes   _____
  combining forms   _____
  inflectional endings   *ignores most*
Compound words   _____
Accent   _____

Special Notes on Strengths and Weaknesses

Jim has word recognition problems that are thwarting his comprehension ability. Jim doesn't attempt to use phonic clues. If he doesn't know the word as a sight word, and if he can't figure it out by using context clues, he skips over the word. His ability to use semantic and syntactic clues is excellent.

Comments on Behavior During the Testing

Jim seemed to like working in a one-to-one relationship. He said that he didn't like to read, but he liked to listen to persons read aloud.

Recommendations

Give Jim a complete word recognition program stressing the use of graphic clues in combination with semantic and syntactic clues. Select books of low readability and high interest content.

2. Student Susan Y, fifth grade (beginning). Begin WRI at 3^1 level.

Level	No. of Errors
3^1	0
3^2	0
4	0
5	0
6	4

Susan begins oral reading at the 5 level.

Since Susan immediately reached the frustration level in comprehension, the teacher would be justified in not having her read the silent reading passage and start going down to lower grade levels to find her instructional and independent levels for comprehension. However, the teacher decides to have Susan read the silent reading passage because she wants to see if Susan was concentrating so hard on pronunciation that she didn't pay attention to what she was reading. Susan is asked to read the fifth-grade silent reading level passage. She makes 60 percent errors. The following chart shows Susan's reading behavior.

	Oral Reading			Silent Reading		Listening Capacity	
	Word Recognition	Comprehension		Comprehension			
Level	No. Errors/ Total No. Words	% Errors	% Correct	% Errors	% Correct	% Errors	% Correct
5	3/270	60	40	60	40		
4	2/232	60	40	60	40		
3^2	2/181	50	50	50	50		
3^1	2/212	40	60	50	50	50	50
2^2	1/148	25	75	25	75	40	60
2^1	1/99	10	90	10	90	25	75
6*	9/276	—		—			

*Susan was asked to read orally only at the sixth level to find her instructional oral reading word recognition level.

From the results, we can see that Susan has excellent word recognition, but she has severe difficulties in reading comprehension. A listening capacity test is given to determine the level at which she can listen to material and comprehend it at the instructional level. From looking at the results of Susan's reading performance, the teacher decides to start reading aloud to Susan at the 3^1 level because this is the level at which she had reached frustration in silent reading. Since Susan is also at her frustration level on the listening capacity test at the 3^1 level, the teacher moves to the 2^2 level and reads aloud the passage. At this level Susan is ap-

proaching frustration. The teacher then reads the 2^1 level passage and finds Susan's listening capacity level. (The selections read aloud to Susan to determine her listening capacity level were different from those in the IRI because Susan had already read those.) It is interesting to note that Susan's listening capacity score is lower than her oral and silent reading scores. She probably has more difficulty concentrating while listening than when reading silently or orally. Her oral and silent reading scores appear to be comparable. The teacher must analyze the kinds of comprehension errors that Susan made. It seems obvious that Susan's ability to read well orally has obscured her comprehension problems. The teacher had decided to give Susan an IRI because she had noticed the discrepancy between her verbalizing in class and her inability to answer even literal questions correctly. Susan can pronounce words very well, but she doesn't have the meanings for many of them. Even when she knows the meaning of the words used in a paragraph, she can't tell you what the paragraph is about. The IRI will give Susan's teacher some insights into Susan's comprehension difficulties; however, it may be that Susan is a slow learner, and as such, is reading close to her reading ability (see Chapters 7 and 16). Since Susan's teacher does not have any IQ score for Susan, she cannot determine this possibility. However, the listening capacity test that was administered to Susan does indicate that Susan's reading potential may only be at a 2^1 grade level. Susan's teacher should probably refer Susan for an individual IQ test, but in the meantime she will have to develop a program for her based on her needs. The first step seems to be concept development.

Pages 131–133 contain a summary sheet, showing a complete record of Susan's reading behavior on the IRI.

PUBLISHED (COMMERCIALLY PRODUCED) IRIs VERSUS TEACHER-MADE IRIs

Teacher-made IRIs are time-consuming to construct, and many teachers do not feel secure about making one. Their prime advantage is that they are directly related to the instructional material used in class. Published IRIs, on the other hand, may not be directly related to the instructional material, but they are usually easier to administer and score because they are generally prepared by experts in the field and with specific directions.

If teachers decide to use a published IRI, they must know what criteria to look for so that they can make a wise choice. A good IRI should have the following features:

1. There should be two forms, so that a pre- and post-test can be given.

2. There should be different passages for oral and silent reading.

3. The comprehension questions should consist of a variety of literal and interpretive questions. (Critical reading questions are optional.)

4. The passages should be selected from the most recent basal reader series.

5. The graded word lists should be representative of the grade level from which they have been taken.

6. The passages selected for oral and silent reading should be representative of the reading material in the book; that is, the readability level should not be higher or lower than the level from which the passages have been selected.

7. Specific directions should be given for administering and scoring the test.

8. There should be a separate set of passages and comprehension questions for the listening capacity test.

Choosing an IRI is in itself not an easy task. Some recently published IRIs appear to be attempting to overcome some of the difficulties prevalent in the earlier published ones. (See the Selected Bibliography at the end of this chapter for a list of some published IRIs.)

WHO SHOULD BE GIVEN AN IRI?

Chapter 7 is devoted to helping you determine who is underachieving in reading so that you can determine who should have further diagnostic testing. Reading expectancy formulas are pre-

Summary Sheet *

Name _____ Susan Y _____ Age _____ 10 _____

Grade _____ 5 _____ Teacher _____ Mr. Jones _____

Level	Word Recognition in Isolation (No. of Errors)	Oral Reading W.R. No. of Errors/ Total No. Wds.	Oral Reading Comp. % Errors	Oral Reading Comp. % Correct	Silent Reading Comp. % Errors	Silent Reading Comp. % Correct	Listening Capacity % Errors	Listening Capacity % Correct
Preprimer								
Primer								
First								
2^1		1/99	10	90	10	90	25	75
2^2		1/148	25	75	25	75	40	60
3^1	0	2/212	40	60	50	50	50	40
3^2	0	2/181	50	50	50	50		
4	0	2/232	60	40	60	40		
5	0	3/270	60	40	60	40		
6	4	9/276						
7								
8								

*For use with the IRI in Appendix A.

†Percentages can be easily calculated using the word recognition formula on page 119, or see the IRI in Appendix A for corresponding reading levels, that is, independent, instructional, or frustration levels.

Level at which WRI was begun _____ 3^1 _____

Level at which oral reading was begun _____ 5 _____

Oral reading—word recognition

    Independent level _____ 5 _____

    Instructional level _____ 6 _____

    Frustration level _____

Oral reading—comprehension
   Independent level 2^1
   Instructional level 2^2
   Frustration level 3^2

Silent reading—comprehension
   Independent level 2^1
   Instructional level 2^2
   Frustration level 3^1
Listening capacity level 2^1

Word analysis
   Consonants—single
      initial   _____
      medial   _____
      final   _____
   Consonants—double
      blends   _____
      digraphs   _____
   Consonants—silent   _____
   Vowels—single
      short   _____
      long   _____
   Vowels—double
      digraphs   _____
      diphthongs   _____
   Effect of final *e* on vowel   _____
   Vowel controlled by *r*   _____
   Structural analysis
      prefixes   _____
      suffixes   _____
      combining forms   _____

inflectional endings   _____

Compound words   _____

Accent   _____

Special Notes on Strengths and Weaknesses

Susan has excellent word recognition skills. She is weak in word meanings. She could not give the meanings of words that she could pronounce. She could not state the main idea of the paragraphs nor could she answer inferential questions. She was able to answer literal questions, but she even missed some of these.

Comments on Behavior During the Testing

She enjoyed reading aloud. She started squirming in her chair whenever comprehension questions were asked. She also squirmed in her chair when I was reading aloud to her.

Recommendations

Help Susan expand her vocabulary. Work on literal and interpretive comprehension skills. Give her a cloze test to further check her use of syntactic and semantic clues to figure out word meanings.

sented, which help you to determine the reading potential of a child. A comparison is then made between the child's reading potential as determined by a reading expectancy formula and his or her score on a standardized reading achievement test. Another formula is then used to analyze the comparison between the child's reading expectancy and his or her score on a reading achievement test. The second formula helps you determine who is underachieving in reading to such an extent that he or she requires further diagnostic testing.

It is emphasized in Chapter 7, and it will again be stressed here, that teachers must be careful about using reading expectancy formulas as absolute determinants of a child's reading potential. A formula is based on intelligence test scores, and many times a child's IQ score is not valid because of a reading problem. As a result a child's reading expectancy would be depressed, that is, lower than it should be. Thus, teachers must use their own judgment concerning whom to test further. There are times when a teacher will want to administer an IRI to a child who scored well on a reading achievement test but who seems to be having some reading problem. There are times, too, when a teacher will want to give an IRI to a student who scored at grade level on a reading achievement test and whose group IQ score was in the average range because the teacher suspects from the child's verbal ability and behavior in class that the child is a highly able child and that his or her word recognition problems may be masking this fact.

It used to be given as a rule of thumb that a child who scores about one or more years below his or her ability level on a standardized reading achievement test should be given an IRI. This is not a good rule to follow in a diagnostic-reading and correction program because the key factor in such a program is to help the child before his or her reading difficulty becomes a big problem. Also, as discussed in Chapter 7, there is a vast difference between a child in second grade with

a one-year underachievement in reading and a child in sixth grade (see Chapter 7).

There are a number of teachers who will not be able to use the reading expectancy formulas that exist because in some school districts, group IQ tests have been made illegal. These teachers will have to depend on other means to determine who in their classes needs an IRI or other diagnostic tests. One good technique is to administer a group standardized listening comprehension test for an estimate of the children's reading potential (see "Standardized Listening Tests" in Chapter 6). The children's reading potential as measured by the standardized listening comprehension test could be compared to their score on a standardized reading achievement test. Along with the results of the standardized listening comprehension test, the teacher should base his or her decision on careful observation of the child's reading behavior and other behaviors that may be related. (See Chapter 11, which discusses observation as a diagnostic technique.)

Special Note

Some persons may say, "Why not give everyone an IRI to be on the safe side?" This would be a good idea; however, time constraints usually weigh against it.

Examples of Candidates for the IRI

The examples that follow should be especially helpful for those teachers who cannot use reading expectancy formulas to determine whether students are underachieving in reading or not because they do not have any IQ scores for their students. It may also be helpful for those teachers who can use reading expectancy formulas because it should make the teacher more sensitive to problems that may exist but are not obvious from the comparison of reading expectancy scores to reading achievement scores.

Example 1. The student answers questions that are posed orally in class very well, but he never raises his hand to read any printed material aloud. When he is called on to read, he makes many oral reading errors. He cannot decode many words that he uses with facility in his speaking vocabulary. Even though this child has scored on grade level on a standardized reading achievement test, he is a good candidate for an informal reading inventory.

Example 2. This student reads orally with excellent facility. He is always raising his hand to read orally; however, whenever he is asked to answer comprehension questions on what he has read either orally or silently, he cannot. This child has scored below grade level on a standardized reading achievement test. He would be a good candidate for an IRI. If the teacher finds that the child's reading level is a few grade levels below his present grade level, she might want to refer this child to the child study team or school psychologist for an individual IQ test.

Example 3. The student stumbles on a number of words when she reads orally. She usually has no difficulty answering questions after she has read silently. She is very verbal and seems to have quite a bit of information on a number of different topics. She has scored a few months below her grade level, which is the fourth grade, on a standardized reading achievement test. She is a candidate for an IRI because her word recognition difficulties may be interfering with her ability to answer comprehension questions.

Example 4. This student has scored below grade level on a standardized reading achievement test; however, she does not seem to have any problems answering difficult reading comprehension questions at the literal, interpretive, and critical levels. The student also reads well orally and volunteers often to read. The teacher decides to give her an informal reading inventory to check at what grade level she is reading and also to determine whether she has reading difficulties that are not obvious. If the IRI does not point out any significant reading problem, this child should take another standardized reading achievement test. It is highly probable that the standardized reading achievement test score is not valid for this child.

MODIFIED IRI APPROACHES: A CAUTION

Many teachers do not have the time to administer a complete IRI to their students so they rely on a modified approach, whereby they use either oral reading in basal readers or graded word lists to determine a student's placement. An approach that teachers use often is the one in which a child is asked to read passages orally from various levels of a basal reader series. The level at which the child is able to read with some proficiency is the one that the teacher usually uses as the child's instructional reading level. The other technique frequently used is to expose the child to a graded list of words that have been selected from a basal reader series and have the child read aloud this list to determine his or her instructional reading level. (One error on a list of twenty words would be at the instructional level.)

The on-the-spot oral reading and word lists are time-savers, and they can be helpful, but teachers must recognize the dangers of these techniques and realize that the information they are receiving may not be valid or reliable. If a teacher only uses a child's oral reading ability to determine his or her reading level, many children may be incorrectly placed. A child may have a word recognition problem but have excellent comprehension, and conversely, a child may have a comprehension problem but no word recognition problems. The latter child with no word recognition problem, who probably has a lower reading potential than the former child with the word recognition problem, would probably be placed in a higher reading group than the child with the word recognition problem.

For the on-the-spot approach to be effective, the teacher should devise some comprehension questions based on the material, or the teacher could test understanding by having the child "retell" what he or she has read in his or her own words. The teacher could also determine comprehension by asking the student to give the main idea of what he or she has read.

The problem with the use of graded word lists to determine a student's reading level is similar to the one just discussed for the on-the-spot oral reading approach. From the graded word list, you are only getting an estimate of the student's ability to pronounce words; you are not getting any information about the child's comprehension. This is dangerous since reading is a thinking act.

The on-the-spot approach is especially effective for students in the upper grades who are reading content material books and are not involved in reading classes. Many times these students are having difficulty because the content books are at too high a readability level for them. The on-the-spot approach would be a viable method for these students. It is a good idea to choose a passage that is representative of the book; a passage from the middle of the book would probably be best for this purpose. Have the student read aloud the passage, which should consist of a paragraph or two, and then have the student answer some comprehension questions on it, or have the student give a summary of what he or she has read.

Some persons have used a group on-the-spot approach to test the readability of textbooks. There are a number of variations to this approach, but for it to be a group approach, all or a number of students must take it at the same time. In the group approach, the students usually read silently a passage close to the middle of the book, and then they write the answers to given questions on the passages, or they write a summary of the passage, or they write the main idea of the passage, and so on. Be *cautious* in using such a test to determine whether the book is at the reading ability level of the student. It may be that the student has difficulty expressing himself or herself in writing. You may be testing a student's writing ability rather than his or her reading ability. From this type of test, you are also not learning whether the student has word recognition problems or comprehension problems.

Examples of Word Lists

Many word lists exist. Some of these are graded word lists that are used to determine reading levels and to analyze word recognition errors. Some are supposed to represent the words children and adults most frequently meet in reading and use in speaking and writing. Teachers usually teach these as sight words for a basic vocabulary. A problem exists, however, in determining which word list to use. Some are better for primary children; some are better for intermediate children; and some are better for adults. Here is a sample catalog to help you determine which word list best suits your purposes.[12]

Large Printed Word Studies
AMERICAN HERITAGE. Caroll, J.B.; Davies, P.; and Richman, B. *American Heritage Word Frequency Book.* Boston, Massachusetts: Houghton Mifflin, 1971.
A word count based on printed school texts (grades three through nine), this list of 86,741 different words was produced from a total of over five million 500-word samples which were taken from 1,045 texts. The inflected

[12]Mary K. Monteith, "A Whole Word Catalog," *The Reading Teacher* 29 (May 1976):845–46.

listing indicates both rank and frequency of use.

KUCERA AND FRANCIS. Kucera, H., and Francis, W.N. *Computational Analysis of Present-Day American English.* Providence, Rhode Island: Brown University Press, 1967.

A count based on 500 samples from fifteen categories of adult printed material, this study lists a total of 50,406 different words produced from 1,014,232 running words. The inflected count indicates rank, frequency of word, and sentence length.

Basic Vocabulary Lists

DOLCH 220, Dolch, Edward W.A. *A Manual for Remedial Reading.* Champaign, Illinois: Garrard Press, 1939.

This basic sight vocabulary list was compiled from two primary-grade reading vocabulary lists—the Wheeler-Howell First Grade Vocabulary List and the Gates Primary Word List—and from the International Kindergarten Union Vocabulary List derived from preschoolers' vocabularies. No nouns are included.

FUNCTIONAL READING LIST FOR ADULTS. Mitzel, M. Adele. "The Functional Reading Word List for Adults." *Adult Education,* No. 2, 1966, pp. 67–69.

A basic vocabulary for adult literacy, this is a 5,000-word list taken from 500,000 running words gathered from reading material which the general public encounters, such as government pamphlets, newspaper and magazine articles, the Yellow Pages, and signs in stores. Divided into four parts according to rank, the 500 most basic words are listed in part one.

HARRIS-JACOBSON SHORT READABILITY WORD LIST. Harris, Albert J., and Sipay, Edward R. *How to Increase Reading Ability.* 6th ed. New York, New York: McKay, 1975. [ED 110 962. Available only from publisher]

This is a list of over 3,000 words compiled from 7,613 different words found in a computerized study of elementary textbooks, grades one through six.

JOHNSON'S BASIC VOCABULARY. Johnson, Dale. "A Basic Vocabulary for Beginning Reading." *Elementary School Journal,* October 1971, pp. 29–34. [EJ 047 894]

This list of 306 words was derived from two sources: the 500 most commonly used words from the Kucera-Francis study and the words used at least fifty times by children who took part in the Murphy study of spontaneous speaking vocabulary.

LA PRAY AND ROSS GRADED WORD LIST. LaPray, M., and Ross, R. "The Graded Word List: Quick Gauge of Reading Ability." *Journal of Reading,* January 1969, pp. 305–07.

This graded word list, PP–12, used to determine reading level and to detect errors in word analysis, is also entitled the San Diego Quick Assessment. It was formed by drawing words randomly from basal reader glossaries and from the Thorndike list.

STARTER WORDS-240. Hillerich, Robert L. "Word Lists—Getting it all Together." *The Reading Teacher,* January 1974, pp. 353–60. [EJ 091 076]

A basic reading and writing vocabulary, this list is based on the 500 most frequently used words from five different counts, including old and new, juvenile and adult writing, and juvenile and adult printed material.

WORD LIST FOR THE 70'S. Johns, Jerry L. "Some Comparisons between the Dolch Basic Sight Vocabulary and the Word List for the 1970's." Study conducted at Northern Illinois University, 1974. [ED 098 541]

This sight vocabulary list was based on four criteria: materials read by children in grades three through nine, materials read by adults, library books read by primary-grade children, and the spontaneous speaking vocabulary of children in kindergarten and first grade. Contains no nouns.

MISCUE ANALYSIS

Some reading authorities have abandoned the traditional method of recording and scoring oral reading errors and have devised their own system based on psycholinguistic theory. (Psycholinguistics is the study of the interrelationships between language and thought. Psycholinguistics applied to reading is the application of what we know concerning language and thought to reading.) Goodman, the prime mover in miscue analysis research, feels that miscue analysis is a viable research process that goes beyond the "superficial behavior of readers" to learn how readers get meaning from language.[13] Goodman objects to the use of the term *errors* because he feels that nothing the reader does in reading is accidental, and *error* implies randomness. If persons can understand how miscues, which are unexpected responses to print, relate to expected responses, they will better understand how the reader is using the reading process. Miscue analysis begins with observed behavior, but it tries to go beyond through analysis.

To analyze readers' miscues, an analytic taxonomy was developed that considers the relationship between the reader's expected response (ER) with his or her observed response (OR). (This taxonomy has been and is continuously modified for new inputs from miscue studies.) The strength of this taxonomy is that it attempts to analyze the causes of a reader's miscues from a number of angles. Its strengths are, however, also its weaknesses for use by the classroom teacher. The Goodman Taxonomy of Reading Miscues consists of about nineteen questions, and each miscue is analyzed in terms of these nineteen questions. The Goodman Taxonomy of Reading Miscues "is a highly complex and sophisticated research instrument calling for considerable background on the part of the

user."[14] This instrument is obviously not for the classroom teacher; however, evolving from the taxonomy is the Reading Miscue Inventory (RMI), which *was* designed to be used by the classroom teacher. The inventory has condensed the nineteen questions, which involved from four to fifteen possible responses for each, to nine questions involving three choices each.

The Reading Miscue Inventory is still too involved and needs more simplification if it is to be used in the regular classroom either in place of the traditional IRI or in conjunction with it. Although the RMI is not widely used, the miscue analysis studies, with the emphasis on reading as a process in which meaning is obtained, have greatly influenced many examiners' interpretations of students' reading errors. They have heightened the consciousness level of testers using the IRI so that many are now concerned not only with the number of errors that a student makes but also with the quality or kind of error. Many recognize that getting meaning is more important than absolute accuracy of word pronunciation. Researchers are working on shortened forms of the RMI. Also, a number of reading authorities are attempting to develop coding systems that incorporate the best of the IRI and that reflect psycholinguistic theory.[15]

POINTS OF CAUTION CONCERNING IRIs

Teachers should recognize that an IRI can yield important information about a student's reading performance, but the results may vary from one IRI to another because of the following factors:

[13]Kenneth S. Goodman, "Miscues: Windows on the Reading Process," in *Miscue Analysis,* Kenneth S. Goodman, ed. (Urbana, Ill.: National Council of Teachers of English, 1973), p. 5.

[14]Carolyn Burke, "Preparing Elementary Teachers to Teach Reading," in *Miscue Analysis,* Kenneth S. Goodman, ed. (Urbana, Ill.: National Council of Teachers of English, 1973), p. 24.

[15]Susanna W. Pflaum, "Diagnosis of Oral Reading," *The Reading Teacher* 33 (December 1979): 278-84.

1. Criteria used to estimate reading levels
2. Amount of information given before the student is asked to read aloud or silently
3. Criteria used to record errors
4. Type of comprehension questions asked and how scored
5. Cut-off point for defining reading levels
6. Readability of material
7. Procedure for reading aloud (Are students asked to look over material before they read aloud?)
8. Order of silent and oral reading passages (Do students read orally first and then proceed to the silent reading passage, or do students read silently first and then proceed to the oral reading passage?)

The remainder of this chapter will discuss some of the points on this list.

Criteria for Estimating Reading Levels

The criteria as established by Betts for estimating reading levels were given in an earlier section. Although Betts's criteria are used by many, they are not universally accepted. One of the problems in using IRIs is that variability exists in the criteria for identifying reading levels. Two researchers summarized the criteria that various persons advocated for IRIs and illustrated the discrepancies among them.[16] They claim that differences exist in administrative procedures as well as in error classification; however, the researchers stated that the procedural differences are not enough to explain the discrepancies among the criteria put forth by

[16]William R. Powell and Colin G. Dunkeld, "Validity of the IRI Reading Levels," *Elementary English* 48 (October 1971):637–42.

authorities to estimate the instructional reading level.

Surprisingly, very little research exists to validate criteria for estimating reading levels. Of the studies that have been done to support the criteria, hardly any agree on levels of criteria.

In the 1970s, many authorities began to question whether the emphasis in determining reading levels should be on error count or on the type of error that is made. It appears that both should be taken into consideration. For example, read the following sentence, and then read how three different children have read it:

The horse went into the stable.

Student 1: The horse went into the *store.*

Student 2: The *big* horse went *in* the *barn*.

Student 3: The horse went *in a* stable.

If we were to count all errors without consideration to type, Student 1 would have the fewest errors, and Student 2 would have the most. However, if we were to look at the readings of the three sentences, we would have to conclude that Student 3, with two errors, has a better understanding of the writer's message than Student 1, with one error; and Student 2, with three errors, is also a better reader than Student 1. The omission and insertion by Student 2 did not affect the meaning of the sentence, nor did the substitution of *barn* for *stable*; however, the substitution of *store* for *stable* did affect the meaning of the sentence. Student 1 made fewer errors and stuck closer to graphic cues than Student 2, but he sacrificed the meaning of the sentence. Student 1, with the fewest errors, has to be judged the poorest reader of the three.

Even though many authorities agree that both number and type of error should be taken into account, it is very difficult to devise a scoring procedure that incorporates these two concepts that would be easy and quick to use and that would eliminate subjectivity.

How Should Oral Reading Errors Be Scored?

How to score the word recognition on the graded oral passages is probably one of the biggest controversies concerning the use of IRIs. How a child is scored will determine his or her placement in a reading level; different criteria for determining reading levels will result in different reading placements, and even if similar criteria are used, different methods of scoring will affect placements. One study revealed that experienced examiners, recording the oral reading errors of an excellent-quality tape of one child slowly reading a 115-word passage, disagreed sharply on the error count. The error count of the fourteen examiners, who were reading specialists, ranged from one to fourteen.[17]

The problem seems to be twofold. It involves the classification or definition of errors and the scoring of them. There is no agreement on what should be considered an error and how the error should be scored, or even whether it should be scored. For example, some authorities note when a student has repeated a part of a word, a word, or words, but they do not count the repetitions as errors; others do. Some examiners count hesitations as errors; some do not. Some count every error made, even if it is on the same word; that is, it is possible to have multiple errors on one word, and rather than count them as one error, some testers will count each error on that word. If a student meets the same word five times in the oral reading, and each time makes an error, some examiners will count this

as five errors; however, some may count this only as one error. Some testers do not count errors on proper nouns; some do.

Categories of errors are also not similar among examiners. Some include reversals; some do not. Some include help from the tester; some do not. Some include provisions for dialect differences; some do not; and so it goes. Some examiners also include information about semantic, syntactic, and graphic cues and suggest that teachers should analyze their students' errors with these in mind so that they can distinguish between the trivial and the significant.[18]

What does this all mean? It means that there is a lot of subjectivity in the scoring of errors, and you must be careful to choose a system that agrees with your philosophy and research findings.

A Special Look at Repetitions

An oral reading error that has caused a great amount of discussion and confusion among users of IRIs is that of repetitions. As already stated, some recommend that repetitions be counted as errors, whereas a number of others do not. One research study using the polygraph to determine the frustration level of a student found that if repetitions are not counted as errors, a child will reach the frustration level before the examiner is able to count enough errors to designate it.[19] It must be remembered that each child in this study was monitored by a polygraph. It is possible that the polygraph, itself, may have caused anxiety.

The author feels that it is not realistic to count every repetition as an error for a number of reasons. Most normal reading aloud is subject to errors even by well-known excellent readers. There

[17]William D. Page, ''Miscue Research and Diagnosis,'' *Findings of Research in Miscue Analysis: Classroom Implications,* P. David Allen and Dorothy J. Watson, eds. (Urbana Ill.: National Council of Teachers of English, 1976), pp. 140–41.

[18]Paul C. Burns and Betty D. Roe, *Informal Reading Assessment* (Chicago: Rand McNally, 1980), p. 7.

[19]Eldon E. Ekwall, ''Should Repetitions Be Counted as Errors?'' *The Reading Teacher* 27 (January 1974):365–67.

are a number of reasons why a student would repeat a word or words or make some short hesitations. The student may be nervous; he or she may be unused to reading aloud or not be familiar with the type of material being read; rapport with the examiner may not be very good; the student may be shy; and, more significantly, the student may be concentrating on the meaning of what he or she is reading because the student has been told that questions will be asked after the oral reading.

Oral and Silent Reading Comprehension

Betts, in developing the IRI, suggested that silent reading be given before oral reading. However, most IRIs today present the oral reading passage before the silent one at the same level because the oral reading is used as a gauge to determine whether a student should read silently at the same level. If a student makes many oral reading errors, it is assumed that he or she will have difficulty reading silently at the same level. When the child is asked the questions after reading the silent passage, if he or she has not read orally at the same level, the teacher will not be able to determine whether the child could not answer the comprehension questions because of a comprehension problem or because of a word recognition problem.

Most IRIs use the same criteria for scoring oral reading comprehension as for scoring silent reading comprehension, even though some persons have suggested that the former should be scored less stringently because readers concentrate more on word pronunciation during oral reading than on comprehension. Many persons feel that students would score higher on comprehension after reading silently than after reading orally; however, this has not been borne out by research. The comparative studies of

silent and oral reading comprehension scores have been inconclusive.[20] As a result, the oral and silent comprehension criteria have remained the same.

It would appear that good readers would do better in comprehension after reading silently than after reading orally. However, there are some children who may do better in comprehension after reading orally because they need to hear the words in order to understand them. Their auditory modality may be more developed than their visual modality.

SUMMARY

Chapter 9 presents a discussion of diagnostic reading tests and techniques with an emphasis on the informal reading inventory. An IRI is a valuable diagnostic aid because it can provide information about a student's reading levels as well as help the teacher gain insight into a child's reading strengths and weaknesses. This chapter provides information on the IRI, its purposes, the criteria for estimating reading levels, how to construct one, how to administer one, how to mark oral reading errors, and how to score them. This chapter also presents information on research concerning IRIs and some information on word lists. Teachers are cautioned about the subjectivity of IRIs and are again reminded that any test, and especially the IRI, is only as good as the person administering and interpreting it. A comparison between teacher-made and published IRIs is given, with a criteria chart for choosing the latter. A section is also presented on miscue analysis and how research in this area has heightened the consciousness level of testers using the IRI so that many are now concerned

[20]E. H. Rowell, "Do Elementary Students Read Better Orally or Silently?" *The Reading Teacher* 29 (January 1976):367–70.

not only with the number of errors a student makes but also with the quality of the errors that are made.

SUGGESTIONS FOR THOUGHT QUESTIONS AND ACTIVITIES

1. Administer an IRI to a child who has a reading problem.

2. Review three different commercial IRIs.

3. Construct an IRI using a basal reader series from the 1980s.

4. Practice marking errors on an oral reading passage by listening to a tape of a child reading a passage.

5. Have a group of persons mark errors on an oral passage while listening to a tape of a child reading an oral passage. Compare the results.

6. You have been appointed to a committee to develop a coding and scoring system of oral reading that takes into account the research done on miscue analysis and the traditional coding and scoring system of most IRIs. What will you come up with?

7. What coding system would you devise for diagnosing oral reading errors?

8. Choose a few paragraphs from a basal reader series and make up comprehension questions for them, including literal, interpretive, and critical reading questions.

SELECTED BIBLIOGRAPHY

Allen, P. David, and Dorothy J. Watson, eds. *Findings of Research in Miscue Analysis: Classroom Implications.* Urbana, Ill.: National Council of Teachers of English, 1976.

Betts, Emmett A. *Foundations of Reading Instruction.* New York: American Book Co., 1946.

Bruinsma, Robert. "Should Lip Movements and Subvocalization During Silent Reading Be Directly Remediated?" *The Reading Teacher* 34 (December 1980):293–95.

Durr, William K., ed. *Reading Difficulties: Diagnosis, Correction, and Remediation,* "The Informal Reading Inventory, pp. 67–132. Newark, Del.: International Reading Association, 1970.

Ekwall, Eldon E. *Ekwall Reading Inventory.* Boston: Allyn and Bacon, 1979.

Goodman, Kenneth S. "Analysis of Oral Reading Miscues: Applied Psycholinguistics." *Reading Research Quarterly* 5 (Fall 1969):9–30.

———., ed. *Miscue Analysis.* Urbana, Ill.: National Council of Teachers of English, 1973.

Guiszak, Frank J. "Dilemmas in Informal Reading Assessments." *Elementary English* 47 (May 1970):666–70.

Harris, Albert J., and Milton D. Jacobson. "Some Comparisons Between Basic Elementary Reading Vocabularies and Other Word Lists." *Reading Research Quarterly* 9 (1973–1974): 87–109.

Jacobs, Donald, and Lyndon Searfoss. *Diagnostic Reading Inventory.* Dubuque, Iowa: Kendall/Hunt Publishing Co., 1978.

Johns, Jerry L. *Basic Reading Inventory.* Dubuque, Iowa: Kendall/Hunt Publishing Co., 1978.

——— et al. *Assessing Reading Behavior: Informal Reading Inventories: An Annotated Bibliography.* Newark, Del.: International Reading Association, 1977.

Johnson, Marjorie S., and Roy A. Kress. *Informal Reading Inventories.* Newark, Del.: International Reading Association, 1965.

Jongsma, Kathleen S., and Eugene A. Jongsma. "Test Review: Commercial Reading Inventories." *The Reading Teacher* 34 (March 1981):697–705.

Pikulski, John. "A Critical Review: Informal Reading Inventories." *The Reading Teacher* 28 (November 1974):141–61.

Rae, Gwenneth, and Thomas C. Potter. *Informal*

Reading Diagnosis: A Practical Guide for the Classroom Teacher, 2nd ed. Englewood Cliffs, N.J.: Prentice-Hall, 1981.

Silvaroli, N. *Classroom Reading Inventory,* 3rd ed. Dubuque, Iowa: W.C. Brown, 1976.

Spache, George D. *Diagnostic Reading Scales.* Monterey: California Test Bureau, 1972.

Woods, Mary L., and Alden J. Moe. *Analytical Reading Inventory.* Columbus, Ohio: Merrill, 1977.

CHAPTER 10

Diagnostic Reading Tests and Techniques II

INTRODUCTION

©1965 United Feature Syndicate, Inc.

Figure 10.1

Charlie Brown may have received a D minus on his book report, but his teacher should receive an A. From an analysis of Charlie's work, she was able to discern that his report was done as an afterthought in a slipshod manner. The *Peanuts* cartoon portrays Charlie Brown's teacher as a remarkably perceptive person. Such perceptivity is important in diagnosis because the teacher is looking for the cause or causes of the student's poor performance in order to help the student improve.

The teacher in a diagnostic-reading and correction program is also concerned with determining a student's independent, instructional, frustration, and capacity levels, so that the student can be given material to read that is best suited for him or her.

In Chapter 9 you learned about the importance of oral reading in diagnosing a student's reading behavior and you were introduced to the informal reading inventory, which is an important diagnostic instrument. This chapter will continue to present diagnostic instruments and techniques that you can use.

The sections that follow will introduce you to a variety of diagnostic instruments. Some will be standardized, and some will be classroom-prepared. After you finish reading this chapter, you should be able to answer the following questions:

1. What are examples of some standardized norm-referenced diagnostic tests that only measure oral reading ability?

2. What are examples of some standardized norm-referenced diagnostic reading tests that measure a number of different skills?

3. What are examples of some standardized criterion-referenced reading tests?

4. What are examples of some teacher-made diagnostic tests?

5. Why are teachers interested in developing their own criterion-referenced tests?

6. What do teachers have to know about behavioral objectives in order to construct criterion-referenced tests?

7. What is the cloze procedure?

8. How is the cloze procedure used as a diagnostic technique?

STANDARDIZED DIAGNOSTIC ORAL READING TESTS

Standardized oral reading tests are individually administered and help teachers analyze the oral reading of their students. Whether the test is part of a battery of tests or is the entire test, the teacher must learn rules for recording errors and the marking symbols used in the particular test. It takes time and practice to learn a system for recording errors and the marking symbols.

It is important that teachers know that they cannot just pick up and administer a standardized oral reading test with which they are unfamiliar. This caution is not given to intimidate you from using a standardized oral reading test but rather to forewarn you that time is needed to become acquainted with it. It is also important that you recognize that all oral tests do not use the same recording system, symbol system, or scoring system. Obviously, if you find a test that you like and that you feel is effective for diagnosing students' oral reading strengths and weaknesses, you should stick with it. Some often used standardized oral reading tests follow. (See the previous chapter for a discussion of oral reading errors.)

Gilmore Oral Reading Test[1]

This is an individually administered test designed to measure three aspects of oral reading ability: accuracy, comprehension, and rate. There are two forms—Form C and Form D—and each form contains paragraphs of a continuing story about a family. The paragraphs are based on graduated levels of difficulty; that is, each paragraph is a little longer and a little more difficult than the preceding one. The paragraphs begin at a first-grade level and proceed to the eighth-grade level.

Each paragraph is followed by five comprehension questions. The pupil is asked these questions as soon as he or she has finished reading each paragraph. The questions on the *Gilmore Oral Reading Test* are primarily concerned with literal comprehension. "Despite its shortcomings, the updated Gilmore is among the best standardized tests of accuracy in oral

[1]John V. Gilmore and Eunice C. Gilmore. New York: The Psychological Corp. © 1968.

reading of meaningful material now available.''[2]

Gray Oral Reading Tests[3]

This is a series of standardized oral reading paragraphs for individual administration. The two major functions of the *Gray Oral Reading Tests* are to provide an objective measure of growth in oral reading from early first grade to college and to aid in the diagnosis of oral reading problems. The paragraphs in this test, as in the Gilmore, are based on graduated levels of difficulty.

Each reading paragraph is followed by four comprehension questions. As in the *Gilmore*, the pupil is asked these questions as soon as he or she has finished reading each paragraph, and, as in the *Gilmore*, the questions are primarily concerned with literal comprehension.

The *Gray Oral Reading Tests* are very highly reviewed in Buros's *Mental Measurements Yearbooks*.

STANDARDIZED DIAGNOSTIC READING TESTS

The standardized diagnostic reading tests that are presented in this section are comprehensive tests in that they consist of a number of subtests. Many of the diagnostic test batteries contain oral reading tests as well as silent reading tests and word analysis tests. Some of the tests, such as the *Botel Reading Inventory*, determine oral

reading grade levels, but the tests consist of word lists rather than paragraphs. (See Chapter 9 for a discussion of the use of word lists to determine reading levels.) The tests presented in this section are also individually administered and they, too, require some sophistication in administration and scoring. Teachers will have to study the examiner's manual carefully before administering any of the tests. It would probably be a good idea if the teacher were to practice giving the test in a simulated situation to some other person before actually giving it to children for diagnostic purposes.

Gates/McKillop/Horowitz Reading Diagnostic Tests[4]

These are individual tests, in one form only, designed to assess the oral reading, writing, and spelling skills of children in grades 1 through 6, but they can also be used to diagnose the reading difficulties of older students. The subtests consist of the following: Oral Reading, Reading Sentences, Isolated Word Recognition, Knowledge of Word Parts (Syllabication), Recognizing and Blending Common Word Parts, Reading Words, Giving Letter Sounds, Naming Letters (Capital and Lower-case), Identifying Vowel Sounds, Auditory Blending and Discrimination, Spelling, Informal Writing Sample. (Not all children will need to be given all the tests.)

From looking at the subtests, it can be seen that the *Gates/McKillop/Horowitz Tests* stress word analysis skills rather than comprehension.

The test manual contains detailed information for administering, scoring, and interpreting results. The Test Kit is composed of Test Materials (contains two Tachistoscopes for

[2]Oscar K. Buros, ed., *The Seventh Mental Measurements Yearbook* (Highland Park, N.J.: Gryphon Press, 1972), p. 1147.

[3]William S. Gray (author), Helen M. Robinson (editor). New York: The Psychological Corp., 1963–1967.

[4]Arthur I. Gates, Anne S. McKillop, and Elizabeth C. Horowitz, Teachers College Press, 1981.

Words: Flash Test), Pupil Record Booklet, and Manual of Directions.

Durrell Analysis of Reading Difficulty, 3rd ed.[5]

This test contains the following subtests: Oral Reading, which consists of five primary and three intermediate paragraphs with literal comprehension questions; Silent Reading, which consists of eight paragraphs equivalent in difficulty to the oral reading paragraphs; Listening Comprehension, which consists of six graded paragraphs with literal comprehension questions; Word Recognition/Word Analysis, which consists of a tachistoscope and word cards, one list for Grade 1 and three lists for Grades 2 through 6; Listening Vocabulary; Pronunciation of Word Elements; Spelling, which consists of one spelling list for primary and one spelling list for the intermediate grades; Visual Memory of Words; Auditory Analysis of Words and Elements; and Prereading Phonics Abilities Inventories. The prereading phonics tests are available for nonreaders, pupils with initial reading difficulties, and kindergartners whose readiness for reading is in doubt. The prereading phonics tests consist of Syntax Matching, Identifying Letter Names in Spoken Words, Identifying Phonemes in Spoken Words, Naming Lower Case Letters, and Writing Letters from Dictation.

The analysis also contains a Profile Chart, a Checklist of Instructional Needs, a General History Data Form, Supplementary Paragraphs, Supplementary Tests, and Suggestions for Supplementary Tests and Observations.

The primary purposes of the analysis are to estimate the general level of reading achievement and to discover weaknesses and faulty reading habits that may be corrected in a remedial program.

The Manual of Directions provides instruction on who should be given the tests as well as directions on how to administer each. It is stated in the manual that norms are provided for most of the tests, but an analytic record of the difficulties the child displays is critical if specific help is to be given to correct weaknesses. It is also stated that the checklists for recording observations of difficulties are a very important feature. The Checklist of Instructional Needs, an excellent guide for observing a child's reading behavior, is on page 148 (see Chapter 11).

Here are examples of some often used comprehensive standardized norm-referenced diagnostic reading tests.

Botel Reading Inventory by Morton Botel, c1966, 1970; Grades 1–junior high school; Follett Educational Corporation.

> Provides estimate of student's instructional level, free-reading level, and frustration level, and identifies basic word attack skills. Subtests are: Word Recognition; Word Opposites; Phonics Mastery; Spelling Placement.

Doren Diagnostic Reading Test of Word Recognition Skills: 1973 Edition by Margaret Doren; c1956–73; Primary grades—useful for anyone who has not yet developed independent reading ability; American Guidance Service, Inc.

> Measures the degree to which children have mastered a variety of word recognition skills: letter recognition, beginning sounds, whole word recognition, words within words, speech consonants, ending sounds, blending, rhyming, vowels, sight words, discriminate guessing.

Stanford Diagnostic Reading Test: 1976 Edition by Bjorn Karlsen, Richard Madden, Eric F. Gardner; c1976; Grades 1.6–3.5 (Red Level); The Psychological Corporation.

[5]Donald D. Durrell and Jane H. Catterson, *Durrell Analysis of Reading Difficulty: Manual of Directions* (New York: The Psychological Corp., 1980).

Check List of Instructional Needs[6]

NON-READER OR PREPRIMER LEVEL

Needs help in:

1. Listening comprehension and speech
   - ____ Attention in listening
   - ____ Understanding of directions
   - ____ Speaking vocabulary
   - ____ Speech correction
2. Prereading phonics abilities
   - ____ Awareness of separate words in sentences
   - ____ Syntax matching
   - ____ Letter name sounds in spoken words
   - ____ Phonemes in spoken words
   - ____ Naming lower case letters
   - ____ Writing letters from dictation
   - ____ Writing letters from copy
3. Visual perception of word elements
   - ____ Visual memory of words
   - ____ Identifying letters named
   - ____ Copying letters
4. Auditory perception of word elements
   - ____ Initial or final single sounds
   - ____ Initial or final blends
   - ____ Phonograms
5. Reading interest and effort
   - ____ Attention and persistence
   - ____ Self-directed work
6. Other
   - ____ _____
   - ____ _____
   - ____ _____

PRIMARY GRADE READING LEVEL

Needs help in:

1. Listening comprehension and speech
   - ____ Understanding of material heard
   - ____ Speech and spoken vocabulary
2. Word analysis abilities
   - ____ Visual memory of words
   - ____ Auditory analysis of words
   - ____ Solving words by sounding
   - ____ Sounds of blends and phonograms
   - ____ Use of context clues
3. Oral reading abilities
   - ____ Speed of oral reading
   - ____ Comprehension in oral reading
   - ____ Phrasing (Eye-voice span)
   - ____ Errors on easy words
   - ____ Repetition of words or phrases
   - ____ Ignoring punctuation
   - ____ Ignoring word errors
   - ____ Attack on unfamiliar words in context
   - ____ Expression in reading
   - ____ Speech, voice, enunciation
   - ____ Security in oral reading
   - ____ _____
   - ____ _____
   - ____ _____
4. Silent reading and recall
   - ____ Speed of silent reading
   - ____ Comprehension in silent reading
   - ____ Attention and persistence
   - ____ Recall on questions
   - ____ Phrasing (Eye movements)
   - ____ Lip movements and whispering
   - ____ Head movements or frowning
   - ____ Position of book; posture
   - ____ _____
   - ____ _____
   - ____ _____
5. Reading interest and effort
   - ____ Attention and persistence
   - ____ Voluntary reading
   - ____ Self-directed work; workbooks

INTERMEDIATE GRADE READING LEVEL

Needs help in:

1. Listening comprehension and speech
   - ____ Understanding of material heard
   - ____ Speech and oral expression
2. Word analysis abilities and spelling
   - ____ Visual memory of words
   - ____ Auditory analysis of words
   - ____ Solving words by sounding syllables
   - ____ Sounding syllables and word parts
   - ____ Attack on unfamiliar words
   - ____ Spelling ability
   - ____ Accuracy of copy
   - ____ Speed of writing
   - ____ _____
   - ____ _____
   - ____ _____
3. Oral reading abilities
   - ____ Speed of oral reading
   - ____ Comprehension in oral reading
   - ____ Phrasing (Eye movements)
   - ____ Expression in reading; speech skills
   - ____ Security in oral reading
   - ____ Word and phrase meaning
   - ____ _____
   - ____ _____
   - ____ _____
4. Silent reading and recall
   - ____ Speed of silent reading
   - ____ Comprehension in silent reading
   - ____ Unaided oral recall
   - ____ Recall on questions
   - ____ Attention and persistence
   - ____ Word and phrase meaning difficulties
   - ____ Sentence complexity difficulties
   - ____ Imagery in silent reading
5. Study abilities
   - ____ Outlining
   - ____ Unaided written recall
     - ____ Main ideas
     - ____ Details
     - ____ Organization
6. Composition
   - ____ Sentence sense
   - ____ Spelling
   - ____ Handwriting
7. Reading interest and effort
   - ____ Attention and persistence
   - ____ Voluntary reading
   - ____ Self-directed work

[6]Donald D. Durrell and Jane H. Catterson, *Durrell Analysis of Reading Difficulty* (New York: The Psychological Corp., 1980), p. 2.

Designed to measure the major components of the reading process and to diagnose pupils' specific needs. The test covers: Auditory Vocabulary, Auditory Discrimination, Phonetic Analysis, Word Reading, and Reading Comprehension.

STANDARDIZED CRITERION-REFERENCED READING TESTS

Criterion-referenced tests are considered standardized if they are published, have been constructed by experts in the field, and have been developed with specific instructions for administration and scoring. Criterion-referenced tests do not supply norms.

The present trend in the field of reading, as well as in other fields, is toward greater use of criterion-referenced tests for both evaluation and diagnosis. Not only are test publishers developing more criterion-referenced tests but also publishers of basal reader series are developing criterion-referenced instruments for use with their basal readers. As already discussed in Chapter 3, criterion-referenced tests are based on a set of instructional objectives, which are stated in behavioral terms and are concerned with an individual's progress in relation to himself or herself. Before developing a criterion-referenced reading test, the test-makers must decide on an inventory of desired student behaviors in reading. These must be identified, the conditions under which they are to occur must be identified, and often the standard or criterion of acceptable performance must also be identified. (See "Teacher-made Criterion-Referenced Tests" and "Behavioral Objectives" for a discussion on behavioral objectives.)

The reason norms are not necessary for criterion-referenced tests is that they measure a student's mastery or nonmastery of explicitly stated behavioral objectives in a specific subject rather than compare the student to a national group in a subject.

Criterion-referenced reading tests are helpful diagnostic aids because they present a set of behaviorally stated objectives that describe reading behaviors at rather specific levels. Some criterion-referenced tests are more specific than others (see "Teacher-Made Criterion-Referenced Tests").

The PRI Reading Systems

Published in 1980 by CTB/McGraw-Hill, these succeed the *Prescriptive Reading Inventory*. A criterion-referenced approach to reading, the *PRI Reading Systems* include assessment and instructional materials that are supposed to supply detailed diagnostic and prescriptive information about a student's reading proficiency. The systems go beyond testing in that instructional materials, including lesson plans and activities, are provided as part of the systems.

The systems have five levels, spanning from kindergarten through grade 9. There are four skill clusters into which all *PRI Reading Systems* objectives are grouped. The objectives are presented at three different levels of specificity. Every kit includes a Systems Overview Chart, a Teacher's Guide, Teacher Resource Files, Tutor Activities, Student Worksheets, Mastery Tests, Reading Passage Books (for use with the Mastery Tests), and a Continuous Progress Monitoring Log.

Here are examples of some other criterion-referenced reading tests:

Individual Pupil Monitoring System—Reading; c1974; Grades 1–6; The Riverside Publishing Company.

A series of criterion-referenced tests measuring pupil's performance on specified behavioral objectives. The system is available in

 Reading Systems [7]

Individual Diagnostic Map

Category Objectives Test
System 1, Level C

Name _____

Teacher _____

Grade _____ Date _____

DIRECTIONS

The items that test a specific category objective are listed by number in the ITEM NUMBERS column. To fill in the box under each item number, refer to the student's corrected test booklet for the *PRI Reading Systems Category Objectives Test*. Record C for correct, X for incorrect, or O for item omitted. Add the number of correct items for each objective and enter that number on the line in the RAW SCORE column. Refer to the guide in the CRITERIA column to determine Mastery (+), Review (R), or Nonmastery (−). Enter +, R, or − for each objective in the box in the last column.

SKILL AREA	OBJECTIVE NUMBER AND NAME	ITEM NUMBERS Enter C, X, or O	RAW SCORE	CRITERIA	+ R −
Word Analysis	7 Word Recognition	1 2 3 4	_____	+ = 3, 4 R = 2 − = 0, 1	☐
	8 Symbol & Sound Correspondence	5 6 7 8 9 10	_____	+ = 5, 6 R = 3, 4 − = 0, 1, 2	☐
	9 Structural Analysis	11 12 13 14 15 16	_____	+ = 5, 6 R = 3, 4 − = 0, 1, 2	☐
Vocabulary	10 Word Picturing	17 18 19 20	_____	+ = 3, 4 R = 2 − = 0, 1	☐
	11 Word Matching	21 22 23 24 25 26	_____	+ = 5, 6 R = 3, 4 − = 0, 1, 2	☐
	12 Word Meaning	27 28 29 30	_____	+ = 3, 4 R = 2 − = 0, 1	☐
Word Usage	13 Language Mechanics	31 32 33 34	_____	+ = 3, 4 R = 2 − = 0, 1	☐
	14 Sentence Parts	39 40 41 42 43 44	_____	+ = 5, 6 R = 3, 4 − = 0, 1, 2	☐
	15 Syntax	35 36 37 38	_____	+ = 3, 4 R = 2 − = 0, 1	☐
Literal Comprehension	16 Story Detail	45 47 48 50 51 53	_____	+ = 5, 6 R = 3, 4 − = 0, 1, 2	☐
	17 Paraphrasing	46 49 52 54	_____	+ = 3, 4 R = 2 − = 0, 1	☐
Interpretive & Critical Comprehension	18 Main Idea	55 59 63 65	_____	+ = 3, 4 R = 2 − = 0, 1	☐
	19 Inference	56 60 61 62	_____	+ = 3, 4 R = 2 − = 0, 1	☐
	20 Figurative & Descriptive Language	57 58 64 66	_____	+ = 3, 4 R = 2 − = 0, 1	☐
Study Skills	22 Reference Skills	79 80 81 82	_____	+ = 3, 4 R = 2 − = 0, 1	☐
Content Area Reading	23 Social Studies	67 68 69 70	_____	+ = 3, 4 R = 2 − = 0, 1	☐
	24 Science	75 76 77 78	_____	+ = 3, 4 R = 2 − = 0, 1	☐
	25 Mathematics	71 72 73 74	_____	+ = 3, 4 R = 2 − = 0, 1	☐

six overlapping levels, each of which assesses in three reading skill categories: Word-Attack Vocabulary and Comprehension, and Discrimination/Study Skills. Information is provided to enable teachers to individualize instruction by objective.

IOX Objectives-Based Tests Collection: Reading; not dated; Grades K–6; Instructional Objectives Exchange, Los Angeles, Calif.

Consists of 38 word-attack criterion-referenced tests and 40 comprehensive criterion-referenced tests.

Woodcock Reading Mastery Tests by Richard W. Woodcock; c1973; Grades K–12; American Guidance Service, Inc.

A battery of five individually administered reading tests: Letter Identification, Word Identification, Word Attack, Word Comprehension, and Passage Comprehension.

Special Note

It is important to state that criterion-referenced tests are *not* norm-referenced tests,

even though some are reporting normative data. The normative data are estimated data only.

TEACHER-MADE (INFORMAL) DIAGNOSTIC READING TESTS

Any test that you develop to help you learn more about a student's specific strengths and weaknesses is an informal diagnostic test. Every day teachers use informal techniques, such as word recognition tests or word lists collected from the back of a basal reader, oral reading tests, cloze tests, criterion-referenced tests, and word analysis tests, to help them learn more about their students' reading. Informal tests are excellent in giving quick feedback. They can also be structured to specifically fulfill an individual need. The classroom test that you develop will vary according to the particular situation.

Here are a number of informal reading tests you will find useful in diagnosing your students' strengths and weaknesses.

INFORMAL DIAGNOSTIC TESTS

Auditory Discrimination
(Before administering this test, make sure the child knows the difference between *same* and *different.* Also, pronounce each pair of words very distinctly, and ask the child to turn away from you when you are presenting the words to him or her so that there will not be any possibility of lip-reading.)

Listen carefully. Tell me whether I say the same word twice or if I say two different words.

1.	Jim	Jim		
2.	Tod	Ted		
3.	bend	band		
4.	top	tip		
5.	lime	line		
6.	chop	shop		

7.	rain	rain
8.	hit	hat
9.	owl	our
10.	fond	found
11.	washing	watching

1. Listen carefully. Give me another word that begins with the same sound as

   top   _____

   car   _____

   boy   _____

2. Listen carefully. Give me another word that ends with the same sound as

   bat   _____

   bed   _____

   lamb   _____

   can   _____

3. Listen carefully. Tell me a word that rhymes with the following words.

   1. walk   _____

   2. bake   _____

   3. tall   _____

   4. fell   _____

   5. let   _____

4. Listen carefully. Tell me the letter that stands for the first sound you hear in each of the following words.

   1. bury _____   2. level _____   3. fierce _____

   4. wiry _____   5. jealous _____   6. nephew _____

   7. quarrel _____   8. tissue _____   9. curb _____

   10. zone _____   11. yield _____

5. Listen carefully. Tell me the two letters that stand for the first two sounds you hear in each word.

   1. pledge _____   2. floral _____   3. snarl _____

   4. twirl _____   5. dreary _____   6. blush _____

   7. statue _____   8. brag _____   9. crystal _____

   10. swagger _____   11. project _____   12. glimpse _____

6. Listen carefully. Tell me the two letters that stand for the first sound you hear in each word.

    1. chair ———————   2. shoe ———————   3. shame ———————

    4. thumb ———————   5. church ———————

7. Listen carefully. Tell me the letter that stands for the sound you hear at the end of the word.

    1. hum ———————   2. hear ———————   3. mom ———————

    4. buzz ———————   5. thug ———————   6. rain ———————

    7. leak ———————   8. burr ———————

Visual Discrimination

Following are a number of letters. Underline the letter that is different from the first one in the line.

Example: E E <u>D</u> E E

1. U R U U U U

2. P P P P P D

3. d d d b d d

4. p p p p d p

5. m m n m m m

6. o o o o e o

7. K K H K K K

Following are a number of letters. Underline the letter that is the same as the first one in the line.

Example: R S S T <u>R</u>

1. D B D B O S

2. B R D D B P

3. M N M N O R

4. O C O P R B

5. G D G S T U

6. W K M N W N

7. N M N M S L

Following are a number of words. Draw a circle around the word that is the same as the first word.

Example: fun   far   fix   fat   (fun)   fall

1. was   saw   sat   won   wet   was

2. bark   dark   bark   hard   barn   bar

3. other   order   ought   other   about   ether

4. saw   set   sun   sat   saw   was

5. shame   same   shone   shame   shorn   slam

6. five   fair   find   fill   five   fix

Following are groups of letters. Draw a circle around the letter group that is the same as the first in the line.

Example: iot   tio   (iot)   oit   oti

1. tio   oit   iot   iot   tio

2. trg   rgt   tgr   trg   grt

3. sab   bsa   sab   bas   sba

4. pdb   bdp   bpd   pdb   pbd

5. oci   ico   coi   oic   oci

6. bpk   kpd   dpb   bpk   bkp

7. mbn   nbm   mbn   bmn   nmb

Memory Digit-Span Test
I am going to say some numbers, and I want you to say them just the way I do. Listen carefully, and get them just right. (Before each series repeat, "Listen carefully, and get them just right." Rate: one per second.) (See Chapter 14 for a digit-span scale.)

_____   85

_____   62

_____   84

_____ 374

_____ 195

_____ 837

_____ 7295

_____ 4962

_____ 6384

_____ 58274

_____ 39481

_____ 72583

_____ 362915

_____ 725816

_____ 817492

_____ 8514739

_____ 7281594

_____ 7359628

_____ 92413758

_____ 86152973

_____ 59814732

_____ 391752684

_____ 147925638

_____ 741592683

I am going to say some numbers, and I want you to say them in reverse order. For example, if I should say 5–1, you would say 1–5. Let's try another. 6–2—you say 2–6. (Before each series repeat, "Ready now, listen carefully and be sure to say the numbers in reverse order." Rate: one per second.)

_____ 92

_____ 71

_____ 38

_____ 197

_____ 638

_____	592
_____	7935
_____	2976
_____	3159
_____	72859
_____	47613
_____	94265
_____	728159
_____	597314
_____	412793
_____	8159637
_____	1742695
_____	6935148

Word Analysis Test—Auditory
Listen carefully. Each of the words I am going to pronounce has one or more syllables. Tell me the number of syllables you hear in each word.

1. mother (2)
2. reached (1)
3. baby (2)
4. bicycle (3)
5. vocabulary (5)

Listen carefully. Tell me the vowel sound you hear in each word.

1. bake (ā)
2. coat (ō)
3. rid (ĭ)
4. not (ŏ)
5. bat (ă)

6. cute (ū)
7. leap (ē)
8. neck (ĕ)
9. nut (ŭ)
10. lip (ĭ)

Word Analysis Test—Visual
Can you pronounce the following nonsense words?

1. l o a p (l ō a̸ p)
2. h a k e (h ā k e̸)
3. c h i n e (c h ī n e̸)
4. p h a s (f ă s)
5. l i p o (l ī p ō)

TEACHER-MADE CRITERION-REFERENCED TESTS

Many school systems are developing their own criterion-referenced tests because these can provide a better match than published tests between the skills tested and the skills taught by the curriculum to which the children have been exposed. The criterion-referenced tests are correlated with student behavioral objectives that have been generated for every measurable reading comprehension and word recognition skill in the curriculum. After the behavioral objectives have been generated, tests are prepared for each behavioral objective. (See Chapter 13, which presents criterion-referenced tests for a number of comprehension skills.)

Many teachers in their everyday lessons utilize behavioral objectives and then prepare tests to determine whether students have achieved them. The test that is correlated to the specific behavioral objective would be considered a criterion-referenced test. The section that follows will present information on behavioral objectives so that you will be able to develop your own criterion-referenced tests. (See also "Criterion-Referenced Tests" in Chapter 3.)

BEHAVIORAL OBJECTIVES

Defining Behavioral Objectives

Behavioral objectives describe what students will be able to do after they have achieved their goals. With the use of behavioral objectives, teachers can very readily evaluate students' performances. Behavioral objectives help teachers clarify their thinking in the preparation of lesson plans because they have to identify precisely what learning behaviors should be exhibited at the end of a lesson. For example, if instructors were to state as an objective, "to develop the understanding that . . . ," how would they know whether students had gained such understanding? They wouldn't, because the phrase *to develop* implies an ongoing process, and the term *understanding* is a construct—something which cannot be directly observed or directly measured. The teacher must avoid using terms which defy direct observation. All stated learning outcomes must be of observable rather than covert (hidden) behavior. A good behavioral objective should include terminal behavior; that is, the objective should state what behavior the student would exhibit in order to demonstrate his accomplishment of the desired end. It should state the criterion or test by which the end can be evaluated.

Objectives in the Cognitive Domain

Bloom's *Taxonomy of Educational Objectives,*[8] which is concerned with the cognitive domain, is helpful in determining those objectives

[8]B.S. Bloom, ed. *Taxonomy of Educational Objectives—The Classification of Educational Goals, Handbook I: Cognitive Domain* (New York: McKay, 1956).

concerned with thinking that students should achieve in any discipline. This taxonomy is based on an ordered set of objectives ranging from the more simplistic thinking skills to the more complex ones. Bloom's objectives are cumulative in that each one includes the one preceding it. As a result, evaluation, the highest level in the taxonomy, includes all the preceding objectives in the hierarchy.

Here are the six major categories in Bloom's taxonomy of objectives in the cognitive domain:

1. *Knowledge:* deals with definitions and statements of facts in various subject matter fields

2. *Comprehension:* enables people to explain or summarize a statement

3. *Application:* enables people to use knowledge and understanding to solve a problem

4. *Analysis:* enables people to separate a whole into its elemental parts

5. *Synthesis:* enables people to put the elements together into a whole

6. *Evaluation:* enables people to make judgments using all preceding cognitive skills

To facilitate the writing of behavioral objectives, samples of some verbs, which describe various cognitive behaviors, follow:

Verbs to Use in Writing Behavioral Objectives in the Cognitive Domain

recognize, identify, find
illustrate, examine
prove, construct, differentiate, relate
estimate, compare, distinguish between
analyze, generalize from data
deduce, formulate hypotheses, integrate
synthesize, evaluate

Taxonomy of Objectives in the Affective Domain

The affective environment is concerned with the feelings and emotional learnings of students. Affective learnings are longer lasting than much of the subject matter of the course and usually exert a dynamic and directive influence on the individual's future involvement with the subject matter. Because knowledge in the affective domain is so important, teachers must have a better understanding of these emotional learnings and also some means of evaluating whether students' affective learnings are favorable or not in specific areas. Before teachers can determine what changes should take place, they must know what is happening in their classrooms and also what kinds of objectives are involved in the affective domain.

A taxonomy of educational objectives in the affective domain is presented in a helpful handbook for the teacher.[9] These objectives in the affective domain are ordinally arranged or ranked according to the degree of "internalization" involved; that is, the first category, *receiving,* is one which has a lesser degree of internalization than that of *responding,* and responding has a lesser degree of internalization than *valuing,* and so forth. In other words, each successive level in the affective domain is in a continuum employing a greater amount of internalization as the categories move on. The fifth category, *characterization by a value,* or value complex, has the greatest degree of internalization; at this level it would involve behavior that is an important or essential part of individuals and their life styles.

Following are samples of verbs which can be

[9]David R. Krathwohl, Benjamin S. Bloom, Bertram B. Masia, *Taxonomy of Educational Objectives—The Classification of Educational Goals, Handbook II: Affective Domain* (New York: McKay, 1964).

used to describe various behaviors in the affective domain:

Verbs to Use in Writing Behavioral Objectives in the Affective Domain

volunteer, take part, choose, offer, give help, share, practice, respond, accept

Constructing and Generating Behavioral Objectives

Cognitive Domain

In formulating behavioral objectives the exact outcomes must be stated in observable terms for ease of evaluation. Following are examples of behavioral and nonbehavioral objectives at different levels of the cognitive domain, which illustrate how much easier it is to evaluate in terms of behavioral objectives:

1. Behavioral objective: knowledge level
   Students will be able to state three words that rhyme with *man* with 100 percent accuracy.
   Nonbehavioral objective:
   To develop the understanding of rhyming words.

2. Behavioral objective: knowledge and application level
   Students should be able to state four meanings for *run* and write a sentence using each meaning.
   Nonbehavioral objective:
   To develop the understanding of word meanings.

3. Behavioral objective: evaluation level
   Students will determine whether the author should have ended the story in the way he or she did, based on what had previously taken place.

Nonbehavioral objective:
To develop the understanding of story endings.

Affective Domain

1. Behavioral objective: responding level
   Students will volunteer to read aloud a story.
   Nonbehavioral objective:
   Students enjoy reading aloud.

2. Behavioral objective: organization level
   Students will formulate standards for reading aloud, and use these to evaluate a tape recording of their oral reading.
   Nonbehavioral objective:
   Students appreciate good oral reading.

CLOZE PROCEDURE

Can you supply the _____ that fits this sentence? When you came to the missing word in this sentence, did you try to gain closure by supplying a term such as *word* to complete the incomplete sentence? If you did, you were involved in the process of *closure,* which involves the ability of the reader to use context clues to determine the needed word. To gain closure, we must finish whatever is unfinished.

The cloze procedure was primarily developed by Wilson Taylor in 1953 as a measure of readability, that is, to test the difficulty of instructional materials and to evaluate their suitability for students. It has since been used for a number of other purposes, especially as a measure of a student's comprehension.

Cloze procedure is not a comprehension skill; it is a technique that helps teachers gain information about a variety of language facility and comprehension skills. A cloze test or exercise is one in which the reader must supply words that have been systematically deleted from a text at a particular grade level.

There is no set procedure for determining the length of the passage or the number of deletions that a passage should have. However, if you wish to apply the criteria for reading levels that have been used in research with the traditional cloze procedure, you must follow certain rules. First, only words must be deleted, and the replacements for each word must be the *exact* word, not a synonym. Second, the words must be deleted in a systematic manner. The researchers who have developed the criteria for scoring cloze tests state that "any departure from these rules leaves the teacher with uninterpretable results."[10]

The traditional cloze procedure consists of deleting every fifth word of a passage that is representative of the material being tested. The passage that is chosen should be able to stand alone; for example, it should not begin with a pronoun which has its antecedent in a former paragraph. The first sentence of the passage should remain intact. Then beginning with either the first, second, third, fourth, or fifth word of the second sentence, every fifth word of a 250-word passage should be deleted.

At the intermediate-grade level and higher, the passage is usually 250 words, and every fifth word is generally deleted. At the primary-grade level, the passage is usually shorter, and every eighth or tenth word is deleted. For maximum reliability, a passage should have at least fifty deletions. If we were to use this figure as our criterion, we can see that we need a passage to be at least 250 words long with every fifth word deleted. Obviously, a cloze technique would not yield as reliable a score for the primary-grade level as for the intermediate-grade level because passages for the former are shorter and have fewer deletions.

[10]John R. Bormuth, "The Cloze Procedure: Literacy in the Classroom," in *Help for the Reading Teacher: New Directions in Research,* William D. Page, ed. (Urbana, Ill.: National Conference on Research in English, 1975), p. 67.

Scoring the Cloze Test

If you have deleted fifty words, the procedure for scoring the cloze test is very easy. All you have to do is multiply the number of correct insertions by two and add a percentage symbol. For example, twenty-five correct insertions would be equal to 50 percent. If you have not deleted exactly fifty words, use the following formula, in which the number of correct insertions is divided by the number of blanks and multiplied by 100 percent.

$$\text{Formula:} \quad \frac{\text{Number of Correct Insertions}}{\text{Number of Blanks}} \times 100\%$$

$$\text{Example:} \quad \frac{40 \text{ correct insertions}}{60 \text{ blanks}} \times 100\%$$

$$\frac{40}{60} \times 100\% = (40 \div 60) \times 100\%$$
$$= 67\% \text{ (rounded to}$$
$$\text{nearest digit)}$$

For a traditional cloze test in which only exact words are counted as correct and every fifth word has been deleted, a score below 44 percent would indicate a frustration level. A score between 44 and 57 percent would indicate the instructional level, and scores above 57 percent would indicate the independent level. It is important to note that these criteria should be used only if the exact words are used and if every fifth word has been deleted from the passage. (See Chapter 9 for an in-depth discussion of reading levels.)

Reading Levels Scale for Cloze Procedure

Independent level	58% and above
Instructional level	44% through 57%
Frustration level	43% and below

Variations of the Traditional Cloze Procedure: An Emphasis on Diagnosis

Variations of the cloze technique are usually used. For example, rather than deleting every fifth or tenth word, every noun or verb is deleted, or every function or structure word (definite and indefinite articles, conjunctions, prepositions, and so on) is deleted. This technique is used when the teacher wishes to gain information about a student's sentence sense. For example:

Jane threw _____ ball _____ Mary. (the, to)

Another variation of the cloze technique is to delete key words in the passage. This technique is useful for determining whether students have retained certain information. For example:

A technique in which the reader must supply words is called the _____ procedure. (cloze)

Cloze technique can also be adapted for other uses. Students can be presented with a passage in which they must complete the incomplete words. For example:

Dick r_____ his bike every day. (rides)

Another adaptation is to present the students with a passage in which every nth word is deleted. They must then choose words from a given word list that *best* fit the blanks.

Cloze exercises are easy to construct, and teachers can use them for diagnosis, review, instruction, and testing. In constructing the exercise, the key thing to remember is its *purpose*. If the purpose is to test a student's retention of some concepts in a specific area, the exact term is usually necessary; however, if the purpose is to gain information about a student's language facility, ability to use context clues, vocabulary development, or comprehension, the exact term is not as important because often many words will make sense in a passage.

Here is an example of an exercise using the cloze technique for an upper primary grade. Notice how explicitly the instructions are stated for the students, and also notice that the first and last sentences of the passage are given intact.

Directions: Read the first and last sentences that have no missing words in them to get a clue to what the story is about. Then read very carefully each sentence that has a missing word or words in it. Using context clues, find a word that would make sense in the story and put it in the blank.

In the forest there live a kind old man and woman. (1) _____ have been living in (2) _____ forest for almost ten (3) _____ . They had decided to (4) _____ to the forest because they (5) _____ nature.

The kind old (6) _____ and woman make their (7) _____ by baking breads and cakes and (8) _____ them to the people who (9) _____ the forest. Everyone who (10) _____ the forest usually buys (11) _____ bread or cake from the old (12) _____ . The kind old man and woman are happy in the forest.

Answers: 1. They, 2. the, 3. years, 4. move, 5. love, like, 6. man, 7. living, 8. selling, 9. visit, 10. visits, 11. some, 12. couple.

Note that the deletion pattern was not the same throughout the passage.

Here is an example of an exercise using cloze technique for an intermediate grade.[11]

Directions: Read the first sentence of the story to get a clue to what the story is about. Then read each sentence that has a missing word or words very carefully. Using context clues, insert a word in each blank so that the story makes sense.

Everyone was looking forward to Friday night because that was the night of the big basketball game. This (1) _____ would determine the championship (2) _____ Deerville High and Yorktown (3) _____. For years Deerville High and (4) _____ High have been rivals. This (5) _____ was very (6) _____ because so far (7) _____ school had won (8) _____ equal number of games. (9) _____ game on Friday night would break the (10) _____.

Friday night finally arrived. The game (11) _____ the championship title (12) _____ being played in the Deerville High (13) _____ because the game (14) _____ year had been played (15) _____ the Yorktown High gym. (16) _____ gym was so (17) _____ that many spectators were without (18) _____. When the two teams (19) _____ the gym from the dressing areas, (20) _____ were thunderous (21) _____ and whistles from the (22) _____. Each team went through (23) _____ warm-up drills of (24) _____ baskets and passing. Then the buzzer (25) _____. The game would begin (26) _____ a moment. Just as the referee (27) _____ the ball in the (28) _____ for the starting jumpball, the lights (29) _____ the gym went (30) _____. There was complete darkness. Everyone (31) _____ taken by surprise. Almost immediately a (32) _____ on the loudspeaker (33) _____ that the game would have (34) _____ be postponed because of a (35) _____ failure. The game would take (36) _____ next Friday. All were (37) _____

[11]Dorothy Rubin, *The Teacher's Handbook of Reading/Thinking Exercises* (New York: Holt, Rinehart and Winston, 1980).

to remain where they (38) _____ until someone with a flashlight came to help them.

Answers: (1) game, (2) between, (3) High, (4) Yorktown, (5) game, (6) important, (7) each, (8) an, (9) The, (10) tie, (11) for, (12) was, (13) gym, (14) last, (15) in, (16) The, (17) crowded, (18) seats, (19) entered, (20) there, (21) cheers, (22) spectators, audience, *or* crowd, (23) its, (24) shooting, (25) sounded *or* rang, (26) in, (27) threw, (28) air, (29) in, (30) out, (31) was, (32) voice, (33) announced, (34) to, (35) power, (36) place, (37) told, (38) were

KNOWLEDGE OF RESULTS AND CLOZE PROCEDURE

Knowledge of results is essential if the cloze procedure is to be used for instruction or diagnosis. Students need feedback. Unless students recognize that they have made a mistake, they will continue to make the same error. Knowledge of results should be given as soon as possible, as well as an explanation for the correct response. Student involvement in the diagnostic process is important, and a student's recognition that he or she has a problem is a positive step in correcting it.

SUMMARY

Chapter 10 continues to discuss and present a number of different kinds of diagnostic tests and techniques. These tests help teachers gain detailed information about their students' reading. Oral reading, if properly used, is an essential diagnostic tool. An astute teacher can gain a great amount of information about a student's reading by listening to the child read aloud. A number of standardized oral reading and diagnostic tests were presented and described. Standardized criterion-referenced tests that are also used for diagnostic purposes were also given and described. The section on teacher-made tests gave examples of a number of diagnostic tests that teachers could use to learn more about their students' reading. In order to help teachers to develop their own criterion-referenced tests a section was presented on behavioral objectives because each test item on a criterion-referenced test must be keyed to a specific behavioral objective. The last section included a discussion on cloze procedure and examples of how this technique can be adapted for various purposes.

SUGGESTIONS FOR THOUGHT QUESTIONS AND ACTIVITIES

1. You have been appointed to a committee whose objective is to develop criterion-referenced tests for a reading program. You are responsible for the primary grades. How would you go about completing this task?

2. Generate a number of behavioral objectives for word recognition, and then construct some test items to determine whether a student has achieved each specific objective.

3. Look up the reviews on three diagnostic reading tests in Buros's *Mental Measurements Yearbooks*.

4. Develop a cloze test to learn how well a child uses syntactic clues.

5. Administer some of the teacher-made tests that are presented in this chapter to a child who is having word recognition problems.

6. Construct some of your own diagnostic tests to learn about a specific reading behavior of a student.

SELECTED BIBLIOGRAPHY

Buros, Oscar. *Reading: Tests and Reviews.* Highland Park, N.J.: Gryphon Press, 1968.

_____, ed. *The Eighth Mental Measurements Yearbook.* Highland Park, N.J.: Gryphon Press, 1978.

Gill, Doren, et al. *Defining Reading Diagnosis: Why, What, and How?* Research Series No. 46 (ED 176 211). East Lansing: Institute for Research on Teaching, Michigan State University, 1979.

Harris, Albert. *How to Increase Reading Ability,* 7th ed., Chapter 8, "Assessing Reading Performance, pp. 163–208. New York: Longman, 1980.

Jongsma, Eugene, ed. *The Cloze Procedure as a Teaching Technique.* Newark, Del.: International Reading Association, 1971.

Marino, Jacqueline L. "Cloze Passages: Guidelines for Selection." *Journal of Reading* 24 (March 1981): 479–83.

Miller, Wilma H. *Reading Diagnostic Kit,* 2nd ed. New York: Center for Applied Research in Education, 1978.

Rae, Gwenneth, and Thomas C. Potter. *Informal Reading Diagnosis: A Practical Guide for the Classroom Teacher,* 2nd ed. Englewood Cliffs, N.J.: Prentice-Hall, 1981.

Schreiner, Robert, ed. *Reading Tests and Teachers: A Practical Guide.* Newark, Del.: International Reading Association, 1979.

CHAPTER 11

Observation and Other Child Study Procedures as Diagnostic Techniques

INTRODUCTION

Read the following conversation overheard in the faculty lounge:

MS. ANDERSON: I don't know what to do with Billy. His behavior is driving me crazy.

MR. JOHNSON: Why? What does he do?

MS. ANDERSON: What doesn't he do? He's forever getting up from his seat. He can't seem to sit still for a moment. He's always disturbing his neighbor. If there is any commotion or problem in the room, you can be sure that Billy is the cause of it.

MR. JOHNSON: Have you spoken to Billy's parents about his behavior?

MS. ANDERSON: Yes, but they say that they do not see the same kind of behavior at home, so they feel that it's something at school. I've just about had it.

MR. JOHNSON: I've had Billy in my class, and I remember him as a pretty bright boy. I think that before you refer him for testing that you should try to observe when Billy starts to act up. I know that I had a child who acted just as Billy does, and I thought that she was misbehaving all the time, and just to make my life miserable. Well, I had just finished a course in diagnosis, and the professor had discussed the uses of observation techniques to learn about the behavior of students. I decided to try it. My sanity was at stake. Was I surprised at the results! It also made me aware of how unfounded my statements about Susan were. Let's go to my room, and I'll show you what I did.

This chapter concerns the use of direct observation and other child study techniques such as questionnaires and inventories. After you read this chapter, you should be able to answer the following questions:

1. What is the purpose of direct observation?

2. When should teachers make generalizations about students' behavior?

3. How can observations be made as objective as possible?

4. What should teachers record as worthy of observation?

5. What is an anecdotal record?

6. What are checklists?

7. What kinds of checklists are there?

8. What are some examples of checklists?

9. How can a rating scale be used with a checklist?

10. What are the advantages of informal interviews?

11. What is an interest inventory?

12. What are some examples of interest inventories?

13. What are projective techniques?

14. How can a teacher use projective techniques in the classroom?

15. What are the kinds of projective techniques that teachers can use?

16. What are the purposes of reading autobiographies?

THE USES OF OBSERVATION

Direct observation is an essential part of any diagnostic program, and it is especially helpful in diagnosing reading problems. Observation is also useful for evaluation because it helps teachers become aware of students' attitudes, interests, and pleasures. It is one thing for a student to say that he or she enjoys reading, but it is another thing for the student to actually read. Through observation, teachers can observe whether students are voluntarily choosing to read in their free time and whether they voluntarily raise their hands to answer questions. The best method to determine whether students have learned something is to observe whether they are actually doing what they have learned.

Making Observations Objective

Observation is a technique; it is a means for collecting data. So that observations are of value, teachers must be as objective as possible

and avoid making generalizations about a student's behavior too early. For example, by observing that Sharon on one or two occasions is reading mystery stories, the teacher states that Sharon likes mysteries. This may be so, but it may be that she is just trying them out. Sharon may actually like only a few of them, and she may read only one or two a year. Here are some helpful suggestions on how to make observations as objective and useful as possible:

1. Use checklists and anecdotal records (observed behavior without interpretations) to record observations (see next section).

2. Observe the student over an extended period of time before making any inferences about the student's behavior.

3. Avoid the projection of one's own feelings or attitudes onto the student's behavior.

4. Observations should be used in conjunction with other measurement techniques.

5. Make sure that only observed behavior is recorded.

6. Look for a pattern of behavior before making any inferences about behavior.

7. Record observed behavior immediately or as soon as possible.

8. Recognize that checklists and anecdotal records do not reveal the cause or causes of the observed behavior(s); they only help to identify patterns of behavior from which one can try to deduce the existence of possible problems.

9. Do not oversimplify a student's observed behavior.

10. Date observations.

ANECDOTAL RECORDS

Teachers are often confused about what to record as worthy of observation. Because of this, checklists (see next section) are very helpful; however, it is not possible for checklists to contain an inclusive list of student behavior. Therefore, teachers usually supplement checklists with anecdotal information, which is the recording of *observed behavior* as objectively as possible. In recording observed behavior, teachers should attempt to put down exactly what has taken place *as soon as possible*. The date and time of the incident should be recorded, and the teacher's interpretation of the observed behavior may be given; however, the teacher's interpretation or possible explanation for the student's behavior should be put in brackets or set off in some way to avoid confusion with the actual observed behavior. It is best for the teacher to record merely the observed behavior and to observe the student over an extended period of time before making any hypotheses about the cause or causes for the behavior. If the teacher observes the student over an extended period of time, the teacher is more likely to see a pattern of behavior.

Determining the Information to be Recorded

What information should be recorded? This is a difficult question to answer, and as already stated, is often confusing for the teacher. As a result, anecdotal information usually consists of unusual observed behavior. However, teachers may be losing important information, which could help them to gain insights into a child's problem, if they record only unusual behavior. Here is an example of a teacher who uses checklists and anecdotal records. Notice how he was losing significant information because he was only recording unusual behavior.

Mr. Jackson has a reading checklist for each student, and after each reading lesson and at other appropriate times, he checks off what he has observed. To supplement his checklist, Mr. Jackson also employs anecdotal information.

Whenever he notices anything unusual, he records the observed behavior. For example, yesterday, Jerry started a fight with his best friend, and then for the rest of the day, he refused to do any work.

Mr. Jackson should have recorded Jerry's unusual behavior, but he should also be recording other kinds of observed behavior that are not on the reading checklists. For example, Mr. Jackson should be recording the following:

1/9   Jerry puts head on desk—reading period

1/13 Jerry puts head on desk—reading period

1/16 Jerry puts head on desk—reading period

1/20 Jerry puts head on desk—reading period

1/23 Jerry puts head on desk—reading period

1/27 Jerry puts head on desk—reading period

Jerry's behavior of putting his head on the desk has become such a normal occurrence that Mr. Jackson may have overlooked it. Yet, this behavior is extremely important. Jerry, over an extended period of time, puts his head on the desk *during the reading period*. Why? Mr. Jackson may not have noticed this behavior because of its frequency and because he may have thought that Jerry put his head on the desk because he was tired or sleepy. Only by recording when Jerry put his head on the desk could Mr. Jackson see that it was always during a reading period. By recording the dates, Mr. Jackson could check to see what kinds of reading lessons were involved. It may be that Jerry was tired or sleepy, but it is most unlikely. It is more probable that by checking further, Mr. Jackson will find that Jerry is bored because the work is too easy for him or that he is frustrated because the work is too hard for him. It may be that Jerry cannot do sustained silent reading because of an eye problem. It may be many things. The point is that the teacher would not be aware of these problems unless he has recorded what appeared to be "common" behavior.

From this discussion, it is obvious that exact guidelines cannot be given about what should or should not be recorded. Alert teachers, however, who are aware of the individual differences of the students in their classes will recognize those situations that warrant recording. Here are some more examples:

1. Susan always seems to want to go to the lavatory. Record when she goes and the frequency. It may be a physiological or emotional problem, or it may be that she wants to "escape" from a certain situation.

2. Frank is always causing disruptions in class. Record when Frank acts up to see whether there is a pattern. It may be that that is Frank's way of avoiding work. What is he avoiding? Is he bored or is he frustrated? Is something bothering him?

3. Marcia starts walking around the room and chatting to other children who want to finish doing their work. Record when Marcia does this, and try to figure out why.

It's important to note that observations do not explain the causes of behavior. As stated earlier, observation is a technique for gathering information; it helps teachers learn more about the behavior of students. If used carefully in conjunction with other techniques and test data, it can help teachers hypothesize possible causes for behavior. The possible causes must then be verified by more extensive and scientifically collected data, such as standardized and teacher-made tests.

Special Note

Teachers should be extremely careful about what anecdotal information becomes part of a child's permanent records because federal legislation now allows parents access to their children's records.

CHECKLISTS

Checklists usually consist of lists of behaviors that the observer checks as present or absent. Checklists are a means for systematically and quickly recording a student's behavior. They are not tests, although it is possible to present or devise a test to enable the rapid filling out of a checklist of behaviors; in other words, the test is administered to get the result, which is the student's profile.

Checklist formats may vary: Some use rating scales, some are used for a whole class or group, and some are used for an individual child. The purpose for the checklist should determine the kind of checklist that is used. An example of a diagnostic checklist for a child's speech problems is on page 169.

Group and Individual Checklists

Checklists that are used to display the behavior of a whole class or of a group of students in a specific area are sometimes preferred by teachers because they do not have to go to individual folders to record a student's behavior; thus teachers can, at a glance, determine who needs help in a specific area and who does not. A group checklist is helpful in planning instruction for the group as well as for the individual, whereas the individual checklist is useful in assessing the strengths and weaknesses of an individual student only. Both types of formats are helpful. A teacher who, at a glance, wishes to see a complete profile of a child may prefer the individual approach, whereas the teacher who wishes to see a profile of students' strengths and weaknesses in specific skills for instructional planning will probably prefer a group checklist.

Child's Name: _____

Grade: _____

Date: _____

Diagnostic Checklist of Speech Problems

	Yes	No
1. Is child's voice		
a. loud?		
b. too low?		
c. nasal?		
d. hoarse?		
e. monotonous?		
f. pitched abnormally high?		
g. pitched abnormally low?		
2. Is child's rate of speech		
a. too slow?		
b. too rapid?		
3. Is child's phrasing poor?		
4. Is child's speech hesitant?		
5. Does the child show evidence of articulatory difficulties such as		
a. the distortion of sounds?		
b. the substitution of one sound for another?		
c. the omission of sounds?		
6. Does the child show evidence of vocabulary problems such as		
a. the repetition of phrases?		
b. a limited vocabulary?		
7. Does the child show evidence of negative attitudes toward oral communication such as		
a. not engaging in discussions or conversations?		
b. not volunteering to give a talk or oral report?		

Whether a group or individual checklist is used, it should contain an itemized list of behaviors in a particular area; there should be space for dates; and there should be space for special notes.

Special Note

Group checklists usually do not have the space for notes that individual checklists have. This may be one of their disadvantages.

Checklists and Rating Scales

A checklist that uses a rating scale is actually an assessment instrument. This type of checklist serves different purposes from one that records observed behavior. An assessment checklist can be used by the teacher at the end of a unit to help to determine a student's progress. It can be used with the student so that the student is aware of his or her progress in a specific area. When the assessment checklists are used, the checklists of observed behavior and the anecdotal records should be used as supplementary information or as aids in verifying the student's rating.

If rating scales are used, it is important that criteria be set up beforehand to help teachers determine what rating to give to a particular student. For example, if a student consistently makes errors in recognizing words that begin with certain blends, that student would receive a rating of 3 on a scale of 1 to 3 in which 1 is the highest and 3 is the lowest. If the student almost never makes an error in recognizing words that begin with certain blends, that student should receive a rating of 1 on a scale of 1 to 3. If a student sometimes makes errors in recognizing words that begin with certain blends, the student would receive a rating of 2 on a scale of 1 to 3. Here is an example of a group checklist with a rating scale.

Phonic Analysis Skills (Consonants) Rating Scale (Group)

	Mary	John	Jack	Susan
	1 2 3	1 2 3	1 2 3	1 2 3

Single consonants
  initial
  medial
  final				

Consonant blends (clusters)				
Consonant digraphs				
Silent consonants				

Special Note

There are diagnostic checklists in each of the chapters in Part IV, as well as in a number of other chapters in this book.

OTHER HELPFUL CHILD STUDY TECHNIQUES

There are some important student characteristics that cannot be gained through direct observation. Attitudes or feelings and interests are examples of essential characteristics that cannot be directly observed. Projective techniques, informal interviews, and inventory-type measures can help teachers learn about those aspects of students that cannot be directly observed. Achievement tests can help teachers learn about the amount of knowledge students have, and intelligence tests can help teachers learn about the students' rate of learning or their approximate potential for doing work in school; projective techniques, informal interviews, and interest inventories can help teachers understand their students better.

In a diagnostic-reading and correction program it is important for teachers to look at both the cognitive and noncognitive characteristics of their students, because students' attitudes and interests will affect what they learn and whether they learn. Reading helps reading; unfortunately, many students are not choosing to read. The reasons for this are varied and many (see Chapter 17). However, if teachers know about their students' attitudes and interests, they can help motivate their students and instill in them a positive attitude toward reading. For example, if a teacher has a child who is doing poorly in reading and who never chooses to read voluntarily, the teacher can learn about that child's interest and use it to motivate the child to read.

Special Note

Teachers must be cautioned against assuming the role of psychologist or therapist and should avoid any suggestion that they are searching for underlying psychological causes for a student's behavior. Teachers should avoid administering any psychiatrically oriented instrument to their students.

Informal Interviews

The easiest way to learn about students' likes or dislikes is to ask them. Teachers have many opportunities during the school day to converse with their students and learn about their feelings and interests. Teachers can also set up special times during the school day to meet with students for a consultation in the form of an informal interview. This is a good technique because it helps the teacher to build rapport with students, as well as to gain information about them. This technique is especially helpful for the lower primary grades and for those students who have reading problems. However, the in-

formal interview is very time consuming, so other techniques are needed also.

Special Note

Teachers should avoid setting up special interviews to discuss students' interests after school. Students may look upon this as a punishment of some sort. Of course, if teachers, by chance, meet some of their students after school and converse with them, this is an excellent opportunity to learn about their interests.

Interest Inventories

Interest inventories can be standardized or teacher-made. The purpose of an interest inventory is to help teachers learn about the likes and dislikes of their students. In this book, we are particularly interested in a student's likes or dislikes so that we can use this information to help stimulate them to read. For example, if we learn from an interest inventory that a student who is a reluctant reader likes mechanics and cars, we could choose books in this area at the student's ability level (see Chapter 17).

Interest inventories usually employ statements, questions, or both to obtain information. The statement or questionnaire method enables the teacher to gain a great amount of information in a relatively short period of time, but there is a major difficulty with this method. When persons fill out an inventory they are not always truthful. Many times individuals give "expected responses"; that is, they answer with responses that they feel the tester expects or wants rather than with responses based on what they actually do or based on how they feel. Students who wish to create a favorable impression on their teacher may especially answer in an expected direction. Teachers cannot completely avoid the faking that is done on inventories, but they can help to control it. Teachers who have good rapport with their students and who have a good affective environment in their classrooms will be able to gain the trust of their students. Before administering the inventory, these teachers can discuss its purpose and try to impress upon the students how important it is for them to put down exactly the way they feel rather than what they think they should feel.

Interest inventories can be individually administered, administered to a small group, or administered to the whole class. The interest inventory is usually used in a group, but it is individually administered if the student's reading problem prevents him or her from filling it out. In the lower primary grades teachers can use a checklist type of questionnaire, whereby they read the question to the children and the children mark the appropriate box. Here are examples of some interest inventories that you can use with your students to ascertain their reading interests.

LOWER PRIMARY GRADES (Read aloud by teacher)

Name_____Grade_____

1. Do you like to read?   Yes _____   No _____   Sometimes _____

2. What kinds of books do you like to read? Books about a. animals _____ b. children _____ c. sports _____ d. adventure _____ e. fairy tales _____

3. What do you like to do after school? a. watch TV _____ b. read a book _____ c. play _____ d. do schoolwork _____ e. work around the house _____ d. work on a hobby _____

4. What do you like to do when there is no school? a. watch TV _____ b. read a book _____ c. play _____ d. do schoolwork _____ e. work around the house _____ f. go shopping with your parents _____ g. visit the zoo _____

5. What are your favorite television shows? a. cartoons _____ b. comedy shows _____ c. movies _____ d. mysteries _____ e. musicals _____ f. game shows _____ g. adventure _____

6. What are your favorite games? a. group games played outside _____ b. indoor games _____ c. electronic (television) games _____

(For numbers 2 through 6, the child may check more than one.)

UPPER PRIMARY GRADES

Name_____ Grade_____

1. Do you like to read? _____

2. When do you like to read the best? _____

_____

3. What is your favorite subject? _____

_____

4. What is your favorite book? _____

_____

5. What do you like to do after school? _____

_____

6. What is your favorite game? _____

_____

7. What is your favorite television show? _____

_____

8. What kinds of books do you like to read? _____

_____

9. What is your hobby? _____

_____

10. Do you take out books from the library? _____

_____

INTERMEDIATE GRADES

Name_____ Grade _____

1. Do you like to read? _____

2. What kinds of books are your favorites? _____

_____

3. What do you like to do after school? _____

_____

4. What are your favorite subjects? _____

_____

5. Name your favorite hobby. _____

6. How often during the month do you go to the public library? _____

7. How often during the week do you go to your school library? _____

8. Name your favorite book. _____

9. What do you enjoy doing the most? _____

10. What is your favorite television show? _____

11. Name your favorite movie. _____

12. What is your favorite sport? _____

13. If you could go anywhere in the world, where would you like to go? _____

14. If you could visit any book character you wanted to, whom would you like to visit?

    _____

15. Name the magazines and newspapers that you read. _____

16. What part of the newspaper do you like to read the best? _____

17. What book is the most popular among you and your friends? _____

18. What would you like to be when you grow up? _____

Projective Techniques

Projective techniques are subtle procedures whereby individuals put themselves into a situation and reveal how they feel. Projective techniques are more revealing than inventories because the student is less likely to fake an answer. The student does not know what the *correct* or *best* answer is, for there is no correct or best answer. On a projective test students are more likely to give the answer that is natural for them, and as a result, reveal how they really feel.

There are, however, a number of problems with projective techniques. The major problem concerns the interpretation of the student's responses. Because of difficulty with interpretation, projective tests are not very trustworthy; however, they do have some definite benefits for teachers with children who have reading problems. They can help teachers gain some insights into the way students who have reading problems feel about themselves without the students realizing it. Teachers may also gain information about why the students think they have a reading problem. The teacher could then use this information to try to help the students.

The examples of projective tests that follow are simple ones that classroom teachers can administer to their students. These tests can be group- or individually administered.

Special Note

Teachers should use projective tests with caution and not try to read too much into the responses. Also, teachers should not administer those tests which require clinical analysis by a psychologist.

Sentence Completion Test

The sentence completion test is easy to administer in a relatively short period of time. Students are given some unfinished sentences that they are asked to complete as rapidly as possible. This test can be given orally to those students who have trouble reading or writing, or it can be given to a whole group at once. Here are some typical incomplete sentences:

> Reading is . . .
> I believe I can . . .
> I prefer . . .
> My favorite . . .

Wish Test

The wish test is similar to the sentence completion test except that the phrase *I wish* precedes the incomplete sentence. Here are some typical examples:

> I wish I were . . .
> I wish I could . . .
> I wish reading were . . .
> I wish school were . . .
> I wish my friends were . . .
> I wish my teacher . . .

Reading Autobiography

The reading autobiography is not as subtle as a projective technique because the students are aware that they are writing or telling about their feelings and trying to analyze why they have a reading problem. It is a helpful technique, however, and probably not as prone to faking as an interest inventory because the students are partners in an attempt to analyze their reading difficulties. The reading autobiography is the student's own life story of his or her reading ex-

periences. It can be presented in a number of ways, and it can be individually or group-administered.

Open-Ended Reading Autobiography

One technique that could be used is simply to have the students write their reading autobiography. They are given the following instructions:

> Since this is the life story of your reading experiences, you must go back as far as you can remember. Try to recall your earliest reading experiences, what they were, and how you felt about them. Try to recall what books you liked when you were very small, and whether you still like those kinds of books. Try to remember when you first started to read. How did you feel? Try to recall how you first learned to read, and what you think helped you the most in learning to read. If you have a reading problem, try to remember when you think it first started and why it started. Put down anything that you feel is important in helping others to understand your reading problem if you think you have one.

Students who have trouble writing could orally relate their autobiographies to the teacher, or they could tape-record them.

Questionnaire Reading Autobiography

The questionnaire autobiography is also helpful in gaining information about a student's reading history, but it is more limiting than the open-ended reading autobiography. Also, it is only as good as the questions on it because students' responses are determined by the questions. Here is an example:

READING AUTOBIOGRAPHY

1. Do you like to read?
2. When do you read? (Write answer in blank.)
3. Do you like someone to read to you?
4. Do you feel you understand what you read?

Yes	No	Sometimes

	Yes	No	Sometimes
5. Did anyone try to teach you to read before you came to school?			
6. Did anyone read to you when you were younger?			
7. Are there lots of books in your house?			
8. Do you think you have a reading problem?			

If you answered *yes* to question 8, answer the following questions:

1. What do you think your reading problem is?

2. Why do you think you have a reading problem?

3. Has anyone tried to help you with your problem?

4. When do you feel your reading problem began?

5. Who do you think has helped you the most in reading?

6. What do you think has helped you the most in reading?

7. Have you ever left the class to attend a special reading class?

If you answered *yes* to question 7, answer questions 8 and 9.

8. How do you feel about being in a special reading class?

9. Do you think the special reading class has helped you?

10. Are your parents interested in helping you in reading?

11. Do you like to read to anyone?

12. What do you do when you come across a word you do not know?

13. What do you do when you do not understand something you are reading?

14. Do you have a library card?

15. If you have a library card, how often do you go to the library?

16. What kinds of books do you like to read?

SUMMARY

Chapter 11 concerns the use of observation and other child study methods as essential diagnostic techniques that help teachers learn about their students' behavior. Direct observation is helpful in diagnosing reading problems and also for evaluation. This chapter discusses how observations can be made as objective as possible and presents techniques, such as checklists and anecdotal records, for recording students' behavior. The purposes and uses of checklists and anecdotal records are given, as well as information on the kinds of behavior that should be recorded. It is stressed throughout the chapter that observation is merely a technique for gathering information; it does not explain the causes of behavior.

Other child study techniques such as the informal interview, interest inventories, projective techniques, and the reading autobiography were also presented as viable methods to help teachers gain information about student characteristics that could not be obtained through direct observation. Interest inventories, which provide knowledge about students' likes and dislikes, help teachers plan activities and choose materials to motivate the students. Projective techniques and reading autobiographies help give teachers insight into students' feelings about themselves and reading.

SUGGESTIONS FOR THOUGHT QUESTIONS AND ACTIVITIES

1. Construct a checklist for a reading skill to use for instruction.
2. Construct a reading checklist that uses a rating scale.
3. Construct an individual checklist that lists all the reading behaviors that you feel are important.
4. Use one of the checklists given either in this chapter or in the chapters in Part IV to learn more about the behavior of a particular child.
5. Observe a child at various times in class. Record his or her behavior by using a checklist.
6. Observe a child at various times in class. Record his or her behavior by using an anecdotal record.

SELECTED BIBLIOGRAPHY

Cohen, Dorothy H., and Virginia Stern. *Observing and Recording the Behavior of Young Children.* New York: Teachers College Press, 1978.

Forness, Steven R., and Karen C. Esveldt. "Classroom Observations of Children with Learning and Behavior Problems." *Journal of Learning Disabilities* 8 (1975): 382–85.

McAvoy, Rogers. "Measurable Outcome with Systematic Observations." *Journal of Research and Development in Education* 4 (1970): 10–13.

Medinnus, Gene. *Child Study and Observation Guide.* New York: Wiley, 1976.

Miller, Wilma H. *Reading Diagnostic Kit,* 2nd ed., Chapter 2, "Teacher Observation as a Diagnostic Technique," pp. 25–51. New York: The Center for Applied Research in Education, 1978.

Strang, Ruth. *Diagnostic Teaching of Reading.* New York: McGraw-Hill, 1969.

Part IV

A REVIEW OF WORD RECOGNITION, COMPREHENSION, VOCABULARY EXPANSION, AND STUDY SKILLS, INCLUDING DIAGNOSTIC TESTS, CHECKLISTS, AND CORRECTIVE TECHNIQUES

CHAPTER 12

Word Recognition Skills

INTRODUCTION

This chapter and the two that follow will present an analytical review of some of the word recognition, comprehension, vocabulary expansion, and study skills that a good teacher must have. It seems obvious that teachers will not be able to diagnose reading problems unless they know the components of reading.

Word recognition is necessary to be able to read. No one would disagree with that statement; however, persons do disagree on what word recognition encompasses. In this book word recognition is seen as a twofold process that includes both the recognition of printed symbols by some method so that the word can be pronounced and the attachment or association of meaning to the word after it has been properly pronounced.

This chapter will concentrate on helping you better understand word recognition strategies and will present a developmental sequence of phonic skills. It is important in a diagnostic-reading and correction program that teachers have the word analysis skills at their fingertips,

as well as techniques for teaching them, so that they can interweave diagnosis with instruction and correction. After you read this chapter, you should be able to answer the following questions:

1. What does word recognition encompass?
2. How is word recognition defined in this book?
3. What strategies are used to help students pronounce words?
4. What strategies are used to help students get word meanings?
5. What skills are taught in phonic instruction?
6. What are consonant and vowel digraphs?
7. What are diphthongs and consonant blends (clusters)?
8. What is a phonogram?
9. How are vowel rules taught?
10. What is the procedure for teaching accenting?

11. What is a schwa?

WORD RECOGNITION STRATEGIES FOR PRONUNCIATION

When we read, we are intent on getting the message and appear to do so automatically and in one step. We don't notice the individual letters, groups of letters, or even every word if we are good readers. It isn't until we stumble on an unfamiliar word that we become aware of the individual letters that are grouped together to form a word. The reason we stopped reading is because the word we stumbled on has interfered with the message. The question is: Do you remember what you did when a word interfered with your understanding of what you were reading? To understand better the concept that word recognition is a twofold process, that there are a number of strategies that can be used to figure out how to pronounce a word as well as to determine its meaning, and tnat these strategies are not necessarily the same, we will be involved in a number of exercises containing nonsense and actual words. Read the following sentence:

I don't like *cland* food.

You should have stumbled on the nonsense word *cland*. Imagine that you do not know that *cland* is a nonsense word. Let's look at the kinds of strategies we could and could *not* use to help us pronounce a word *independently.*

Strategy 1: Phonic Analysis and Synthesis

Definition: Phonics is a decoding technique that depends on students' being able to make the proper grapheme (letter)–phoneme (sound) correspondences. *Analysis* involves breaking down something into its component parts. *Synthesis* involves building up the parts of something into a whole. (In this chapter a sequential development of phonic skills will be presented.)

Analysis: Break down *cland* into the blend *cl* and the phonogram (graphemic base) *and*. We have met the blend *cl* before in such words as *climb* and *club*. We have met the phonogram *and* before in such words as *sand* and *band*. We therefore know the pronunciations of *cl* and *and*.

Synthesis: Blend together the *cl* and *and*.

Using this technique, we should be able to pronounce *cland*.

Strategy 2: Whole-Word or "Look-and-Say" Method

Definition: The whole-word or "look-and-say" method has the teacher or any other individual directing a student's attention to a word and then saying the word. The student must make an association between the oral word and the written word, and he or she shows this by actually saying the word.

This technique, also referred to as the sight method, is a useful word recognition strategy to help us learn to pronounce words, but it will not help us figure out the pronunciation of unfamiliar words independently.

Strategy 3: Ask Someone to Pronounce the Word for You

This could be done, but it would be similar to the "look-and-say" method and it would not help us figure out the word independently.

Strategy 4: Context Clues

Definition: By context we mean the words surrounding a word that can shed light on its meaning. When we refer to context clues, we mean clues that are given in the form of definitions, examples, comparisons or contrasts, explanations, and so on, which help us figure out word meanings. (For more on context, see Chapter 13.)

This is a word recognition technique, but it is not one that helps us figure out the pronunciation of words. It is one used to help us gain the meaning of a word.

Strategy 5: Structural Analysis and Synthesis (Word Parts)

Definition: Structural analysis and synthesis involve the breaking down (analysis) of words into word parts and the building up (synthesis) of word parts into words. Word parts are prefixes, suffixes, roots (bases), and combining forms (see Chapter 13).

Structural analysis is most often used in conjunction with phonic analysis. Knowing word parts, such as prefixes, suffixes, and roots, helps us to isolate the root of a word. After the root of a word is isolated, phonic analysis is applied. If the word parts are familiar ones, we can blend together the word parts to come up with the pronunciation of the word.

Structural analysis is a helpful word recognition technique that can also help with the pronunciation of words, but it will not help us to figure out the pronunciation of *cland* unless we apply phonic analysis because as a nonsense word, it is an unfamiliar root (base) word.

Structural analysis is helpful in figuring out the pronunciation of an unfamiliar word if the word is composed of familiar word parts such as prefixes, suffixes, and roots. The technique we would use is similar to that used with phonic analysis and synthesis. For example, let's see how we would go about figuring out how to pronounce the italicized word in the following sentence by using structural analysis and synthesis.

The salesperson said that the goods were not *returnable.*

Structural analysis: Break down the word into its parts to isolate the root.

re turn able

If we had met *re* before and if we had met *able* before, we should know how to pronounce them. After we have isolated *turn*, we may recognize it as a familiar word and know how to pronounce it.

Structural synthesis: Blend together *re, turn,* and *able.*

If *turn* were not a familiar root word, we could apply phonic analysis and after that blend it together with the prefix *re* and the suffix *able.*

Strategy 6: Look Up the Pronunciation in the Dictionary

This is a viable method, but you may not have a dictionary handy, and by the time you look up the pronunciation of the word, you may have lost the trend of what you were reading.

Let's list those techniques that can help us to figure out the pronunciation of words:

1. Phonic analysis and synthesis
2. Whole word or "look-and-say"
3. Asking someone
4. Structural analysis and synthesis
5. Looking up the pronunciation in the dictionary

Notice that of all the techniques, phonic analysis and synthesis does give you a great amount of power in figuring out the pronunciation of words *independently.*

Figure 12.1

© 1975 United Feature Syndicate Inc.

WORD RECOGNITION STRATEGIES FOR WORD MEANING

Being able to pronounce a word is important, but it does not guarantee that we will know its meaning. As stated previously, word recognition is a twofold process; the first involves correct pronunciation, and the second involves meaning. After we have pronounced the word, we have to associate the word with one in our listening capacity in order to determine the meaning of the word; that is, we have to have heard the word before and know what the word means. Obviously, the larger our stock of listening vocabulary, the better able we will be to decipher the word. Since *cland* is a nonsense word, we would not have heard the word before, and we can not associate any meaning to it. Even though we can pronounce a word such as *misanthropic,* it doesn't mean that we can associate any meaning to it. If we have never heard the word before, it would not be in our listening vocabulary; therefore the pronunciation would not act as a stimulus and trigger an association with a word that we have stored in our memory bank. Let's see the techniques that we can use to help us unlock words we have never heard of or met before.

Strategy 1: Context

By context we mean the words surrounding a particular word that can help shed light on its meaning. (Context clues are especially important in determining the meaning of words, and because of their importance, special emphasis is given to them in Chapter 13.) Read the following sentence:

> Even though my *trank* was rather long, I wouldn't take out one word.

From the context of the sentence you know that the nonsense word *trank* must somehow refer to a sentence, paragraph, paper, or report of some sort. Even though you have never met *trank* before, the context of the sentence does throw light on it. You know from the word order or position of the word (syntax) that *trank* must be a noun, and words such as *word* and *long* give you meaning (semantic) clues to the word itself. There are times, however, when context is not too helpful, so other strategies must be used.

Strategy 2: Structural Analysis and Synthesis for Word Meaning

Read the following sentence:

> We asked the *misanthrope* to leave.

From the position of the word *misanthrope* in the sentence, we know that it is a noun; however, there is not enough information to help us figure out its meaning. Structural analysis could be very useful where there are insufficient context clues and the word consists of a number of word parts.

> *Analysis:* Break down *misanthrope* into its word parts. *Mis* means either "wrong" or "hate," and *anthropo* means "mankind."
> *Synthesis:* Put together the word parts. It doesn't make sense to say wrong mankind, so it must be hate and mankind. Since misanthrope is a noun, its meaning would have to be "hater of mankind."

Structural analysis is a powerful tool, but it is dependent on your having at your fingertips knowledge of word parts and their meanings. If you do not have these at hand, you obviously need another strategy. (More will be said about structural analysis in Chapter 13.)

Strategy 3: Ask Someone the Meaning of the Word

This at times may be the most convenient strategy if someone is available who knows the meaning of the word.

Strategy 4: Look Up the Meaning in the Dictionary

If you cannot figure out the word independently rather quickly so that your train of thought is not completely broken, the dictionary is a valuable tool for word meanings.

Let's list those techniques that can help us figure out the meaning of words:

1. Context of a sentence
2. Structural analysis and synthesis
3. Asking someone
4. Looking up the meaning in the dictionary

There are times when it is possible for context clues to help with the correction of mispro-

nounced words that are in the listening capacity of the reader but not yet in his or her reading vocabulary. For example, a child is asked to read the following sentence:

> The horse went into the barn.

The child reads the sentence as follows:

> The *harse* went into the barn.

The child then corrects himself, and rereads the sentence correctly. What has taken place? The first pronunciation of *harse* was obtained from graphic clues. As the student continued to read, the context of the sentence indicated that the mispronounced word should be *horse* rather than *harse*. Since *horse* was in the listening capacity of the child, he was able to correct his mispronunciation of *horse*.

It is important to state that the child would not have been able to correct his mispronunciation if the word *horse* had not been in his listening capacity and if he had not heard it correctly pronounced.

Special Notes

Many foreign students who are learning English as another language or students who speak nonstandard English may pronounce a number of words incorrectly because they have heard them pronounced that way, but they may know the meanings of the words. The teacher must be careful in determining the cause of the child's mispronunciation; that is, is the mispronunciation due to a pronunciation problem or a comprehension problem?

Configuration has not been presented as a viable word recognition strategy because of its limited value. Configuration, which has to do with the shape or outline of a word (can mother night), cannot be used to figure out unfamiliar words. Configuration is supposed to help the children remember the word because of its shape. It may be useful in a few limited cases where the shape of the word is unique. Time, however, would better be spent on students learning more useful cues such as semantic, syntactic, and graphic ones.

WORD RECOGNITION STRATEGIES: SOME FURTHER REMARKS

It is important that teachers be aware of the different word recognition strategies and the purpose for each so that effective teaching can take place. For example, a teacher must realize that helping a child to become proficient in phonics will not help him or her to be a good reader unless the child has developed a stock of vocabulary and has adequate concept development. A child may be able to decode all the words in a passage, but as stated in Chapter 1 when defining reading, this child would not be reading unless he or she could determine the meaning of the passage. A teacher should not only be aware of the different strategies for figuring out word pronunciation and meanings but also recognize that some strategies work better with different children. This advice should not, however, preclude teachers from helping children to become proficient in using all the strategies and from helping children to determine which strategy or strategies are best to use in a specific situation. Usually, a combination of strategies is used.

Because phonics is a powerful tool that helps students become more self-reliant readers, the remainder of this chapter will concern itself with this area. Also, unless teachers have phonic skills at their fingertips, they will not be able to analyze many of their students' difficulties with word analysis. In the chapter that follows more

will also be said about structural analysis and context.

THE IMPORTANCE OF DECODING IN READING

As we have seen, students who have difficulty in listening will have problems in oral language as well as in reading. Since reading is a process of interpreting printed symbols that are based on arbitrary speech sounds, it depends on a foundation of previously learned speech symbols. Usually, beginning readers have a substantial oral vocabulary before they begin to read, when they learn that each word they speak or listen to has a printed symbol. Students who become effective readers must be able to automatically decode written symbols which represent speech sounds. Inability to do so will prevent readers from bringing anything to or getting any message from the printed page.

DEFINING PHONICS

Phonics, which is the study of relationships between the letter symbols (graphemes) of a written language and the sounds (phonemes) they represent, is a method used in teaching word recognition in reading. It is a pedagogical term. Phonics is used in the classroom as an aid to decoding words. It helps students gain independence and reliance in reading, but it is only one aspect of the reading process.

LEARNING PHONIC SKILLS

Learning phonics is necessary so that children are able to gain independence in reading. If children do not learn phonic analysis and synthesis, they will be at a disadvantage in learning to read. The teacher, however, must not assume that all children can learn to make the proper grapheme–phoneme relationships. Some children can benefit from another method of word recognition. It should be recognized that phonics is but one part of word recognition, which itself is but one part of the whole reading program.

The best way for teachers to understand how children learn phonic word attack skills is to experience the phenomenon themselves. To simulate this experience, teachers must know the steps involved. First the child learns a few sight words. Then, when the child learns that some words look alike and/or sound alike, the mastering of phonic word attack skills has begun. This task is not a simple one. Below is a technique which helps put the teacher into the "skin" of the child learning word attack skills.

A DEVELOPMENTAL SEQUENCE OF PHONIC INSTRUCTION[2]

Although the teaching of phonics will vary according to the needs and readiness levels of the students, in a developmental sequence certain skills must be achieved before others. So that teachers can properly diagnose the needs and readiness levels of their students in phonics, teachers must be proficient in this area.

An outline of the developmental sequence of phonic instruction is on page 191. Each area listed will be defined, and examples for each skill will be presented.

In the illustration which follows you will learn a new set of phonic signals. English speech will be represented by symbols other than those of the usual Roman alphabet. Play along with the game. When you finish, you will better understand the task which children face and which you help them master.[1]

STEP ONE

Objective: Learn sight words.

Learn to pronounce the six words below at sight. Test yourself by covering the pictures.

[1] Carl J. Wallen, *Word Attack Skills in Reading* (Columbus, Ohio: Merrill, 1969), pp. 13–18.
[2] For ease of reading, the author has omitted slashes (//), which are often used to enclose phonemic symbols.

STEP TWO

Objective: Test yourself on knowledge of sight words.

Match words and pictures. Check yourself by referring back to step one.

STEP THREE

Objective: Test auditory discrimination readiness.

Answer the following questions with *yes* or *no*.

1. Do the two words represented by the pictures have the same ending sound?

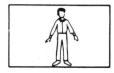 

2. Do the two words represented by the pictures have the same ending sound?

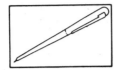 

3. Do the two words represented by the pictures have the same beginning sound?

STEP FOUR

Objective: Test visual discrimination readiness.

Circle the *words* in each column which have the same letters in the same places as those underlined in the word at the top of the column. Column 1 has been completed.

I	II	III
boy	५५7X	⊗⊥Ī∆
big	⊗⊥ℲW	५५57X
toy	⊗⊥7X	⊗⊥ℲW
rub	W3५7X	५५ 7X
bold	५५५7X	⊗⊥Ƴ7X

STEP FIVE

Objective: Use phonic word attack to pronounce a new word.

Follow the directions given below.

1. Pronounce these three words.
2. How do the three words look alike?
3. How do the three words sound alike?

4. Pronounce these three words.
5. How do the three words look alike?
6. How do the three words sound alike?

7. Here is a new word.
8. How does it look like the other two groups of words?
9. Can you pronounce the new word?

(If you cannot pronounce the new word, do steps one, two, three, and four again. Then follow the directions given in step five.)

Notice that you pronounced the new word by comparing the look of the new word with the look of familiar words. You assumed that if words have a similar spelling they will have a similar pronunciation.

Thus: 1. *oride*   probably begins like *or* and rhymes with *hide.*
      2. *smeek* probably begins like *smile* and rhymes with *seek.*
      3. *virgule* probably begins like *virtue* and rhymes with *mule.*

In phonic word attack the child compares new words with familiar ones. When he finds words having a similar spelling he assumes that the words will also have a similar pronunciation. Phonic signals are the letters and groups of letters which the reader compares. The reader learned two nonsense phonic signals in the previous exercise and used them in applying phonic word attack to the new word.

| Phonic Signals Learned | New Word Attacked |

1. Auditory discrimination.
2. Visual discrimination.
3. Sounds of initial consonants and written representations of initial consonants.[3]
4. Substitution of initial consonants in sight vocabulary words.
5. Final consonants and their substitution in sight vocabulary words.
6. Consonant clusters (blends) (*bl, st, str*).
7. Initial consonant blends (clusters); final consonant blends (clusters).
8. Initial consonant digraphs (*th, ch, sh*).
9. Final consonant digraphs (*ng, gh*).
10. Silent consonants (*kn, pn, wr*).
11. Vowel sounds.
    a. Long vowel sounds.
    b. Short vowel sounds.
12. Effect of final *e* on vowel.
13. Double vowels.
    a. Digraphs.
    b. Diphthongs.
14. Vowel controlled by *r*.
15. Special letters and sounds.
16. Phonograms (graphemic bases).
17. Syllabication.
    a. Meaning of syllable.
    b. Rules.
       (1) Double consonant vc/cv.
       (2) Vowel-consonant-vowel v/cv.
       (3) Consonant with special *le* the vc/cle or v/cle.
    c. Syllable phonics.
       (1) Open syllable.
       (2) Closed syllable.
    d. Accent.

Auditory and Visual Discrimination

As has already been stated, unless children are able to hear sounds correctly, they will not be able to say them correctly, read them, or write them. Not only must children be able to differentiate between auditory sounds and visual symbols in order to be ready for reading, they must also learn that the sounds they hear have written symbols.

Since they must have good auditory and visual discrimination, these samples of exercises should help in determining such discrimination.

AUDITORY DISCRIMINATION
DIRECTIONS:

Listen carefully and see if you can tell which pair of words are the same.

```
can      can
hurt     hut
```

DIRECTIONS:

Listen carefully and give me another word that begins like:

T—Top   _____ _____

C—Car   _____ _____

---

[3]Consonants are usually taught before vowel sounds.

DIRECTIONS:

Listen carefully and give me another word that ends like:

AY—Day   _____   _____

OW—Cow   _____   _____

VISUAL DISCRIMINATION
DIRECTIONS:

Draw a circle around the word that is like the first word:

far   fun   fix   car   far

DIRECTIONS:

Draw a circle around all groups of letters and groups of numbers that are alike. This exercise is excellent for picking up reversals.

tio   toi   iot   ito   tio   ot

3523   2533   2452   3523   5234   3352

Initial Consonants

Initial consonants are single consonants (one speech sound represented by one letter), for example *b(bird), g(go), k(kite), p(pet), t(Tom), y(yellow), z(zoo).*

Presentation

Teachers should not present initial consonants in isolation from words. Since letters do not have sounds, but are merely representations of them, it is not correct to refer to the sound of *b* or *g.* Teachers may state a number of words beginning with the initial consonant. They may ask the children to listen to the words *ball, book,* and *bee.* They should write the words on the board. Then they should ask how *ball, book,* and *bee* are similar. They all have the same beginning letter *b.* They all start with the same sound. Teachers can then give a list of words that begin with *b* and ask students to state some others like *big, book,* and *balloon.*

For variety, the children can be given a series of words which begin with the same initial consonant and be told to match these words with those in a second column that start with the same letter by drawing a line from one to the other. For example:

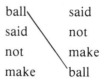

Substitution of Initial Consonants

After children have learned to recognize and are able to state single consonants, they are ready to substitute those in already learned words to generate new words. The new words must be in their listening capacity; that is, they must have heard the word and know the meaning of it in order to be able to *read* it. For example, children have learned the consonant letter *c* and they also know the word *man*. They should then be able to substitute *c* for *m* and come up with the word *can*.

Final Consonants and Substitution of Final Consonants

Final consonants are similar to the list given for initial consonants, except that they appear at the end of the word. Examples of the most frequent single consonants are *b(rob), d(road), g(pig), k(brook), l(tool), m(mom), n(hen), p(top), r(car), s-z(has), t(hot)*.

Some teachers teach final consonants at the same time that they teach initial consonants. This approach is preferable, since teachers are working with a particular sound that they want the children to overlearn; that is, they want students to be able to recognize and state the sound-letter combination over an extended period of time. By emphasizing the initial and final consonants in words, the children are gaining extra practice in both the particular sound and the letter which represents the sound being studied. Since the children have learned that the letter *Gg* stands for a certain sound, and can recognize this sound in *girl, go, game, get,* and so on, they should also be given words such as *pig, log, leg, tag,* and so on to see whether they can recognize the same sound at the end of the word.

In order to gain skill in the substitution of final consonants, the children are given a list of words that they can already decode and recognize—such as *bat, pet, let, tan*. Then they are asked to substitute the final letter *g* in all the words to make new words. For example, *bat* would become *bag, pet* would become *peg, let* would become *leg,* and *tan* would become *tag*. Pupils can also be asked to substitute other consonants to make new words. For example, *d* for *g* in *bag* to make *bad,* and *d* in *let* to make *led*.

Consonant Clusters (Blends)

Consonant clusters are simply a way of combining the consonant sounds of a language. Clusters are a blend of sounds. (In some basal reader series, the term *consonant cluster* has replaced the term *consonant blend*.)

Initial Consonant Blends (Clusters)

Consonant blends (clusters) are a combination of sounds, not letters. They are two or more consonant sounds blended together so that the identity of each sound is retained. For example: *bl(blame), pl(play), cr(crack), tr(try), sk(skate), sl(sled), sm(smile), sn(snow), sp(spot), sw(swim), scr(scream), str(stream), spr(spread), spl(splash)*.

Consonant blends are generally introduced in the first grade at the primer level in basal readers and are then developed throughout the primary grades. The teaching of the initial consonant blends depends on the readiness levels of the children, who may be at the stage where they can benefit from added instruction in order to help them more readily decode words. The children must be able to recognize, sound, and substitute initial consonants in words before proceeding to blends. They should be given a list of sight words that have blends, such as *spin, snow, play, stop,* asked to say these words, and then tell what sounds they hear at the beginning of the words. They should also be asked to say a list of words such as *go, get, me,* and *mother* and then be asked what the difference between the two groups of words is. The children should be able to discern that in the group consisting of *play, stop,* and *spin,* they were able to hear two consonant sounds rather than one. Thus the concept of a blend is introduced. The teacher should then give the children exercises similar to those presented in the section on initial consonants. For example, the pupils could be given a list of words which they may not necessarily know as sight words:

1	2	3	4
black	big	mother	happy
ball	play	great	broom
blue	draw	farm	track
chain	down	spin	grow
train	go	run	help

Teachers would tell the children to underline only those words they pronounce—such as *black, play, spin,* and *broom.*

This exercise can also be used to see how well children listen, follow directions, and recognize blends. For example, the teacher can instruct the children to *listen carefully* and not to do anything until he or she has completed the sentence. Then, the teacher can say: Put a circle around *black* and a cross on *blue.* Put a circle around *draw* and a line under *play.* Put a line under *great* and a circle around *spin.* Put a cross on *track* and a circle around *broom.*

Final consonant blends are usually taught after initial consonant blends, using similar techniques.

Initial Consonant Digraphs

Consonant digraphs usually consist of two consonants which represent one speech sound. For example: *ch(chair), sh(show), th(thank), ph(phone).*

Final Consonant Digraphs

Examples of final consonant digraphs are *th(booth), ng(sing), sh(mash), ch(cinch), gh(rough).* Note: It is possible to have a digraph represent one of the sounds in a cluster. In the word *cinch, nch* represents a cluster (blend) because *nch* represents a blend of *two* sounds.

The letter *n* represents a sound, and the digraph *ch* represents another sound.

Silent Consonants

Silent consonants refer to two consonants in which one is silent. Examples are *kn(know), gh(ghost), wr(wreck).* These are analogous to consonant digraphs, since the two consonants represent one speech sound.

Vowel Sounds

Working with vowel sounds is more difficult than working with consonants because of the inconsistency of vowel sounds. There are exceptions for almost every vowel rule. Most children have met many of the vowel rules in sight words and have learned to pronounce the words properly before they are able to state the rule. Vowel rules are generally introduced some time in the first grade and usually taught through the primary grades. Again, when to teach vowel rules would depend on the readiness level of the pupils in the class. The purpose of teaching vowel rules is to help students become more proficient in analyzing words, so that they can be more effective independent readers.

Should long or short vowels be taught first?[4] Since the long vowel sound is the name of the vowel, children might have less difficulty in hearing this sound. Therefore, it would be better to start with long vowel sounds, even though there are more words with short vowel sounds.

Whichever kind of vowel is taught first, it is important that the teacher use the children's experiences to help them acquire new skills.

Teachers should familiarize children with the schwa sound, represented by (ə) of the phonetic

[4]Although some linguists frown at the use of the terms *long* and *short* vowels, because they claim there are only gradations of vowel sounds, it is helpful to use these terms in the teaching of phonics.

alphabet. The schwa is important in phonic instruction because it frequently appears in the unstressed (unaccented) syllables of words with more than one syllable (see "Special Letters and Sounds").

Long Vowel Sounds—a e i o u (and sometimes) y

In teaching this concept, attention should be drawn to the sound element. A number of sight words illustrating the long vowel sound can be placed on the board:

āpe	bē	gō
āge	hē	nō
Āpril	ēven	ōpen
āte	mē	

The children are told to listen to the words as they are sounded. Can they hear the name of any of the vowels in the words? If they can, they can tell which ones they hear. After they correctly state the vowel they heard, "saying its name," it is explained that these vowels are called long vowels and they are marked, for example, ā.

A list of words containing long vowels should be read to the children, and the students should then say which vowel is long in each word. They can be given a list of words and asked to mark all the vowels that are long after everyone has said the words aloud. For example:

āble	gāme	hāte	mōst
boy	get	hid	nāme
cāke	girl	hīde	nō
cāme	gō	man	nōte
father	hat	mē	pet

After children have had practice in recognizing long vowel sounds in spoken words the teacher presents written exercises in which the children must work independently at marking the long vowel sounds. The words in these exercises should all be sight vocabulary words—those the children have already met and are able to recognize.

Y represents a long vowel sound when it occurs at the end of a word or syllable and when all the other letters in the word or syllable are consonants, for example, *by, cry, baby, deny*. Note that *y* in these words represents different vowel sounds. It stands for a long *i* sound in one-syllable words containing no other vowels (see "Special Letters and Sounds").

Short Vowel Sounds

Since the children have already had practice in long vowel sounds, a list of words with short vowel sounds can next be placed on the board and each one pronounced:

not	get	man
got	let	can
pin	put	mad
tin	cut	cap
met	hat	had

The list containing long vowels can be presented so that children can hear the differences between long and short vowel sounds. The children's attention should also be brought to the *position* of the short vowel in such words as the following:

fat	man	net	got
mat	mad	get	not
cat	can	let	
hat		pet	

Children should be helped to notice the vowel rule—*a single vowel in the middle of a word or syllable is usually short*. As this concept is usually introduced in the first grade, the presentation of the term *syllable* would be deferred. The concept of closed syllable is reviewed in the intermediate grades in conjunction with syllabication.

Words like *gō, nō, mē,* and *hē* should also be noticed. The vowels are all long; there is only one vowel in the word; and *a vowel at the end of a one-vowel word (or syllable) usually has the long sound.*

The Effect of the Final e

Words that the children know as sight words should be listed on the board and sounded:

note	cake	cute
made	take	mile

The children are asked to listen to the vowel sound, and it is stressed that in each of the sounded words the first vowel stands for a long sound. The children are then asked to notice what all the words have in common: All the words have two vowels; one of the vowels is an *e,* which is always at the end of the word, and this *e* always has a consonant preceding it; the first vowel is long, and the final *e* is silent. The teacher then lists the following words on the board:

hat	cap	tub
kit	Tim	rob
can	not	hug
tap	cut	hop

The students read the words and tell what the vowel is and what kind of vowel sound the word has. The teacher then asks the children to put an *e* at the end of the words, so that the word list becomes the following:

hate	cape	tube
kite	time	robe
cane	note	huge
tape	cute	hope

The pupils are asked to read the words aloud. If they need help, the teacher reads the word. Again they are asked to notice what all the words have in common and what happened to the words when the final *e* was added to each of them.

The teacher, through observation and discussion, helps children develop the final *e* rule which states that *in words or syllables containing two vowels, separated by a consonant, one of which is a final* e, *the first vowel is usually long and the final* e *is silent.*[5]

Some practice exercises include a list of words to which children are instructed to add a final *e* to make a new word. The children then use both words in a sentence to show that they understand the difference in meaning between them. Another exercise shows their ability to recognize differences between words:

Directions: Put in the correct word.

1. He _____ himself. (cut, cute)
2. She is _____. (cut, cute)
3. I _____ you like my pet. (hop, hope)
4. I like to _____ on my foot. (hop, hope)
5. My friend's name is _____. (Tim, time)
6. What _____ is it? (Tim, time)

---

[5]When we say that a letter is silent, we mean that it does not add a sound to the syllable; however, it is just as important as any other letter in the syllable. It signals information about other letters, and it helps us to determine the sound represented by other letters.

Double Vowels

Digraphs

Two vowels adjacent to one another in a word (or syllable) stand for a single vowel sound and are called vowel digraphs. For example: *ea, oa, ai, ei, oe, ie* in words like *beat, boat, hail, receive, believe.* In first grade the children usually learn the rule that when two vowels appear together, the first is usually long and the second is silent. This rule usually does hold true for a number of vowel combinations such as *ai, oa, ea, ay,* and *ee;* however, there are exceptions, such as *ae, uy, eo, ew.* These digraphs are sounded as a single sound, but not with the long sound of the first. Some examples are *sew, buy, yeoman, Caesar.* Note that in the word *believe,* it is the *second* vowel that is long. Some vowel digraphs combine to form one sound that is not the long sound of either vowel. For example, in the words *neighbor, weigh,* and *freight,* the digraph *ei* is sounded as a long *a,* and in the word *sew* the digraph *ew* is sounded as a long *o,* with the *w* acting as a vowel. Note that in the word *rough* the digraph *ou* is not sounded as a long vowel.

Obviously, the teacher should spend time on those vowel combinations which are the most useful. These are *ea, oa, ai, ay,* and *ee.*

Diphthongs

Diphthongs are blends of vowel sounds beginning with the first and gliding to the second. The vowel blends are represented by two adjacent vowels. Examples include *ou, oi, oy, ow.* Some of these diphthongs can be confusing to children because the *ou* in *house* is a diphthong but the *ou* in *rough* is not a diphthong but a digraph. Note that in the word *how* the *w* acts as a vowel in the diphthong *ow.* (Even though a diphthong is a *blend* of two vowel sounds, for syllabication purposes you should consider it as one vowel sound.)

Vowel Controlled by *r*

A vowel followed by *r* in the same syllable is controlled by the *r.* As a result, the preceding vowel does not have the usual long or short vowel sound. For example: *car, fir, or, hurt, perch.* If a vowel is followed by *r,* but the *r* begins another syllable, the vowel is not influenced by the *r.* For example: $\bar{\imath} \cdot r\bar{a}t\not{e}$, $t\bar{\imath} \cdot r\bar{a}d\not{e}$.

Review of Vowel Generalizations

1. A long vowel is one which sounds like the name of the vowel.

2. A single vowel followed by a consonant in a word or syllable usually has a short vowel sound.

3. A single vowel at the end of a word or syllable usually has a long vowel sound.

4. A vowel digraph consists of two adjacent vowels with one vowel sound. Many times the first vowel is long and the second is silent. There are exceptions, such as *believe,* in which the two vowels form a single sound where the first vowel is not long, and *weigh,* in which the two vowels form a single sound but neither vowel is long.

5. In words or syllables containing two vowels separated by a consonant, and one vowel is a final *e,* the first vowel is usually long and the final *e* is silent, as in $b\bar{a}k\not{e}$.

6. A vowel followed by *r* in the same syllable is controlled by the consonant *r.*

7. When *y* is at the end of a word containing no other vowels, the *y* represents the long sound of *i,* as in *my, sky.*

8. Diphthongs are blends of vowel sounds beginning with the first and gliding to the second, as in *boy, boil, house.*

Review Exercise

Clues to Vowel Sounds

Here are five clues that will help in determining which vowel sound you would expect to hear in a one-syllable word:

1. A single vowel letter at the beginning or in the middle is a clue to a short vowel sound—as in *hat, let, it, hot,* and *cup.*
2. A single vowel letter at the end of a word is a clue to a long vowel sound—as in *we, by,* and *go.*
3. Two vowel letters together are a clue to a long vowel sound—as in *rain, day, dream, feel,* and *boat.*
4. Two vowel letters, separated by a consonant, and one vowel is a final *e,* are a clue to a long vowel sound—as in *age, ice, bone,* and *cube.*
5. A vowel letter followed by *r* in the same syllable is a clue to a vowel sound that is neither long nor short—as in *far, bird, her, horn, care,* and *hair.*

In the blank before each word write the number of the statement in the list that would help you determine the vowel sound in the word.

_____ she	_____ grave	_____ curb
_____ pill	_____ plot	_____ up
_____ oak	_____ drain	_____ pair
_____ lung	_____ harsh	_____ coax
_____ mane	_____ whine	_____ charm
_____ hurl	_____ freak	_____ plead
_____ bean	_____ ask	_____ flag

Special Letters and Sounds

Y

As already mentioned, *y* is used both as a consonant and a vowel. When *y* is at the beginning of a word or syllable, it is a consonant. For example: *yes, yet, young, your, canyon, graveyard.* In the words *canyon* and *graveyard, y* begins the second syllable; therefore it is a consonant.

When *y* acts as a vowel, it represents the short *i* sound, the long *i* sound, or the long *e* sound. *Y* usually represents the short *i* sound when *y* is in the middle of a word or syllable that has no vowel letter. For example: *hymn, gym, synonym, cymbal. Y* usually represents the long *i* sound when it is at the end of a single-syllable word that has no vowel letter. For example: *by, try, why, dry, fly. Y* usually represents the long *e* sound when it is at the end of a multisyllabic word. For example: *baby, candy, daddy, family.*

C and G

Some words beginning with *c* or *g* can cause problems because the letters *c* and *g* each stand for both a hard and a soft sound. The letter *g* in *gym, George, gentle,* and *generation* stands for a soft *g* sound. A soft *g* sounds like *j* in *Jack, jail,* and *justice.* The initial letter *c* in *cease, center, cent,* and *cite* stands for a soft *c* sound. A soft *c* sounds like *s* in *so, same,* and *sew.* The initial letter *g* in *go, get, game, gone,* and *garden* stands for a hard *g* sound. The initial letter *c* in *cat, came, cook, call,* and *carry* stands for a hard *c* sound. A hard *c* sounds like *k* in *key, king, kite, kettle.* Note that the letter *c* represents a sound that is either like the *s* in *see* or like the *k* in *kitten.*

Q

The letter *q* is always followed by the letter *u* in the English language. The *qu* combination represents either one speech sound or a blend of two sounds. At the beginning of a word, *qu* almost always represents a blend of two sounds, *kw.* For example: *queen, quilt, quiet, queer, quack.* When *qu* appears at the end of a word in the *que* combination, it represents one sound, *k*. For example: *unique, antique, clique.*

The Schwa (ə)

The *schwa* sound is symbolized by an upside down *e* (ə) in the phonetic (speech) alphabet. The schwa sound frequently appears in the unstressed (unaccented) syllables of words with more than one syllable. The schwa, which usually sounds like the short *u* in *but,* is represented by a number of different vowels, for example, believe (bə · lǰēvȼ ′), police (pə · lēs′), divide (də · vīdȼ ′), robust (rō´bəst), Roman (rō´mən). In these examples the italicized vowels represent the schwa sound. Although the spelling of the unstressed syllable in each word is different, the sound remains the same for the different vowels. (Note: The pronunciations presented here come from *Webster's New Collegiate Dictionary,* but it should not be inferred that these are the only pronunciations for these words. Pronunciations may vary from dictionary to dictionary and from region to region.)

Phonograms (Graphemic Bases)

A phonogram or graphemic base is a succession of graphemes that occurs with the same phonetic value in a number of words. For example: *at, ack, ake, ight, et, an, ook, am, ock,* and so on. All phonograms begin with a vowel, and words that contain the same phonogram rhyme, for example, *cake, bake, rake, lake, take,* and so on.

Phonograms may also be referred to as "word families." Knowledge of phonograms helps students build and unlock a large number of words on their own. For example, if a child knows the word *can,* he or she can build a number of words by merely changing the initial consonant. Children can use phonograms to unlock words in the following manner:

1. The child meets the unfamiliar word *tank.*
2. The child recognizes *ank* as a phonogram he has met in *bank.*
3. The child substitutes *t* for *b.*
4. The child blends *t* and *ank* to get *tank.*

In analyzing a student's word recognition strategies, the teacher usually tries to assess the child's ability to use phonograms to decode words (see page 182).

Syllabication—Intermediate Grades

A syllable is a vowel or a group of letters containing one vowel sound. Syllabication of words is the process of breaking down an unknown multisyllabic word into single syllables. This is important in word recognition because in order to be able to pronounce the word, a child must first be able to syllabicate it. Knowledge of syllabication is also helpful in spelling and writing. In attacking multisyllabic words, the pupil must first analyze the word, determine the syllabic units, apply phonic analysis to the syllables, and then blend them into a whole word.

Syllabication Rules

Since a multisyllabic word must be syllabicated before applying phonic analysis, syllabication rules will be given first. The vowel rules that the students have learned since first grade should be reviewed because these same rules will be used in the application of phonic analysis.

Rule 1: Vowel followed by two consonants and a vowel (vc/cv). If the first vowel in a word is followed by two consonants and a vowel, the word is divided between the two consonants.

Examples: but/ter can/dy com/ment

Rule 2: Vowel followed by a single consonant and a vowel (v/cv). If the first vowel is followed by one consonant and a vowel, the consonant usually goes with the second syllable.

Examples: be/gin ti/ger fe/ver pu/pil

There is an exception to the v/cv syllabication rule. If the letter *x* is between two vowels, the *x* goes with the first vowel rather than with the second one.

Examples: ex/it ex/act ox/en

Rule 3: Vowel or consonant followed by a consonant plus *le* (v/cle) or (vc/cle). If a consonant comes just before *le* in a word of more than one syllable, the consonant goes with *le* to form the last syllable.

Examples: sam/ple can/dle an/kle bun/dle pur/ple daz/zle bea/gle ca/ble

Rule 4: Compound words. Compound words are divided between the two words.

Examples: girl/friend base/ball

Rule 5: Prefixes and suffixes. Prefixes and suffixes usually stand as whole units.

Examples: re/turn kind/ly

Phonics Applied to Syllabicated Syllables

After the word has been divided into syllables, the student must determine how to pronounce the individual syllables. The pronunciation is determined by whether the syllable is open or closed and whether it contains a vowel digraph or diphthong:

Open syllable: one which contains one vowel and ends in a vowel. The vowel is usually sounded as long, as in *go*.
Closed syllable: one which contains one vowel and ends in a consonant. The vowel is usually sounded as short, as in *mat*.

Application of Vowel Rule to Syllabication Rule 1—Double Consonant Rule (vc/cv)

The closed-syllable vowel rule would apply to a syllable that contains one vowel and ends in a consonant. The vowel sound is usually short.
Examples: ăs/sĕt, căn/dy

Application of Vowel Rule to Syllabication Rule 2—Vowel Consonant Vowel Rule (v/cv)

The open-syllable rule would apply to a syllable that contains one vowel and ends in a vowel. The vowel sound is usually long.
Examples: bē/gin tī/ger ō/ver
    fā/tal dē/tour pū/pil

Application of Vowel Rule to Syllabication Rule 3—Special Consonant *le* Rule (v/cle) or (vc/cle)

If the syllable is closed as in *sad/dle* and *can/dle*, the vowel sound is usually short in the first syllable since it ends in a consonant. If the syllable is open as in *fā/ble* and *bū/gle*, the vowel sound is usually long in the first syllable, since it ends in a vowel. The letter combinations containing *le*—such as *cle, ble, gle, dle, kle, ple, tle,* and so on—usually stand as the final syllable. The final syllable is not accented; it is always an unstressed syllable containing the schwa sound.
Examples: sĭm/pəl fā/bəl săd/dəl
    ăp/pəl bū/gəl căn/dəl

Accenting Words

In order to pronounce words of more than one syllable the students must syllabicate the word, apply phonic analysis, and then blend the syllables into one word. In order to be able to blend the syllables into one word correctly, students must know something about accenting and how accents affect vowel sounds. Pupils should know that unaccented syllables are usually softened and, as already stated, if the syllable of a multisyllabic word is an unstressed syllable, it will often contain the schwa sound. Note: When syllables are blended together, the pronunciation may not be exactly the same as the syllable by syllable pronunciation.

Examples: (kĭt) (tĕn)—(kĭt ′tən); (bē) (lēvé)—(bə · lēvé′)

(Stressed syllables never contain the schwa sound.)

There may be differences between pronunciation of homographs (words that are spelled the same but have different meanings) due to a difference in accent.

Example: con′duct (noun) con duct′ (verb)

Accenting and accent marks are taught in conjunction with syllabication in the intermediate grades. Since children at this level do not meet too many words which require a secondary accent, the teaching emphasis should be on the primary accent.

Procedures for Teaching Accenting

A number of two-syllable words are placed on the board and syllabicated:

pi/lot	a/ble	ap/ple	va/cant
den/tist	rea/son	help/ful	bot/tle
sub/due	bun/dle	wis/dom	tai/lor
lo/cal	can/dle	jour/nal	

The teacher explains that even though students are able to syllabicate the individual words and are able to apply the proper phonic analysis, in order to be able to pronounce the word correctly, they still must know something about accenting the words.

Students are asked to listen while the teacher pronounces each word, to determine which syllable is stressed. The teacher then asks individual students to volunteer to pronounce the words, explaining that the syllable which is sounded with more stress in a two-syllable word is called the accented syllable. The teacher explains that the accent mark (′) is used to show which syllable is stressed, that is, spoken with greater intensity or loudness. This mark usually comes right after and slightly above the accented syllable. The teacher further explains that the dictionary has a key to pronunciation of words, and that the marks that show how to pronounce words are called *diacritical marks.* The most frequent diacritical marks are the breve (˘) and the macron (¯), which pupils have already met as the symbols for short and long vowel sounds. The accent (′) is also in the class of diacritical marks.

A list of words correctly syllabicated are put on the board:

pi′ lot	a′ ble	ap′ ple	pro′ gram
rea′ son	help′ ful	bot′ tle	jour′ nal
wis′ dom	tai′ lor	lo′ cal	den′ tist

Syllabication and vowel rules are then reviewed. The two-syllable words in the list above are all accented on the first syllable. Another group of words in which the second syllable is stressed are then listed:

ap point′	pro ceed′	as tound′
sub due′	pa rade′	po lite′
re ceive′	com plain′	pro vide′

Students are again asked to listen while each word is pronounced to determine which syllable is being stressed and to see if they notice any similarity among all the second syllables. They should notice that all stressed second syllables have two vowels. From their observations they should be able to state the following generalization: *In two-syllable words the first syllable is usually stressed, except when the second syllable contains two vowels.*

In three-syllable words it is usually the first or second syllable which is accented, as in *an' ces tor, cap' i tal, ho ri' zon.*

These skills for decoding of words are useful for all children, including those who speak nonstandard English. However, for those speaking nonstandard English or a foreign language the teacher must be especially certain to utilize the aural–oral approach before attempting to teach reading (see, for example, sections in Chapters 5 and 6). Obviously, the child must have the words that are to be decoded in both his or her hearing and speaking vocabularies in order to make the proper grapheme–phoneme associations.

Children who speak nonstandard English or a foreign language will need more practice in auditory discrimination and sound production, as was discussed in the previous chapters, before being able to read. This approach will facilitate the acquisition of phonic and word attack skills which will help these children to become proficient and independent readers. As was stated earlier, individual differences will determine when an approach is preferable with a given child or group. Teachers must be cautioned against attempting to teach such skills to all children, for they are not all able to learn phonic or syllabication rules. Students at low ability levels usually have difficulty with syllabication and accenting. (See Chapter 10 for some examples of teacher-made diagnostic tests for word recognition skills.)

Student's Name: _____

Grade: _____

Teacher: _____

Diagnostic Checklist for Word Recognition Skills

	Yes	No

1. The student uses
  a. context clues.
  b. picture clues (graphs, maps, charts).		

2. The student asks someone to state the word.		
3. The student uses the dictionary to try to unlock unknown words.		

4. The student uses phonic analysis by recognizing
  a. consonants.
    (1) single consonants: initial, final.
    (2) consonant blends (clusters) (*br, sl, cl, st,* and so on).
    (3) consonant digraphs (*th, sh, ph, ch,* and so on).
    (4) silent consonants (kn, gn, pn).		

Student's Name: _____

Grade: _____

Teacher: _____

Diagnostic Checklist for Word Recognition Skills (Cont.)

	Yes	No

    b. vowels.
       (1) short vowels (*cot, can, get,* and so on).
       (2) long vowels (*go, we, no,* and so on).
       (3) final silent *e* (*bake, tale, role*).
       (4) vowel digraphs (*ea, oa, ee, ai,* and so on).
       (5) diphthongs (*oi, oy*).
    c. the effect of *r* on the preceding vowel.
    d. special letters and sounds (*y, c, g,* and *q*).
    e. known phonograms or graphemic bases (a succession of graphemes that occurs with the same phonetic value in a number of words [*ight, id, at, ad, ack*]).

5. The student is able to apply the following syllabication rules to words:
    a. vowel consonant/consonant vowel rule (*vc/cv*) (*but/ter, can/dy*).
    b. vowel/consonant vowel rule (*v/cv*) (*na/tive, ca/bin*).
    c. special consonant *le* rule (*vc/cle*) or (*v/cle*) (*ca/ble, can/dle*).

6. The student is able to apply phonic analysis to syllabicated words with
    a. an open syllable (*no/ble*).
    b. a closed syllable (*can/dy*).
    c. a vowel digraph (*re/main*).
    d. a diphthong (*foi/ble*).

7. The student is able to apply the following accent rule to two-syllable words:
    Accent falls on the first syllable except when the second syllable has two vowels (tailor, career).

Student's Name: _____

Grade: _____

Teacher: _____

Diagnostic Checklist for Word Recognition Skills (Cont.)

	Yes	No

8. The student is able to use structural analysis to recognize
   a. compound words (*grandmother, caretaker*).
   b. the root or base of a word (*turn, state*).
   c. suffixes (*tion, al, ic, y*).
   d. prefixes (*re, un, non*).
   e. combining forms (*bio, cardio, auto*).
   f. derivatives.
      (1) root plus prefix (*return*).
      (2) root plus suffix (*turned*).
      (3) root plus prefix and suffix (*returned*).

(See Chapter 13 for an elaboration of the terms above.)

SUMMARY

Chapter 12 has presented an analytical look at word recognition skills. Word recognition in this book is looked on as a twofold process that includes both the recognition of printed symbols by some method so that the word can be pronounced and the association of meaning to the word after it has been pronounced. The emphasis in the chapter is on helping you to gain a better understanding of the word recognition process and the skills necessary to teach word recognition skills. After the strategies for word recognition are presented, a sequential development of phonics instruction and syllabic word attack skills are given. The emphasis on the phonics area is warranted because knowledge of phonics helps readers become more self-reliant in decoding words.

Also, unless teachers have the word analysis skills at their fingertips, they will not be able to diagnose a student's word recognition problems. You should be cautious, however, to note that phonics is but one part of the reading process and that knowledge of phonics does not mean that the student understands what he or she has read. A diagnostic checklist of word recognition skills was also presented.

SUGGESTIONS FOR THOUGHT QUESTIONS AND ACTIVITIES

1. You have been appointed to a special primary-grade reading committee. Your task is to help teachers better understand the role that phonics plays in the word

recognition process. How would you go about doing this?

2. You have been asked to give a workshop on creative activities that would help correct some students' word recognition problems. What are some activities you would present?

3. The administration in your school district has asked you to develop criterion-referenced tests for specific word recognition skills. What kind of tests would you construct for a primary grade? For an intermediate grade?

4. You have a child in your class who seems to have great difficulty retaining information. He needs extensive practice in order to overlearn his letters and words. You need to develop some activities that would be fun and that would help this child in a primary grade overlearn his initial consonants. What kind of activities would you develop to help this child?

5. Present a lesson that would help a primary-grade student correct a word recognition problem.

6. Present a lesson that would help you to determine the syllabication skills of an intermediate-grade level student.

SELECTED BIBLIOGRAPHY

Chall, Jeanne S. *Learning to Read: The Great Debate.* New York: McGraw-Hill, 1967.

Cuyler, Richard C. "Guidelines for Skill Development: Word Attack," *The Reading Teacher* 32 (January 1979):425–33.

Durkin, Dolores. *Strategies for Identifying Words: A Workbook for Teachers and Those Preparing to Teach,* 2nd ed. Boston: Allyn and Bacon, 1980.

Eeds-Kniep, Maryann. "The Frenetic Frantic Phonic Backlash." *Language Arts* 56 (November/December 1979):909–17.

Heilman, Arthur. *Phonics in Proper Perspective,* 3rd. ed. Columbus, Ohio: Merrill, 1976.

Jenkins, Barbara L., et al. "Children's Use of Hypothesis Testing When Decoding Words." *The Reading Teacher* 33 (March 1980):664–67.

Juel, Connie. "Comparison of Word Identification Strategies with Varying Context, Word Type, and Reader Skill." *Reading Research Quarterly* 15 (1980):358–76.

Rosso, Barbara, Rak Emans, and Robert Emans. "Children's Use of Phonic Generalizations." *The Reading Teacher* 34 (March 1981):653–57.

Speckels, Judith. "Poor Readers Can Learn Phonics." *The Reading Teacher* 34 (October 1980):22–26.

Wulz, S. Vanost, and John H. Hollis. "Word Recognition: A Task-based Definition for Testing and Teaching." *The Reading Teacher* 32 (April 1979):779–86.

Reading Comprehension and Vocabulary Expansion: An Emphasis on Diagnosis and Correction

INTRODUCTION

TEACHER X: John, in what year does this story take place?

JOHN: In 1945.

TEACHER X: Good.

TEACHER W: Maria, what conclusion can you draw from the story you have just read?

MARIA: Humans are at times inhumane.

TEACHER W: Good.

TEACHER S: Susan, how do you feel about the author's portrayal of the main character?

SUSAN: The character is portrayed in an unrealistic manner because . . .

TEACHER S: Good.

TEACHER Y: Tom, can you supply an ending to the story we have just read that is different from the author's?

TOM: I'll try. Everyone had left. He was now alone. However, he . . .

TEACHER Y: Good.

Although the questions posed by Teachers X, W, S, and Y are all comprehension questions, there is a wide range of difference in the difficulty of the questions. Teachers who persist in ask-ing only questions similar to the one asked by Teacher X are hindering their students and not helping them reach higher levels of thinking. Background knowledge of reading comprehension is important for teachers to be able to develop a reading program that includes higher levels of cognition. Also, in a diagnostic-reading and correction program, teachers must be able to diagnose their students' ability to comprehend what they read so that they can provide corrective measures for those students who need them. This chapter gives special emphasis to the diagnosis and correction of comprehension skills.

After you have finished reading this chapter you should be able to answer the following questions:

1. What are the categories of reading comprehension as presented in this chapter?

2. What are some of the reading comprehension skills?

3. What is the main idea of a paragraph?

4. How do you find the main idea of a paragraph?

5. What is inference?

6. How do context clues help in getting word meanings?

7. What are analogies?

8. What do you need to know to complete analogy proportions?

9. How can questioning be used as a diagnostic technique?

10. How can comprehension skills be presented using a diagnostic and corrective approach?

11. Why is skill in vocabulary expansion important?

12. What is the place of the dictionary in vocabulary expansion?

13. Why would you help students learn combining forms?

READING COMPREHENSION SKILLS

Reading comprehension is a complex intellectual process involving a number of abilities. The two major abilities concern word meanings and reasoning with verbal concepts.

Various writers have suggested different lists of skills that they feel are basic to understanding. The skills usually listed are as follows:

1. Associate experiences and meaning with the graphic symbol.

2. React to the sensory images (visual, auditory, kinesthetic, taste, smell) suggested by words.

3. Interpret verbal connotations and denotations.

4. Understand words in context and how to select the meaning that fits the context.

5 Give meaning to units of increasing size: the phrase, clause, sentence, paragraph, and whole selection.

6. Detect and understand the main ideas.

7. Recognize significant details.

8. Interpret the organization.

9. Answer questions about a printed passage.

10. Follow directions.

11. Perceive relationships: part-whole; cause-effect; general-specific; place, sequence, size, and time.

12. Interpret figurative expressions.

13. Make inferences and draw conclusions, supply implied details, and evaluate what is read.

14. Identify and evaluate character traits, reactions, and motives.

15. Anticipate outcomes.

16. Recognize and understand the writer's purpose.

17. Recognize literary and semantic devices and identify the tone, mood, and intent or purpose of the writer.

18. Determine whether the text affirms, denies, or fails to express an opinion about a supposed fact or condition.

19. Identify the antecedents of such words as *who, some,* or *they.*

20. Retain ideas.

21. Apply ideas and integrate them with one's past experience.[1]

CATEGORIZING READING COMPREHENSION

Comprehension involves thinking. As there are various levels in the hierarchy of thinking, so are there various levels of comprehension. Higher levels of comprehension would obviously include higher levels of thinking. The following model adapted from Nila Banton Smith divides the comprehension skills into four categories.[2] Each category is cumulative in that each builds on the others. The four comprehension categories are (1) literal comprehension, (2) interpretation, (3) critical reading, (4) creative reading.

Literal Comprehension

Literal comprehension represents the ability to obtain a low-level type of understanding by using only information explicitly stated. This category requires a lower level of thinking skills than the other three levels. Answers to literal questions simply demand that the pupil recall what the book says.

Interpretation

Interpretation is the next step in the hierarchy. This category demands a higher level of thinking because the questions are concerned with answers not directly stated in the text but suggested or implied. To answer questions at the interpretive level, readers must have problem-solving ability and be able to work at various levels of abstraction. Obviously, children who are slow learners will have difficulty working at this level as well as in the next two categories (see Chapter 16).

The interpretive level is the one at which the most confusion exists when it comes to categorizing skills. The confusion concerns the term *inference. Inference* may be defined as something derived by reasoning; something that is not directly stated but suggested in the statement; a logical conclusion that is drawn from statements; a deduction; an induction. From the definitions we can see that inference is a broad reasoning skill and that there are many different kinds of inferences. All the reading skills in interpretation rely on the reader's ability to "infer" the answer in one way or another. However, by grouping all the interpretive reading skills under inference, "some of the most distinctive and desirable skills would become smothered and obscured."[3]

Some of the reading skills that are usually found in interpretation are as follows:

> determining word meanings from context
> finding main ideas
> "reading between the lines" or drawing inferences[4]
> drawing conclusions
> making generalizations
> recognizing cause and effect reasoning
> recognizing analogies

Critical Reading

Critical reading is at a higher level than the other two categories because it involves evaluation, the making of a personal judgment on the accuracy, value, and truthfulness of what is read. To be able to make judgments, a reader must be able to collect, interpret, apply, analyze, and synthesize the information. Criti-

---

[2]Nila Banton Smith, "The Many Faces of Reading Comprehension," *The Reading Teacher* 23 (December 1969): 249-59, 291.

[3]Ibid., pp. 255-56.

[4]Although, as already stated, all the interpretive skills depend on the ability of the reader to infer meanings, the specific skill of "reading between the lines" is the one that teachers usually refer to when they say they are teaching *inference.*

cal reading includes such skills as the ability to differentiate between fact and opinion, the ability to differentiate between fantasy and reality, and the ability to discern propaganda techniques. Critical reading is related to critical listening because they both require critical thinking.

Creative Reading

Creative reading uses divergent thinking skills to go beyond the literal comprehension, interpretation, and critical reading levels. In creative reading, the reader tries to come up with new or alternate solutions to those presented by the writer.

TIME SPENT IN COMPREHENSION INSTRUCTION

Hardly any person would disagree with the statement that children need to be helped to acquire comprehension skills; without the ability to comprehend, reading would not take place. The question is: How much time is spent on comprehension instruction in the schools? Durkin, a noted reading researcher, undertook a study to determine the answer to this question. She found that teachers spend very little time on comprehension instruction; they attend to written assignments; and none of the teachers in the study views social studies as a time to help with reading instruction.[5] In that part of the study dealing with fourth grade, the researcher reports that "less than 1 per cent (28 minutes [out of 4,469 minutes]) went to comprehension instruction."[6] The results are startling;

however, another researcher reexamined Durkin's data and found that by broadening the definition of comprehension instruction, she could state that "some teachers are attempting to teach reading comprehension approximately one-fourth of the time they are involved in teaching reading and social studies."[7] These findings seem more realistic.

What is devastating is that reading authorities do not expect to find comprehension instruction in the primary grades. For example, Durkin did not initiate her study in the primary grades because she felt that there is less comprehension instruction "in the primary grades because of the concern there for decoding skills. . . ."[8] Durkin also states that she chose fourth grade as one part of her three-prong study "because it is commonly believed that at that level a switch is made from *learning to read* to *reading to learn*. It is also at that level that content subjects begin to be taken seriously."[9]

As has already been stated in Chapter 5, *learning to read* and *reading to learn* are not two mutually exclusive processes; they can and should take place together. Children in the lower grades as well as in the higher grades should be involved in both. The following section will help you gain a better insight on how to help primary-grade and intermediate-grade level children acquire comprehension skills.

HELPING CHILDREN ACQUIRE COMPREHENSION SKILLS

All children need help in developing higher level reading comprehension skills. If teachers persist in asking only literal comprehension

---

[5]Dolores Durkin, "What Classroom Observations Reveal About Reading Comprehension," *Reading Research Quarterly* 14, No. 4 (1978–1979): 533.
[6]Ibid., p. 497.

[7]Carol A. Hodges, "Toward a Broader Definition of Comprehension Instruction," *Reading Research Quarterly* 15, No. 2 (1980): 305.
[8]Durkin, op. cit., p. 493.
[9]Ibid., p. 494.

questions that demand a simple convergent answer, higher-level skills will not be developed.

Unfortunately, much of what goes on in school is at the literal comprehension level. Teachers usually ask questions that require a literal response, and children who answer this type of question are generally seen as being excellent students. It is to be hoped that this perception will change now that many reading task forces across the country are emphasizing the teaching of higher-level comprehension skills.

The kinds of questions the teacher asks will determine the kinds of answers he or she will receive. Rather than asking a question that would call for a literal response, the teacher must learn to construct questions that call for higher levels of thinking. This should begin as early as kindergarten and first grade. For example, the children are looking at a picture in which a few children are dressed in hats, snow pants, jackets, scarves, and so on. After asking the children what kind of clothes the children in the picture are wearing, the teacher should try to elicit from his or her students the answers to the following questions: "What kind of day do you think it is?" "What do you think the children are going to do?"

This type of inference question is at a very simple level because it is geared to the readiness and cognitive development level of the children. As the children progress to higher levels of thinking they should be confronted with more complex interpretation or inference problems. It is important that the teacher work with the children according to their individual readiness levels. The teacher should expect all the children to be able to perform, but he or she should avoid putting them in situations which frustrate rather than stimulate them.

Critical reading skills are essential for good readers. Teachers can use primary-graders' love of fairy tales to begin to develop some critical reading skills. For example, after the children have read "Little Red Riding Hood," the teacher can ask such questions as the following:

1. Should Little Red Riding Hood have listened to her mother and not spoken to a stranger? Explain.

2. Would you help a stranger if your mother told you not to speak to a stranger? Explain.

3. Do you think a wolf can talk? Explain.

4. Do you think that this story is true? Explain.

5. Do you think Little Red Riding Hood is a good girl? Explain.

Creative reading questions are probably the most ignored by teachers. To help children in this area, teachers need to learn how to ask questions that require divergent rather than convergent answers. A teacher who focuses only on the author's meaning or intent and does not go beyond the text will not be encouraging creative reading. Some questions which should stimulate divergent thinking on the part of the reader would be the following:

1. After reading "Little Red Riding Hood," can you come up with another ending for the story?

2. After reading about John, can you come up with a plan for the kind of vacation he would like?

3. After reading the story about the cat that escaped from the well, can you come up with some ideas as to how he was able to escape?

4. Based on your reading about John and his family, what kind of trip would you plan to make them happy?

Divergent answers, of course, require more time than convergent answers. Also, there is no one correct answer.

Following are a short reading selection and examples of the four different types of comprehension questions. These are being presented so that the teacher can have practice in recognizing the different types of questions at the four levels.

> One day in the summer, some of my friends and I decided to go on an overnight hiking trip. We all started out fresh and full of energy. About halfway to our destination, when the sun was almost directly overhead, one-third of my friends decided to return home. The remaining four of us, however, continued on our hike. Our plan was to reach our destination by sunset. About six hours later as the four of us, exhausted and famished, were slowly edging ourselves in the direction of the setting sun, we saw a sight that astonished us. There, at the camping site, were our friends who had claimed that they were returning home. It seems that they did indeed go home, but only to pick up a car and drive out to the campsite.

The following are the four different types of comprehension questions:

Literal comprehension: What season of the year was it in the story? What kind of trip were the persons going on?

Interpretation: What time of day was it when some of the people decided to return home? How many persons were there when they first started out on the trip? In what direction were the hikers heading when they saw a sight that astonished them? At what time did the sun set?

Critical reading: How do you think the hikers felt when they reached their destination? Do you feel that the persons who went home did the right thing by driving back to the site rather than hiking? Explain.

Creative reading: What do you think the exhausted hikers did and said when they saw the four who had supposedly gone home?

QUESTIONING AS A DIAGNOSTIC TECHNIQUE

Asking questions is an important part of teaching, learning, and diagnosing. Teachers' questions, which can stimulate students to either low- or high-level thinking, give teachers an insight into students' ability to comprehend information. Teachers can learn from their questions whether students need help, whether they are able to see relationships and make comparisons, and whether what the students are reading or listening to is too difficult or too easy.

Students' questions are important in helping students to learn, and they are essential diagnostic aids in giving teachers feedback on students' ability to understand information. In order to ask good questions, students must know their material. As a result, those students who ask the best questions usually are those who know the material best. Confusing questions are a signal that the teacher needs to slow down or reteach certain material.

Teachers can use questioning as a diagnostic technique to learn about their students' thinking ability. Here are some examples.

The teacher has the children read a short story. The story is about a little boy who wants to go to school, but he can't because he is too young. The teacher tells the children that she is going to make up some questions about the story, and the children have to tell her whether the questions that she makes up are able to be answered or not. If a question is able to be answered, the student should answer it; if a question is not able to be answered, the student must tell why. The teacher makes up the following questions:

1. What are the names of Ben's sister and brother who go to school?

2. Why does Ben want to go to school?

3. Make up an adventure for Ben.

4. Why can't Ben go to school?

5. What are the names of the bus driver's children?

6. What does Ben do in the summer?

This technique can help the teacher learn which children are able to concentrate, as well as which children are able to do different kinds of thinking. Questions 1 and 4 are literal questions; question 2 is an inferential question; question 3 is a creative question; and questions 5 and 6 are not able to be answered because no such information was given in the story either directly or indirectly.

A more difficult questioning technique that the teacher could use with highly able children is to have them make up questions for a selection that they have read.

After students have read a selection, the teacher can ask them to make up three different questions. The first question should be one for which the information is directly stated in the passage. The second question should be one for which the answer is not directly stated in the passage. The third question should be one that requires an answer that goes beyond the text.

In early primary grades the teacher can use pictures as the stimuli for questions, or the teacher can relate a short story to the children and have them devise questions for it.

Here are some questions that a group of fourth-grade children made up after reading a story about Melissa and her friend Fred, who were always getting into trouble.

1. Who is Melissa's best friend? (literal)

2. What is the main idea of the story? (inferential)

3. From the story what can we infer about the main character's personality? (inferential)

4. Relate an episode that you think Melissa could get into. (creative)

The children who made up the questions challenged their classmates with their questions and then they were responsible for determining whether their classmates had answered them correctly.

SOME IMPORTANT COMPREHENSION SKILLS: A DIAGNOSTIC AND CORRECTIVE APPROACH

This section presents some comprehension skills that need special emphasis. Because this book emphasizes a diagnostic-reading and correction program, the interpretive reading skills will be presented using a diagnostic and corrective approach for both primary- and intermediate-grade children. Even though only some interpretive level skills have been chosen to demonstrate this approach, you can, of course, use it with literal, critical, and creative reading skills.

Because of the ambiguity of language, the first portion of this section will deal with *homographs.* Unless teachers can help students discern that words have multiple meanings and help them to determine the correct meaning from the context, students will not be able to read. Because *context clues* are a vital aid to comprehension, a brief discussion of some often used context clues is also being presented. *Finding the main idea of a paragraph* is the comprehension skill on which teachers probably spend the most time. It is also a skill that is many times taken for granted—it is assumed that preservice teachers can find the main idea of a paragraph and that teachers can help their students do the same. This assumption is often not borne out. Other interpretive skills that are often neglected by teachers because of their own insecurities in these areas will be presented, as well as a diagnostic checklist for selected reading comprehension skills.

Determining Meanings of Words with Multiple Meanings (Homographs)[10]

Because many words have more than one meaning, the meaning of a particular word is determined by the position (syntax) of the word in a sentence and from meaning (semantic) clues of the surrounding words. You must help students to be careful to use correctly those words with many meanings. In the following pairs of sentences, notice how the same italicized word conveys different meanings:

> That is a large *stack* of books.
> *Stack* the books here.
>
> The *train* had a lot of passengers.
> Do you *train* your own dog?
>
> The dogs *bark* at night in my neighborhood.
> The *bark* of the tree is peeling.

From these, you can see that the way the word is used in the sentence will determine its meaning. Words that are spelled the same but have different meanings are called *homographs.* Some homographs are spelled the same but do not sound the same. For example, *refuse* means "trash," but it also means "to decline to accept." In the first sentence, *refuse* (ref ' use) meaning "trash" is pronounced differently from *refuse* (re fuse ') meaning "to decline to accept" in the second sentence. In reading you can determine the meaning of *refuse* from the way it is used in the sentence (context clues). For example:

[10] Dorothy Rubin, *The Vital Arts—Reading and Writing* (New York: Macmillan, 1979).

1. During the garbage strike there were tons of uncollected *refuse* on the streets of the city.
2. I *refuse* to go along with you.

As already shown, readers should be able to grasp the meaning of homographs from the sentence context (the words surrounding a word that can shed light on its meaning). For example, note the many uses of *capital* in the following sentences.

> That is a *capital* idea.
> Remember to begin each sentence with a *capital* letter.
> The killing of a policeman is a *capital* offense in some states.
> Albany is the *capital* of New York State.
> In order to start a business, you need *capital.*

Each of the preceding sentences illustrates one meaning for *capital.*

> In sentence 1 *capital* means "excellent."
> In sentence 2 *capital* means "referring to a letter in writing that is an uppercase letter."
> In sentence 3 *capital* means "punishable by death."
> In sentence 4 *capital* means "the seat of government."
> In sentence 5 *capital* means "money or wealth."

Special Note

Confusion may exist among the terms *homonym, homophone,* and *homograph* because some authors are using the more scientific or linguistic definition for the terms, and others are using the more traditional definition. *Homonyms* have traditionally been defined as words that sound alike, are spelled differently, and have different meanings, for example, *red, read.* However, many linguists use the term *homophone* rather than homonym for this meaning. Linguists generally use the term *homonym* for words which are spelled the same, pronounced the same, but have different meanings, for example, *bat* (the mouselike winged mammal) and *bat* (the name for a club used to hit a ball). *Bat* (baseball bat) and *bat* (animal) would traditionally be considered homographs (words that are spelled the same but have different meanings), but linguists usually define *homographs* as words that are spelled the same but have *different pronunciations and different meanings,* for example, *lead* (dense metal) and *lead* (verb).

The teacher should be aware that different textbooks may be defining the three terms somewhat differently and should be familiar with the various systems and definitions in use. An attempt to find out which terms students have been exposed to and continued use of them will establish consistency, at least until pupils are old enough to understand the differences.

In this book the generic definition of homograph is used; that is, homographs are words that are spelled the same but have different meanings, and the words may or may not be pronounced the same.

UPPER PRIMARY-GRADE LEVEL

SKILL: MULTIPLE MEANINGS (HOMOGRAPHS)
Diagnostic Analysis

Objective: The students will be able to state the one word that has multiple meanings to fit the blanks in each sentence.

Criterion-Referenced Test

Directions: Read each sentence carefully. Choose a word from the list that is spelled the same but has different meanings that would fit all the blanks of the sentence. The sentence must make sense. There are more words given as answers than you need.[11]

Word list: tall, fall, spring, feed, train, cat, pet, cry, bark, can.

1. I _____ carry that heavy _____ of beans.

2. My dog will _____ if you pick the _____ off the tree.

3. I need to _____ my dog not to bark when he hears the _____ .

4. During the _____ , the leaves begin to _____ in some parts of the country.

5. My _____ doesn't like you to _____ it too much.

> Answers: 1. can   2. bark   3. train   4. fall   5. pet
> Tell students the results.

[11]Dorothy Rubin, *The Teacher's Handbook of Primary-Grade Reading/Thinking Exercises* (New York: Holt, Rinehart and Winston, 1982).

UPPER PRIMARY-GRADE LEVEL

SKILL: MULTIPLE MEANINGS (HOMOGRAPHS)
Diagnostic Analysis

Objective: The students will be able to state the one word that has multiple meanings that will fit each set of given meanings.

Criterion-Referenced Test

> **Directions: Read each set of meanings carefully. Think of a word that is spelled the same but has different meanings that would fit each set of meanings. Put the word in the blank.**[12]

1. You weigh yourself on these. A fish has these. _____

2. You call pennies, nickels, and dimes this. You do this to your clothing. _____

3. You do this to an envelope. This animal lives in the water, and it can balance a ball on

   its nose. _____

4. You can lie on this in the water. You can do this in the water. _____

Answers: 1. scales   2. change   3. seal   4. float
Tell students the results.

Correction: Here are some instructional techniques and materials you can use with your students to help them recognize that words can have more than one meaning.

1. Hold up two pictures. The first picture is that of a train, and the second picture shows a boy trying to train his dog. Ask the children what the two pictures have in common. Try to get them to make up sentences about what is taking place. Write the sentences about the two pictures on the board. Try to get them to use the word *train* for both pictures.

2. Hold up a number of pictures that depict the words *slip, root,* and *bark* in more than one way. Try to get the children to recognize that each set of pictures is different, but that the word telling what each picture in the set is about is the same. You can tell the students that words

with more than one meaning are usually called *homographs.*

3. Put the following sentences on the chalkboard and have the students fill in the blanks with one word that fits all the blanks in each sentence. Go over the sentences with the children.

1. I _____ my father _____ the tree in the woods. (saw)

2. In the _____ our flowers look very pretty near our _____ . (spring)

3. My mother says that I _____ help her _____ some vegetables from her garden. (can)

4. Don't you _____ when you change a flat _____ ? (tire)

5. After we drank water from the _____ , we did not feel _____ . (well)

[12]Ibid.

4. Challenge the children with riddles such as the following: I can make things brighter, I am part of a camera; and plants develop from me. What am I? Hint: One word fits all three things.

5. Ask the children to use their dictionaries to try to make up riddles to challenge their classmates.

INTERMEDIATE-GRADE LEVEL

SKILL: MULTIPLE MEANINGS (HOMOGRAPHS)
Diagnostic Analysis

Objective: The students will be able to state the one word that has multiple meanings to fit the blanks in each sentence.

Criterion-Referenced Test

Directions: Read each sentence carefully. Think of a word that is spelled the same but has different meanings that would fit all the blanks of the sentence and make sense. Insert this word in the blanks.[13]

1. My mind goes _____ every time I have to fill in any _____.

2. In England, I paid two _____ for a book to help me shed some _____.

3. The lawyer knew that he had won his _____ when he produced the _____ containing the murder weapon.

4. A certain _____ of dogs is easier to _____ than others.

5. After he had drunk a lot of _____, he wasn't in very good _____ because he thought that he saw _____.

6. Part of the _____ was to _____ a course that no one could follow after we hid the jewels in the chosen cemetery _____.

7. The police said that they would _____ everyone who was standing by the barbeque _____ at the time of the murder.

8. I always _____ by some _____ when I deliver a speech about my _____ on something.

Answers: 1. blank 2. pounds 3. case 4. breed 5. spirits 6. plot 7. grill 8. stand
Tell students the results.

---

[13]Dorothy Rubin, *The Teacher's Handbook of Reading/Thinking Exercises* (New York: Holt, Rinehart and Winston, 1980).

INTERMEDIATE-GRADE LEVEL

SKILL: MULTIPLE MEANINGS (HOMOGRAPHS)
Diagnostic Analysis

Objective: The students will be able to state the one word with multiple meanings that will fit each set of meanings.

Criterion-Referenced Test

> **Directions: Read each *set* of meanings carefully. Find the one word that fits all the definitions in each set. Insert this word in the blank.**[14]

1. I'm a fruit that's good to eat, but I can also be a very desirable position or thing.

   _____

2. I can be a great many things, and usually I'm the chief or leader. I play a prime position in any activity, including a play; even in finance I'm a capital sum. _____

3. I'm what you do to tea; I'm hard to climb; and I make prices very high.

   _____

4. I'm a geographical feature; I'm produced by an orchestra; and I mean fine, good, or logical. _____

> Answers: 1. plum   2. principal   3. steep   4. sound
> Tell students the results.

Correction: Here are some techniques and instructional materials you can use to help students recognize that words can have more than one meaning.

1. Present students with a number of phrases. Tell them that the same word can fit in each set of phrases. The meaning of the word changes based on the words surrounding it (context). For example: a *brush* with the law; *brush* your teeth; a *brush* for your hair. Have them do the following exercise:

> **Directions: Read each set of phrases carefully. Think of a word that is spelled the same but has different meanings that would fit all the blanks in each set of phrases. Insert the word in the blanks.**[15]

1. _____ call; jelly _____ ; _____ of wallpaper; _____ back; _____ up.

[14]Dorothy Rubin, *The Intermediate-Grade Teacher's Language Arts Handbook* (New York: Holt, Rinehart and Winston, 1980).
[15]Rubin, *The Teacher's Handbook of Reading/Thinking Exercises.*

2. Flower _____ ; from _____ to stern; a goblet _____ ; _____ the leak.

3. A high _____ ; _____ card; four _____ and twenty; a musical _____ .

4. _____ colors; _____ asleep; to break a(n) _____ ; run _____ .

5. A(n) _____ person; to _____ someone; a(n) _____ fever; a(n) _____ amount.

6. _____ of a whip; _____ shut; not a(n) _____ ; _____ one's finger at; a(n) _____ decision.

7. A(n) _____ decision; a skin _____ .

8. A strong _____ ; _____ a ship.

9. _____ straw; at _____ ; _____ word; _____ night; the _____ person.

10. A monkey _____ ; to _____ free; to _____ a part of the body.

2. State a word such as *run*. Present the following sentences to your students and ask them to give the meaning of *run* in each sentence. Have them note that the meaning is different for each. Have them look up *run* in the dictionary. Have them write four other sentences using *run* in different ways.

1. I have a _____ in my stocking. _____

2. My brother will _____ for office in the next election. _____

3. Don't _____ so fast. _____

4. Let's give them a _____ for their money. _____

Present the following exercise to your students:

Directions: Read each *set* of sentences carefully. Figure out the one word that fits in each set of sentences. Insert this word in the blank. Then give the meaning of the word as it is used in each different sentence.[16]

SET I

1. At that _____ a waiter came to take our order. _____

2. What was your _____ ? _____

---

[16]Rubin, *The Intermediate-Grade Teacher's Language Arts Handbook.*

3. We went to the _____ for our vacation. _____

4. The _____ of the dagger scratched my arm. _____

SET II

1. What is the tax _____ ? _____

2. Play that in the major _____ of C. _____

3. A fish has _____ s. _____

4. Don't use that _____ to weigh yourself because it's broken.

Context Clues

Sentence context also helps readers figure out words that are not homographs. For example, in the following sentence see if you can figure out the meaning of *hippodrome*.[17]

> In ancient times the Greek people would assemble in their seats to observe the chariot races being held in the *hippodrome*.

From the context of the sentence, you should have realized that *hippodrome* refers to some arena (place) where races were held in ancient Greece.

Sometimes readers can actually gain the definition of the word from the sentence or following sentences. For example:

> The house had a cheerful atmosphere. At any moment I expected *blithe* spirits to make their entrance and dance with joy throughout the house.

From the sentences, readers can determine that *blithe* refers to something joyful, gay, or merry.

Alert readers can also use contrasts or comparisons for clues to meanings of words. For ex-

SMIDGENS   by Bob Cordray

I'M TOO WEAK TO STOP AND TALK, LEON! I CAUGHT THE FLU AT WORK TODAY!

WHY DON'T YOU GO TO THE DOCTOR?

CAN'T AFFORD IT!

DON'T YOU HAVE GROUP INSURANCE AT WORK?

SURE... BUT THEY WON'T PAY ANYTHING UNLESS THE WHOLE **GROUP** GETS SICK!

© 1975 National News Syndicate

Figure 13.1.

---

[17] Dorothy Rubin, *Gaining Word Power* (New York: Macmillan, 1978).

ample, try to determine the meaning of *ethereal* in the following sentence:

> He was impressed by the *ethereal* grace of Jane's walk rather than Ellen's heavy-footed one.

If you guessed "light and airy" for the meaning of *ethereal,* you were correct. You know that *ethereal* is somehow the opposite of *heavy*. This is an example of contrasts.

In the next example, see how comparisons can help you:

Maria was as *fickle* as a politician's promises before election.

In this sentence *fickle* means "not firm in opinion" or "wavering." Because politicians try to court all their constituents (voters) before an election, they often are not firm in their opinions, make many promises, and are wavering. By understanding the comparison, readers can get an idea of the meaning of *fickle.*

Good readers use all these kinds of clues to help them determine word meanings.

UPPER PRIMARY-GRADE LEVEL

SKILL: CONTEXT CLUES
Diagnostic Analysis

Objective: The students will be able to use context clues to choose the word that best fits the sentence.

Criterion-Referenced Test

> **Directions: Read each sentence carefully. Use context clues to help you choose the word that *best* fits the sentence. Put the word in the blank. A word may be used only once. All words are used as answers.**[18]

Word List: rose, point, suit, box, play.

1. That was a good _____ she made in the game.

2. The pitcher stood in the _____.

3. We _____ late yesterday.

4. That color does not _____ you.

5. What is the _____ of the story?

> Answers: 1. play   2. box   3. rose   4. suit   5. point
> Tell students the results.

[18]Rubin, *The Teacher's Handbook of Primary-Grade Reading/Thinking Exercises.*

UPPER PRIMARY-GRADE LEVEL

SKILL: CONTEXT CLUES
Diagnostic Analysis

Objective: The students will be able to use context clues to figure out the meaning of the underlined word in a sentence.

Criterion-Referenced Test

> **Directions: Read each sentence carefully. Use the context clues to help you figure out the meaning of the underlined word. Sometimes the clue to help you figure out the word meaning is in the next sentence.**[19]

1. It is <u>difficult</u> for me to climb a rope. _____

2. It seemed <u>incredible</u> that he could do all that work in one hour. _____

3. The <u>valiant</u> knight fought the dragon. _____

4. The doctors said that they had no quick <u>remedy</u> for the child's illness.

_____

5. The material was so <u>coarse</u> that it hurt my skin. _____

> Answers: 1. hard 2. unbelievable 3. brave 4. cure 5. rough
> Tell students the results.

Correction: Here are some techniques and instructional materials to help students recognize how context clues can help them figure out word meanings.

1. Present the following sentence to your students, which should have an unfamiliar word in it.

Mary is usually a prudent person.

Ask them if they can give you the meaning of *prudent.* If not, ask them what would help. Then present this sentence.

However, yesterday she was very foolish.

Now ask them if they can figure out the meaning of *prudent.* Elicit from the children how the second sentence gave them a clue to the word *prudent.* From the second sentence, they should have realized that prudent must mean "wise," the opposite of *foolish.*

2. Present the following exercise to the students.

[19]Ibid.

Directions: Read each sentence carefully. Use the context clues to help you figure out the meaning of the underlined word. Sometimes the clue to help you figure out the word meaning is in the next sentence.[20]

1. My kitten is very tame. She will not hurt anyone. _____

2. Everyone seems to know her. She must be a famous writer. _____

3. That is such an enormous ice-cream cone. You will have to get lots of people to help you eat some of it. _____

4. That street is so broad that we can all walk side by side. _____

5. The lion is a fierce animal. _____

INTERMEDIATE-GRADE LEVEL

SKILLS: CONTEXT CLUES
Diagnostic Analysis

Objective: The students will be able to use context clues to choose a word that makes sense in each sentence.

Criterion-Referenced Test

Directions: Read each sentence carefully. Use context clues to help you choose the word that *best* fits the sentence. A word may only be used once. (More words are given in the word list than you need.) Insert the word in the blank.[21]

Word List: buy, browse, pine, economy, suit, take, play, box, bore, pinch, coat, blade, post, rose, idle, work, iron, spectacles, posture, run, flowed, clothing, happy, fast, sell, dress

1. Good looks _____ in her family.

2. At the stadium the crowd _____ through the gate.

3. The pitcher was still in his or her _____.

4. At the library, I usually _____ through lots of books.

5. They said that they would try to _____ out their difficulties.

6. The children _____ for their dog who is missing.

7. During holidays, I usually feel the money _____.

---

[20]Ibid.
[21]Rubin, *The Teacher's Handbook of Reading/Thinking Exercises.*

8. Unless my mother wears her _____ , she has difficulty seeing.

9. The senators surveyed the _____ of foreign affairs.

10. It is not good to allow your car motor to _____ .

11. That color doesn't _____ you.

12. In our science class we examined a(n) _____ of grass under the micro-scope.

13. After she _____ from her chair, we noticed that she was hurt.

14. The carpenter _____ a hole in a classroom wall.

15. A number of people went on a(n) _____ to protest conditions at their place of work.

> Answers: 1. run 2. flowed 3. box 4. browse 5. iron 6. pine 7. pinch 8. spectacles
> 9. posture 10. idle 11. suit 12. blade 13. rose 14. bore 15. fast
> Tell students the results.

INTERMEDIATE-GRADE LEVEL

SKILL: CONTEXT CLUES
Diagnostic Analysis

Objective: The students will be able to use context clues to figure out the meanings of words in sentences.

Criterion-Referenced Test

> **Directions: Using the context clues, determine the meaning of the underlined word as it is used in each sentence. Sometimes the clue to help you figure out the word meaning is in the next sentence. Write your answer in the space provided.**[22]

1. In the alphabet, the letter *r* <u>precedes</u> the letter *s*. _____

2. Jane is the <u>recipient</u> of three science awards. She received the awards because of her work in controlling air pollution. _____

3. Mary plays a <u>dual</u> role in the play. In the first act she's a teen-ager, and in the second act she's middle-aged. _____

[22]Ibid.

4. John is a very <u>conscientious</u> person; that is, he is very particular, thorough, and careful about everything he does. _____

5. It's interesting that in the same family you can have brothers and sisters, <u>siblings</u>, who are so different from one another. _____

6. Ellen has much more <u>stamina</u> than her sister Judy, who has no endurance for exertion. _____

7. When you <u>pilfer</u> something, you steal in small quantities or amounts.

_____

8. He is a <u>candid</u> person; that is, he is always frank and open. _____

9. We didn't want Mr. Jones at our assembly because he is always so long-winded and <u>verbose</u>. _____

10. It seems odd to be <u>clad</u> in such heavy clothes in the month of July. _____

Answers: 1. comes before 2. receiver 3. double 4. careful, thorough 5. brothers or sisters 6. resistance to fatigue 7. steal in small quantities 8. frank 9. wordy 10. dressed Tell students the results.

Correction: Here are some instructional materials and techniques to use with your students.

1. Present your students with the following sentence that has an unfamiliar word.

Jim behaved in a very *rash* manner.

Ask your students why this sentence does not help them figure out the meaning of *rash*. Then present them with this sentence:

He rushed in too quickly and almost lost his life.

Now ask them to try to determine the meaning of *rash*. From the second sentence, they should recognize that *rash* refers to something that is done quickly and not very carefully.

2. Give them a sentence which uses comparison and ask them to see if they can figure out the meaning of an unfamiliar word.

Fred is as *obstinate* as a mule.

Ask the students to give you the meaning of *obstinate*. Since a mule is an animal that is considered stubborn, your students should get an idea of *obstinate* as meaning "stubborn."

3. Here is another exercise you can use with your students.

Directions: Read the first sentence of the story to get a clue to what the story is about. Then read each sentence that has a missing word or words very carefully. Using context clues, insert a word in each blank so that the story makes sense.[23]

In the year 2022 many families live on the moon. Life on the (1) _____ is a great (2) _____ different (3) _____ earth (4) _____.

To give (5) _____ an idea (6) _____ life (7) _____ the moon, let's follow Alison, a nine-(8) _____-old. Most (9) _____ Alison awakens (10) _____ 7:00 A.M. Moontime. (11) _____ puts on (12) _____ special moonsuit (13) _____ moonshoes, and then she goes to (14) _____ community bathroom. (You see, everyone (15) _____ the (16) _____ lives together in (17) _____ huge bubblelike enclosure.) In (18) _____ community bathroom, Alison enters (19) _____ special room in which she (20) _____ off her moon (21) _____. After (22) _____ bath, Alison redresses (23) _____ goes to the large community social (24) _____ to meet with (25) _____ family (26) _____ plan for the day. Alison wonders (27) _____ exciting (28) _____ she (29) _____ do (30) _____ learn today.

Finding the Main Idea of a Paragraph[24]

In reading and writing, finding the main idea is very useful. In reading, the main idea helps you to remember and understand what you have read. In writing, the main idea gives unity and order to your paragraph.

The main idea of a paragraph is the central thought of the paragraph. It is what the paragraph is about. Without a main idea, the paragraph would just be a confusion of sentences. All the sentences in the paragraph should develop the main idea.

To find the main idea of a paragraph, you must find what common element the sentences share. Some textbook writers place the main idea at the beginning of a paragraph and may actually put the topic of the paragraph in bold print in order to emphasize it. However, in literature this is not a common practice. In some paragraphs the main idea is not directly stated but implied. That is, the main idea is indirectly stated, and you have to find it from the clues given by the author.

Although there is no foolproof method for finding the main idea, there is a widely used procedure that has proved to be helpful. In order to use this procedure you should know that a paragraph is always written about something or

[23]Ibid.
[24]Rubin, *The Vital Arts—Reading and Writing.*

someone. The something or someone is the topic of the paragraph. The writer is interested in telling his or her readers something about the topic of the paragraph. To find the main idea of a paragraph, you must determine what the topic of the paragraph is and what the author is trying to say about the topic that is special or unique. Once you have found these two things, you should have the main idea. This procedure is useful in finding the main idea of various types of paragraphs.

Reread the preceding paragraph and state its main idea. *Answer:* A procedure helpful in finding the main idea of a paragraph is described.

Now read the following passage from "Fight Fat with Behavior Control" by Michael J. Mahoney and Kathryn Mahoney, in *Psychology Today* (May 1976). After you have read the passage, choose the statement that *best* states the main idea.

> In our society, food is often connected with recreation. We go out for coffee, invite friends over for drinks, celebrate special occasions with cakes or big meals. We can't think of baseball without thinking of hot dogs and beer, and eating is so often an accompaniment to watching TV that we talk of TV snacks and TV dinners. Just as Pavlov's dogs learned to salivate at the sound of a bell, the activities we associate with food can become signals to eat. Watching TV becomes a signal for potato chips; talking with friends becomes a signal for coffee and doughnuts; nodding over a book tells us it's time for pie and milk.

1. Watching TV signals a need for food.
2. All persons connect food with recreation.
3. Eating is a social activity.
4. Recreation, in our society, often serves as a signal for food.
5. In all societies food is often connected with recreation.

The answer is statement 4. Statement 1 is a fact in the paragraph, but it is too specific to be the main idea. Statement 2 is too general. The paragraph is not discussing all persons. Statement 3 can be inferred from the paragraph, but it is not the main idea of the paragraph. Statement 5 is too general. Statement 4 is what the paragraph is about. The sentences in the paragraph elaborate this idea by giving examples of various recreations that are connected or associated with food.

Special Note

The main idea is a general statement of the content of the paragraph. You must be careful, however, that your statement is not so general that it goes beyond the information that is directly or indirectly given in the paragraph.

Finding the Central Idea of a Group of Paragraphs

We generally use the term *central idea* rather than *main idea* when we refer to a *group* of paragraphs, a story, or an article. The procedure, however, for finding the main idea and for finding the central idea is the same.

The central idea of a story is the central thought of the story. All the paragraphs of the story should develop the central idea. To find the central idea of a story, students must find what common element the paragraphs in the story share. The introductory paragraph is usually helpful because it either contains or anticipates what the central idea is and how it will be developed. The procedure for finding the central idea of a story is similar to that for finding the main idea of a paragraph.

It is important to help your students recognize that the title of a story and the central idea are not necessarily the same. The ability to state the title of a story is related to the skill of finding the central idea; however, many times the title merely gives the topic of the story. The central idea is usually more fully stated than the title.

UPPER PRIMARY-GRADE LEVEL

SKILL: MAIN IDEA
Diagnostic Analysis

Objective 1: The students will be able to choose a statement that best states the main idea of a short one-paragraph story.

Objective 2: The students will be able to state a title for a story that gives an idea of what the story is about.

Criterion-Referenced Test

Directions: Read the short story. Then read the statements that follow the story. Choose the one that *best* states the main idea of the story. Also, state a title for the story. Then write the title in the blank.

Tom and Jim are not feeling very good. They have just had their first fight. Tom and Jim have never had a fight before. Tom thought about the fight. Jim thought about the fight. They both felt sad.

1. Tom and Jim are sad.
2. Tom and Jim have never fought before.
3. Tom and Jim's first fight makes them feel sad.
4. Tom and Jim fight.
5. Tom and Jim feel ill.

———————————

Answers: Number 3.   *Sample title:* Tom and Jim's First Fight
Tell students the results.

UPPER PRIMARY-GRADE LEVEL

SKILL: CENTRAL IDEA OF A SHORT STORY
Diagnostic Analysis

Objective 1: The students will be able to state the central idea of a short story.
Objective 2: The students will be able to state a title for a story.

Criterion-Referenced Test

Directions: Read the story. Write the central idea of the story. Then write a title for the story that gives readers an idea of what the story is about.[25]

Once upon a time in the deep green jungle of Africa, there lived a cruel lion.

[25]Rubin, *The Teacher's Handbook of Primary-Grade Reading/Thinking Exercises.*

This lion frightened all the animals in the jungle. No animal was safe from this lion. One day the animals met and came up with a plan. The plan was not a very good one, but it was the best they could think of. Each day one animal would go to the lion to be eaten by him. That way the other animals would know that they were safe for a little while. The lion agreed to the plan and that is how they lived for a time.

One day it was the sly fox's turn to be eaten by the lion. Mr. Fox, however, had other plans. Mr. Fox went to the lion's cave an hour late. The lion was very angry. "Why are you so late? I am hungry," he said. Mr. Fox answered, "Oh, I am so sorry to be late, but another very, very big lion tried to catch me. I ran away from him so that you could eat me." When the lion heard about the other lion, he became more angry. "Another lion?" he asked. "I want to see him." The fox told the lion that he would take him to see the other lion. The fox led the lion through the jungle. When they came to a well, the fox stopped. "Look in there," said the fox. "The other lion is in there." The lion looked in the well, and he did indeed see a lion. He got so angry that he jumped in the well to fight the lion. That was, of course, the end of the lion.

Answers: *Central idea:* A clever fox outsmarts a cruel lion.
Sample title: The Clever Fox and the Cruel Lion *or* A Fox Outsmarts a Lion
Tell students the results.

Correction: Here are some instructional techniques and materials to use with your students.
1. Present the following paragraph to your students:

Sharon was sad. She felt like crying. She still couldn't believe it. Her best friend, Jane, had moved away. Her best friend had left her. What would she do?

Ask your students what the topic of the paragraph is or about whom or what the paragraph is written.

Answer: Sharon

Ask your students what the writer is saying that is special about Sharon.

Answer: Sharon is sad because her best friend moved away.

Tell your students that the main idea of the story is finding who or what the story is about and what is special about the who or what of the story.
2. Present your students with the following exercise:

Directions: Read the short story. Read the statements that follow the short story. Choose the one that *best* states the main idea of the story. Then write a title for the story that gives readers an idea of what the story is about.

Tom and Jim live on the moon. They spend a lot of time in their house. They have to because it is very hot when the sun is out. It is also very cold when the sun is not out. On the moon, daylight lasts for fourteen earth days. Darkness or nighttime lasts for fourteen earth days, too.

1. It's cold on the moon.
2. Tom and Jim stay in their house a lot.
3. The moon's weather.
4. Tom and Jim's house.
5. The moon's weather forces Tom and Jim to stay in their house.
6. Tom and Jim like to stay in their house.

Answers: Number 5.   *Sample title:* The Moon's Weather

3. Discuss with the children the difference between the title and the main idea. Help them to see that the title and the main idea are not necessarily the same. Help them to see that the main idea is usually more fully stated than the title.

INTERMEDIATE-GRADE LEVEL

SKILL: MAIN IDEA OF A PARAGRAPH
Diagnostic Analysis

Objective: The students will be able to state the main idea of a paragraph.

Criterion-Referenced Test

Directions: Read the paragraph carefully. Write the main idea of it in the space below.

Jim and his friends planned to go on a camping trip. For weeks, he and his friends talked about nothing else. They planned every detail of the trip. They studied maps and read books on camping. Everything was set. Everything, that is, except for asking their parents to let them go. Jim and his friends had planned everything. They had not planned on their parents not letting them go. However, that is what happened. Jim's and his friends' parents did not allow them to go.

Answer: Jim and his friends' plans to go camping are blocked by their parents. Tell students the results.

INTERMEDIATE-GRADE LEVEL

SKILL: CENTRAL IDEA OF A SHORT STORY
Diagnostic Analysis

Objective 1: The students will be able to state the central idea of a short story.
Objective 2: The students will be able to state a title for a story.

Criterion-Referenced Test

Directions: Read carefully the following short story to determine the central idea of the story. Finding the central idea of a story is similar to finding the main idea of a paragraph. (To find the central idea of the story, find the topic of the story and what is

special about the topic.) After you have found the central idea of the story, choose a title for the story that gives readers an idea of what the story is about.[26]

A man and his son went to the market one morning. They took along a donkey to bring back whatever they would buy.

As they walked down the road, they met a woman who looked at them with a sour face.

"Are you not ashamed," she called to the father, "to let your little boy walk in the hot sun, when he should be riding on the donkey?"

The father stopped and lifted his boy to the donkey's back. So they went on.

After a little while they met an old man. He began at once to scold the boy. "You ungrateful son!" he shouted. "You let your poor old father walk while you sit there on the donkey like a lazy good-for-nothing!"

When the old man had passed, the father took his frightened son from the donkey and got onto the animal himself.

Further on they met another man who looked at them angrily. "How can you let your child walk in the dusty road?" he asked. "And you sit up there by yourself!"

The father was troubled, but he reached down and lifted his son up where he could sit on the donkey in front of him.

A little later they met a man and his wife, each of them riding a donkey. The husband called out, "You cruel man! How can you let the poor donkey carry such a heavy load? Get off at once! You are big enough and strong enough to carry the little animal instead of making it carry two of you."

The poor man was now really perplexed. He got off the donkey and took his son off, too.

Then he cut down a young tree for a pole and trimmed it. He tied the donkey's four feet to the pole. Then he and his son lifted the pole. They trudged along, carrying the donkey between them.

As they were crossing a bridge over a stream, they met with a crowd of young men. Seeing the donkey being carried on a pole, they started to laugh and shout. Their noise startled the poor donkey who started to kick violently and broke the ropes holding his feet. As he frisked about, he tumbled off the bridge and was drowned.

The man looked sadly into the stream and shook his head.

"My son," he said to the boy, "you cannot please everybody."

Answers: *Central idea:* A man and his son learn that you cannot please everyone.
Sample title: You Can't Please Everyone
Tell students the results.

Correction: Here are some instructional techniques and materials that you can use with your students.

1. Have your students read the following paragraph. After they read the paragraph, have them choose the word or words that *best* answer the two questions that follow the paragraph.

All through school, John's one goal was athletic success so that he could be in the Olympics. John's goal to be in the Olympics became such an obsession for him that he could not do anything that did not directly or indirectly relate to his goal. He practiced for hours every day. He exercised, ate well, and had at least eight hours of sleep every night. Throughout school, John allowed nothing and no one to take him away from his goal.

a. What is the topic of the paragraph?
   (1) exercise and practice
   (2) work
   (3) Olympics
   (4) John's goal
   (5) athletic success
   (6) attempts

Answer: 4

b. What is the author saying about John's goal to be in the Olympics (the topic) that is special and that helps tie the details together?
   (1) That it needed time and patience.
   (2) That it was a good one.
   (3) That it was not a reasonable one.
   (4) That it was the most important thing in John's life.
   (5) That it required good health.
   (6) That it was too much for John.

Answer: 4

Tell your students that if they put the two answers together, they should have the main idea of the paragraph. Main idea: The goal, being in the Olympics, was the most important thing in John's life.

2. Choose a number of paragraphs from the students' social studies or science books. First have them find the topic of each and then have them state the main idea of each. Go over the procedure for finding the main idea with them.

3. Choose some short stories and follow the same procedure for finding the central idea. Present the short stories without the titles. Have the students make up a title for each short story. Discuss the fact that the title and the central idea are not necessarily the same. Discuss what the differences are.

Drawing Inferences

Many times writers do not directly state what they mean but present ideas in a more indirect, roundabout way. That is why inference is called the ability to "read between the lines." *Inference* is defined as *understanding that is not derived from a direct statement but from an indirect suggestion in what is stated.* Readers draw inferences from writings; authors make implications or imply meanings.

The ability to draw inferences is especially important in reading fiction, but it is necessary for nonfiction, also. Authors rely on inferences to make their stories more interesting and enjoyable. Mystery writers find inference essential to the maintenance of suspense. For example, Sherlock Holmes and Perry Mason mysteries are based on the ability of the characters to uncover evidence in the form of clues that are not obvious to others around them.

Inference is an important process that authors rely on. Good readers must be alert to the ways that authors encourage inference.

Implied Statements

As has been said already, writers count on inference to make their writing more interesting and enjoyable. Rather than directly stating something, they present it indirectly. To under-

PEANUTS ®   **By Schulz**

© 1956 United Feature Syndicate, Inc.

stand the writing, the reader must be alert and be able to detect the clues that the author gives. For example, in the sentence *Things are always popping and alive when the twins Herb and Jack are around,* you are given some clues to Herb's and Jack's personalities, even though the author has not directly said anything about them. From the statement you could make the inference that the twins are lively and lots of fun to be around.

You must be *careful,* however, that you *do not read more* into some statements than is intended. For example, read the following statements and put a circle around the correct answer. *Example:* Mary got out of bed and looked out of the window. She saw that the ground had something white on it. What season of the year was it? (a) winter, (b) summer, (c) spring, (d) fall, (e) can't tell.

The answer is "(e) can't tell." Many persons choose "(a) winter" for the answer. However, the answer is (e) because the "something white" could be anything; there isn't enough evidence to choose (a). Even if the something white was snow, in some parts of the world, including the United States, it can snow in the spring or fall.

Good readers, while reading, try to gather clues to draw inferences about what they read. Although effective readers do this, they are not usually aware of it. As Sherlock Holmes says in *A Study in Scarlet,* "From long habit the train of thought ran so swiftly through my mind that I arrived at the conclusions without being conscious of intermediate steps."

UPPER PRIMARY-GRADE LEVEL

SKILL: INFERENCE OR "READING BETWEEN THE LINES"
Diagnostic Analysis

Objective: The students will be able to read a short story and answer inference questions about it.

Criterion-Referenced Test

Directions: Read the short story. Then answer the questions.[27]

Zip and Zap are a cat and rat. They are good friends. They live on the moon. Zip and Zap love to ride in space. Their school goes on a space trip every

[27]Rubin, *The Teacher's Handbook of Primary-Grade Reading/Thinking Exercises.*

month. Zip and Zap wear their space clothes and their air masks in the space ship. All the other moon cats and rats wear them, too. Zip and Zap want to be space ship pilots. This is the same space ship that brought Zip and Zap to the moon. The space ship has its own landing place. It is well taken care of. Special cats and rats take care of the space ship. Zip and Zap are happy that they can ride in the space ship.

1. Is there air in the space ship? Explain.

2. Were Zip and Zap born on the moon? Explain.

3. Is the space ship important to the moon cats and rats? Explain.

4. Is travel an important part of school learning? Explain.

5. Do Zip and Zap know what they want to do when they grow up? Explain.

Answers: 1. No. Zip and Zap wear their space clothes and their air masks in the space ship.
2. No. It is stated that the space ship is the same one that brought Zip and Zap to the moon.
3. Yes. It is their means of travel. It is stated that there are special cats and rats who take care of the space ship and that the space ship is well taken care of.
4. Yes. Every month the school goes on a space trip.
5. Yes. It is stated that they want to be space ship pilots.

Tell students the results.

UPPER PRIMARY-GRADE LEVEL

SKILL: INFERENCE OR "READING BETWEEN THE LINES"
Diagnostic Analysis

Objective: The students will be able to read a short story and then determine whether there is enough information in the story to make inferences about it.

Criterion-Referenced Test

> **Directions: Read the short story carefully. Read each of the statements below the story. For each of the statements, see if there is enough information in the story to write *true* or *false*. If there is not enough information to write *true* or *false*, write "can't tell."**[28]

Zip and Zap go to school when it is dark out. Darkness lasts for fourteen earth days. Daylight lasts for fourteen earth days, too. Zip and Zap do lots of things in school. They learn to read and write. Zip and Zap have their own robot who helps them. The robot can answer any question that Zip and Zap ask. Zip and Zap enjoy learning about the earth and other planets. They keep their robot busy. They like school.

1. Zip and Zap go to school for fourteen earth days in a row.
2. One moon day lasts for twenty-eight earth days.
3. Zip and Zap sleep for fourteen days in a row.
4. Zip and Zap ask their robot lots of questions.
5. Zip and Zap do not want to go to school.
6. Zip and Zap have lots of tests in school.
7. Zip and Zap get good grades in school.
8. Zip and Zap's robot can do lots of things.
9. Zip and Zap are interested in geography.
10. Zip and Zap do not have a teacher.

Answers: 1. true 2. true 3. can't tell 4. true 5. false 6. can't tell 7. can't tell 8. can't tell 9. true 10. can't tell
Tell students the results.

Correction: Here are some instructional procedures and materials to use with your students.
1. Present the following short selection to your students:

Sharon and Carol are going out to play. They are dressed very warmly.

Ask your students what they can say about the weather outside. They should say that it must be cold outside because the children are dressed very warmly. Even though it didn't say that it was cold outside, there was enough evidence to make this inference.

Now ask your children to tell you what season of the year it is. They should say that you can't tell because there is not enough evidence. It could be cold in the fall and spring. Some children might be able to state that you can't tell because different places of the country and world have different climates.

2. Give your students a number of opportunities to make inferences from stories they are reading if enough evidence exists.

INTERMEDIATE-GRADE LEVEL

SKILL: INFERENCE OR "READING BETWEEN THE LINES"
Diagnostic Analysis

Objective: The students will be able to make inferences about short selections if enough evidence exists for the inferences.

Criterion-Referenced Test

Directions: Read the following selection *very carefully*. Without looking back at the selection, try to answer the questions.

The two men looked at each other. They would have to make the decision that might cost many lives. They kept rubbing their hands together to keep warm. Although they were dressed in furs and every part of them was covered except for their faces, they could still feel the cold. The fire that had been made for them from pine trees was subsiding. It was getting light. They had promised their men a decision at dawn. Should they go forward or should they retreat? So many lives had already been lost.[29]

a. Did this take place at the North Pole or South Pole? _____

How do you know? _____

_____

_____

b. Circle the word that best fits the two men. The two men were: (1) trappers (2) officers (3) soldiers (4) guides. Explain why you made your choice.

Explain: _____

_____

_____

[29]Rubin, *The Teacher's Handbook of Reading/Thinking Exercises.*

c. What inference can you draw from this short passage? Circle the answer.
(1) The men were on a hunting trip.
(2) The men were at war with Indians.
(3) The decision that the two men had to make concerned whether to take an offensive or defensive position in some kind of battle.
(4) The men were on a hunting trip, but they got caught in a bad storm.

Explain: _____

_____

_____

Answers:
(a) No. There are no pine trees at the North or South Pole. (b) Officers. Guides would not talk about *their* men. Guides usually act as advisers. They do not make decisions. Trappers trap animals for fur. Also, it is stated that the fire had been made for them. Officers do not usually prepare the camp. (c) The term *retreat* would be a commander's term. Nothing was stated about a storm nor was anything stated or suggested about Indians. Hunters would not usually hunt under such adverse conditions. It was too cold to hunt big game, and hunters would very rarely lose so many lives.
Tell students the results.

INTERMEDIATE-GRADE LEVEL

SKILL: INFERENCE OR "READING BETWEEN THE LINES"
Diagnostic Analysis

Objective: The students will be able to determine whether enough evidence exists to make inferences.

Criterion-Referenced Test

Directions: Read the following paragraph carefully. Read each given statement carefully, and then determine whether the statement is true or false. If there is not enough evidence for an answer, write, "can't tell." Write your answers in the space provided.[30]

Walking under the blazing sun, which was almost directly overhead, I felt content and almost joyous. The delicious sun seemed to go right through me. How good it felt! The warmth of the sun always makes me feel good. I wonder if it's because it somehow makes up for the human warmth I crave.

_____ 1. The person is a female.

[30]Ibid.

_____ 2. The person is hitchhiking.

_____ 3. It's summer.

_____ 4. It's about noon.

_____ 5. The person needs affection.

Answers: 1. can't tell   2. can't tell   3. can't tell   4. True (If the sun is almost directly overhead, it is about noon.)   5. True (The person said he or she craves warmth.)

Tell students the results.

Correction: Here are some instructional procedures and materials that you can use.

1. Present your students with the following statements:

> Jack looks out of the train window. All he sees are miles and miles of leafless trees.

Ask them whether Jack just began to look out of the window. The students would answer "no." Ask them how they know this. They should say because it says that he saw miles and miles of trees. He couldn't see "miles and miles of trees" unless he had been looking out the window for a while.

Ask them whether Jack is traveling through a densely populated or sparsely populated area. They should say that Jack is traveling through a sparsely populated area. Ask them how they know this. They should say because the area has so many trees. Ask them what kind of area it is. The students should say that it could be a forest or a park or a preserve. Enough evidence isn't given to determine this. Ask them if they can determine what season of the year it is since there are leafless trees. They should say "no." It could be any season of the year. It is not stated in what part of the country or world Jack is

traveling. The trees could be leafless as a result of a forest fire, a disease, a drought, or some other cause.

2. Have students read a number of stories and see what inferences they can draw from them. Help them to recognize that enough evidence should exist to make an inference. Tell them that many times persons "jump to conclusions" before they have enough evidence. This can cause problems. Taking an educated guess is helpful in scientific activities and in searching for the truth of difficult questions. Students are encouraged to make educated guesses, but they need to recognize when they do not have enough evidence to do so.

Categorizing

The ability to divide items into categories is a very important thinking skill. As children advance through the grades they should be developing the skill of categorizing; that is, children should be able to differentiate and group items into more complex categories. Primary-grade children should be able to categorize a cat as distinct from a mouse or a rabbit. They should be able to group cat, dog, and cow together as animals. As these children develop their thinking skills, they should to be able to proceed from more generalized classifications to more specialized classifications.

You should help your students to recognize that every time they put things into groups— such as pets, farm animals, wild animals, cities, states, countries, capitals, fruits, vegetables, colors, and so on—they are using the skill of categorizing. When they categorize things, they are classifying things. To be able to classify things, they must know what belongs together and what does not belong together. You can help your students to classify or categorize things into more general or more specific categories. For example, the category of food is more general than the categories of fruits, vegetables, or nuts. The category of animals is more general than the categories of pets, wild animals, or tame animals. The category of pets is less general than the category of animals but more general than the categories of dogs or cats.

EXAMPLES:
1. Group these words: apple, peach, potato, rice, oats, cucumber, barley, peanuts, acorn, pecans, almonds, pear.

Answer:

Nuts	Fruits	Vegetables	Grains
peanuts	apple	potato	rice
acorn	peach	cucumber	oats
pecans	pear		barley
almonds			

2. Circle the word that does not belong.

Airedale   Persian   Angora   Siamese

Answer: You should have circled *Airedale* because all the others words refer to *cats*.

PRIMARY-GRADE LEVEL

SKILL: CATEGORIZING
Diagnostic Analysis

Objective: The students will be able to categorize pictures of various objects into groups.

Criterion-Referenced Test

Directions: The teacher will orally give directions to students. The children are given a page which consists of pictures of things that would be found in a house. Underneath each picture will appear the name of the object. These items are presented in random order on the page. The children are asked to cut out the pictures and paste them according to their groups on another sheet of paper, which has these headings: *Furniture, Appliances,* and *Eating Utensils*. The teacher reads these headings aloud to the children.

The pictures on the page are as follows: sofa, bed, desk, dresser with mirror; iron, toaster, refrigerator, oven; fork, knife, plate, cup.

Tell students the results.

PRIMARY-GRADE LEVEL

SKILL: CATEGORIZING
Diagnostic Analysis

Objective: The students will be able to group a list of words in a number of different ways.

Criterion-Referenced Test

Directions: First read the list of words. Then group them in at least seven different ways.[31]

hen	*dog*
drake	*turkey*
sow	*duck*
mare	*elephant*
colt	*ape*
gander	*tiger*
puppy	*goat*
kitten	*mule*
goose	*horse*
pig	

Answer:
Children will arrange the words into a number of different groups. Here are some:
   Wild animals: elephant, ape, tiger
   Tame animals: all the others
   Fowl: hen, drake, gander, goose, turkey, duck
   Female animals: hen, sow, mare
   Male animals: drake, colt, gander
   Pets: colt, mare, puppy, kitten, dog (many of the other animals can be pets)
   Baby animals: puppy, kitten
   Farm animals: hen, drake, sow, mare, colt, gander, and so on except for the elephant, ape, and
      tiger
   Animals: all would be included

Tell students the results.

Correction: Here is information that should help you plan corrective activities for your children.

Young children tend to overgeneralize and, until they are able to make discriminations, they will not be able to classify. By the time children come to school, they are able to make many discriminations and are beginning to classify.

1. Five-year-olds learn to put things together which belong together—blocks of the same size

[31]Rubin, *The Teacher's Handbook of Primary-Grade Reading/Thinking Exercises.*

in the same place; clothes for each doll in the right suitcase; parts of a puzzle in the right box; scissors, brushes, and paints in the spaces designated for these materials.

2. First-graders may separate things that magnets can pick up from things they do not pick up by using two boxes—one marked "yes" and the other marked "no." They can think of two kinds of stories—true and make-believe stories. They can make booklets representing homes, dividing the pictures they have cut from magazines into several categories—living rooms, dining rooms, bedrooms, and so on. They can make two piles of magazines labeled "To Cut" and "To Read."[32]

3. Second-grade pupils continue to put things together which belong together—such as outdoor temperature readings and indoor temperature readings, valentines in individual mail boxes in the play post office, and flannel graph figures made to use in telling a story in the envelope with the title of the story. In addition, seven-year-olds begin to understand finer classifications under large headings; for example, in a study of the work of a florist, plants may be classified as "plants which grow indoors" and "plants which grow outdoors." Indoor plants may be further subdivided into "plants which grow from seeds," "plants which grow from cuttings," "plants which grow from bulbs," and so on. After visiting the local bakery, second-graders, who are writing and drawing pictures of the story of their trip, can list the details in two columns—in one, "things we saw in the store" in the other, "things we saw in the kitchen."

4. Third-grade boys and girls have many opportunities to classify their ideas and arrange them in organized form. During a study of food in their community one group put up a bulletin board to answer the question "What parts of plants do we eat?" The pictures and captions followed this tabulation formulated by the third-graders:

Leaves	Seeds	Fruits	Roots
cabbage	peas	apples	carrots
lettuce	beans	oranges	radishes
spinach	corn	plums	

The file of "Games We Know" in one third grade was divided into two parts by the pupils—"indoor games" and "outdoor games." Each of these categories was further subdivided into "games with equipment" and "games without equipment." After a visit to the supermarket a third-grade class booklet was made by the children with stories and pictures of the trip. The organization of the booklet with its numbered pages was shown in the Table of Contents:

OUR VISIT TO THE FOOD MARKET

1. The Fruit and Vegetable Department   1
    Kinds of Fruits   3
    Kinds of Vegetables   4
    Where the Fruits and Vegetables
      Come From   6
    Making the Packages   8
    Finding the Prices   9
    Storing the Fruits and Vegetables   11
2. The Meat Department   14
    Different Animals Meat Comes From   16
    Kinds of Meat   18
    Keeping Meat   21
    Storing Meat   22
    Packaging Meat   24
  And so on.

(See "Outlining" in Chapter 14.)

---

[32]Although grade designations are given, teachers must take the individual differences of students into account. Some first-graders may be at a third-grade level; others may be at a first-grade or lower skill-development level.

INTERMEDIATE-GRADE LEVEL

SKILL: CATEGORIZING
Diagnostic Analysis

Objective: The students will be able to group items that belong together.

Criterion-Referenced Test

> **Directions: First find what the items in a group have in common, and then choose a word or phrase from the list below that *best* describes the group. There are more words and phrases than are needed. Put the word or phrase on the line after each group of words.**[33]

Words and Phrases: books, fiction books, nonfiction books, fruit, vegetables, food, cooked food, desserts, dairy products, long books, writing, fowl, animals, tame animals, female animals, wood, wood products, meat, beef, pork, lamb.

1. pears, apples, bananas _____

2. meat, tomatoes, apples _____

3. milk, cheese, butter _____

4. jello, applesauce, ice cream _____

5. liver, pork chops, lamb chops _____

6. hen, mare, doe _____

7. biography, autobiography, novel _____

8. biography, autobiography, dictionary _____

9. novel, comics, fairy tales _____

10. paper, telephone pole, furniture _____

Answers: 1. fruit   2. food   3. dairy products   4. desserts   5. meat   6. female animals
7. books   8. nonfiction books   9. fiction books   10. wood products
Tell students the results.

---

[33]Rubin, *The Teacher's Handbook of Reading/Thinking Exercises.*

INTERMEDIATE-GRADE LEVEL

SKILL: CATEGORIZING
Diagnostic Analysis

Objective: The students will be able to recognize when an item does not belong in a group.

Criterion-Referenced Test

> **Directions: First read the words in each set to see what they have in common; then circle the word in each set that does not belong. You may use the dictionary to look up unfamiliar words.**[34]
>
> 1. Indiana, Connecticut, Seattle, Maine
> 2. large, huge, immense, heavy
> 3. trumpet, bell, bray, chirp
> 4. devil, warlock, wizard, witch
> 5. occult, mysterious, weary, secret
> 6. dachshund, Siamese, poodle, Schnauzer
> 7. spiders, ticks, flies, scorpions
> 8. frogs, snakes, turtles, lizards
> 9. Albany, Harrisburg, San Francisco, Nashville
> 10. stove, coal, oil, wood

Answers: 1. Seattle   2. heavy   3. bell (not a characteristic cry or sound of a bird, insect, or animal)   4. witch   5. weary   6. Siamese   7. flies (do not have eight legs)   8. frogs (not reptiles)
9. San Francisco (not a capital)   10. stove
Tell students the results.

Correction: Here are some instructional procedures and materials to use.

1. Present students with the following list of words and have them group them in as many ways as they can think of.

chalk	book
checkers	library
pencil	auditorium
paper	science books
student	baseball
teacher	nurse
chalkboard	jump rope
desk	basketball

classroom	pen
principal	chess
history books	spelling books

2. Present the following exercise to your students. This activity is a more difficult one because of the vocabulary. Have students look up any words they are not sure of in the dictionary. Make sure that students remember that words may have more than one meaning so that they are not confused when they see words such as *minute*.

After students have finished the exercise, go over it carefully, discussing why they did what they did.

[34]Ibid.

Directions: Here is a group of words. Put them into ten groups according to a common feature and state the common feature for each group.[35]

small, wood, brass, round, silk, oil, wheat, stockings, hexagon, skim, tin, triangle, wool, satin, meter, coal, nylon, peds, gram, iron, rectangle, barley, socks, octagon, scan, oats, huge, liter, survey, mammoth, oval, minute, cylindrical.

1. _____

_____ Common feature _____

2. _____

_____ Common feature _____

3. _____

_____ Common feature _____

4. _____

_____ Common feature _____

5. _____

_____ Common feature _____

6. _____

_____ Common feature _____

7. _____

_____ Common feature _____

8. _____

_____ Common feature _____

9. _____

_____ Common feature _____

10. _____

_____ Common feature _____

Answers: 1. wood, oil, coal—fuels   2. brass, tin, iron—metals   3. silk, wool, satin, nylon—fabrics   4. round, cylindrical, oval—shapes   5. wheat, barley, oats—grains   6. stockings, peds, socks—footwear   7. skim, scan, survey—fast reading   8. meter, gram, liter—metric terms   9. hexagon, triangle, rectangle, octagon—geometric figures   10. small, huge, mammoth, minute—sizes

[35]Rubin, *The Intermediate-Grade Teacher's Language Arts Handbook.*

COMPLETING ANALOGIES (WORD RELATIONSHIPS)

Working with analogies requires high-level thinking skills. Students must have a good stock of vocabulary and the ability to see relationships. Students who have difficulty in classification will usually have difficulty working with analogies.

Some primary-grade children can be exposed to simple analogies based on relationships with which they are familiar.[36] Analogies are relationships between words or ideas. In order to be able to make the best use of analogies or to complete an analogy statement or proportion, the children must know the meanings of the words and the relationship of the pair of words. For example: *Sad is to happy as good is to* _____. Many primary-grade children know the meanings of *sad* and *happy* and that *sad* is the opposite of *happy;* they would, therefore, be able to complete the analogy statement or proportion with the correct word—*bad.*

Some of the relationships that words may have to one another are similar meanings, opposite meanings, classification, going from particular to general, going from general to particular, degree of intensity, specialized labels, characteristics, cause-effect, effect-cause, function, whole-part, ratio, and many more. The preceding relationships do not have to be memorized. Tell your students that they will

[36]See Sister Josephine, C.S.J., "An Analogy Test for Preschool Children," *Education* (December 1965): 235–237.

gain clues to these from the pairs making up the analogies; that is, the words express the relationship. For example: *"pretty* is to *beautiful"*—the relationship is degree of intensity (the state of being stronger, greater, or more than); *"hot* is to *cold"*—the relationship is one of opposites; *"car* is to *vehicle"*—the relationship is classification.

It would probably be a good idea for teachers to review the word lists of the analogy exercises to determine whether their students are familiar with the vocabulary. Teachers can encourage students to use dictionaries to look up any unfamiliar words.

The analogy activities can be done in small groups or with the entire class orally as well as individually. If children work individually, it would help to go over the answers together in a group so that interaction and discussion can further enhance vocabulary development.

Special Notes

1. The term *word relationships* should be used with your primary-grade students rather than *analogies.* You might want to introduce the term *analogy* to some of your highly able upper primary-grade children. Highly able children especially enjoy working with analogies.

2. In introducing some of the relationships that pairs of words can have to one another, you should, of course, use words that are in your students' listening capacity. The list of some possible relationships is presented as an aid for you, the teacher.

LOWER PRIMARY-GRADE LEVEL

SKILL: PICTURE RELATIONSHIPS (ANALOGIES)
Diagnostic Analysis

Objective: The students will be able to choose a picture from the given pictures that will best complete the analogy.

Criterion-Referenced Test

Directions: (These will be given orally by the teacher.) Present the following picture sets to your children. Tell them that the sets of pictures belong together in some way. Each set has a missing picture. Have them look at the first pair of pictures in the set. Tell them to try to figure out how they belong together. Then have them choose a picture from the large box that would *best* complete the second pair in the set. Have them draw a line from the picture in the large box to the empty box. *All the pictures in the box are used as answers.* Do the first set with the children.[37]

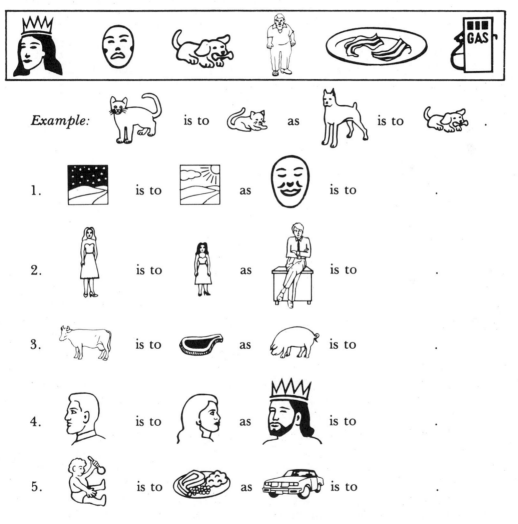

Tell students the results.

[37]Rubin, *The Teacher's Handbook of Primary-Grade Reading/Thinking Exercises.*

UPPER PRIMARY-GRADE LEVEL

SKILL: WORD RELATIONSHIPS (ANALOGIES)
Diagnostic Analysis

Objective: The students will be able to complete each analogy statement with the *best* word.

Criterion-Referenced Test

> **Directions: Here are sets of words that have a certain relationship to one another. Each set has a missing word that you have to supply. Look at the first pair or words. Try to figure out what the relationship is. Then choose a word from the list that *best* completes the second pair in the set. (All words do not fit in.) The first is done for you.**[38]

Word List: hide, house, nice, proud, sire, hay, sow, stallion, ewe, gander, drake, stable, water, milk, drink, cruel, tired, great, hot.

1. *Bird* is to *nest* as *horse* is to _____stable_____ .

2. *Cool* is to *cold* as *warm* is to _____ .

3. *Cow* is to *bull* as *duck* is to _____ .

4. *Deer* is to *doe* as *pig* is to _____ .

5. *Hungry* is to *eat* as *thirsty* is to _____ .

6. *In* is to *out* as *kind* is to _____ .

Answers: 1. stable   2. hot   3. drake   4. sow   5. drink   6. cruel
Tell students the results.

Correction: Here are some instructional procedures and materials that you can use.

1. Present students with the words *hot* and *cold*. Ask them what the relationship between the two words is. Help them to recognize that *hot* and *cold* are opposites. Present students with the words *tall* and *short*. Ask them what the relationship between the words is. Again help them to recognize that they are opposites. Tell them that they are going to work with word relationships. The first relationship will be opposites. Put the following on the chalkboard:

Thin is to *fat* as *little* is to _____ .

Ask them to give you a word that would fit the blank. Present a number of opposite relationships to your students.

2. Present students with the words *little* and *small*. Ask them what the relationship between the words is. Help them to recognize that these are words that have the same meaning; they are synonyms. Present students with the words *big* and *large*. Ask them what the relationship between the words is. Again help them to recognize that the words are similar in meaning. Tell them that they are going to work with word

[38]Ibid.

relationships. Put the following on the chalk-board:

Sad is to *gloomy* as *happy* is to _____ .

Ask them to give you a word that would fit the blank. Present a number of such relationships to your students.

3. Do the same as above for different kinds of relationships.

4. Present the following word relationship to them.

Directions: Here are sets of words that have a certain relationship to one another. Each set has a missing word that you have to supply. Look at the first pair of words. Try to figure out what the relationship is. Then choose a word from the list that *best* completes the second pair in the set. (All words are used as answers.)[39]

Word List: quiet, less, bean, cub, doe, always, yesterday, heavy, young, weak.

1. *Night* is to *day* as *old* is to _____ .
2. *Fruit* is to *plum* as *vegetable* is to _____ .
3. *Thin* is to *light* as *fat* is to _____ .
4. *Cat* is to *kitten* as *bear* is to _____ .
5. *Horse* is to *mare* as *deer* is to _____ .
6. *Loud* is to *soft* as *noisy* is to _____ .
7. *Wrong* is to *right* as *never* is to _____ .
8. *Stop* is to *go* as *strong* is to _____ .
9. *Most* is to *least* as *more* is to _____ .
10. *Tomorrow* is to *today* as *today* is to _____ .

Answers: 1. young 2. bean 3. heavy 4. cub 5. doe 6. quiet 7. always 8. weak 9. less 10. yesterday

Go over each analogy with the students. Have them explain why they chose the word that they did.

[39]Ibid.

INTERMEDIATE-GRADE LEVEL

SKILL: ANALOGIES (WORD RELATIONSHIPS)
Diagnostic Analysis

Objective: The students will be able to complete each analogy statement with the *best* word.

Criterion-Referenced Test

> **Directions: Find the relationship between a pair of words and then complete each analogy with the *best* word. There are more words given in the list than you need.**

Word List: sun, moon, light, cold, kilometer, pour, year, rate, ship, day, compass, rain, cards, blizzard, doe, time, era, kind, drove, dame, ram, century, place, ewe, love, cub, binary, meter, ecstasy, chirp, moo, friend, hate, millimeter.

1. *Happy* is to *sad* as *night* is to _____.

2. *Rain* is to *downpour* as *snow* is to _____.

3. *Horse* is to *mare* as *deer* is to _____.

4. *Chicken* is to *rooster* as *sheep* is to _____.

5. *Sad* is to *miserable* as *joy* is to _____.

6. *One* is to *thousand* as *meter* is to _____.

7. *Hint* is to *disclose* as *drip* is to _____.

8. *Distance* is to *odometer* as *direction* is to _____.

Answers: 1. day   2. blizzard   3. doe   4. ram   5. ecstasy   6. kilometer   7. pour   8. compass
Tell students the results.

Correction: Here are some instructional procedures and materials that you can use.

1. Discuss the various relationships that words can have to one another and have the students give examples of these. Put the examples on large newsprint so that students can refer to them. As students learn new relationships, have them add to the list.

For example:

Opposites: *hot* is to *cold*

Similarities: *thin* is to *lean*

Degree of intensity: *pretty* is to *beautiful*

Classification: *boat* is to *vehicle*

Ratio: *5* is to *10*

Part is to whole: *eye* is to *pupil*

Whole is to part: *finger* is to *hand*

Bear is to cub: *parent* is to *child*

2. Have students construct their own analogies by using the dictionary. Then have them

challenge their classmates by deleting the final term of the analogy statement.

Special Note

It should again be emphasized that the skill areas covered in this chapter illustrating a diagnostic and corrective approach are a sampling of some interpretive comprehension skills rather than an inclusive set. Teachers using the given examples as a guide can develop diagnostic and corrective materials for other interpretive comprehension skills, as well as for critical and creative comprehension skills. (See the diagnostic checklist on page 250.)

DIAGNOSIS AND CORRECTION IN CONTENT AREAS

Diagnosis and correction in reading should not be relegated merely to the reading period. Reading is taking place all through the day at school, and teachers would be losing valuable opportunities to learn about students' reading strengths and weaknesses if they did not observe their students' reading behavior in content areas. It's in these areas that teachers can observe whether students are applying what they have learned during the reading period.

A student's problem in mathematics may not be caused by an inability to do quantitative reasoning or basic mathematical operations; it may be a reading problem. Similarly, a problem in science or social studies may be a reading problem. The teacher should have students find the main idea of various paragraphs in their content books to discern whether they understand what they are reading. Teachers should give students opportunities to read aloud from their books to determine whether the books are at the proper readability level for the students. (See "A Modified Informal Reading Inventory Approach: A

Caution" in Chapter 9.) Also, teachers should be alert to students' attitudes toward a subject. It may be that the student does not like the subject because the student cannot read the textbook. A student who is not reading at grade level would probably have difficulty reading a social studies, science, or math textbook whose readability level is at the same grade level. If teachers cannot get books for their students at their reading ability levels, they will have to make special provisions. They will have to provide a special guide that would have an outline of the material the students are supposed to read. It would also list all those vocabulary words that the teachers feel would cause difficulty. Before the students are asked to read the material, the teachers should go over the vocabulary words with the students. The words should be pronounced, presented in a sentence, and defined. After the students have read the material, the teachers should go over it with them in the same way that they would in a reading lesson. The emphasis, however, would be on gaining content concepts.

Special Note

It would be very difficult to find a subject matter book for a student who is reading below grade level at the student's reading ability that would cover the same material. If a student is in fourth grade, the subject matter book for third-grade mathematics covers different material. Also, the student may be good in mathematics but have a reading problem, and if a book from a lower grade level is used, the student would be penalized in mathematics.

VOCABULARY EXPANSION

Good vocabulary and good reading go hand in hand. Unless readers know the meanings of

Student's Name:_____

Grade:_____

Teacher:_____

Diagnostic Checklist for Selected Reading Comprehension Skills

	Yes	No
1. The student is able to state the meaning of a word in context.		
2. The student is able to give the meaning of a phrase or a clause in a sentence.		
3. The student is able to give variations of meanings for homographs (words spelled the same but with more than one meaning, for example, *train, mean, saw, sole,* and so on).		
4. The student is able to give the meaning of a sentence in a paragraph.		
5. The student is able to recall information that is explicitly stated in the passage (literal questions).		
6. The student is able to state the main idea of a paragraph.		
7. The student is able to state details to support the main idea of a paragraph.		
8. The student is able to summarize a paragraph.		
9. The student is able to answer a question that requires reading between the lines.		
10. The student is able to draw a conclusion from what is read.		
11. The student can complete analogy proportions.		
12. The student can hypothesize the author's purpose for writing the selection.		
13. The student can differentiate between fact and opinion.		
14. The student can differentiate between fantasy and reality.		
15. The student can detect bias in a story.		
16. The student can detect various propaganda tactics that are used in a story.		
17. The student can go beyond the text to come up with alternate solutions or ways to end a story or solve a problem in the selection.		
18. The student shows that he or she enjoys reading by voluntarily choosing to read.		

words, they will have difficulty understanding what they are reading. It should be stressed that just knowing the meanings of the words will not ensure that individuals will be able to state the meanings of sentences, nor does knowing the meanings of sentences assure that readers can give the meanings of whole paragraphs, and so forth. However, by not knowing the meanings of the words, the individual's chances of being able to read well are considerably lessened. Without an understanding of words, comprehension is impossible.

As children advance in concept development, their vocabulary development must also advance because the two are interrelated (see Chapter 4). Children deficient in vocabulary will usually be deficient in concept development. Studies have shown that "vocabulary is a key variable in reading comprehension and is a major feature of most tests of academic aptitude. . . ."[40]

Most teachers are aware of the importance of building sight vocabulary, and word attack skills are a large part of the beginning reading program. However, the development of a larger meaning vocabulary is often neglected.

Primary-Grade Children

The development of vocabulary is too important to the success of a child in school to be left to chance. Teachers should, therefore, provide a planned vocabulary expansion program for children when they first enter school.

For a vocabulary program to be successful, the teacher must recognize that individual differences exist between the amount and kind of words that kindergarten and first-grade children have in their listening capacity (ability to understand a word when it is spoken). Some children come to school with a rich and varied vocabulary, whereas others have a more limited and narrow vocabulary. Some children may have a rich and varied vocabulary that can be used with their peers and at home, but it may not be useful to them in school. For example, some children may possess a large lexicon of street vocabulary and expressions, and some others may speak an English dialect that contains its own special expressions and vocabulary.

Teachers should recognize also that young children's listening vocabulary is larger than their speaking vocabulary and obviously larger than their reading and writing vocabulary. All four areas of vocabulary need to be developed. However, since children first learn language through the aural-oral approach, the teacher should begin with these areas first.

Developing Vocabulary from Literature

Reading literature aloud to children is a viable means of increasing vocabulary and reading achievement.[41] (See Chapters 6 and 16.) The teacher should choose books that appeal to children. The authors of these books must be aware of what is important to a child and what is likely to be confusing so that they can build meaning out of words through the kind of imagery that makes sense to a child. For example, in *Mike Mulligan and His Steam Shovel,* the meaning of *steam shovel* is clarified by giving numerous examples in which a steam shovel is used. In Margaret Wise Brown's book *The Dead Bird,* the meaning of *dead* is given by a description of the bird's state.[42]

[40]Walter M. MacGinitie, "Language Development," in *Encyclopedia of Educational Research,* 4th ed. (London: Collier-Macmillan, 1969), p. 693.

[41]Dorothy H. Cohen, "The Effect of Literature on Vocabulary and Reading Achievement," *Elementary English* 45 (February 1968): 209–13, 217.

[42]See Dorothy H. Cohen, "Word Meaning and the Literary Experience in Early Childhood," *Elementary English* 46 (November 1969): 914–25, for a listing of books and examples.

Vocabulary Consciousness

In the primary grades children are beginning to meet words that are spelled the same but have different meanings, based on their context in the sentence. Pupils learn that the word *saw* in "I saw Jane" does not carry the same meaning as in "Dick will help Father saw the tree." When primary-graders recognize that *saw, train, coat,* and many other words have different meanings based on surrounding words, they are beginning to build a vocabulary consciousness. This consciousness grows when they begin to ask about and look up the meanings of new words they come across in their everyday activities.

Teachers ought to challenge primary-grade children's budding vocabulary consciousness in enjoyable ways. One way to do so is to use word riddles or fun-with-word activities. Examples:

1. From a six-letter word for what you put on bread, remove two letters to get what a goat does with his horns.
2. To a four-letter word for something liquid that falls from the sky, add two letters to make a kind of damage you can do by twisting a part of the body.
3. From a five-letter word for an animal with a shell, take one letter away to make a word for something that holds things together.
4. The plural of an insect, when you add a letter to it, becomes something you wear.

Answers: (1) butter, butt; (2) rain, sprain; (3) snail, nail; (4) ants, pants.

Another way to challenge primary-grade children and to help them to expand their vocabulary is through the learning of word parts. The primary grades are not too soon to begin to help children learn about word parts such as prefixes, suffixes, and roots in order to expand their vocabulary. (See "Defining Word Part Terms" in this chapter.)

The Dictionary as a Tool in Vocabulary Expansion

Although children use picture dictionaries in the primary grades more as an aid to writing than in vocabulary expansion, if young readers discover the wonders of the dictionary they can enrich their vocabulary. Primary-grade picture dictionaries consist of words that are generally in the children's listening, speaking, and reading vocabularies. They consist of alphabetized lists of words with pictures and can serve as the children's first reference tool, helping them to unlock words on their own and making them more independent and self-reliant. The children can also learn multiple meanings from a picture dictionary, when they see the word *saw,* for example, with two pictures which represent a tool and the act of seeing.

Intermediate-Grade Children

As students become more advanced in reading, more words which previously only had one meaning are being met in new and strange situations. In the intermediate grades, students should be guided to a mastery of vocabulary. If they are fascinated with words, they generally want to know the longest word in the dictionary, and many enjoy pronouncing funny or nonsense-sounding words such as *supercalifragilisticexpialidocious.* These students should be helped to

1. Become aware of words they do not know.
2. Try to guess the meaning from the context and their knowledge of word parts.
3. Learn the most used combining forms.
4. Jot down words that they do not know and look them up in the dictionary later.

5. Keep a notebook and write down the words they have missed in their vocabulary exercises, giving them additional study. Learn to break words down into word parts in order to learn their meaning.

6. Maintain interest in wanting to expand vocabulary.

Defining Word Part Terms

In order to help students use word parts for increasing vocabulary, some terms should be defined. There are a great number of words in our language which combine with other words to form new words, for example, *grandfather* and *policeman* (compound words). You may also combine a root (base) word with a letter or a group of letters either at the beginning (prefix) or end (suffix) of the root word to form a new, related word, for example, *replay* and *played*. *Affix* is a term used to refer either to a prefix or a suffix.

In the words *replay* and *played, play* is a root or base, *re* is a prefix, and *ed* is a suffix. A *root* is the smallest unit of a word that can exist and retain its basic meaning. It cannot be subdivided any further. *Replay* is not a root word because it can be subdivided to *play*. *Play* is a root word because it cannot be divided further and still retain a meaning related to the root word.

Derivatives are combinations of root words with either prefixes or suffixes or both. *Combining forms* are usually defined as roots borrowed from another language that join together or that join with a prefix, a suffix, or both a prefix and a suffix to form a word. Many times the English combining forms are derived from Greek and Latin roots. In some vocabulary books, in which the major emphasis is on vocabulary expansion rather than on the naming of word parts, a *combining form* is defined in a more general sense to include any word part that can join with another word or word part to form a word or a new word.[43]

Vocabulary Expansion Instruction

Vocabulary expansion instruction depends on the ability levels of students, their past experiences, and their interests. If they are curious about sea life and have an aquarium in the classroom, this could stimulate interest in such combining forms as *aqua,* meaning "water," and *mare* meaning "sea." The combining form *aqua* could generate such terms as *aquaplane, aqueduct,* and *aquanaut.* Since *mare* means "sea," students could be given the term *aquamarine* to define. Knowing the combining forms *aqua* and *mare,* many will probably respond with "seawater." The English term actually means "bluish-green." The students can be challenged as to why the English definition of aquamarine is bluish-green.

A terrarium can stimulate discussion of words made up of the combining form *terra.*

When discussing the prefix *bi,* children should be encouraged to generate other words that also contain *bi,* such as *bicycle, binary, bilateral,* and so on. Other suggestions follow.

Write the words *biped* and *quadruped* in a column on the board, along with their meanings. These words should elicit guesses for groups of animals. The teacher could ask such questions as, "What do you think an animal that has eight arms or legs would be called?" "What about an animal with six feet?" And so on. When the animals are listed on the board, the children can be asked to look them up in the dictionary so that they can classify them.[44]

[43]Dorothy Rubin, *Vocabulary Expansion I* (New York: Macmillan, 1982).

[44]See Loraine Dun, "Increase Vocabulary with the Word Elements, Mono through Deca," *Elementary English* 47 (January 1970): 49–55.

When presenting the combining forms *cardio, tele, graph,* and *gram,* place the following vocabulary words on the board:

cardiograph	telegraph
cardiogram	telegram

After students know that *cardio* means "heart" and *tele* means "from a distance," ask them to try to determine the meaning of *graph,* as used in *cardiograph* and *telegraph.* Have them try to figure out the meaning of *gram,* as used in *telegram* and *cardiogram.* Once students are able to define *graph* as an "instrument or machine," and *gram* as "message," they will hardly ever confuse a cardiograph with a cardiogram.

When students are exposed to such activities, they become more sensitive to their language. They come to realize that words are man-made, that language is living and changing, and that as people develop new concepts they need new words to identify them. *Astronaut* and *aquanaut* are good examples of words which came into being because of space and undersea exploration.

Children come to see the power of combining forms when they realize that by knowing a few combining forms they can unlock the meanings of many words. For example, by knowing a few combining forms, students can define correctly many terms used in the metric system, as well as other words.

deca:	ten
deci:	tenth
cent, centi:	hundred, hundredth
milli:	thousand, thousandth
decameter:	ten meters
decimeter:	1/10 meter
centimeter:	1/100 meter
millimeter:	1/1000 meter
decade:	period of ten years

century:	period of one hundred years
centennial:	one hundredth-year anniversary
millennium:	period of 1,000 years
million:	one thousand thousands

(*Centi, milli, deci* are usually used to designate "part of.")

You should caution your students that many times the literal definitions of the prefixes, suffixes, or combining forms may not be exactly the same as the dictionary meaning. For example, *automobile.*

Vocabulary Expansion Instruction for Students Weak in Vocabulary

Working with upper-elementary-grade students who are especially weak in vocabulary requires a relatively structured approach, one that emphasizes the systematic presentation of material at graduated levels of difficulty in ways somewhat similar to those used in the teaching of English as a second language. Each day, roots, combining forms, prefixes, and suffixes should be presented with a list of words made up from these word parts. Emphasis is placed on the meanings of the word parts and their combinations into words rather than on the naming of the word parts. For example, *bi* and *ped* are pronounced and put on the chalkboard. Their meanings are given. When *biped* is put on the board, the students are asked by the teacher if they can state its meaning.

The terms presented for study should be those which students will hear in school, on television, or on radio, as well as those they will meet in their reading. The word parts should be presented in an interesting manner, and those that combine to form a number of words should be given. When students realize that they are seeing these words in their reading, they will be greatly reinforced in their learning.

To provide continuous reinforcement, daily

"nonthreatening" quizzes on the previous days' words may be given. Students should receive the results of such quizzes immediately, so that any faulty concepts may be quickly corrected. The number of words that are presented would depend on individual students.

The possibilities for vocabulary experiences in the classroom are unlimited. Teachers must have the prefixes, suffixes, and combining forms at their fingertips in order to take advantage of the opportunities that present themselves daily. Here is a list of some often used word parts and vocabulary words derived from them.

Prefixes	Combining Forms	Vocabulary Words
a—without	anthropo—man	anthropology, apodal
ante—before	astro—star	astronomy, astrology
arch—main, chief	audio—hearing	audiology, auditory, audition, audible
bi—two	auto—self	automatic, autocracy, binary, biped
cata—down	bene—good	benefit, catalog
circum—around	bio—life	biology, biography, autobiography
hyper—excessive	chrono—time	chronological, hypertension
hypo—under	cosmo—world	microcosm, cosmology
in—not	gamy—marriage	monogamy, bigamy, polygamy
inter—between, among	geo—earth	interdepartmental, geology
mis—wrong, bad	gram—written or drawn	telegram, mistake
mono—one, alone	graph—written or drawn,	telegraph, monarchy
post—after	instrument	
re—backward, again	logo—speak	theology, logical, catalog
trans—across	macro—large	macrocosm
	micro—small	microscope, transatlantic
	mis—hate	misanthrope, misogamist
	poly—many	polyglot
Suffixes	retro—backward	retrorocket
	pod—foot, feet	pseudopod
able—able to	scope—instrument for seeing	microscope
ible—able to	phobia—fear	monophobia
ology—the study of	theo—god	theocracy
tion—the act of	pseudo—false	pseudoscience

The Dictionary as a Tool in Vocabulary Expansion

In the intermediate grades dictionaries serve more varied purposes, and there is emphasis on vocabulary expansion. Children delight in learning new words. If properly encouraged by the teacher, vocabulary expansion can become an exciting hunting expedition, where the unexplored terrain is the vast territory of words.

At any grade level teachers can show by their actions that they value the dictionary as an important tool. If a word seems to need clarification, students should be asked to look it up in the dictionary. Although at times it may seem more expedient simply to supply the meaning, students should be encouraged to look it up for themselves. If the pupil discovers the meaning of the word on his or her own, he or she will be more apt to remember it.

In order to build a larger meaning vocabulary, the teacher could use a number of motivating techniques to stimulate vocabulary expansion. Each pupil can be encouraged to keep a paper bag attached to his or her desk, in which he or she puts index cards with words on one side and the meaning of the word he or she has looked up on the other. Sometime during the day students can be encouraged to challenge one another, with one student calling out the meanings of a word and another student supplying the word. This technique should make the dictionary one of the students' most treasured possessions. (See Chapter 14 for more on the dictionary.) (See the diagnostic checklists that follow below.)

VOCABULARY EXPANSION IN CONTENT AREAS

Unless students know word meanings, they will not be able to understand what they are reading. No one will dispute this statement. However, many teachers may not recognize that a student's problem in a content area is that he or she does not have the prerequisite vocabulary to understand the concepts being presented.

Using word parts to help students expand vocabulary in the content areas is a viable approach (see previous sections). Another approach is to directly select words from students' content areas. Each week the teacher could choose a certain number of words from various books and highlight them as the words of the week. Each word would be pronounced, put into a sentence, and defined. During the week students can use these words to make up word riddles, challenging their classmates for answers. The words would become part of the week's spelling words, and students would be asked to put them into sentences that show the students understand their meaning; or the teacher could present the words in sentences to the students and ask them to define the word as used in the sentence. Here is an example of how one teacher correlates the content area of social studies to vocabulary, spelling, and other language arts.

A fifth-grade group of children in a social

Student's Name:_____

Grade:_____

Teacher:_____

Diagnostic Checklist for Vocabulary Development (Primary Grades)

	Yes	No
1. The child shows that he or she is developing a vocabulary consciousness by recognizing that some words have more than one meaning.		
2. The child uses context clues to figure out word meanings.		
3. The child can state the opposite of words such as *stop, tall, fat, long, happy, big.*		

Student's Name:_____

Grade:_____

Teacher:_____

Diagnostic Checklist for Vocabulary Development (Primary Grades) (Cont.)

	Yes	No
4. The child can state the synonym of words such as *big, heavy, thin, mean, fast, hit.*		

5. The child can state different meanings for homographs (words that are spelled the same but have different meanings based on their use in a sentence). Examples:
    I did not *state* what *state* I live in.
    Do not *roll* the *roll* on the floor.
    Train your dog not to bark when he hears a *train.*		

6. The child is developing a vocabulary of the senses by being able to state words that describe various sounds, smells, sights, tastes, and touches.		
7. The child is expanding his or her vocabulary by combining two words to form compound words such as *grandfather, bedroom, cupcake, backyard, toothpick, buttercup, mailman.*		
8. The child is expanding his or her vocabulary by combining roots of words with prefixes and suffixes. Examples: *return, friendly, unhappy, disagree, dirty, precook, unfriendly.*		
9. The child is able to give the answer to a number of word riddles.		
10. The child is able to make up a number of word riddles.		
11. The child is able to classify various objects such as fruits, animals, colors, pets, and so on.		
12. The child is able to give words that are associated with certain objects and ideas. Example: hospital—*nurse, doctor, beds, sick persons, medicine,* and so on.		
13. The child is able to complete some analogy proportions such as *Happy is to sad as fat is to* _____.		
14. The child shows that he or she is developing a vocabulary consciousness by using the dictionary to look up unknown words.		

Student's Name:_____

Grade:_____

Teacher:_____

Diagnostic Checklist for Vocabulary Development (Intermediate Grades)

	Yes	No
1. The student recognizes that many words have more than one meaning.		
2. The student uses context clues to figure out the meanings.		
3. The student can given synonyms for words such as *similar, secluded, passive, brief, old, cryptic, anxious*.		
4. The student can give antonyms for words such as *prior, most, less, best, optimist, rash, humble, content*.		
5. The student can state different meanings for homographs (words that are spelled the same but have different meanings based on their use in a sentence), for example: It is against the law to *litter* the streets. The man was placed on the *litter* in the ambulance. My dog gave birth to a *litter* of puppies.		
6. The student is able to use word parts to figure out word meanings.		
7. The student is able to use word parts to build words.		
8. The student is able to complete analogy statements or proportions.		
9. The student is able to give the connotative meaning of a number of words.		
10. The student is able to work with word categories.		
11. The student is able to answer a number of word riddles.		
12. The student is able to make up a number of word riddles.		
13. The student uses the dictionary to find word meanings.		

studies unit is working with famous people from other continents. The spelling and vocabulary words for the children include three sets of words:

General Words	Continents	Countries
continent	North America	Brazil
globe	South America	Canada
atlas	Africa	India
hemisphere	Asia	Japan
meridian	Australia	Israel
latitude	Europe	France
longitude		England
		Argentina
		Algeria
		China
		United States

He tells the students that the words on the board are words they will meet when they read their social studies assignment. He points to the globe and atlas and says that students have probably seen these but have probably not worked with them. Today they will. First he will pronounce each general word, put it into a sentence, and explain certain of the terms. After that he will pronounce each continent and country that is listed on the board. Then he will have some students look at the map, some at the globe, and some in the atlas to find the continents and countries that are listed on the board.

During the lesson the teacher asks a question concerning two women leaders about whom they have read and about whom the class has already talked. The teacher says, "I'll give you a hint. One of the women's first names is spelled almost like the country she now heads." Many children are able to correctly give Indira Gandhi as the woman, and India as her country.

A discussion ensues about why India has been in the news so much. The teacher than asks the name of the other famous woman leader who has been in the news. A girl is called on and answers correctly.

The teacher says, "Good. You really seem to know your world affairs and your countries. Let's see how good you are in categorizing countries according to their continents. I have an outline map for each one of you, and I'd like you to see if you can put the continents in the right areas and then insert the countries that I have listed on the board. Does anyone have any questions? Let's do one together to make sure everyone understands."

He points to an area on one of the outline maps, and asks, "Can everyone see where I am pointing? Okay, what is this continent?"

"Correct," says Mr. Jones. "Looking at the list on the board, which country would you place in this continent and approximately where would you put it?"

Again, many of the children call out the correct answer.

"Good. Let's see how many of you can finish this on your own."

The children start working and Mr. Jones walks around checking their papers and stopping to help those who need it. After some time has elapsed, the teacher goes over the correct answers with the group to give them feedback on the results. He helps students summarize what they have done and asks them to check the news for exciting things that are happening in other areas of the world so that they can add those to their list.

"Tomorrow," Mr. Jones says, "we're going to be combining outlining with our study of continents and countries. Then we're going to use the outline as a guide to learn more about the country we choose to study. I would like you to think about which country you want to get to know better. At your seats, review some of the things we talked about concerning outlines. This sheet should help you."

Comments: Mr. Jones is helping his students not only to expand their vocabulary but also to see how skills such as categorizing and outlining are related and how these skills can help students learn and retain information. As stated earlier in this book, if students are given opportunities to work with categorizing and other important thinking skills, they will be more prone to use them when they are reading alone. Mr. Jones is also able to diagnose a student's ability to work with certain concepts because he is working with a group of children rather than with the whole class. Mr. Jones can quickly see whether a student is confused or not and help that student immediately.

SUMMARY

Chapter 13 is concerned with helping you better understand reading comprehension and vocabulary expansion skills, as well as with helping you gain techniques for the diagnosis and correction of these skills. Reading comprehension is a complex intellectual process involving a number of abilities. The two major ones involve word meanings and reasoning with verbal concepts. It was emphasized that comprehension involves thinking, and as there are various levels of thinking, so are there various levels of comprehension. Reading comprehension was categorized into a hierarchy of four levels: literal comprehension, interpretation, critical reading, and creative reading. Then a special section on diagnosis and correction was presented for selective interpretive skills. The skills that were chosen to demonstrate the diagnostic and corrective approach were the following: determining meanings of homographs, using context clues, finding the main idea of a paragraph and the central idea of a group of paragraphs, drawing inferences, categorizing, and recognizing analogies. An explanation and examples, as well as diagnostic tests and correction, were given for each presented skill. In the vocabulary section of the chapter, it was stressed that good vocabulary and good reading go hand in hand and that children who are deficient in vocabulary development will have difficulty in reading because comprehension is impossible without an understanding of words. Because of this teachers should have a planned vocabulary program in their classes rather than leaving it to chance.

Diagnostic checklists were presented for both comprehension and vocabulary skills.

SUGGESTIONS FOR THOUGHT QUESTIONS AND ACTIVITIES

1. State the four levels of comprehension presented in this chapter. State one skill for each level. Then prepare a behavioral objective and a criterion-referenced test for the behavioral objective for each skill you have chosen (primary grades).

2. Do the same for the intermediate grades.

3. You have been appointed to a special reading curriculum committee at your school. The committee is interested in revamping their primary reading program. What suggestions would you make.

4. You are appointed to a committee that is charged with developing a diagnostic testing and correction program for reading comprehension. What suggestions would you make to the committee to proceed?

5. Generate reading comprehension questions for a selection that would elicit high-level reading/thinking responses.

6. You have been asked to generate a number of diagnostic tests for intermediate-grade students in vocabulary development. What kind of diagnostic tests would you develop?

7. There are a number of children in your first-grade class who are weak in concept development. How would this affect their vocabulary development? What can you

do to help them acquire the concepts they need?

8. You are interested in developing a vocabulary expansion program using combining forms. How would you go about doing it? What kinds of activities would you develop for students weak in vocabulary?

9. How important is vocabulary development? Explain.

10. How can you diagnose vocabulary problems in content areas?

11. Construct a pretest to determine whether your intermediate-grade students have knowldege of some often used combining forms.

12. You have a student in your class who has difficulty answering comprehension questions. How would you go about determining what his or her problem or problems are? What can you do to help this student?

13. Present a reading comprehension lesson and videotape it. Note the kinds of questions you ask. Critique your lesson and state some ways in which you can improve it.

14. Compare your students' reading behavior in the content areas to their behavior when reading in reading groups. Try to determine whether interest in a subject affects the students' reading performance.

SELECTED BIBLIOGRAPHY

Burke, Eileen M. "Using Trade Books to Intrigue Children with Words." *The Reading Teacher* 32 (November 1978): 144–48.

Cuyler, Richard C. "Guidelines for Skill Development: Vocabulary." *The Reading Teacher* 32 (December 1978): 316–22.

Durkin, Dolores. "What Is the Value of the New Interest in Reading Comprehension." *Language Arts* 58 (January 1981): 23–43.

Goodman, Yetta, and Dorothy J. Watson. "A Reading Program to Live With: Focus on Comprehension." *Language Arts* 54 (November/December 1977): 868–79.

Guszak, Frank J. "Teacher Questioning and Reading." *The Reading Teacher* 21 (1967): 227–34, 252.

Hansen, Jane. "An Inferential Comprehension Strategy for Use with Primary Grade Children." *The Reading Teacher* 34 (March 1981): 665–69.

Hoban, Tana. *Push, Pull, Empty, Full: A Book of Opposites.* New York: Macmillan, 1972.

Karbal, Harold T. "Keying In on Vocabulary." *Elementary English* 52 (March 1975): 367–69.

Rubin, Dorothy. *Gaining Word Power.* New York: Macmill

_____. *The Vital Arts—Reading and Writing.* New York: Macmillan, 1979.

_____. *Reading and Learning Power.* New York: Macmillan, 1980.

_____. *The Teacher's Handbook of Reading/Thinking Exercises.* New York: Holt, Rinehart and Winston, 1980.

_____. "Developing Vocabulary Skills." In *The Primary-Grade Teacher's Language Arts Handbook.* New York: Holt, Rinehart and Winston, 1980.

_____. "Developing Vocabulary Skills." In *The Intermediate-Grade Teacher's Language Arts Handbook.* New York: Holt, Rinehart and Winston, 1980.

_____. *The Teacher's Handbook of Primary-Grade Reading/Thinking Exercises.* New York: Holt, Rinehart and Winston, 1982.

_____. *Vocabulary Expansion I.* New York: Macmillan, 1982.

_____. *Vocabulary Expansion II.* New York: Macmillan, 1982.

Singer, Harry. "Active Comprehension: From Answering to Asking Questions." *The Reading Teacher* 31 (May 1978): 901–908.

Smith, Frank. *Understanding Reading,* 2nd ed. New York: Holt, Rinehart and Winston, 1978.

Smith, Nila Banton. "The Many Faces of Reading Comprehension." *The Reading Teacher* 23 (December 1969): 249–59, 291.

Sullivan, JoAnna. "Comparing Strategies of Good and Poor Comprehenders." *Journal of Reading* 21 (May 1978): 710–15.

Tatham, Susan M. "Comprehension Taxonomies: Their Uses and Abuses." *The Reading Teacher* 32 (November 1978): 190–94.

Thorndike, E. L. "Reading as Reasoning: A Study of Mistakes in Paragraph Reading." *Journal of Educational Psychology* 8 (June 1917): 323–32.

Thorndike, Robert L. "Reading as Reasoning." *Reading Research Quarterly* 9 (1973–74): 135–47.

Vaughan, Sally, et al. "A Multiple-Modality Approach to Word Study: Vocabulary Scavenger Hunts." *The Reading Teacher* 32 (January 1979): 434–37.

CHAPTER 14

Reading and Study Skills

INTRODUCTION[1]

How many times have you heard students make the following statements?

"I spent all night studying, but I did very poorly on my exams."
"I reread the chapter ten times, but I still don't understand it."
"I reread the chapter about fifteen times, and I don't even remember what I read."
"I always listen to music when I study."
"I like to be relaxed when I study."
"I don't need to study."
"I don't know how to study."
And so it goes . . .

Many students do poorly in school because they have never learned how to study. Elementary-school teachers usually do not spend time helping children acquire study skills

because they themselves may lack the skills,[2] or because they feel that this is the job of high school teachers. Also, many high school teachers do not spend time in this area because they make the assumption that their students have already acquired the study skills they need. As a result, many students go through the grades without ever being helped to acquire study skills. This is a mistake. Children should be helped to acquire good study habits as soon as possible before they develop either poor study habits or erroneous concepts about studying. Children should be helped to learn that with good study habits, they could spend less time studying and learn more.

This chapter is concerned with helping you gain the information and skills that are necessary for you to help your students become better learners. This is important in a diagnostic-reading and correction program where the emphasis is on the *prevention* of reading and

[1]Portions of this chapter are adapted from Dorothy Rubin, *Reading and Learning Power* (New York: Macmillan, 1980).

[2]Eunice N. Askov et al., "Study Skill Mastery Among Elementary Teachers," *The Reading Teacher* 30 (February 1977):485-88.

learning problems. After you finish reading this chapter, you should be able to answer the following questions:

1. What does studying require, and what is the key to building good study habits?
2. What is SQ3R?
3. What is the role of concentration in studying?
4. How do attitudes influence our studying?
5. What is skimming?
6. What role does skimming play in study techniques?
7. How do you summarize a paragraph?
8. Why should children be good question-askers?
9. How can the teacher help his or her students to be better notetakers?
10. How can the teacher help his or her students to be better test-takers?

WHAT ARE SOME GOOD STUDY PROCEDURES?

Although there is no simple formula that will apply to all students, educational psychologists have found that some procedures will help all students. The key is in building good habits, devising a system that works for the individual student, and keeping at it.

A person cannot relax and study at the same time. Studying requires a certain amount of tension, concentration, and effort in a specific direction. Of course, the amount of tension varies with different individuals. The point is that studying is hard work, and students who are not

prepared to make a proper effort are wasting their time.

Building Good Study Habits

The first step in building good study habits is to determine *when to study.* Some students study only just before an announced test. Some may even stay up until all hours and cram. All of us have probably done this once or twice. However, if this is a student's normal way of doing things, he or she will not do well in school. Cramming does not bring about sustained learning. It can be justified only as a last resort. To be a good student, the student must plan his or her study time and spread it out over a period of time. Students must realize that a regular plan will prevent confusion and help them retain what they are studying. Students, even in the

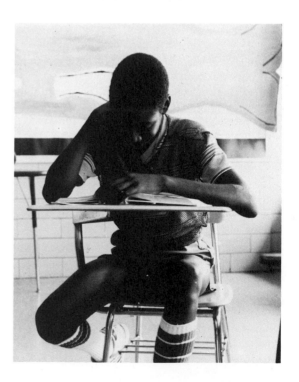

elementary grades, should be helped to plan an overall time schedule in which they allow for social and physical activities. It is to be hoped that their time schedule also allows for some recreational reading (see Chapter 17). Students must recognize that a rhythm of activities is important. It does not matter whether they study in the evening, before or after dinner, or right after class during free periods. The important thing is for the student to follow a schedule and spread out the studying over the week.

The second step in building good study habits is to determine *where to study.* Some students are able to study well in a school or public library, but there are others who cannot. Most elementary-school students study at home. Regardless of where the student studies, he or she should choose a place that is comfortable and convenient, has enough light, and is *free from distractions.* Consistency is important.

To help children establish a comfortable, convenient, and suitable place for study at home, the teacher and the children can design such a place in the classroom. A special area can be set aside as a study area. It should be as free from distractions as possible, comfortable, and well lighted. Students should be free to go to this area whenever they wish to study. If a student is in this area, other students should recognize that it is "off bounds"; that is, other students should respect the student's desire to study and not interrupt or bother the student.

Teachers must recognize that there are some students in class who may not have a place at home to study. There may be many children in the house and not enough rooms, so that the only place to study may be the kitchen. This place, however, is not very good because it usually has too many distractions. Teachers should be aware of the home situations of their students and try to help them as much as possible without embarrassing them. One thing the teacher could do is discuss the possibility of studying at the library or at a friend's house. If these are not

feasible, and if the student does not have to ride a bus to school, the teacher might make some arrangements whereby the student can study in the school. A teacher must be sensitive to the fact that students who do not have a place to do homework or study at home are actually being penalized twice—once, because they do not have a place to study, and twice, because they will probably be penalized for not doing the homework and they will also probably not do well in school.

The third step in building good study habits is to determine the *amount of time* to spend in studying. You must help students recognize that the amount of time they spend will depend on the subject and how well they know it. It is unrealistic to set up a hard-and-fast rule about the amount of time to study in a specific subject because the amount of time will vary. In some subjects a student may need to spend a lot of time studying because he or she is weak in that area, whereas in others the student may only have to spend a short time studying. You should help students understand the concept of *overlearning* because some students feel that if they know something, they do not have to study it at all. In order to overlearn something, students must recognize that they must practice it even after they feel that they know it. *Overlearning* is not bad like *overcooking* the roast. Overlearning helps persons retain information over a long period of time. Overlearning happens when individuals continue to practice even after they think they have learned the material.

HOW TO STUDY

After you have helped students attain positive attitudes toward their learning tasks and helped them recognize that they must exert effort to study, find a suitable place to study, and spend time in studying, you must still help them learn *how to study.* There are a number of study techniques; however, SQ3R[3] will be presented rather than some of the others because it is a widely used technique developed by a well-known psychologist that has proved helpful to many students. Here are the five steps in this technique:

1. *Survey*—Students should get an *overall* sense of their learning task before proceeding to details. They should skim the whole assignment to obtain some idea(s) about the material and how it is organized.

2. *Question*—Students should check section headings and change these to questions to set their purposes for reading.

3. *Read*—Students should read to answer the questions that they have formulated for themselves. While reading they should notice how the paragraphs are organized because this will help them remember the answer.

4. *Recite*—*This step is very important.* Without referring to their book, students should try to answer the questions that they have formulated for themselves. (Writing down key ideas will provide necessary notes for future review. See section on notetaking.)

5. *Review*—Students should take a few moments to review the major headings and subheadings of their previous assignment before starting to study the new assignment. (How well they are able to combine or incorporate the new learning with their previous learning will determine how well they will remember the new material.) After they have completed their entire new assignment, they should take a few moments to go over its major ideas before they go on to something else.

Make sure students understand that they can survey a reading assignment to determine its organization and to obtain some ideas about it, but they cannot study unfamiliar material by skimming or reading rapidly. Help your students to recognize that the key factor in remembering information is recall or recitation and not the rereading of their assignment. The time they spend answering the questions that they have formulated is crucial in learning.

Here is an example of how you can help your students adapt the SQ3R technique to suit their personal needs.

Example: Assignment—Reading a Chapter in a Textbook

Step 1. Students should quickly look over the entire chapter for an overview and to see the organization and relationships. In doing this it's a good idea for students to read quickly the first

© 1975 United Features Syndicate, Inc.

[3]Adapted from Francis P. Robinson, *Effective Study,* 4th ed. (New York: Harper & Row, 1970).

sentence of each paragraph because textbook writers generally put the topic sentence at the beginning of the paragraph. (Students should notice section headings and authors' marginal notes.)

Step 2. Students should choose a part of the chapter to study. (The amount of material they choose will depend on their concentration ability and their prior knowledge in the area. See section on concentration in this chapter.)

Step 3. Students should look over the first part of the chapter that they have chosen to study and formulate questions on it. (Most textbooks have section headings that are very helpful for formulating questions.)

Step 4. Students should read the material to answer their questions. While reading, they should keep in mind the way that the author has organized the details.

Step 5. Students should attempt to answer questions formulated before reading.

Step 6. Students should go on to the next section of their chapter and follow the same steps. After they have finished their whole assignment, they should review or go over *all* that they have studied. (When they review, they should go back to the beginning of the chapter, look at each section heading, and try to recall the main idea of each paragraph in the section.)

Activities

Here are some sample activities to give your students practice in using the SQ3R technique.

1. Choose a selection your students have not read before, and have them do the following:
    a. Survey the selection to determine what it's about.
    b. Use the given six questions to set purposes for reading.
    c. Read the selection carefully.
    d. Without looking back at the selection, try to answer the questions. (Prepare six questions that can be used to set purposes for reading.)

2. Choose another selection that your students have not read before, and have them do the following:
    a. Survey the selection to determine what it's about.
    b. Use the given five questions to set purposes for reading.
    c. Read the selection carefully.
    d. Without looking back at the selection, try to answer the questions. (Prepare five questions that can be used to set purposes for reading and that students can answer.)

3. Choose a selection that your students have not read before, and have them formulate questions that could help them in studying.

CONCENTRATION

You need to help your students recognize that even though they are acquiring some good study habits, they may still have difficulty studying because they cannot *concentrate*. Concentration is necessary not only for studying but also for listening in class. Concentration is sustained attention. If you are not feeling well, if you are hungry or tired, if you are in a room that is too hot or cold, if your chair is uncomfortable, if the lighting is poor or if there is a glare, if there are visual or auditory distractions, you will not be able to concentrate.

Skill in concentration can be developed, and teachers should plan to have their students spend time in this area, which is essential for both reading and listening skills.

Concentration demands a mental set or attitude, a determination that you will block everything out except what you are reading or listening to. For example, how many times have you looked up a phone number in the telephone directory and forgotten the number almost immediately? How many times have you had to look up the *same* number that you had dialed a number of times? Probably very often. The reason for your not remembering is that you did not *concentrate.* In order to remember information, you must concentrate. Concentration demands active involvement; it is hard work. You must help your students recognize that it is a contradiction to say that you will concentrate and relax at the same time. Concentration demands wide-awake and alert individuals. It also demands persons who have a positive frame of mind toward their work. Teachers need to have a good affective environment in their classrooms and be encouraging because the students' attitude or mental set toward what they are doing will greatly influence how well they will do. Obviously if students are not interested in the lecture or reading assignment, they will not be able to concentrate. Teachers should, therefore, try to make the lectures and assignments as interesting as possible.

Of course, it is necessary to help your students understand that paying attention does not guarantee they will comprehend what they have read or heard, but it is an important first step. Without concentration, there is no hope of understanding the information. The following types of activities will help your students develop their concentration.

Activities

Activity 1: Word Concentration (Listening)[4]

In playing this game, just two persons are needed—a speaker and a listener. It can also be played with teams. The speaker says, "Listen

[4]Dorothy Rubin, *The Primary-Grade Teacher's Language Arts Handbook* (New York: Holt, Rinehart and Winston, 1980).

carefully. I am going to say some words and when I am through, I want you to repeat them. I will state the words only once and at a rate of one per second. Remember. Listen carefully and do not say them until I am finished. I'll start with two words and then I'll keep adding one word. Let's do one together."

Example: Speaker says, "Train, nail." The listener repeats, "Train, nail." And the speaker says, "Good," if the words are repeated correctly.

Set 1: can/dog . . . red/map . . .

Set 2: mail/milk/book . . . cake/pen/sad . . .

Set 3: sad/none/in/may . . . chair/help/two/ six . . .

Set 4: name/sail/bike/pen/man . . . worm/boat/ sick/has/more . . .

Set 5: chair/name/key/same/hop/note . . . leg/ rope/teach/dance/dog/name . . .

Set 6: witch/rob/sleep/some/read/check/nuts . . . ball/ape/mind/sleep/dog/king/hair . . .

Set 7: spoon/mate/can/man/all/book/sad/ show . . . love/rode/room/all/door/can/ girl/pad . . .

Set 8: boat/lamp/paint/long/dock/teach/knife /win/chair . . . draw/food/pat/car/sand/pan /size/spring/farm . . .

In this game, the words that are presented are not related to one another, so that the listener must concentrate very hard in order to be able to repeat them immediately. This game can be played each day or a few times during the week. Children enjoy playing this game and are delighted when they find that they are able to pay attention for longer periods of time and are, therefore, able to repeat more and more of the words.

The following paragraph presents a scale that should help in determining how well your children are doing.

Digit-Span Scale for Digits Forward and Digits Backward

On the average, two-and-one-half-year-olds are able to repeat two digits in order, and three-year-olds are able to repeat three digits in order. Children from about the age of four and one-half to about seven years of age are able to repeat four digits in order. Seven- to ten-year-olds are usually able to repeat five digits in order. Ten- to fourteen-year-olds are usually able to repeat six digits in order. Fourteen-year-olds to more able adults usually can repeat seven, eight, and nine digits in order. (Digits refer to numbers. One-syllable words may be substituted for digits.)

On the average, seven-year-olds can repeat three digits in reverse order, and nine-year-olds to twelve-year-olds can repeat four digits in reverse order. Twelve-year-olds up to able adults can repeat five digits in reverse order. More able adults can usually repeat six and seven digits in reverse order.

Activity 2: Digit-Span Concentration (Listening)[5]

Digit-span exercises based on a graduated level of difficulty are helpful in developing concentration. The instructions for the digits are similar to those in Activity 1 for words; however, in place of words the term *number* is inserted. (See Chapter 10.)

Activity 3: Adding Word Concentration (Listening)[6]

The teacher says, "I'm going to say two sets of words. The second set has all the words from Set 1 but it also has a new word. You have to write what the new word is. Example: *Set 1:*

pen, dog, tall. *Set 2:* tall, dog, pen, snow. (The new word is *snow.*)"

Set 1: stamp, week, red
Set 2: week, stamp, red, (smoke)

Set 1: child, help, dark, nice
Set 2: child, (grow), help, nice, dark

Set 1: sun, spoon, mouth, five, bet
Set 2: spoon, mouth, five, (game), bet, sun

Set 1: wild, rose, bread, couch, pill, cup
Set 2: rose, bread, couch, pill, (crumb), cup, wild

Set 1: pin, fat, net, pine, wind, swing, dog
Set 2: fat, net, pine, wind, (damp), swing, pin, dog

FOLLOWING DIRECTIONS

Being able to follow directions is an important skill that we use all our lives. Scarcely a day goes by without the need to obey directions. Cooking, baking, taking medication, driving, traveling, repairing, building, planning, taking examinations, doing assignments, filling out applications, and a hundred other common activities require the ability to follow directions.

You can help your students to be better at following directions through practice and by having them heed the pointers given below.

1. Read the directions *carefully*. Do *not* skim directions. Do not take anything for granted and, therefore, skip reading a part of the directions.

2. If you do not understand any directions, do not hesitate to ask your teacher and/or another student.

3. Concentrate! People who follow directions well tend also to have the ability to concentrate well.

4. Follow the directions that *are* given, not the ones you think ought to be given.

[5]Dorothy Rubin, *The Intermediate-Grade Teacher's Language Arts Handbook* (New York: Holt, Rinehart and Winston, 1980).
[6]Ibid.

5. Reread the directions if you need to, and refer to them as you follow them.

6. Remember that some directions should be followed step by step.

7. Practice following directions. Try this activity, which will give you experience in following directions.

Directions: Read carefully the entire list of directions that follows before doing anything. You have four minutes to complete this activity.[7]

1. Put your name in the upper right-hand corner of this paper.

2. Put your address under your name.

3. Put your telephone number in the upper left-hand corner of this paper.

4. Add 9370 and 5641.

5. Subtract 453 from 671.

6. Raise your hand and say, "I'm the first."

7. Draw two squares, one triangle, and three circles.

8. Write the opposite of *hot.*

9. Stand up and stamp your feet.

10. Give three meanings for *spring.*

11. Write the numbers from one to ten backward.

12. Write the even numbers from two to twenty.

13. Write the odd numbers from one to twenty-one.

14. Write seven words that rhyme with *fat.*

15. Call out, "I have followed directions."

16. If you have read the directions carefully, you should have done nothing until now. Do only directions 1 and 2.

[7]Dorothy Rubin, *The Teacher's Handbook of Reading/Thinking Exercises* (New York: Holt, Rinehart and Winston, 1980).

Answer: The directions stated that you should read the entire list of directions carefully *before doing anything.* You should have done only directions 1 and 2. When you take timed tests, you usually do *not* read the directions as carefully as you should.

Activities

Here is a sample activity in following directions.

Directions: Read each numbered instruction once only, and then carry out the instructions on the boxed material. (This activity requires a great amount of concentration.)[8]

1	7	3	4	play	dog	man	M	N	O
P	Q	35	32	63	15	10	stop	under	big

Instructions

1. If there are two numbers that added together equal 7 and a word that rhymes with *may,* put a line under the rhyming word.

2. If there is a word that means the same as *large,* a word opposite to *go,* and a word that rhymes with *fan,* put a circle around the three words.

3. If there are two numbers that added together equal 8, two numbers that added together equal 67, and a word the opposite of *over,* underline the two numbers that added together equal 8.

4. If there are five consecutive letters, four words that each contain a different vowel, and at least four odd numbers, put a cross on the five consecutive letters.

5. If there are six words, three even numbers, two numbers that added together equal 45,

[8]Ibid.

and three numbers that added together equal 16, circle the word *dog*.

6. If there are two numbers that added together equal 25, two numbers that added together equal 95, and three numbers that added together equal 79, put a circle around the three numbers that added together equal 79.

SKIMMING

Setting purposes for reading is a crucial factor. Students need to learn that they read for different purposes. If they are reading for pleasure, they may either read quickly or slowly based on the way they feel. If they are studying or reading information that is new to them, they will probably read very slowly. If, however, they are looking up a telephone number, a name, a date, or looking over a paragraph for its topic, they will read much more rapidly. Reading rapidly to find or locate information is called *skimming*. All skimming involves fast reading; however, there are different kinds of skimming. Skimming for a number, a date, or a name can usually be done much more quickly than for the topic of a paragraph or to answer specific questions. (Some persons call the most rapid reading *scanning* and the less rapid reading skimming.) Teachers should help students recognize that they read rapidly to locate some specific information, but that once they have located what they want, they may read the surrounding information more slowly.

Teachers should also make sure that students do not confuse skimming with studying. Although skimming is used as part of the SQ3R technique when students survey a passage, skimming material is not the same as studying. Studying requires much slower and more concentrated reading.

Skimming is an important skill because it is used so often throughout one's life, and it is many times the only way to get a job done in a reasonable amount of time. Some skimming activities for upper-intermediate-grade students follow:

1. Skim newspaper headlines for a particular news item.
2. Skim movie ads for a particular movie.
3. Skim tape or record catalogs for a specific title.
4. Skim the Yellow Pages of the phone book for some help.
5. Skim the television guide to find a particular show.

OUTLINING

Outlining helps students organize long written compositions or papers. An outline should serve as a guide for the logical arrangement of material. Closely related to classification and categorizing, outlining should begin to be developed in the primary grades (see Chapters 4 and 13).

Sets and Outlining

An exercise involving sets can be used with both primary- and intermediate-grade students to help them recognize that outlining and classification are closely related. Ask students to think of the set of all the books in the library. This is a very general set:

Books in
the library

Next ask students to state the kinds of books one would find in the library. By doing this we are becoming less general:

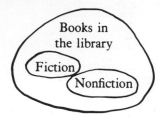

Now ask students to state what kinds of books one would find in the set of fiction books and what kinds of books one would find in the set of nonfiction books:

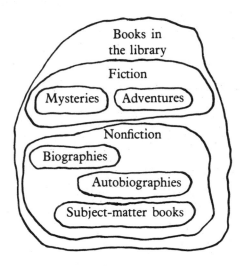

Ask the children to name a particular mystery or adventure book. At this point we are becoming very specific:

Now ask the students to put this information in outline form.

Here are samples of exercises, according to grade levels, which should help children develop the skill of outlining through understanding classification.

PRIMARY GRADES

FAMILY NAMES

Directions

On the line above each group write the appropriate family name or main topic. Although the different groups in each exercise belong to the same general class, the differences between the groups may be indicated by adding a descriptive word to the family name you choose.

Horse
Cow
Dog

Tiger
Wolf
Bear
Moose
Fox

FOURTH OR FIFTH GRADE

ORGANIZING

Directions

At the head of the exercise is a list of words. Take each word and ask: "Does this word belong in Group I or Group II?'' When you are sure of your answer, write the word under its main topic.

EXERCISE

Chicago, Arizona, Vermont, California, Los Angeles, Tulsa, Georgia, Baltimore

I. States
   A.
   B.
   C.
   D.

II. Cities
   A.
   B.
   C.
   D.

OUTLINES—TIME ORDER

Directions

Study the following list. Select your main topics, and arrange them in time order. Then arrange your subtopics.

EXERCISE

Changes in Transportation

horseback, pioneer forms, modern forms, covered wagon, railway express, pony express, motor truck, airplane

   I.
      A.
      B.
      C.

   II.
      A.
      B.
      C.

FIFTH OR SIXTH GRADE

LEVELS OF ABSTRACTION

Here are some items in columns. Each column describes one item. Each word tells you more, or less, information about the item than all the others. Put a 1 in front of the word that tells the least, a 2 in front of the word that tells the next least, and so on until the highest number is placed beside the word telling the most. The word that tells the least is the most general word—such as *animal*—whereas the word that tells the most is the most specific—such as *John Doe.*

Example

3	A—John Doe
1	B—Animal
2	C—Human
____	A—Animal
____	B—Lassie
____	C—Collie
____	D—Dog
____	A—Rock
____	B—Nonliving
____	C—Rock formations
____	D—Mt. Everest
____	A—Tree
____	B—Living organism
____	C—Spruce
____	D—Plant

_____ E—Evergreen

_____ A—Mammal

_____ B—Living organism

_____ C—Arthur Hale

_____ D—Human

_____ E—Animal

_____ A—Machinery

_____ B—Automobile

_____ C—Cadillac

_____ D—Vehicle

_____ A—Wheat

_____ B—Grain

_____ C—Plant

_____ D—Living organism

SUMMARIES

Many teachers are helping intermediate- and higher-grade level students learn how to summarize passages because they recognize this as a viable means of gaining the essential information. Summarizing material helps persons retain the most important facts in a long passage, and if the summary is a written summary, it helps integrate the reading and writing process.

Teachers can help elementary children learn how to summarize by beginning with paragraphs and then working up to longer passages. Children should know that a good summary should be brief and should include only essential information. The main idea of the paragraph (if only a paragraph is being summarized) or the central idea of an article and the important facts should be stated but not necessarily in the se-

quence presented in the article. The sequence in the paragraph or article must be followed in the summary only if that sequence is essential. Teachers need to help their students include only the information stated in the paragraph or article and not what they think should have been included or their opinions.

Before teachers work with summaries, it might be a good idea for them to review with their students how to find the main idea of passages.

KNOWING YOUR TEXTBOOK

Helping children to learn about the various parts of their textbooks is an important study skill that can save students valuable time and effort. Here are some things that teachers should have students do after they have acquired their textbooks.

1. *Survey the textbook.* This helps students see how the author presents the material. Students should notice whether the author presents topic headings in bold print or in the margins. Students should also notice if there are diagrams, charts, cartoons, pictures, and so on.

2. *Read the preface.* The preface or foreword, which is at the beginning of the book, is the author's explanation of the book. It presents the author's purpose and plan in writing the book. Here the author usually describes the organization of the book and explains how the book either is different from others in the field or is a further contribution to the field of knowledge.

3. *Read the chapter headings.* The table of contents will give students a good idea of what to expect from the book. Then when they begin to study they will know how each

section they are reading relates to the rest of the book.

4. *Skim the index.* The index indicates in detail what material students will find in the book. It is an invaluable aid because it helps students find specific information that they need by giving them the page on which it appears.

5. *Check for a glossary.* Not all books have a glossary; however, a glossary is helpful because it gives students the meanings of specialized words or phrases used in the book.

Activities

Have the students skim to answer the following:

1. Using the index of one of the students' textbooks, the students state the pages on which they would find various topics.

2. Using one of their textbooks, the students give the meaning(s) of some of the terms that are presented in the glossary.

3. Using the table of contents of one of their textbooks, the students state the pages that some chapters start on.

ASKING QUESTIONS

A section on asking questions is being presented because this is an area in which students need special help. Many students become intimidated early in school about asking questions and as a result hardly ever ask any. Asking questions is an important part of learning. Children must be helped to recognize this, and teachers must provide an environment that is nonthreatening so that students will feel free to ask questions. Knowing how and when to ask questions helps students to gain a better insight

into a subject, gives the teacher feedback, and slows the teacher down if he or she is going too fast. Unfortunately, as has already been stated, many students are afraid to ask questions. Sometimes their fear may be caused by a teacher's attitude; however, often it's because a student doesn't know how to formulate the question or is "afraid of looking like a fool."

Here are some pointers that teachers should try to get across to their students:

1. Persons who ask the best questions are usually those who know the material best.

2. Asking questions is not a substitute for studying the material.

3. Questions help to clarify the material for students.

4. Teachers usually want and encourage questions.

5. The questions students ask will probably help a number of other students.

Here are suggestions on the kind of questions students should ask about examinations:

1. What kind of test will it be? Will it be an objective or subjective test?

2. How long will the test be? (This will help the students to know whether it's a quiz (a minor exam) or a test (one that usually counts more than a quiz).

3. Will dates, names, formulas, and other such specifics be stressed? (This is important for the student to know because it will influence the type of studying that he or she will do.)

4. Will it be an open-book or closed-book exam? (This is important because it will influence the type of studying a student will do.)

5. What chapters will be covered?

Here are some suggestions on other kinds of questions students should ask:

1. In going over an examination, they should ask general questions or those that relate to everyone's papers. Tell students that if they have specific questions on their papers, they should ask the teacher their questions in private.
2. Tell students that they should not hesitate to ask questions about the marking of their papers if they do not understand it. They should especially ask the teacher about a comment on their papers that they do not understand. Help them to recognize that they learn from knowing the results and understanding their mistakes.

Here are some suggestions on how students should ask questions:

1. They should be as specific as possible.
2. They should state the question clearly.
3. They should not say, "I have a question," and then go into a long discourse before asking it. (The question may be forgotten.)
4. They should make sure that the question is related to the material.

NOTETAKING FOR STUDYING

Notetaking is a very important tool; it is useful not only in writing long papers but also in studying. Students are usually not concerned with notetaking until they begin writing long reports or papers. Teachers should help students learn how to take notes. Here is information on notetaking that teachers should convey to their upper-intermediate-grade students.

Notes consist of words and phrases that help persons remember important material. They do not have to be complete sentences; however, un-

less an individual's notes are clear and organized, he or she will have difficulty in using them for study. For example, examine this set of notes on an article entitled "Why Home Accidents Occur":

Student's Notes

1. slippery floors
2. bathroom light switch
3. cellar stairs dark
4. ladder broken
5. medicines on shelf
6. light cord bare
7. pots on stove with handles out
8. throw rugs
9. using tools carelessly
10. toys on floor
11. box on stairs
12. putting penny in fuse box
13. thin curtains over stove

Student's List of Main Topics of Article

I.   Failure to see danger
II. Failure to use things correctly
III. Failure to make repairs

It is difficult to make sense of these notes because the main topics are vaguely stated. The items in the list of notes can fit under more than one main topic; they are not precise enough; that is, they do not contain enough information to unmistakably identify or distinguish them.

Notetaking for study can be incorporated in the SQ3R study technique. Here is a suggested procedure combining SQ3R and notetaking:

1. Students should read the whole selection to

get an overview of what they have to study. A preliminary reading helps them see the organization of the material.

2. Students should choose a part of the selection to study, basing their choice on their concentration ability.

3. Students should survey the part chosen and note the topic of the individual paragraph or group of paragraphs. They should write the topic(s) in their notebook instead of the questions they would write in a normal SQ3R procedure.

4. Students should read the part.

5. After they finish reading each paragraph, they should state its main idea. Students should put down *only* important supporting details under the main idea.

   a. Although students do not have to use a formal outline for their notes, they should *indent* their listing so that the relation of supporting material to main ideas is clear.

   b. Students should try not to take any notes until after they have finished reading the whole paragraph. They should remember that *recall* is the essential step in the SQ3R technique. By not taking notes until they have finished reading, they are more actively involved in thinking about the material as they try to construct notes.

Good notes are very helpful for review, and they can save students a great amount of time.

You should help your students recognize that for study, if the material is new to them, it's usually a good idea to write the topic for each paragraph unless the paragraph is a transitional one. You should also tell your students that textbook writers sometimes list the topics of their paragraphs in the margins and the students should be on the lookout for these helpful clues.

TEST-TAKING

The term *tests* seems to make most students shudder. However, tests are necessary to help students learn about their weaknesses so that they can improve and also learn about their strengths; they help give students a steady and encouraging measure of their growth; and tests are helpful for review.

The more students know about tests, the better they can do on them. The general test-taking principles that follow are provided for you the teacher so that you can help your students to be better test-takers. The principles you present to your students will depend on the grade level you are teaching as well as the students with whom you are working. Many intermediate-grade students are ready to learn about test-taking techniques and how to study for them. As a matter of fact, so are some primary-grade children. Although children today seem to be test-wise, most really are not.

Teachers should help students to be better test-takers. The first thing that teachers should try to help students understand is that the best way to do well on a test is to be *well prepared*. There are no shortcuts to studying. However, research has shown that persons do better on tests if they know certain test-taking techniques and if they are familiar with the various types of tests.

Here are some general test-taking principles:

1. Students should plan to do well. They should have a *positive* attitude.

2. Students should be well rested.

3. Students should be prepared. The better prepared an individual is, the less nervous and anxious he or she will be.

4. Students should look upon tests as a learning experience.

5. Students should look over the whole test before they begin. They should notice the

types of questions asked and the points allotted for each question. (Students have to learn not to spend a long time on a one- to five-point question that they know a lot about. They should answer it and go on.)

6. Students should know how much time is allotted for the test. (Students need to learn to allot their time wisely and to check the time.)

7. Students should concentrate!

8. Students should read instructions very carefully. (Students need to be helped in this area because many times they read into the questions things that are not there. Students must learn that if a question asks for a description and *examples,* they must give the examples. Students also need to learn that if they do not understand something or if something does not make sense, they should ask the teacher about it because there may be a mistake on the test.)

9. Students should begin with the questions they are sure of. This will give them a feeling of confidence and success. However, as already advised, they must learn not to dwell on these at length.

10. If students do not know an answer, they should make an intelligent guess. As long as the penalty for a wrong answer is the same as for no answer, it pays to take a calculated guess. (Of course, if the guess is wrong, students will not get any points for it.)

11. After students answer the questions they are sure of, they should work on those that count the most, that is, that are worth the greatest number of points.

12. Students should allow time to go over the test. They should check that they have answered all the questions. They should be leery about changing a response unless they have found a particular reason to while going over the test. For example, they may have misread the question, they may have misinterpreted the question, or they may not have realized that it was a "tricky" question. If the question is a straightforward one, it's probably better for students to leave their first response.

13. After the test has been graded and returned, students should go over it to learn from the results. Unless students find out why an answer is wrong and what the correct answer is, they may continue to make the same mistake on other tests.

14. Students should study the test after they get it back to determine what their teacher emphasizes on tests.

THE SCHOOL LIBRARY AND LIBRARY SKILLS

The school library should be an integrated part of the students' ongoing activities. A number of schools have designed their physical plants so that the library is actually in the center of the building, easily accessible to all classrooms. The library, properly utilized, becomes the students' storehouse of information and a reservoir of endless delight.

The atmosphere in the library should be such that children feel welcome, invited, and wanted. The librarian is the individual who is responsible for setting this tone. A friendly, warm person who loves children and books will usually have a library which has similar characteristics. Children should feel free to visit the library at all times, not just during their regularly scheduled periods.

An enthusiastic and inventive librarian will, by various means, act as an invitation to children to come to the library. Some librarians engage in weekly storytelling for all grade levels.

author card, a title card, and the subject card. The teacher should have samples of these for the children to see and handle. By simulating this activity in the classroom, children will be better prepared for actual library activity. Also, their chances for success in using the catalog properly to find a desired book will be increased. This utilitarian activity can also be programmed to reinforce knowledge of alphabetizing.

Intermediate and Upper-Elementary Grades

By the fourth grade children can learn about other categories of books in the library, such as biographies and reference books.

Reference Books

Children in the elementary grades ask many questions about many topics. Teachers should use some of these questions to help children learn about reference sources. Teachers should help children understand that it is impossible for one person to know everything today because of the vast amount of knowledge that already exists, compounded each year by its exponential

Librarians should encourage teachers and children to make suggestions for storytelling, as well as to share the kinds of books they enjoy and would like. The librarian should also act as a resource person in helping the classroom teacher develop library skills in students. Once students gain the "library habit," it is hard to break, and it will remain with them throughout life.

Following are some of the library skills that children should receive in the elementary school.

Primary Grades

In the primary grades children are ready to acquire some library skills which will help them become independent library users. First, the teacher can help primary-grade children learn the kinds of books that are available in the library, for example, fiction and nonfiction books. Definitions of the terms should be given, as well as examples of each type of book. For best results, the examples used should be books with which the children are familiar.

Primary-grade children who have learned to read and can alphabetize can also learn to use the card catalog. They should learn that there are three kinds of cards for each book: an

growth. However, a person can learn about any particular area or field if he or she knows what source books to go to for help. For example, the *Readers' Guide to Periodical Literature* will help one to find magazine articles written on almost any subject of interest. There are reference books on language and usage, such as Roget's *Thesaurus of English Words and Phrases,* which would help upper-grade students find synonyms and less trite words to use in writing.

The dictionary, which is a very important reference book, is probably the one with which the students are the most familiar. It is helpful in supplying the following information to a student:

1. Spelling.
2. Correct usage.
3. Derivations and inflected forms.
4. Accents and other diacritical markings.
5. Antonyms.
6. Synonyms.
7. Syllabication.
8. Definitions.
9. Parts of speech.
10. Idiomatic phrases.

The most often used reference book in elementary school, besides the dictionary, is the encyclopedia. Children should be helped to use the encyclopedia as a tool and as an aid, rather than as an end in itself. That is, children should be shown how to extract information from the encyclopedia without copying the article verbatim.

In the upper elementary grades children should learn that there are many reference books available in the library which can supply information about a famous writer, baseball player, scientist, celebrity, and so forth. The key factor is knowing that these reference sources exist and knowing which book to go to for the needed information.

Teachers can help their upper-grade children familiarize themselves with these reference books by giving them assignments in which they have to determine what source books to use in fulfilling the assignment.

Student's Name:_____

Grade:_____

Teacher:_____

Diagnostic Checklist for Reading and Study Skills

I. Dictionary	Yes	No	Sometimes

A. GRADES 1, 2

The student is able to
1. supply missing letters of the alphabet.
2. arrange words none of which begin with the same letter in alphabetical order.
3. list words several of which begin with the same letter.

Student's Name:_____

Grade:_____

Teacher:_____

Diagnostic Checklist for Reading and Study Skills (Cont.)

I. Dictionary	Yes	No	Sometimes
4. list words according to first and second letters.			
5. list words according to third letter.			
6. find the meaning of a word.			
7. find the correct spelling of a word.			

B. GRADES 3, 4, 5, 6

The student is able to

1. locate words halfway in the dictionary.			
2. open the dictionary by quarters and state the letters with which words begin.			
3. open the dictionary by thirds and state the letters with which words begin.			
4. open the dictionary at certain initial letters.			
5. use key words at the head of each page as a guide to finding words.			
6. use the dictionary to select meanings to fit the context (homographs).			
7. use the dictionary to build up a vocabulary of synonyms.			
8. use the dictionary to build up a vocabulary of antonyms.			
9. answer questions about the derivation of a word.			
10. use the dictionary to learn to pronounce a word.			
11. use the dictionary to correctly syllabicate a word.			
12. use the dictionary to get the correct usage of a word.			
13. use the dictionary to determine the part(s) of speech of the word.			
14. use the dictionary to gain the meanings of idiomatic phrases.			

Student's Name:_____

Grade:_____

Teacher:_____

Diagnostic Checklist for Reading and Study Skills (Cont.)

2. Library Skills	Yes	No	Sometimes

A.   PRIMARY GRADES

The student is able to
1. use the card catalog to find a book.
2. state the kinds of books that are found in the library.

B.   INTERMEDIATE GRADES

The student is able to
1. state the kinds of reference materials that are found in the library.
2. use the encyclopedia as an aid to gaining needed information.
3. find books in the school library.

3. Building Good Study Habits	Yes	No	Sometimes

INTERMEDIATE GRADES

The student is able to
1. plan his or her studying time.
2. choose a place to study that is free from distractions.
3. recognize that he or she needs to study.

4. Study Procedures	Yes	No	Sometimes

INTERMEDIATE GRADES

The student is able to
1. use the SQ3R technique when studying.
2. apply the SQ3R technique when studying a chapter in a textbook.

Student's Name:_____

Grade:_____

Teacher:_____

Diagnostic Checklist for Reading and Study Skills (Cont.)

5. Concentration and Following Directions	Yes	No	Sometimes

A. PRIMARY GRADES

The student is able to
1. listen carefully and follow directions.
2. read directions and follow them carefully.
3. show that concentration is increasing by being able to pay attention for longer periods of time.

B. INTERMEDIATE GRADES

The student is able to
1. listen carefully and follow directions.
2. read directions and follow them correctly.
3. fill out some application forms.

6. Skimming	Yes	No	Sometimes

A. PRIMARY GRADES

The student is able to
1. find some information quickly by skimming.
2. skim a paragraph and state its topic.

B. INTERMEDIATE GRADES

The student is able to
1. differentiate between skimming and studying.
2. recognize the role that skimming plays in studying.
3. locate information such as the departure time of trains by skimming train schedules.

Student's Name:_____

Grade:_____

Teacher:_____

Diagnostic Checklist for Reading and Study Skills (Cont.)

7. Knowing Your Textbook	Yes	No	Sometimes

A.   PRIMARY GRADES

The student is able to
1. use the table of contents to find chapter headings.
2. use the glossary to gain the meaning of a word.
3. list the parts of a textbook.

B.   INTERMEDIATE GRADES

The student is able to
1. read the preface to learn about the author's purpose in writing the book.
2. skim the index to learn about the material that will be found in the book.
3. skim the index to find the page on which a specific topic is found.

8. Asking Questions	Yes	No	Sometimes

A.   PRIMARY GRADES

The student is able to
1. formulate questions that will obtain the wanted information.
2. ask questions that are pertinent to the topic under discussion.

B.   INTERMEDIATE GRADES

The student will be able to
1. ask questions that will help in studying for a test.
2. ask questions that will help in learning about what to study.

Student's Name: _____

Grade: _____

Teacher: _____

Diagnostic Checklist for Reading and Study Skills (Cont.)

9. Test-Taking	Yes	No	Sometimes

A. PRIMARY GRADES

The student is able to
1. read questions very carefully so that they are answered correctly.
2. follow directions in taking a test.

	Yes	No	Sometimes
1.			
2.			

B. INTERMEDIATE GRADES

The student is able to
1. recognize that he or she studies differently for objective and essay tests.
2. take objective tests.
3. take essay tests.
4. go over the test to learn why he or she did not do well.
5. ask questions about a test to learn from the mistakes.

	Yes	No	Sometimes
1.			
2.			
3.			
4.			
5.			

10. Summaries	Yes	No	Sometimes

INTERMEDIATE GRADES

The student is able to
1. summarize a passage.
2. use a summary for study.

	Yes	No	Sometimes
1.			
2.			

11. Notetaking	Yes	No	Sometimes

INTERMEDIATE GRADES

The student is able to
1. explain why notetaking is a useful study tool.

	Yes	No	Sometimes
1.			

Student's Name:_____

Grade:_____

Teacher:_____

Diagnostic Checklist for Reading and Study Skills (Cont.)

II. Notetaking	Yes	No	Sometimes
2. explain why notetaking is helpful in writing long papers.			
3. take notes while listening to a talk.			
4. take notes while reading to help remember important information.			

SUMMARY

Chapter 14 is concerned with presenting information and procedures to help teachers develop a study skills program for their students because the emphasis in a diagnostic-reading and correction program is on *prevention*. The importance of building good study habits, which includes when to study, where to study, and the amount of time to spend in studying, was discussed. In discussing how to study, the SQ3R technique was explored. Examples of how to use this technique and activities were also given. Teachers were shown how to help their students gain competence in concentration and questioning. Skimming, reading rapidly to find information, was discussed, as well as how the ability to summarize passages helps students retain information. Since this chapter is a comprehensive one on study skills, topics such as "Knowing Your Textbook," "Notetaking for Studying," and "Test-Taking" were presented, as was a diagnostic checklist for reading and study skills.

SUGGESTIONS FOR THOUGHT QUESTIONS AND ACTIVITIES

1. You have been appointed to a special committee to help develop a study skills program for your elementary school. What suggestions would you make? What kinds of skills and activities would you recommend for the primary grades? For the intermediate grades?

2. Develop some concentration activities for primary-grade children.

3. Develop some activities for intermediate-grade students.

4. You have students who seem to make careless errors on tests. What would you do to help them be better test-takers?

5. What kind of program would you develop to help your students be better notetakers?

6. Some teachers in your school system feel that primary-grade children are too immature to learn study skill techniques. What do you think? How would you con-

vince these teachers that this is not so for many children?

SELECTED BIBLIOGRAPHY

Heilman, Arthur W. *Principles and Practices of Teaching Reading,* Chapter 13, "Teaching Reading-Study Skills," pp. 457–500. Columbus, Ohio: Merrill, 1977.

Niles, O.S. "Organization Perceived." In *Developing Study Skills in Secondary Schools, Perspectives in Reading,* No. 4, pp. 57–76. Newark, Del.: International Reading Association, 1965.

Rae, Gwenneth, and Thomas C. Potter. *Informal Reading Diagnosis: A Practical Guide for the Classroom Teacher,* 2nd ed., Chapter 9, "Function: Study and Reference Skills," pp. 107–23. Englewood Cliffs, N.J.: Prentice-Hall, 1981.

Robinson, Francis P. *Effective Study,* 4th ed. New York: Harper & Row, 1970.

Rubin, Dorothy. *Reading and Learning Power.* New York: Macmillan, 1980.

Part V

THE DIAGNOSTIC-READING AND CORRECTION PROGRAM IN ACTION

CHAPTER 15

Helping Children Overcome Reading Difficulties

INTRODUCTION

John has trouble reading orally.
Marie needs help in learning English.
Frank needs help in concept development.
Jim has word recognition problems.
Debbie can't answer any high-level comprehension questions.
Betty's nonstandard English may be interfering with her ability to read.
Jeff has word recognition and comprehension problems.
Mike has acquired some very bad reading habits.
And so it goes. . .

The teacher must decide which of these children need individual attention and which can work in a group setting. Whether she decides to work with the child individually or in a group, she must take the individual differences of each child into account and try to provide for his or her individual needs.

By now you should recognize that Ms. Mills needs to gather more data about each of the above children before she can determine what to do to help them. Then she must provide each student with activities that will help him or her gain enough practice to acquire the skill. This chapter will present a number of scenarios showing Ms. Mills in action. After you finish reading this chapter, you should be able to answer the following questions:

1. What techniques can a teacher use to help a child overcome his or her reading difficulty?

2. How does a teacher conduct an individual conference?

3. What steps are involved in helping a child in an individualized setting?

4. What is a learning center?

5. What steps are involved in the development of a learning center?

6. What is the role of record-keeping?

7. What are individualized programs?

8. For whom do individualized programs work?

9. What is the place of student involvement in diagnosis?

10. What is a reading management system?

11. How can peer tutoring be used in the classroom?

STUDENT INVOLVEMENT

The primary purpose for diagnosis is to determine what is causing a student's problem so that a program can be developed to help the student overcome the difficulty. Student involvement is crucial. Unless the student recognizes that he or she has a problem, unless the student understands what that problem is, and unless the student is interested in overcoming the problem, it is likely that nothing much will be accomplished.

The teacher can help the student to become involved in the following ways:

1. The teacher should help the student recognize his or her strengths as well as weaknesses.

2. The teacher should not overwhelm the student by listing all of his or her difficulties at once.

3. The teacher should try to elicit from the student what the student thinks his or her reading problems are, why the student feels that he or she has these problems, and what the student feels are the causes of his or her reading problems.

4. The teacher and the student together should set attainable goals to overcome a specific problem.

5. Together, the learning steps are determined.

SCENARIO 1

In listening to Susan, a fifth-grader, read orally, Ms. Mills finds that the pupil consistently makes many word recognition errors. Ms. Mills decides to have a conference with Susan about this problem. Ms. Mills begins the conference by praising Susan's ideas and by telling Susan that she enjoys the endings Susan makes up for many different stories. "However," Ms. Mills says, "you have a number of word recognition problems, and these problems are preventing you from reading a lot of books that you probably want to read." Susan replies that she has always had trouble reading. "I guess I just can't read," Susan says. Ms. Mills says that Susan has a good mind and that she could be a good reader if she could overcome some of her word recognition difficulties. Ms. Mills tells Susan that she would like to give her some tests to try to determine what her word recognition problems are. Ms. Mills asks Susan if that would be all right with her. Ms. Mills also tells Susan that the tests are nothing to worry about and that Susan will not be graded on them. Susan says that she definitely does want to read better because she wants to be a writer when she grows up. "Good!" says Ms. Mills. "The first step in improving in something is knowing that you have a problem. The second step is determining what the problem is. Let's meet again tomorrow, and then I'll give you an informal reading test."

The next day Ms. Mills meets with Susan and administers an informal reading inventory (see Chapter 9). After Ms. Mills analyzes the results, she notices that there is a pattern in the word recognition errors Susan makes. The informal reading inventory also confirms Ms. Mills's other observations of Susan, namely, that she is a highly able child who has excellent comprehension skills but difficulties in word recognition.

Ms. Mills tells Susan that she will meet with her again the next day, and then they will set up a program to help her to overcome her word recognition problems.

The next day Ms. Mills meets again with Susan. Ms. Mills asks Susan if she has noticed anything special about the words she seems to have the most difficulty with. Susan says that she seems to get stuck on words that have certain vowel combinations. Ms. Mills discusses with Susan what she has discovered about her problems. One of Susan's problems does indeed deal with certain vowel combinations. Ms. Mills tells Susan that there are a number of phonic rules that she can learn to help her to be a better independent reader. "As a matter of fact," Ms. Mills says, "in the word recognition learning center there is a program just for you. Let's go to the center so that we can look at it together."

Ms. Mills and Susan proceed to the learning center where Ms. Mills shows Susan a modularized instructional word recognition program. The teacher chooses the module that deals entirely with vowel combinations. Ms. Mills and Susan go over each step of the module together. The word recognition module is composed of the following steps: (1) directions for using the module, (2) pretest, (3) behavioral objectives, (4) learning activities, (5) student self-assessment, (6) postassessment, and (7) recycling.

After going over each step of the module with Susan, Ms. Mills makes sure that Susan is able to operate the audio equipment that is used in the module. Ms. Mills then tells Susan that she can work at her own pace, and that if she needs any help, she should not hesitate to come to her. Susan thanks Ms. Mills and says that she is looking forward to starting as soon as possible. "It looks like fun," she says, "because there are so many different kinds of activities, and I especially enjoy doing word riddles and puzzles."

It is probable that Susan is on her way to becoming a better reader. However, Ms. Mills's job is not over. She must continue to check on Susan's progress and then, together with Susan, determine whether she is ready to go on to another area or whether she needs further help in the same area.

RECORD-KEEPING

Since Susan is only one of many students in Ms. Mills's class, and since many of the students are working in different areas at different levels, Ms. Mills cannot rely on her memory to recall exactly what each student is doing and at what level each student is working. Ms. Mills, therefore, has established a record-keeping system. She has a folder for each student in the class. In the folder she keeps a record of each student's progress in each area. For example, Ms. Mills, after meeting with Susan, went back to her file drawer to pull Susan's folder. She wanted to record that Susan is attempting to accomplish certain behavioral objectives in the area of word recognition. She also wanted to record the specific program Susan is working in and the date that she started.

Susan's folder contains a number of items: a checklist of activities, a record of standardized

Outline of Steps in Individualizing a Reading Program for Susan Based on Her Needs

1. Susan has a reading problem.
2. Susan's reading problem is observed by Ms. Mills.
3. A conference is set up between Susan and Ms. Mills.
4. At the conference Susan recognizes that she has a reading problem.
5. Both Susan and Ms. Mills decide to diagnose Susan's reading problem.
6. In diagnosing Susan's reading problem, Ms. Mills and Susan analyze the types of reading errors Susan consistently makes to determine if a pattern exists.
7. Another conference is set up between Susan and Ms. Mills.
8. Susan and Ms. Mills, following an analysis of Susan's word recognition errors, determine one of Susan's problems.
9. Ms. Mills decides on a program to help Susan overcome one of her word recognition problems.
10. Ms. Mills introduces Susan to the program.
11. Susan begins work in the program.
12. Ms. Mills periodically checks on Susan's progress.
13. Ms. Mills keeps records on Susan's progress.

achievement test scores, intelligence test scores, and criterion-referenced test information, as well as other diagnostic test information. In the folder there is also a sheet listing the particular behavioral objectives that Susan has attempted to accomplish up to that time. Next to each behavioral objective is the program chosen to achieve it, as well as the starting and completion dates.

SCENARIO 2

Alan Y is a fifth-grader who scored at a 4.2 level on the reading comprehension subtest of the *California Achievement Tests,* which is given in the fall of the school year and is used as a screening device for instructional purposes. Ms. Mills knows that Alan has a problem in comprehension, but she does not know in exactly what skill or skills. Therefore, Ms. Mills must choose a diagnostic test that will help locate Alan's specific comprehension problem or problems. The standardized diagnostic reading tests seem to be good in isolating specific word analysis difficulties, but they are not very good in isolating specific comprehension problems. From observing Alan in his reading group and from individual sessions, Ms. Mills knows that Alan does not have problems at the literal comprehension level. His problem appears to be at the interpretive and critical reading levels. Ms. Mills administers a criterion-referenced test to Alan to determine what specific interpretive and critical reading skills are causing problems. The *PRI Reading Systems* test reveals a number of specific skills that are causing problems for Alan, one of which is finding the main idea. Ms. Mills decides that she will probe further to find out what strategies Alan is using to find the main idea of paragraphs. She chooses a few paragraphs at Alan's independent word recognition level so that there is no interference from any word recognition problems. Alan reads the first paragraph silently and then attempts to state its main idea. He then reads the second paragraph silently and states its main idea. Ms. Mills notices that Alan gives the topic as the main idea. She asks Alan what he thinks the main idea of any paragraph should tell him. Alan answers, "What the paragraph is about." Ms. Mills says, "Good, but that is only part of it. What the paragraph is about is the topic of the paragraph. No wonder you keep giving the topic as the main idea."

Ms. Mills proceeds to tell Alan that there is a technique that can help him find the main idea of paragraphs. She says, "Every paragraph is written about something or someone. The something or someone is the topic of the paragraph. To find the main Idea of the paragraph, you must determine what the topic of the paragraph is and what the author is saying about it that is special. Once you have found these two things, you should have the main idea. Let's try one together."

Here is the sample activity that Ms. Mills gave to Alan:

SAMPLE ACTIVITY

Read the following paragraph. After you read the paragraph, choose the word or words that *best* answer the two questions that follow.

Paul Smith wasn't a liar; he just exaggerated a lot. Paul exaggerated so much that people always expected him to exaggerate. Paul never disappointed them. Here are some examples of Paul's exaggerations. If Paul ate three pancakes, he'd say, "I ate fifty pancakes." Also, if he walked a mile, he'd say, "I walked a hundred miles today."

1. What is the topic of the paragraph?
   a. Lying
   b. Paul's lying
   c. Paul's exaggeration
   d. Exaggeration

Answer: c

2. What is the author saying about Paul's exaggeration (the topic) that is special and that helps tie the details together?
   a. It is bad.
   b. It is not believed.
   c. It is a problem.
   d. It applies to everything he does.
   e. It should not be allowed.

Answer: d

The topic is Paul's exaggeration, and what is special about it is that it applies to everything he does.

Main idea: d—Paul's exaggeration applies to everything he does.

Ms. Mills set up a program that consisted of a number of activities to help him gain skill in finding the main idea of paragraphs. Here are some of the sample activities:

1. Find the main idea of many paragraphs such as these:

   What makes an airplane fly is not its engine nor its propeller. Nor is it, as many people think, some mysterious knack of the pilot, nor some ingenious gadget inside. What makes an airplane fly is simply its shape. This may sound absurd, but gliders do fly without engines, and model airplanes do fly without pilots. As for the insides of an airplane, they are disappointing, for they are mostly hollow. No, what keeps an airplane up is its shape—the impact of the air on its shape. Whittle that shape out of wood, or cast it out of iron, or fashion it, for that matter, out of chocolate and throw the thing in the air. It will behave like an airplane. It will *be* an airplane.[1]

Main idea: What makes an airplane fly is its shape.

In many parts of Africa, the use of traps, poisons, and dogs has virtually exterminated the leopard. In my youth, we thought that the only good leopard was a hide stretched out for drying. But now we are discovering that the leopard played an important part in maintaining nature's balance. Leopards used to kill thousands of baboons every year, and now that the leopards have been largely wiped out baboons are proving to be a major control problem in many parts of the colony. The perfect way to keep them in check is by allowing their natural enemy, the leopard, to destroy them. So leopards are now widely protected and allowed to increase in numbers. Such is the strange way that man works—first he virtually destroys a species and then does everything in his power to restore it.[2]

Main Idea: Leopards are now widely protected because they play an important part in maintaining nature's balance.

2.   State the topics of each of the preceding paragraphs.

[1]Wolfgang Langwiesche, *Why An Airplane Flys* (n.d.).
[2]J. A. Hunter, *African Hunter* (New York: Harper 1952).

3.   Compare the topics of each of the paragraphs with the main idea.

Ms. Mills used the same approach to help Alan with his other comprehension problems. She also had Alan write a number of paragraphs and then state the main ideas of the paragraphs he wrote. Ms. Mills believes in integrating reading and writing wherever and whenever possible because she knows that the language arts are closely interrelated.

SCENARIO 3

George Y is another student in Ms. Mills's class who scored at a 4.2 level on the reading comprehension subtest of the *California Achievement Tests*. Ms. Mills is confused about this score because George is quite verbal; he always seems to have a lot of information on many topics, and he can answer some very difficult questions. Ms. Mills has also noticed that George never volunteers to read anything aloud. Because of this, Ms. Mills decides to give George an informal reading inventory.

Ms. Mills started George two grade levels below his grade level. George does not reach the zero level of errors for words in isolation until the first level. George started oral reading at the first grade level. Even at this level, he made one error. He had no problems with comprehension. George is able to answer all the comprehension questions for the oral and silent reading passages through the third level, even though he makes a number of errors in the oral reading passages. At the fourth grade level, the number of word recognition errors are at the frustration level, and Ms. Mills suspects that even with his superior comprehension, George would have some difficulty answering the questions; so she decides to give him a listening capacity test. She reads aloud one passage from each level and asks George the questions. George is able to answer all the questions correctly up until the eighth level.

Ms. Mills realizes that George's word recognition problems had masked his ability to answer many questions. Although both George and Alan had made similar scores on the reading comprehension subtest of the *California Achievement Tests,* their reading abilities and needs are entirely different. George's cognitive development is quite advanced, whereas Alan's is about low average. George needs an intensive and extensive program in learning word recognition skills, and Alan needs help in comprehension.

Ms. Mills decides to look at George's school records to see what methods and materials he was exposed to in learning to read. She also decides to discuss his word recognition problems with him.

In talking to George, Ms. Mills learns that George's parents are both professionals and well known in their fields, that George is an only child, and that George goes everywhere with his parents and is included in their interesting conversations. George's information certainly explains his high cognitive and language development, but it does not account for his decoding problems. Ms. Mills realizes from the types of errors he made when he was reading orally that George is probably using context clues to gain the information that he does get. Ms. Mills decides to give him an informal diagnostic word analysis test to see if she can pinpoint his word recognition problems.

Ms. Mills administers the *Informal Diag-nostic Tests* presented in Chapter 10. She wants to test George's auditory discrimination because he had mentioned that he had had many ear infections when he was younger. She wants to make sure that he is able to differentiate among various sounds. George has no difficulties with auditory discrimination; however, from the results of the word analysis tests, it is obvious that he does not have any phonic or structural analysis skills. When Ms. Mills asks George about this, he says that he never had any instruction in phonics in the school that he had gone to. (George had gone to a different school in another state for the first three years of his education.) He hadn't mentioned it earlier in their talk because he didn't know that he was missing these skills.

Ms. Mills decides to set up an intensive word analysis program for George to follow. The program that George is involved in is similar to Susan's in Scenario 1, except that George's program is more extensive because he has not had any instruction in phonics or structural analysis. Ms. Mills feels that George should have no difficulty gaining word analysis and synthesis skills and that he should acquire these skills in a relatively short period of time because he is a very bright individual and highly motivated. Also, when she did some blending activities to probe for his difficulties, she noticed how quickly George caught on and how he was able to apply what he learned; that is, his transfer of knowledge was excellent. George was also very excited when he saw, in his words, "how easy it was to figure out words by using graphic cues."

Here are examples of some of the probing activities Ms. Mills used to discover the strategies George uses to decode words:

1. A nonsense word—*prand*—was pre-

sented in isolation and George was asked to pronounce the word.

When George could not pronounce the word, a familiar word using the cluster *pr* was presented to George. The word was *pretty.*

Then George was presented with the familiar word *hand*, which he had no difficulty pronouncing.

Ms. Mills asked George to blend the *pr* and the *and* to get the pronunciation of the word. George had no difficulty doing this.

Ms. Mills showed George how he could figure out many words using the graphemic base *and* by just changing the initial consonant.

2. A nonsense word was presented in context. George was asked if he could figure out what he thinks the nonsense word is. "The *drend* went into the house, slammed the door, and started to cry."

Using context clues, George knew that *drend* had to be a noun because it came after *the,* and he knew from the surrounding words that *drend* must refer to a person.

3. Ms. Mills gave George a word in isolation that she thought he would have in his listening capacity and asked him to pronounce it. The word was *probe.*

George recognized the *pr* blend and attempted to pronounce the word, but he couldn't.

The word was then presented in context. "The police said that they would *probe* into the crime until they turned up something."

George was asked to read the sentence. He stumbled on the word *probe,* but after he had read the whole sentence, he went back and correctly pronounced *probe.* George was able to give a definition for it.

George's behavior confirmed Ms. Mills's feelings that he relied heavily on context clues, that he lacked most other word recognition strategies, and that he learned

quickly. (See Chapter 12 for a review of word recognition skills and for an analysis of word recognition strategies.)

Ms. Mills introduces George to the learning center program that he will be working with and follows the same steps as with Susan.

SCENARIO 4

This scenario involves a student in Ms. Mills's class who is attending a special reading class conducted by a reading teacher. Ms. Mills is familiar with the research findings about "pull-out" programs (see Chapter 1) and wants to make sure that Jim, the child in the pull-out program, is helped rather than hindered. She knows that for the pull-out program to be effective, Jim must be involved in the developmental reading program that is taking place in the regular classroom. The remedial reading program must be in addition to the regular classroom reading program rather than a substitute for it. Ms. Mills meets regularly with Mr. Jason, the reading teacher, to learn about Jim's progress and to correlate what he is doing in the special reading class with what he is doing in reading in his regular class. Thus Jim's remedial reading program, which takes place outside the regular classroom, is part of the developmental reading program taking place in the regular classroom. Ms. Mills meets regularly with Jim also to go over some skills and to discuss his progress. Because Jim is involved in the regular reading program in class, he feels that he is part of the group; he is also getting the double-barreled help that he needs from his outside class.

Today's meeting with Jim is just to discuss how he thinks he is progressing. Ms. Mills also wants to talk to Jim about the books she had suggested he might enjoy reading because they were about race cars, his favorite topic. Jim appears relaxed and seems to have a good rapport with Ms. Mills. He tells her that he did enjoy reading the books on race cars and proceeds to tell her all about the books. Ms. Mills is ecstatic because this is a child who had never voluntarily chosen to read before. Buoyed by her success, Ms. Mills asks Jim if he would like her to try to get him another book about race cars. Jim says, "Yes." Ms. Mills tells Jim that she is pleased with his progress, and at the rate he is going, he will soon not need to attend the extra reading class.

Ms. Mills will use reference books such as the *Elementary School Library Collection* to help her find another book at Jim's reading ability level.

SCENARIO 5

Vicki L is a new student in Ms. Mills's fifth-grade class. She and her family just moved into the school district. Ms. Mills is trying very hard to make Vicki feel at home because she knows how difficult it is for a young person to leave all her friends and come to a strange school where she does not know anyone. Ms. Mills tries to make a point of speaking to Vicki informally during recess and at other times so that she can get to know her. During some of their conversations Ms. Mills tries to find out what Vicki's interests are and what kinds of books she likes to read.

Vicki's records from her other school haven't arrived yet, so Ms. Mills has to do some informal testing to determine at what level Vicki is reading. Actually, it really doesn't make any difference that Vicki's records haven't arrived because Ms. Mills prefers to do her own informal testing before looking at a child's past records. She feels that often records can bias a teacher.

Ms. Mills chooses a passage from the middle of the basal reader, which is equivalent to a fifth-grade level. She tells Vicki that she wants her to read the passage aloud and that she should concentrate because she will be asked some questions about what she has read. She tells Vicki something about the story before Vicki begins to read. Vicki's voice is loud and clear, but she reads word by word, or rather syllable by syllable. She sounds out every word she comes to. It's as if she does not recognize any word or that she does not trust herself to correctly say it unless she first sounds it out. (Now, Ms. Mills knows what persons meant when they said that a child was "overphonicked." Ms. Mills believes in using phonics to help children become self-reliant and independent readers, but she stresses that phonics is only one part of the word recognition program and that the primary goal is comprehension.) When Ms. Mills asks Vicki questions on the passage, Vicki is able to answer the literal questions, but she has difficulty answering any at the interpretive level. Ms. Mills decides to choose another passage from the same basal reader and read it aloud to Vicki. She wants to see if Vicki would do better in comprehension if she did not have to concentrate so hard on sounding out the words. Ms. Mills tells Vicki to listen carefully and see how well she can answer questions on what Ms. Mills has read aloud. After Ms. Mills finishes reading the passage to Vicki, she asks her some questions. Again, Vicki is able to answer the literal questions but not the ones requiring a higher level of thinking.

Ms. Mills asks Vicki to tell her about her reading experiences. She asks Vicki how she learned to read. Vicki tells Ms. Mills that she had learned to sound out every word and that all they did at her other school was work with words. She says very proudly that she could figure out lots of words by herself. Ms. Mills says that she saw she could and that was very good, but she tells Vicki that she wants her to try to go beyond the words and concentrate more on the message that the words have. She also tells Vicki that she wants her to take a chance and not sound out every word. She gives Vicki another passage to read, and asks her to look at it first and then to try to read it in thought units. Ms. Mills reads the first two sentences aloud first, and then she asks Vicki to read the complete passage aloud. Ms. Mills praises Vicki for reading it with less sounding out of words. She asks Vicki if there are any words in the passage that she does not know. Vicki says that she knows all the words. "Good," says Ms. Mills. "Let's put some in sentences." Ms. Mills asks Vicki to put a few of the words into sentences. Vicki was able to do this. Ms. Mills tells Vicki that she would like to work with her each day for a little while. She will also put her in one of the reading groups. Ms. Mills tells Vicki that her ability to sound out

words is excellent, but she needs to concentrate more on understanding what she is reading and reading more smoothly. She says that she will arrange a meeting with her parents to see if they would work with her too.

Ms. Mills feels that Vicki is a bright child who should be doing much better than she is. She feels that Vicki has not had any experiences in working with higher level thinking skills, so she will plan a program for her which would help her to develop such skills. Ms. Mills also feels that Vicki needs practice in reading for meaning rather than for pronunciation and that she needs to gain confidence in herself. It could be that she has so overrelied on the sounding out of words that she had not paid attention to the whole word. As a result, each time she met the word, it was as if she were meeting it for the first time. (Vicki appeared to lose the whole because of the parts.) Ms. Mills decides that she will have Vicki look at the *whole* word and have her say it. "Vicki is certainly a perfect example of what can happen if you use extremes."

INDIVIDUALIZED INSTRUCTION

A special section on individualized instruction is being presented in this chapter because a teacher in a diagnostic-reading and correction program must know how to individualize instruction for those students who have special needs.

The many different types of individualized programs range from informal ones, developed by teachers or teachers and students together, to commercially produced ones. It is beyond the scope of this book to give a description of the

organizational patterns or the individualized programs that exist; books have been written on these (see the Selected Bibliography). However, a brief description of some of the characteristics of both informal and commercially produced individualized programs would be helpful.

Teacher-Made (Informal) Programs

Informal programs can vary from teacher to teacher. However, most of the programs usually use behavioral objectives, which are taken from curriculum guides, study guides, and instructors' manuals. To accomplish the objectives the teachers usually select activities and materials from a number of sources, the teacher and student confer periodically, and the teacher keeps a check on the student's progress by keeping adequate records.

Commercially Produced or Published Programs

There are a variety of different commercial programs, and they have a number of things in common. Most of them use behavioral objectives for each curriculum. Usually each curriculum is divided into small discrete learning steps based on graduated levels of difficulty. A variety of activities and materials generally combined in a multimedia approach is used, and usually built into the commercial programs is a system of record-keeping, progress tests, and checklists.

Some Common Characteristics of Commercially Produced and Teacher-Made Individualized Programs

In almost all individualized programs, students work at their own pace. Learning outcomes in individualized programs are based on the needs, interests, and ability levels of the students. Activities are interesting and challenging, and they usually employ a multimedia approach. The activities are based on desired outcomes, students work independently, and there is some system of record-keeping.

For Whom Does Individualized Instruction Work?

Students who have short attention spans, who have trouble following directions, and who have reading problems will obviously have difficulty working independently. Teachers will have to help these students set limited, short-range ob-

jectives that can be reached in a short period of time. For those students with reading problems, the teacher will have to rely very heavily on audio tapes to convey directions. Students who are slow learners (see Chapter 16) will also need special help; special programs will have to be devised for them. Students who have no discernible achievement problems but who have never worked in an individualized program before will also have difficulty unless they are properly oriented to the program. (Note: Do not confuse the need to work independently in an individualized program with the need to provide for the individual differences of each student in the class. For example, a child who is a slow learner will usually have trouble working independently, but the teacher still needs to provide an individual program for this child based on his or her special needs.)

Some Common Sense about Individual Programs

Preparing individual outcomes and a specially tailored program for each student in each specific subject can be a monumental task. Therefore, what is generally done is to use outcomes and programs already prepared, either teacher-made or commercially made, and then match these to the needs of individual students. For such an individualized program to work effectively, teachers must have a variety of individualized programs available for their students, and they must know the individual needs of each student (see the section on learning centers).

LEARNING CENTERS IN THE CLASSROOM

The concept of learning centers is not new. Good teachers have always recognized the importance of providing "interest centers" for their students based on their needs and ability levels. However, in the past most of the science, art, library, listening, and fun centers were just "interest attractions"; they usually were marginal to the ongoing teaching-learning program rather than an integral part of it.

As used today, learning centers are an important and integral part of the instructional program. They are more formalized and are recognized as vital to a good individualized program. A place is usually set aside in the classroom for instruction in a specific curriculum area. Aims for learning centers may be developed beforehand by teachers or cooperatively by teachers and students. Some of the requirements for a good learning center are as follows:

1. Is in an easily accessible area.
2. Is attractive.
3. Provides for students on different maturational levels.
4. Has clearly stated behavioral objectives so that students know what they are supposed to accomplish (outcomes).
5. Provides for group and team activities as well as individual activities.
6. Allows for student input.
7. Asks probing questions.
8. Has some humorous materials.
9. Provides activities that call for divergent thinking.
10. Uses a multimedia approach.
11. Has carefully worked out learning sequences to accomplish objectives.
12. Has provisions for evaluation and record-keeping.

Designing a Learning Center

In the following plan for developing a learning center, notice the similarity to the development of a lesson plan.

1. Motivating technique: necessary to attract attention. This could be realia (real objects), pictures, humorous sayings, and so on.

Example: Familiar commercials with pictures are listed on learning center bulletin board (propaganda learning center).

2. Behavioral objectives: necessary so that students know what they are supposed to accomplish (outcomes).

Example: propaganda learning center.

a. Define *propaganda*.
b. Define *bias*.
c. Explain what is meant by a propaganda technique.
d. List five propaganda techniques.
e. Describe each of the five propaganda techniques you chose and give an example of each.
f. Read ten commercials and identify the propaganda technique used in each.
g. Read a political speech and state what propaganda techniques the politician uses.
h. Team up with another student, and using a propaganda technique, role-play a commercial to be presented to the class.
i. Using one or more propaganda techniques, write a commercial about an imaginary product.
j. Tape-record the commercial created by you on the imaginary product.

3. Directions to accomplish objectives: necessary so that students know what to do to accomplish objectives. Step-by-step instructions are given for the students to accomplish the objectives. Students are told to

a. read behavioral objectives so that you know what you are supposed to accomplish.
b. go to file drawer one, which contains the learning activities to accomplish objective one.
c. complete each learning activity and record your progress on each before you go on to the next objective. (This depends on the learning center. In some learning centers, the students must accomplish the objectives in sequence; in others this is not necessary. For the propaganda learning center, some of the learning objectives must

be accomplished in order. Obviously, before students can write a commercial using propaganda and bias, they must be able to define *propaganda* and *bias*, they must be able to explain propaganda techniques, they must be able to recognize them, and they must be able to give examples of them.)

Summary of Steps in Preparing a Learning Center

1. Select a topic.
2. State objectives.
3. Identify experiences.
4. Collect materials.
5. Prepare activities.
6. Make schedules (which children use center and when).
7. Prepare record forms (each student using center must have one).

Multimedia in Learning Centers

Ms. Mills recognizes that successful individualized programs usually have learning centers that use a diversity of instructional materials to accommodate the individual differences of students. As a result, Ms. Mills has included in each of her learning centers learning sequences that use such instructional materials as textbooks, library books, programmed materials, sets of pictures, realia (real things), commercial and teacher-prepared audio tapes, filmstrips, films, TV, radio, tape recorders, maps, globes, manipulative materials, and games.

The media corner itself is not a learning center but a conveniently located storage and extra viewing place. Each learning center has its own viewing area. The media corner has two "homemade" carrels, which are helpful for viewing films and filmstrips if the learning center is occupied.

Ms. Mills realizes that she is extremely fortu-

A media corner in a learning center.

nate to be in a school system that not only recognizes the importance of the use of a variety of media to help students to achieve learning objectives but also provides the funds necessary to acquire the materials. (She also has a friend who helped her make the carrels for the media center.)

COMPUTER-AIDED INSTRUCTION AND READING IN A DIAGNOSTIC-READING AND CORRECTION PROGRAM

Ms. Mills recently went to a professional conference and was exposed to some of the latest technological advances in education. At the conference she was especially impressed with the use of computer-aided instruction in reading. Computer-aided instruction did not frighten her or make her feel unneeded because Ms. Mills realizes that it is mainly a management tool; that is, with the proper program in the computer, a teacher can manage a larger class more effectively. It would, however, be especially effective for her because she believes in a diagnostic-reading and correction approach to reading. For example, during a reading lesson, students would read a passage and then the computer would question each student simultaneously through terminals. The pupils can answer by menu selection, whereby only one single letter or number needs to be keyed in to indicate the answer. The result to the teacher is immediate feedback of the responses of *all* the students. This type of questioning and feedback can be repeated for however much depth or breadth of coverage is required by the teacher. The teacher can not only receive immediate feedback but also see a pattern of the answers. This pattern would help the teacher immediately discern those questions that caused the most or the least difficulty for the students. The computer could also display for the teacher a pattern of an individual's responses or compare what an individual student has done over an extended period of time. The possibilities are innumerable. The teacher could also use the feedback for evaluation and grouping.

Another possibility of computer-aided instruction is to use it in a tutorial manner, that is, in a one-to-one situation with the student. In this manner, the student knows the results in a friendly, nonthreatening way. It also diagnoses the student's problem without the teacher knowing it. (Certain programs can be developed so that only the student is aware of his or her reading difficulties.) Studies indicate that some students respond more favorably to computer diagnostics than to teacher diagnostics. These students feel that the computer is more fair and more private, and as a result, relate better to such an impersonal diagnostic tool.

Ms. Mills was so excited about computer-aided instruction that she wanted to have a terminal immediately; however, this is probably not likely. There are a number of drawbacks that would prevent computer-aided instruction to be mass-produced in the very near future for every classroom. The main drawback is cost. Although the cost of computer hardware (machines) is going down, the cost of the software (programs) is going up.

At the conference Ms. Mills was given a demonstration of a keyboard-actuated device with a voice. The device is the Texas Instrument Speller, and it is an example of some of the simple-minded things that are now possible with low-cost computer technology. The computer voice asks you to spell a word. You key in the letters on a keyboard. If they are correct, it says, "Correct," and then goes on to the next word. If it is incorrect, it says, "Wrong, try again," and gives you another chance. If you still get it wrong, it tells you the correct spelling. The program's vocabulary is made up of approximately fifty words.

Ms. Mills was told that the computers of the future may be able to understand and respond to voice input. If that is the case, students who can't read or write will be able to use the computer as a learning tool. The possibilities are limitless and exciting provided that the software can be designed in a reasonable time frame at an affordable cost.

READING MANAGEMENT SYSTEMS

Ms. Mills has been reading about reading management systems in the professional journals. Also, at one of the faculty meetings at her school, the principal had said that they should look into these systems to determine whether they should purchase a commercially produced one. Therefore, when Ms. Mills saw that there was a session devoted to reading management systems at the conference she was attending, she decided to go to it.

At the meeting, Ms. Mills learned that there were a number of different commercially produced systems available; however, they all seemed to have a common structure. Management systems usually include a set of instructional objectives for skill areas, precriterion- and postcriterion-referenced tests, as well as other diagnostic tests, instructional materials, and a system for record-keeping. It was also stated that management systems seem to be an outgrowth of learning centers, but they are usually more structured, more highly developed, and require more paperwork. However, the paperwork problem may be solved because management systems and computer-aided instruction are being combined to take the burden of record-keeping off the shoulders of the teachers.

Ms. Mills was especially interested in the comments about reading management systems from persons who had used them. Some of the persons felt that these systems were the panaceas they had been waiting for; however, most persons were realistic. They recognized that there were advantages and disadvantages. Some of the points that were stressed are as follows:

1. A management system, whether internally developed in a school system or developed by publishers, is only as good as the persons administering it and using the materials.

2. Reading management systems are especially helpful in a diagnostic-reading and correction program because the system is built around a diagnosis and correction approach. They stress individual differences, and the students are encouraged to compete with themselves rather than with others.

3. Teachers using reading management systems, which stress the acquisition of hundreds of specific skills, must help their students to recognize that reading is more than the acquisition of specific skills; reading requires thinking; it is the comprehension of ideas. Also, students need to interact with others; they need to share and discuss ideas; they need human, as well as inanimate, feedback.

4. A possible major problem is that teachers may begin to see themselves as merely the managers or paper shufflers for the system. Teachers must never abandon their role as the instructor. Teachers must be good classroom organizers and managers, but these are not their only roles. The management system should be an *aid* to the teacher; the teacher should not be an *aide* to the system.

When Ms. Mills came back from her professional trip, she shared what she had seen and heard with her colleagues. The trip had exhilarated her and given her some fresh insights and ideas that she couldn't wait to try out in her class.

PEER INSTRUCTION

Ms. Mills was pleased to learn at the professional meetings she had attended that her idea about using students to help other students was looked on as professionally sound and that it had benefits for both the tutor and the tutee. Peer tutoring usually helps the student who has been having trouble in one area gain skill in that area and also gain confidence in working with the skill. It also helps the tutee feel more at ease about participating in a large group. The tutor also gains because it helps him or her to overlearn the skill that is being taught, and it helps to enhance his or her self-concept. The tutor is looked on with respect by the teacher and his or her peers.

Ms. Mills likes using peer tutors in her class because it helps her to work with more children individually. Ms. Mills is always very careful about the pairing of the tutor and tutee. She is aware of the personalities in her class, and from administering a sociogram, she learned a great deal about the cliques, stars, and isolates. Ms. Mills is also very sensitive to the fact that some peer tutors, because of their popularity, can be overburdened. She does not allow this to happen. She feels strongly that the peer tutoring relationship must be one that is beneficial and satisfying to both parties.

SUMMARY

Chapter 15 has presented a number of scenarios in which a teacher works individually with a child to determine his or her reading difficulties and to develop a program to help the child overcome them. You are taken through the procedure step by step. A scenario is also given for a child who goes to a special reading class. A discussion of individualized programs was presented, and information was given on learning centers and how to set them up as well as on reading management systems. Peer instruction was discussed as a sound technique that can benefit both the tutor and tutee if handled properly.

SUGGESTIONS FOR THOUGHT QUESTIONS AND ACTIVITIES

1. You are a teacher in an innovative school system. You have been appointed to a committee to suggest ways that instruction can be individualized more than it now is so that teachers can be more responsive to students' needs. What suggestions would you make?

2. A student in your class has difficulty reading orally. What would you do to help him?

3. You have thirty students in your class. What techniques would you use to learn more about their reading behaviors?

4. Suggest some reading skills you would like to have in your learning center.

5. You have no group IQ scores on any children in your class. How can you determine whether a child is reading according to his or her ability?

6. What steps would you take in your everyday reading program to assure that continuous diagnosis and correction are taking place?

7. If you have children who go to special pull-out reading classes, how do you incorporate what they do in their special reading classes with what is done in the regular reading class?

SELECTED BIBLIOGRAPHY

Allen, Vernon L. *Children as Teachers: Theory and Research on Tutoring.* New York: Academic Press, 1976.

Blanchard, J. S. "Computer-Assisted Instruction in Today's Reading Classrooms." *Journal of Reading* 23 (February 1980):430–34.

Breyfogle, Ethel, et al. *Creating a Learning Environment: A Learning Center Handbook.* Pacific Palisades, Cal.: Goodyear Publishing Co., 1976.

Charles, C. M. *Individualizing Instruction.* St. Louis, Mo.: C. V. Mosby, 1976.

Davidson, Tom, et al. *The Learning Center Book: An Integrated Approach.* Pacific Palisades, Cal.: Goodyear Publishing Co., 1976.

Durr, William K., ed. *Reading Difficulties: Diagnosis, Correction, and Remediation,* "Reading Difficulties: Correction," pp. 133–213. Newark, Del.: International Reading Association, 1970.

Hiebert, Elfrieda H. "Peers as Reading Teachers." *Language Arts* 57 (November/December 1980): 877–81.

Reeves, Harriet Ramsey. "Individual Conferences—Diagnostic Tools." *The Reading Teacher* 24 (February 1971):411–15.

Spache, George D., Ken Mcilroy, and Paul C. Berg. *Case Studies in Reading Disability.* Boston: Allyn and Bacon, 1981.

CHAPTER 16

Helping Special Children

All the children of all the people have a right to an education.

PUBLIC LAW 94–142

INTRODUCTION

What does it mean to be *average?* Is there really an average child?

Who is a slow learner? Can a slow learner work in the abstract?

Who is a gifted child? How does a gifted child learn?

What is mainstreaming? How will it affect me in my regular class?

What does a teacher in a diagnostic-reading and correction program have to know about exceptional children?

What is Public Law 94–142?

This chapter will provide the answers to these questions as well as to many more—some of which are listed at the end of this introduction.

Public Law 94–142 advocates a free appropriate education for all children in the least restrictive environment. This law has brought to the fore the importance of the uniqueness of each child. In the regular classroom there is usually a wide range of ability, which generally includes the borderline (slow-learning) and the gifted child.[1] As a result of Public Law 94–142, exceptional children may be mainstreamed into the regular classroom. In order to be able to work with such children, all teachers, not just special education teachers, must become more knowledgeable of exceptional children. The more teachers know about the children with whom they work, the better able they will be to provide for their individual differences and needs.

This chapter provides reading and other language arts methods that are most applicable for those children whom teachers currently have in their regular classrooms, such as the borderline child and the gifted child; however, they may also be adapted for children who may be mainstreamed. Public Law 94–142 requires that exceptional children have individualized programs especially prepared for them. These individual-

---

[1]Although gifted children are classified as exceptional children, they are generally found in the regular classroom. Borderline (slow-learning) children are not classified as exceptional children in the revised AAMD definition.

ized programs are too varied to be presented in a text with as broad a scope as this one. Teachers who have mainstreamed children in their classrooms are, therefore, encouraged to go to special education texts for more in-depth coverage. (See the Selected Bibliography for a listing of books that deal specifically with the subject.) After you finish reading this chapter, you should be able to answer the questions presented at the beginning of the introduction as well as the following:

1. Who are "exceptional children"?

2. What does the term *learning disability* mean?

3. What are the levels of mental retardation and the descriptive terminology presently used to classify retarded persons?

4. What is the significance of the phrase *adaptive behavior* in defining mental retardation?

5. What are the identification biases of children labeled "educable mentally retarded"?

6. What should a teacher know about the cognitive styles of students?

7. What are the kinds of reading and other language arts experiences that should be planned for the borderline or slow-learning child?

8. What kinds of instructional provisions should be provided for the gifted child?

9. How can children in the regular classroom be prepared for a mainstreamed child?

THE "AVERAGE" CHILD

The first question that comes to mind whenever anyone labels someone an average child is: Is there really an "average" child? Actually, there probably is not. Every child is an individual and as such is unique and special. However, for research purposes we tend to define the average child as that individual who scores in the IQ range from 90 to 110. Studies are based on averages. Averages are necessary as criteria or points of reference. Only after we have determined the criteria for "average" can we talk about "above or below average."

THE BORDERLINE CHILD OR THE "SLOW LEARNER"

The borderline child is usually described as a dull average child who is borderline in his or her intellectual functioning. These children's IQ scores range from approximately 68 to 85. As a result, they generally have difficulty doing schoolwork. Borderline children are not, however, equally slow in all their activities or abnormal in all their characteristics. It is difficult at times to differentiate borderline children and children with specific learning disabilities from underachievers produced by disadvantaged environments.[2]

Providing Instruction for the Borderline Child

Teachers in regular classrooms have many times been frustrated because they have had children who do not seem to be able to learn material that is considered "average" for the specific grade level. Not only is the teacher frustrated, but so is the child. A child who according to an individual IQ test scores in the 68 to 85 range would have difficulty working at grade level. Because of social promotion (children are promoted according to chronological age rather than achievement) children are moved along each year into a higher grade. As

[2]Samuel A. Kirk, Sister Joanne Marie Kliebhan, and Janet W. Lerner, *Teaching Reading to Slow and Disabled Learners* (Boston: Houghton Mifflin, 1978), p. 3.

slow learners go through the grades, their problems generally become more pronounced and compounded unless they are given special attention.

The term *slow learner* is probably a misnomer because the term implies that a child needs more time to get a concept but eventually will acquire it. Actually, there are some concepts that slow learners cannot acquire no matter how long they work on them, because slow learners usually cannot work in the abstract. Obviously, the teacher should not use inductive or deductive teaching techniques in working with slow learners. Slow learners generally can learn material if it is presented at a concrete level. Slow learners usually must be given many opportunities to go over the same concept; they must continue to practice in an area beyond the point where they think that they know it, in order to *overlearn* it. The practice should be varied and interesting to stimulate the students. Many games and gamelike activities could be used for this purpose. Slow learners have a short attention span, so learning tasks should be broken down into small discrete steps. Slow learners generally need close supervision, and they may have difficulty working independently. Distractions must be kept at a minimum, and each task should be very exactly defined and explained. It is necessary to define short-range goals, which slow learners can accomplish, to give them a sense of achievement. Slow learners are usually set in their ways, and once they learn something in one way, they will be very rigid about changing.

The teacher should recognize that individual differences exist within groups as well as between groups. Obviously, there will be individual differences among slow learners.

READING FOR THE BORDERLINE CHILD

In Chapter 4 you learned that children who are advanced in language development have a

better chance for success in school than those who are not. Slow development of language is a noticeable characteristic of slow-learning children. The teacher recognizes that these children need many opportunities to express themselves orally and that they learn best at a concrete level. The teacher should, therefore, plan his or her program for slow-learning children to include many *first-hand experiences* where the children can deal with real things. The teacher can take the children on trips to visit farm animals, zoo animals, the firehouse, the police station, factories, railroad stations, farms, and so on. In planning for the trip, the teacher should use the same good practices that are used for all children. The teacher should discuss the trip with the children beforehand and give them the opportunity to help plan for it. After the trip the teacher should encourage the children to discuss what they saw. The teacher and children could then cooperatively write a story about the visit.

In helping slow-learning children acquire new words, the teacher should recognize that these children will learn and retain words that they will use in their everyday conversation more readily than abstract words. Therefore it helps for the teacher to associate the new words with their pictorial representations, real objects, or actions. Slow learners must repeatedly hear and see these words in association with objects, pictures, or actions in order to learn them. As mentioned in the previous section, the children must *overlearn* the word. (Overlearning takes place when you continue practice even after reaching the point where you feel you know something quite well.) Slow-learning children have problems not only in working with abstract words but also in dealing with words in isolation. Cohen's study has shown that the slower students are in academic progress, the more difficult it is for them to deal with words in isolation, unrelated to a totally meaningful experience. Her study has also found that the reading aloud of stories that are at the interest, ability, and attention span level of the children is an excellent means of helping them develop vocabulary and sentence sense (see Chapters 6 and 13).[3] After listening to a story, the children should be encouraged to engage in some oral expression activities. All children need many opportunities to express themselves, and slow learners are no exception. A child who feels accepted and is in a nonthreatening environment will feel more free to contribute than one who feels threatened or embarrassed.

In reading and other language arts instruction the teacher should provide opportunities for the slow-learning child to work with other children. Oral expression (speech stimulation) activities such as choral speaking, finger play, and creative dramatics are good for these purposes. The child should be given opportunities to share with the other children; all children seek approval of peers as well as of adults.

GIFTED CHILDREN

Gifted children fall into the category of exceptional children because they deviate greatly from "average" children.

When one talks about the gifted, immediately visions of small children wearing horn-rimmed glasses and carrying encyclopedias come to mind. This is a myth. There are many definitions of the gifted. In recent years the definition has been broadened to include not only the verbally gifted, with an IQ above 130 or 135 on the Stanford-Binet intelligence test, but also those individuals whose performance in any line of socially useful endeavor is consistently superior.

Marland's national definition in a congressional report alerts educators to the multifaceted aspects of giftedness:

> Gifted and talented children are those identified by professionally qualified persons who by virtue of outstanding abilities are capable of high performance. These are children who require differentiated educational programs and services beyond those normally provided by the regular school program in order to realize their contribution to self and society.

Children capable of high performance include those with demonstrated achievement and/or potential ability in any of the following areas:

1. General intellectual ability.
2. Specific academic aptitude.
3. Creative or productive thinking.
4. Leadership ability.
5. Visual and performing arts.
6. Psychomotor ability.[4]

Characteristics of Gifted Children

Gifted children, on the average, are socially, emotionally, physically, and intellectually superior to "average" children in the population. Gifted children have, on the average, superior general intelligence, a desire to know, originality, common sense, willpower and perseverance, a desire to excel, self-confidence, prudence and forethought, and a good sense of humor, among a host of other admirable traits.

Instructional Provisions for Gifted Children

Gifted children need special attention because of their precocious learning abilities. However, when they are not given special attention, they still usually manage to work on grade level. As a result, gifted children are often ignored. Regret-

---

[3]Dorothy H. Cohen, "The Effect of Literature on Vocabulary and Reading Achievement," *Elementary English* 45 (February 1968): 209–13, 217.

[4]S. P. Marland, *Education of the Gifted and the Talented* (Washington, D. C.: U.S. Office of Education, 1972), p. 10.

tably, they are actually the most neglected of all exceptional children. Attention is given to those who have "more need." Margaret Mead, the renowned anthropologist, has written about this attitude toward the gifted:

> Whenever the rise to success cannot be equated with preliminary effort, abstinence and suffering, it tends to be attributed to "luck," which relieves the spectator from according the specially successful person any merit. . . . In American education, we have tended to reduce the gift to a higher I.Q.—thus making it a matter of merely a little more on the continuity scale, to insist on putting more money and effort in bringing the handicapped child "up to par" as an expression of fair play and "giving everyone a break"—and to disallow special gifts. By this refusal to recognize special gifts, we have wasted and dissipated, driven into apathy or schizophrenia, uncounted numbers of gifted children. If they learn easily, they are penalized for having nothing to do; if they excel in some outstanding way, they are penalized as being conspicuously better than the peer group, and teachers warn the gifted child, "Yes, you can do that, it's much more interesting than what the others are doing. But, remember, the rest of the class will dislike you for it."[5]

Gifted children, like all other children, need guidance and instruction based on their interests, needs, and abilities. Although gifted children are intellectually capable of working at high levels of abstraction, unless they receive appropriate instruction to gain needed skills, they may not be able to realize their potential. Gifted children should not be subjected to unnecessary drill and repetition. They gain abstract concepts quickly, they usually enjoy challenge, and they have long attention spans. Teachers who have gifted children in their self-contained classrooms can provide for them to work at their own pace in many areas through individualized programs.

READING FOR THE GIFTED CHILD

Gifted children's language development is usually very advanced. They generally have a large vocabulary and delight in learning new words. According to Terman, a noted psychologist, who did monumental research on the gifted, nearly half of the gifted children he studied learned to read before starting school; at least 20 percent before the age of five years, 6 percent before four, and 1.6 percent before three years. Most of these children learned to read with little or no formal instruction.[6] Other studies seem to corroborate these findings. However, these findings should not be taken to mean that gifted children can fend for themselves and that teachers should spend more time with others. It does mean that the teacher must provide alternate programs for gifted children. To not recognize that these children are reading when they first enter school and to make them go through a program geared to "average" children can be devastating for the gifted children.

Gifted children usually have wide-ranging interests that they pursue in extensive depth; they read voraciously, and they are impatient with detail. They are usually able to work in a number of activities simultaneously; therefore the teacher must provide a rich and varied program for the gifted so that they have the opportunity to work in many areas. Speech stimulation activities such as choral speaking and creative dramatics give gifted children an opportunity to work with children on all ability levels. This is important for both gifted children

[5]Margaret Mead, "The Gifted Child in the American Culture of Today," *The Journal of Teacher Education* 5 (September 1954): 211-12.

[6]Lewis M. Terman and Melita H. Oden, *The Gifted Child Grows Up,* Genetic Studies of Genius, Vol. 4 (Stanford, Cal.: Stanford University Press, 1947).

and for those of various other levels; children who work together in activities that tap the special abilities of all the children will usually learn to understand each other better.

MAINSTREAMING

The impetus of mainstreaming was triggered by Public Law 94–142, a federal law designed to give handicapped children a "free appropriate public education." It requires state and local governments to provide identification programs, a special education, and related services such as transportation, testing, diagnosis, and treatment for children with speech handicaps, hearing impairments, visual handicaps, physical disabilities, emotional disturbances, learning disabilities, and mental retardation handicaps. Public Law 94–142 also requires that whenever possible, handicapped students must be placed in regular classrooms. *Mainstreaming* is the placement of handicapped children in the least restrictive educational environment that will meet their needs.

Handicapped children who are moved to a regular classroom are supposed to be very carefully screened. Only those who seem able to benefit from being in a least restrictive environment are supposed to be put into one. The amount of time that a handicapped child spends in a regular classroom and the area in which the child participates in the regular classroom depend on the individual child. Some children who are moderately mentally retarded (trainables) may spend time each week in a regular classroom during a special activity, such as a story hour.

For mainstreaming to be successful, classroom teachers must be properly prepared for their new role, and teachers must enlist the aid and cooperation of every student in their class. Classroom teachers must prepare their students for the mainstreamed child by giving them some background and knowledge about the child. The amount and type of information given will, of course, vary with the grade level. Regular classroom teachers should also have the students involved in some of the planning and implementation of the program for the mainstreamed child.

For example, if teachers are expecting physically handicapped children to be admitted to their class, they can help to prepare their students by reading some books to them that portray a physically handicapped child in a sensitive and perceptive manner. Teachers might read some excerpts from Helen Keller's *The Story of My Life* or Marie Killilea's *Karen.* After reading the excerpts teachers can engage the students in a discussion of the handicapped child's struggles, fears, hopes, concerns, goals, and dreams. Teachers can then attempt to help the children in their classes recognize that they have feelings, hopes, and fears similar to many handicapped children's. Teachers should also help their students to understand that a child with a physical handicap does not necessarily have a mental handicap. As a matter of fact, many handicapped persons are very intelligent and able to make many contributions to society. The teacher can then discuss with the children how they think they can make the new child who is coming to their class feel at home. The teacher might also use special films and television programs to initiate interest in the handicapped and to help gain better insights about them. (See the bibliographies in Chapter 17 and at the end of this chapter for books on the handicapped.)

Besides preparing the children in the regular classroom for the mainstreamed child, an individualized program must be developed for each mainstreamed child in cooperation with the child's parents, the special education teacher, or consultants. The program should provide a favorable learning experience for both the handicapped child and the regular classroom students. That is, the integration of a handicapped child should not take away from the program of the regular classroom children. To assure that this is not done, it has been advocated that there be modifications in class size, scheduling, and curriculum design to accommodate the shifting demands that mainstreaming creates; that appropriate instructional materials, supportive services, and pupil personnel services are provided for the teacher and the handicapped student; that there be systematic evaluation and reporting of program developments; and that there be adequate additional funding and resources.[7]

WHO ARE THE EXCEPTIONAL CHILDREN?

The phrase *exceptional children* is applied to those children who deviate so much from "average" or normal children that they require special attention. Exceptional children deviate from the "average" child in "(1) mental characteristics, (2) sensory abilities, (3) neuromuscular or physical characteristics, (4) social or emotional behavior, (5) communication abilities, or (6) multiple handicaps. . . ."[8] More specifically, with slight variation from state to state and author to author, exceptional children have been classified as (1) gifted, (2) educable mentally retarded, (3) trainable mentally retarded, (4) custodial mentally retarded, (5) emotionally disturbed, (6) socially maladjusted, (7) speech-impaired, (8) deaf, (9) hard of hearing, (10) blind, (11) partially seeing, (12) crippled, (13) chronic health cases, (14) multiple handicapped, and (15) learning disabled.

Levels of Mental Retardation

Although there are many definitions of mental retardation, the one most generally used is the revised AAMD definition. In defining an individual who is mentally retarded, the American Association on Mental Deficiencies (AAMD) states in its revised 1973 definition that

> Mental retardation refers to significantly subaverage general intellectual functioning existing concurrently with deficits in *adaptive behavior,* and manifested during the developmental period.[9] [italics are author's]

Adaptive behavior is a crucial phrase in this definition, and it is one that is often ignored. Many mildly retarded individuals function quite well outside the school environment, and their mild retardation is not noticeable. They are able to adapt socially, emotionally, and physically; that is, they have sufficient communication skills, sensory-motor skills, and socialization skills to function in society as independent and self-reliant individuals if they are helped to acquire vocational skills.

The AAMD definition classifies individuals according to the severity of their mental retardation. The scale for determining the levels of mental retardation is based on individual intelligence test scores. (The cutoff for the different levels varies according to the IQ test used.) However, there are also available levels of adaptive behavior that correspond to the intellectual categories of mild, moderate, severe, and profound retardation (see Table 16.1).

In the revised AAMD definition, mental retardation refers to an IQ of 67 or below. Children with an IQ above 67 are not considered

[7]Resolution passed by the 1975 Representative Assembly of the NEA.

[8]M. Stephen Lilly, *Children with Exceptional Needs: A Survey of Special Education* (New York: Holt, Rinehart and Winston, 1979), p. 17.

[9]H. Grossman, ed., *Manual on Terminology and Classifications in Mental Retardation,* rev. ed. (Washington, D.C.: American Association on Mental Deficiency, 1973), p. 11. The categories in the 1977 revision of the manual are identical to those in the 1973 edition.

retarded. There is a category in the earlier AAMD definition called *borderline* retardation which has been deleted from the 1973 revision. The IQ range for the borderline level is approximately 68 to 85. This group of children, many times referred to as *slow learners*, is between the "average" child and the mentally retarded child. Special emphasis has been given to this group because most classroom teachers have children in this IQ range in their regular classrooms, but many teachers may not know how to provide for them.

Table 16.1
IQ Ranges for the Levels of Mental Retardation

	Intelligence Tests	
	Stanford-Binet	Wechsler
Mild retardation	67–52	69–55
Moderate retardation	51–36	54–40
Severe retardation	35–20	39–25
Profound retardation	19 and below	24 and below

As was stated earlier, there are a number of different definitions of mental retardation. These definitions usually have different IQ cutoffs for mental retardation, and whether a child is classified as mentally retarded or not is many times dependent on the definition of mental retardation that is being used. Since different school systems or states may use different definitions, a child may be considered mentally retarded in one school system or state but not in another. School systems also usually use the term *educable* to refer to mildly retarded children, *trainable* to refer to moderately retarded children, and *custodial* to refer to severely and profoundly retarded children.

IDENTIFICATION BIASES OF CHILDREN LABELED "EDUCABLE MENTALLY RETARDED"

It appears that the incidence of educable mental retardation is not equally distributed across all segments of the population. There is a tendency to label more boys as educable mentally retarded than girls. This may be because boys are usually more likely to be mischievous than girls and as a result are more likely to be candidates for referral. There also seems to be a highly disproportionate number of children from a lower socioeconomic status. Studies show too that minority children are overrepresented in this group.[10]

The teacher is usually the person who first identifies the child as having a problem. Many times, as already stated, the child is referred for special testing because of nonadaptive social behavior. After the referral the child is given a number of standardized tests, of which the IQ test is the most influential in determining whether the child is retarded or not. Since studies have shown that children from minority groups and from lower socioeconomic classes usually do not do as well on IQ tests as children from the rest of the population, it is not surprising to find children from these groups disproportionately represented in the group of children labeled "educable mentally retarded."

It cannot be emphasized enough how careful teachers must be in using such terms as *mentally retarded, emotionally disturbed,* and *learning disabled* to label a child. Once labeled, the child is hardly ever able to shed that label, even though he or she has been incorrectly labeled. Often children so labeled continue to function at a particular level because they, themselves, have incorporated the image that others have of them

[10]Lilly, op. cit., pp. 61–62.

into their own self-concept (see "Teacher Assumptions" in Chapter 2).

LEARNING DISABILITIES

The definition of *learning disabilities* is one that needs special attention because there is so much confusion concerning this term. Researchers have found that the characteristics of children so labeled vary so much that it is impossible to list common characteristics. The way the term is used seems to vary not only from state to state but from school district to school district within a state.[11]

Although there is a great amount of confusion and controversy concerning the term *learning disability* and although studies have shown that there is in existence a multitude of definitions and synonyms for it, there is one definition that is most widely accepted and acted on. It is the one proposed by the National Advisory Committee on Handicapped Children:

> Children with special learning disabilities exhibit a disorder in one or more of the basic psychological processes involved in understanding or in using spoken or written language. These may be manifested in disorders of listening, thinking, talking, reading, writing, spelling, or arithmetic. They include conditions which have been referred to as perceptual handicaps, brain injury, minimal brain dysfunction, dyslexia, developmental aphasia, etc. They do not include learning problems which are due primarily to visual, hearing, or motor handicaps, to mental retardation, emotional disturbance, or to environmental disadvantage.[12]

[11]Ibid., p. 21.
[12]*National Advisory Committee on Handicapped Children: First Annual Report* (Washington, D.C.: U.S. Office of Education, 1968), p. 34.

SUMMARY

Teachers usually have children with a wide range of abilities in their classrooms, which generally include borderline (slow-learning) and gifted children. Now, because of mainstreaming, many teachers can expect to have physically handicapped children, children with emotional problems, children with learning disabilities, and children who are mildly and moderately mentally retarded in their classes at some time. Therefore, teachers must be prepared for their new role, and an individualized program must be developed for mainstreamed children in cooperation with the children's parents and the special education teacher or the consultant. In this chapter, reading and other language arts methods are provided that are most applicable for dealing with borderline and gifted children; however, they may also be adapted for some of the children who may be mainstreamed.

Exceptional children are those children who deviate so much from the average that they require special attention. The category of exceptional children includes the gifted as well as the physically handicapped, the emotionally disturbed, and the learning disabled. Adaptive behavior is an important factor in defining individuals who are mentally retarded. Teachers must be especially cautious in using such terms as *mentally retarded, emotionally disturbed,* and *learning disabled* to label a child. Labels are difficult to shed.

SUGGESTIONS FOR THOUGHT QUESTIONS AND ACTIVITIES

1. You are a teacher who will soon have a child from a special class mainstreamed into your class. How would you go about preparing for this child? To whom would you go for help? How would you involve the children in your class?

2. You have been appointed to a committee concerned with the issue of mainstreaming. What are your views about mainstreaming?

3. What recommendations would you make concerning the mainstreaming of children?

4. You have just been appointed to a committee concerned with the development of a program for gifted children. What recommendations would you make?

SELECTED BIBLIOGRAPHY

Aiello, Barbara, ed. *Making It Work: Practical Ideas for Integrating Exceptional Children into Regular Classrooms.* Reston, Va.: The Council for Exceptional Children, 1975.

Baskin, Barbara Holland, and Karen H. Harris, eds. *The Special Child in the Library.* Chicago: American Library Association, 1976.

Charles, C. M. *Individualizing Instruction.* St. Louis, Mo.: C. V. Mosby, 1976.

Dexter, Beverly L. *Special Education and the Classroom Teacher: Concepts, Perspectives, and Strategies.* Springfield, Ill.: C. C. Thomas, 1977.

Dunn, Lloyd M., ed. *Exceptional Children in the Schools: Special Education in Transition.* New York: Holt, Rinehart and Winston, 1973.

"The Gifted and the Talented." (Special Feature) *Today's Education* 65 (January/February 1976): 26–44.

Hart, Vera. *Mainstreaming Children with Special Needs.* New York: Longman, 1980.

Kirk, Samuel A., et al. *Teaching Reading to Slow and Disabled Learners.* Boston: Houghton Mifflin, 1978.

Knight, Lester N. *Language Arts for the Exceptional: The Gifted and the Linguistically Different.* Itasca, Ill.: F. E. Peacock, 1974.

Labuda, Michael, ed. *Creative Reading for Gifted Learners: A Design for Excellence.* Newark, Del.: International Reading Association, 1974.

Laycock, Frank. *Gifted Children.* Chicago: Scott, Foresman, 1978.

Lilly, M. Stephen. *Children with Exceptional Needs: A Survey of Special Education.* New York: Holt, Rinehart and Winston, 1979.

Macmillan, Donald L. *Mental Retardation in School and Society.* Boston: Little, Brown, 1977.

"Mainstreaming." (Special Feature) *Today's Education* 65 (March/April 1976):18–32.

Parks, A. Lee, and Thomas N. Fairchild. *Mainstreaming the Mentally Retarded Child.* Austin, Tex.: Learning Concepts, 1976.

Paul, James L., Ann P. Turnbull, and William M. Cruickshank. *Mainstreaming: A Practical Guide.* Syracuse, N.Y.: Syracuse University Press, 1977.

Roucek, Joseph S., ed. *Slow Learner.* New York: Philosophical Library, 1970.

Scofield, Sandra J. "The Language Delayed Child in the Mainstreamed Primary Classroom." *Language Arts* 55 (September 1978):719–23, 732.

Terman, Lewis M., and Melita H. Oden. *The Gifted Child Grows Up,* Genetic Studies of Genius, Vol. 4. Stanford, Cal.: Stanford University Press, 1947.

Turnbull, Ann P., and Jane B. Schulz. *Mainstreaming Handicapped Students: A Guide for Classroom Teachers.* Boston: Allyn and Bacon, 1979.

Ward, Marjorie, and Sandra McCormick. "Reading Instruction for Blind and Low Vision Children in the Regular Classroom." *The Reading Teacher* 34 (January 1981):434–44.

Witty, Paul, ed. *Gifted Child.* Westport, Conn.: Greenwood Press, 1972.

CHAPTER 17

Getting Children to Like Books

INTRODUCTION

Reading helps reading; the problem is that many students are not reading. It is easy to understand why a child who has a reading problem is not reading, but we have a large population of students who have no discernible reading problems who are also not reading. Why?

Read the following typical and atypical statements made by young people:

Typical Statements

"I have baseball practice."
"I have band practice."
"I'm trying out to be a cheerleader."
"I'm meeting the gang at George's house."
"I have to watch a special TV program."
"Let's go see that great movie."
"Let's listen to the new tape."
"I have piano lessons."
And so on . . .

Atypical Statements

"I can't wait to get home to finish that terrific book I'm reading."

"Let's get together to discuss that great book."
And so on . . .

Young people must contend with enculturated attitudes, as well as with competing activities, which vie for their time and attention. Pressure from peers, parents, teachers, and society abound. Be well-rounded . . . socialize . . . join clubs . . . try out for athletic teams . . . attend meetings . . . show class spirit . . . and so on. Studies show that the most popular students are those who are brilliant, athletic, and *non-studious*. And which student doesn't want to be popular?

It used to be that the typical statements given above were generally made by males and the atypical statements by females. However, this is not as true anymore because of the unisex movement. Pressures weigh heavily on females too. It is possible that the statement "I have baseball practice" is being voiced by a female rather than a male. The result is that the population of reluctant readers is probably increasing.

Also, the fact that students are reading less

may be contributing to the recently reported lower SAT scores. The less students read, the less their vocabulary is expanded. Since there is a high correlation between vocabulary and aptitude tests, this may account for the lower SAT scores. In order to try to offset the lower scores, many persons advocate the "cure-all," going "back to the basics." The need for skills in the basics is fine, but it is not the whole answer. Many of the young people who are not reading have no reading problem; they are just not choosing to read in their leisure time. Also, if students' specific reading disabilities are removed, it does not necessarily follow that these students will become readers. In order to become readers, students must have the time and the desire to read; students must have acquired an appreciation for reading.

This chapter is crucial because it helps teachers attain the tools they will need to provide a reading for appreciation program for their students. An important objective for any teacher, and especially for one committed to a diagnostic-reading and correction program, is to instill a love for books in students. The only way a teacher knows whether she or he has been successful in teaching reading skills is to observe whether children are voluntarily choosing to read. After you finish reading this chapter, you should be able to answer the following questions:

1. What is reading appreciation?

2. What must educators do to show that they value a reading for appreciation program?

3. How would you provide an atmosphere conducive to recreational reading in your classroom?

4. What are some techniques that will interest children in books?

5. How would you help children select books?

6. What should you know about sex stereotyping in books?

7. What is bibliotherapy? Explain.

8. How can bibliotherapy be used to interest children in books?

9. What kinds of books would you provide for the culturally different child?

10. How can television be used as a constructive force to interest children in books?

WHAT IS READING FOR APPRECIATION?

Webster's New Collegiate Dictionary defines appreciation as "1a: sensitive awareness; especially the recognition of aesthetic values; b: judgment, evaluation: especially a favorable critical estimate; c: an expression of admiration, approval, or gratitude; 2: increase in value."[1] When we talk about reading appreciation, we usually are talking about sensitive awareness, especially the recognition of aesthetic values. The emphasis in appreciative reading is usually completely on enjoyment. Appreciative reading in this book is defined as deriving pleasure and enjoyment from books that fit some mood, feeling, or interest.

Some persons feel that an individual cannot attain appreciation unless he or she has a complete understanding at the highest level of what is being read. For these persons, reading for appreciation would be at the highest level in a hierarchy of reading. In this book appreciative reading is regarded as a separate domain with a hierarchy of its own. It is therefore possible for an individual to appreciate a piece of literature even though he or she does not completely understand it. Thus, a poem can be enjoyed because of its delightful sounds, rhythm, or

[1]A. Merriam-Webster, *Webster's New Collegiate Dictionary* (Springfield, Mass.: Merriam, 1977), p. 56.

Figure 17.1

language, even though it is not understood. Of course, the greater the understanding, the higher the appreciation, but appreciation is still possible without complete understanding at various lower levels.

THE IMPORTANCE OF PROVIDING TIME FOR A READING FOR APPRECIATION PROGRAM

Every good reading program must have a component dedicated to appreciative reading. Learning to read and reading to learn are important parts of any reading program, but appreciative reading is what determines whether persons will read and continue to read throughout their lives. If children develop an appreciation of books at an early age, it will be more difficult for other activities and media to compete. One important factor is the decision to have a reading for appreciation program. Many educators give lip service to the appreciation component

of the reading program, but they do not implement it. The only way educators can show they value this program is to set aside time for it. By setting time aside, there is a chance for success. As stated earlier, young people have to contend with many enjoyable activities that compete for their time and attention; reading for pleasure is often given a low priority in the competitive battle. By setting time aside during the school day for reading for enjoyment, educators would be giving students a chance to whet their appetites for books. What is especially encouraging is that the Drop Everything and Read Program (DEAR) seems to be sweeping the country. Many school systems have initiated DEAR in their schools, and the response to it has been excellent. DEAR is a very simple program to institute, but it needs the backing and commitment of *all* school personnel for it to work. Certain times during the week are set aside when *all persons* in the school system drop everything and read. (*Sustained Silent Reading* [SSR] rather than *DEAR* is the more familiar phrase used for practice in independent silent reading.)

SETTING THE ENVIRONMENT FOR THE ENJOYMENT OF READING IN THE CLASSROOM

Teachers who are enthusiastic about books will infect their students with that enthusiasm. A teacher who is seen to be deeply immersed in a book during the lunch hour will also have a marked influence on students. But the teacher's responsibility does not end there. The teacher must set the stage, provide the materials, and plan with students for recreational reading.

First, the classroom must be an inviting place to read. It should be airy, light, and physically comfortable. The emphasis on books should be clearly visible. For example, bulletin boards should have recommended booklists at all interest and readability levels. Award-winning books, book jackets from a number of popular children's books, students' recommendations and evaluations of various books, as well as artwork depicting a scene or characters in books, should be on display.

Lots and lots of books should be provided for the children at all interest and readability levels (see section on choosing books). Newspapers, magazines, and other printed matter of interest to children should be available. Filmstrips, records, and films of favorite stories should also be kept handy for the children's use.

Next, a special place to read is necessary. A section or corner of the room should be readily accessible to all the students, where a few comfortable chairs, some large comfortable pillows, and a scatter rug are placed. This is the reading corner.

Now, time must be provided so that children can read. This book period is separate from the weekly visit to the library and is not dependent on whether children have free time only because they have finished all their "other work." Every day the teacher and children should plan for a book time, when the class just enjoys literature. After the teacher has helped students to choose their books and settle down, the teacher too should read.

WHETTING CHILDREN'S INTEREST IN BOOKS

Studies have shown that reading literature aloud to children helps prepare them for reading (see Chapters 6, 13, and 16).

During the week there are many opportunities for the teacher to read to students. Books that are chosen to be read in full should be those that will interest all children. For example, one fifth-grade class loved Sherlock Holmes stories; however, the vocabulary was too difficult for a

Children love to be told stories. For that matter, so do adults. Storytelling is an art and must be practiced to be effective. It is different from reading, and many teachers find this difficult and very time-consuming. Some schools have special librarians who are adept at storytelling.

Another technique that teachers can use to interest children in books is to have several students orally report on books they have read which they feel others would also enjoy. In presenting such reports students must explain why they enjoyed the books, tell about some of the exciting parts, but not give away the endings.

A technique children enjoy using to interest others in books is creative dramatics. A group of students who have read the same book can present skits highlighting exciting parts.

Peer role-modeling is another technique that teachers can use to interest children in books. (See ''Television and Reading for Appreciation'' in this chapter.) If children see other children reading, they, too, may choose to read. Teachers can display pictures of children reading on the walls and bulletin boards. One teacher made a practice of taking photographs of her students while they were reading. Then,

number of the students, even though the stories were at their interest level. Therefore, the teacher either used synonyms for difficult words or defined them. There are a number of books in which the authors seem to be able to use word imagery to clarify the meanings of unfamiliar words. The techniques that the authors use do not take away from the quality of the story as a story but enhance it.[2]

The teachers must read with expression. They should imagine themselves to be actors or actresses and literally ''give it their all.'' If they are reading effectively, the teachers should have gained the complete attention of the students.

[2]See Dorothy H. Cohen, ''Word Meaning and the Literary Experience in Early Childhood,'' *Elementary English* 46 (November 1969): 914–25, for a listing of books and examples.

these snapshots were placed on a special bulletin board for all to view.

CHILDREN'S INTERESTS AND BOOK SELECTION

The interests and needs of the individual child will determine the kinds of books he or she will read. Because children choose and read books for different purposes, they will need a wide selection.

Most reading interest studies have been based on asking children what they would like to read rather than on what they actually have read. A rare study was done on books actually borrowed from the library by children. In grades four through six these books were taken out in order of popularity: *Henry Huggins, Charlotte's Web, Mrs. Piggle Wiggle, Encyclopedia Brown, Homer Price, All-of-a-Kind Family, The Black Stallion, The Tenggren Tell-It-Again Book, John Henry* (Keats), *The Red Balloon, Stuart Little, The Mouse on the Motorcycle, Dot for Short, Pinocchio,* and *Peter Pan* (abridged by Josette Frank).

It was also reported that jokes and riddles were in first place for nonfiction popularity. A reflection of the times was shown in the children's choices of sport books. Judo and jujitsu were the favorites.[3]

Since the middle 1970s, an annual bibliography of children's choices of trade books has been compiled under the direction of the International Reading Association–Children's Book Council Joint Committee. Of all the trade books published in the previous year, approximately five hundred are selected by a group of educators. The books are then sent to designated classrooms. A team of specialists keeps a record of the children's reactions to the various books. Based on the children's choices, a book is either elected to the bibliography or denied placement on it.[4]

CHILD DEVELOPMENT CHARACTERISTICS AND BOOK SELECTION

Teachers who are knowledgeable about the social, emotional, physical, and intellectual development of their students will be better able to help them choose books.

Table 17.1 suggests a listing of books based on children's developmental stages.[5]

SEX DIFFERENCES IN BOOK SELECTION

Most of the studies in this area concerned the discovery of boys' and girls' interests in books by either observing the kinds of books they took out or through questionnaires. All such research was, however, after the fact. That is, boys and girls, by the time they have arrived in school, have already been persuaded by the culture of the kind of interests they should have. The studies confirm and reinforce the enculturation. For example, in a 1950 study of seventh- to twelfth-graders it was found that boys like fierce adventure stories and mysteries, whereas girls prefer stories about love and sentiment, home and family life. A 1967 study corroborated earlier sex difference findings. Fourth-, fifth-, and sixth-grade boys preferred historical fiction, history, social studies, science, and health,

[3]Donald J. Bisset, "Literature in the Classroom," *Elementary English* 50 (February 1973): 235.

[4]Children's Book Council Joint Committee, "Children's Choices for 1981," *The Reading Teacher* 35 (October 1981): 51–72.
[5]Charlotte S. Huck, *Children's Literature in the Elementary School,* 3d ed. updated (New York: Holt, Rinehart and Winston, 1979), pp. 31–36.

Table 17.1

Books for Ages and Stages

Preschool and Kindergarten—Ages 3, 4, and 5

Characteristics	Implications	Examples
Rapid development of language.	Interest in words, enjoyment of rhymes, nonsense, and repetition and cumulative tales. Enjoy retelling folktales and stories from books without words.	*Mother Goose* Burningham, *Mr. Gumpy's Outing* Gág, *Millions of Cats* Hutchins, *Rosie's Walk* Rockwell, *The Three Bears* Spier, *Crash! Bang! Boom!* Watson, *Father Fox's Pennyrhymes* Wezel, *The Good Bird* *The Gingerbread Boy*
Very active, short attention span.	Require books that can be completed in one sitting. Enjoy participation through naming, touching, and pointing. Should have the opportunity to hear stories several times each day.	Burningham, *A B C* Burningham, *The Cupboard* Carle, *Do You Want to Be My Friend?* Carle, *The Very Hungry Caterpillar* Kunhardt, *Pat the Bunny* Wildsmith, *Puzzles*
Children themselves are the center of their world. Interest, behavior, and thinking are egocentric.	Like characters with whom they can clearly identify. Can only see one point of view.	Buckley, *Grandfather and I* Keats, *The Snowy Day* Preston, *Where Did My Mother Go?* Wells, *Noisy Nora*
Curious about their world.	Stories about everyday experiences, pets, playthings, home, people in their immediate environment are enjoyed.	Cohen, *Will I Have a Friend?* Hoban, *Best Friends for Frances* Keats, *Peter's Chair* Rockwell, *My Doctor*
Building concepts through many firsthand experiences.	Books extend and reinforce children's developing concepts.	Anno, *Anno's Counting Book* Hoban, *Big Ones, Little Ones* Hoban, *Count and See* Jensen, *Sara and the Door* Showers, *The Listening Walk*
Children have little sense of time. Time is "before now," "now," and "not yet."	Books can help children begin to understand the sequence of time.	Burningham, *Seasons* Carle, *The Grouchy Ladybug* Tresselt, *It's Time Now* Zolotow, *Over and Over*

Table 17.1 (continued)

Characteristics	Implications	Examples
Children learn through imaginative play.	Enjoy stories that involve imaginative play. Like personification of toys and animals.	Burton, *Mike Mulligan and His Steam Shovel* DeRegniers, *May I Bring a Friend?* Ets, *Just Me* Freeman, *Corduroy* McPhail, *The Train*
Seek warmth and security in relationships with adults.	Like to be close to the teacher or parent during storytime. The ritual of the bedtime story begins literature experiences at home.	Brown, *Goodnight Moon* Clifton, *Amifika* Flack, *Ask Mr. Bear* Hutchins, *Good-Night, Owl!* Minarik, *Little Bear* Sharmat, *I Don't Care*
Beginning to assert their independence. Take delight in their accomplishments.	Books can reflect emotions.	Barrett, *I Hate to Go to Bed* Brown, *The Runaway Bunny* Krauss, *The Carrot Seed* Lexau, *Benjie* Preston, *The Temper Tantrum Book* Watson, *Moving*
Beginning to make value judgments about what is fair and what should be punished.	Require poetic justice and happy endings in the stories.	Bulla, *Keep Running, Allen* Hutchins, *Titch* Piper, *The Little Engine That Could* Potter, *The Tale of Benjamin Bunny* Potter, *The Tale of Peter Rabbit*

Primary—Ages 6 and 7

Characteristics	Implications	Examples
Continued development and expansion of language.	Daily story hour provides opportunity to hear qualitative and creative language of literature.	Preston, *Squawk to the Moon, Little Goose* Steig, *Amos and Boris* Tresselt, *A Thousand Lights and Fireflies* Poetry of Aileen Fisher, Karla Kuskin, David McCord, Stevenson, and others.
Attention span increasing.	Prefer short stories or may enjoy a continued story provided each chapter is a complete incident.	Flack, *Walter the Lazy Mouse* Lobel, *Frog and Toad Together* Parish, *Amelia Bedelia*

Table 17.1 (continued)

Characteristics	Implications	Examples
Striving to accomplish skills demanded by adults.	Children are expected to learn the skills of reading and writing. Need to accomplish this at their own rate and feel successful. First reading experiences should be enjoyable.	Cohen, *When Will I Read?* Conford, *Impossible, Possum* Duvoisin, *Petunia* Guilfoile, *Nobody Listens to Andrew* Kraus, *Leo the Late Bloomer*
Learning still based upon immediate perception and direct experiences.	Use informational books to verify experience. Watch guinea pigs or record changes in a tadpole *prior* to reading a book.	Brady, *Wild Mouse* Hoban, *Look Again!* Selsam, *The Amazing Dandelion* Silverstein, *Guinea Pigs, All about Them*
Continued interest in the world around them—eager and curious. Still see world from their egocentric point of view.	Need wide variety of books. TV has expanded their interests beyond their home and neighborhood.	Aliki, *Green Grass and White Milk* Fuchs, *Journey to the Moon* Koren, *Behind the Wheel* Lionni, *Fish Is Fish* Swinton, *Digging for Dinosaurs*
Vague concepts of time.	Simple biographies and historical fiction may give a feeling for the past, but accurate understanding of chronology is beyond this age group.	Aliki, *A Weed Is a Flower* Dalgliesh, *The Bears on Hemlock Mountain* Hutchins, *Clocks and More Clocks* Turkle, *Obadiah the Bold*
More able to separate fantasy from reality. Developing greater imagination.	Enjoy fantasy. Like to dramatize simple stories.	Ness, *Sam, Bangs, and Moonshine* Sendak, *Where the Wild Things Are* Slobodkina, *Caps for Sale* Tolstoy, *The Great Big Enormous Turnip*
Beginning to develop empathy and understanding for others.	Adults can ask such questions as, "What would you have done?" "How do you think Stevie felt about Robert?"	Hill, *Evan's Corner* Steptoe, *Stevie* Wolf, *Anna's Silent World* Yashima, *Crow Boy*
Have a growing sense of justice. Demand applications of rules, regardless of circumstances.	Expect poetic justice in books.	Freeman, *Dandelion* Hutchins, *The Surprise Party* Udry, *Let's Be Enemies* Zemach, *The Judge*

Table 17.1 (continued)

Characteristics	Implications	Examples
Humor is developing; enjoy incongruous situations, misfortune of others, and slapstick.	Encourage appreciation of humor in literature. Reading aloud for pure fun has its place in the classroom. Enjoy books that have surprise endings, play on words, and broad comedy.	Allard, *The Stupids Have a Ball* Barrett, *Animals Should Definitely Not Wear Clothing* DuBois, *Lazy Tommy Pumpkinhead* Kuskin, *Just Like Everyone Else* Segal, *Tell Me a Mitzi*
Beginning sexual curiosity.	Teachers need to accept and be ready to answer children's questions about sex.	Gruenberg, *The Wonderful Story of How You Were Born* Mayle, *"Where Did I Come From?"* Sheffield, *Where Do Babies Come From?*
Physical contour of the body is changing. Permanent teeth appear. Learning to whistle and develop other fine motor skills.	Books can help children accept physical changes in themselves and differences in others.	Keats, *Whistle for Willie* McCloskey, *One Morning in Maine* Rockwell, *I Did It*
Continue to seek independence from adults.	Need opportunities to select books of their own choice. Should be encouraged to go to the library on their own.	Ardizzone, *Tim to the Rescue* Steptoe, *Train Ride* Taylor, *Henry the Explorer* Waber, *Ira Sleeps Over*
Continue to need warmth and security in adult relationships.	Books may emphasize universal human characteristics in a variety of life styles.	Clark, *In My Mother's House* Gill, *Hush, Jon* Reyher, *My Mother Is the Most Beautiful Woman in the World* Scott, *Sam* Zolotow, *Mr. Rabbit and the Lovely Present*

Table 17.1 (continued)

Middle Elementary—Ages 8 and 9

Characteristics	Implications	Examples
Attaining independence in reading skill, may read with complete absorption. Others may still be having difficulty in learning to read. Wide variation in ability and interest. Research indicates boys and girls developing different reading interests during this time.	Discover reading as an enjoyable activity. Prefer an uninterrupted block of time for independent reading. During this period, many children become avid readers.	Blume, *Tales of a Fourth Grade Nothing* Clymer, *My Brother Stevie* Colver, *Bread-and-Butter Indian* Dahl, *Danny: The Champion of the World* Fox, *Maurice's Room* Greene, *Philip Hall Likes Me, I Reckon Maybe* Konigsburg, *From the Mixed-Up Files of Mrs. Basil E. Frankweiler* Robinson, *The Best Christmas Pageant Ever* Schulz, *Hooray for You, Charlie Brown* Selden, *The Cricket in Times Square* Steele, *Winter Danger*
Interest in hobbies and collections is high.	Enjoy how-to-do it books and series books. Like to collect and trade paperback books. Begin to look for books of one author.	Bond, *A Bear Called Paddington* Cleary, *Ramona and Her Father* Simon, *The Paper Airplane Book* Stein, *The Kids' Kitchen Takeover* Wilder, "Little House" series
Seek specific information to answer their questions. May go to books that are beyond their reading ability to search out answers.	Require guidance in locating information. Need help in use of library, card catalog, and reference books.	Gallob, *City Leaves, City Trees* Macaulay, *Castle* McWhirter, *The Guinness Book of World Records* Sarnoff, *A Great Bicycle Book*

Table 17.1 (continued)

Later Elementary—Ages 10, 11, and 12

Characteristics	Implications	Examples
Rate of physical development varies widely. Rapid growth precedes beginning of puberty. Girls about two years ahead of boys in development and reaching puberty. Boys and girls increasingly curious about all aspects of sex.	Continued sex differentiation in reading preferences. Guide understanding of growth process and help children meet personal problems.	Blume, *Are You There God? It's Me, Margaret* Blume, *Then Again, Maybe I Won't* Donovan, *I'll Get There, It Better Be Worth the Trip* Ravielli, *Wonders of the Human Body* Winthrop, *A Little Demonstration of Affection*
Understanding and accepting the sex role is a developmental task of this period. Boys and girls develop a sense of each other's identity.	Books may provide impetus for discussion and identification with others meeting this task.	Cleaver, *Trial Valley* George, *Julie of the Wolves* Greene, *A Girl Called Al* Jones, *Edge of Two Worlds* L'Engle, *The Moon by Night*
Increased emphasis on peer group and sense of belonging. Deliberate exclusion of others. Expressions of prejudice.	Emphasize unique contribution of all. In a healthy classroom atmosphere discussion of books can be used for clarification of values.	Armstrong, *Sounder* Levoy, *Alan and Naomi* Neville, *Berries Goodman* Westall, *The Machine Gunners*
Family patterns changing. Highly critical of siblings. By end of period may challenge parents' authority.	Books may provide some insight into these changing relationships.	Byars, *The Pinballs* Hopkins, *Mama* Mann, *My Dad Lives in a Downtown Hotel* Rodgers, *Freaky Friday* Wersba, *The Dream Watcher*
Begin to have models other than parents. May draw them from TV, movies, sports figures, and books. Beginning interest in future vocation.	Biographies may provide appropriate models. Career books may open up new vocations and provide useful information.	Carruth, *She Wanted to Read: The Story of Mary McLeod Bethune* Goldreich, *What Can She Be? A Lawyer* Lee, *Boy's Life of John F. Kennedy* Naylor, *How I Came to Be a Writer* Robinson, *Breakthrough to the Big League*

Table 17.1 (continued)

Characteristics	Implications	Examples
Sustained, intense interest in specific activities.	Children spend more time in reading at this age than any other. Tend to select books related to one topic; for example, horses, sports, or a special hobby.	Glubok, *The Mummy of Ramose* Graham, *Great No-Hit Games of the Major Leagues* Moeri, *A Horse for X, Y, Z* Ravielli, *What Is Tennis?* Ross, *Racing Cars and Great Races*
Reflecting current adult interest in the mysterious, occult, and supernatural.	Enjoy mysteries, science fiction, and books about witchcraft.	Christopher, *Wild Jack* Duncan, *A Gift of Magic* Hunter, *The 13th Member* L'Engle, *A Swiftly Tilting Planet* Sleator, *Blackbriar*
Highly developed sense of justice and concern for others. Innate sympathy for weak and downtrodden.	Like "sad stories" about handicapped persons, sickness, or death.	Byars, *Summer of the Swans* Greene, *Beat the Turtle Drum* Platt, *Hey, Dummy* Robinson, *David in Silence*
Increased understanding of the chronology of past events. Beginning sense of their place in time. Able to see many dimensions of a problem.	Literature provides the opportunity to examine issues from different viewpoints. Need guidance in being critical of biased presentations.	Frank, *Anne Frank: The Diary of a Young Girl* Hickman, *The Valley of the Shadow* Hunt, *Across Five Aprils* Lester, *To Be a Slave* Tunis, *His Enemy, His Friend* Uchida, *Journey to Topaz*
Search for values. Interested in problems of the world. Can deal with abstract relationships; becoming more analytical.	Valuable discussions may grow out of teacher's reading aloud prose and poetry to this age group. Questions may help students gain insight into both the content and literary structure of a book.	Babbitt, *Tuck Everlasting* Collier, *My Brother Sam Is Dead* Cunningham, *Dorp Dead* Dunning, *Reflections on a Gift of Watermelon Pickle and Other Modern Verse* Engdahl, *Enchantress from the Stars* Kohl, *The View from the Oak* Slote, *Hang Tough, Paul Mather* Wojciechowska, *Shadow of a Bull*

whereas girls of similar ages preferred realistic fiction, fanciful tales, biography, recreational interests, and poetry. A 1973 study found that boys' interests had not changed in a decade and that boys have a narrower range of reading interests than girls. Boys prefer books dealing with "excitement," "suspense," and "unusual experiences." "Outdoor life," "explorations and expeditions," "sports and games," and "science fiction" are some of the categories boys listed as their favorites.[6] A 1972 study discovered sex differences expressed in television watching also. Boys chose sports, whereas girls chose social empathy.[7]

This is a time of change in society's attitude toward sex roles. The teacher must be careful not to be caught up in stereotypes. However, what we know about children's attitudes toward choosing books should also be taken into account. For example, it has been found that boys usually *will not* read "girl books," whereas girls *will* read "boy books." Therefore, the teacher should make sure that there is a variety of books in the classroom from which both boys and girls can choose, based on their interests. Examples of "girl books" are *Little Women* and *Rose in Bloom* by Louisa May Alcott.

Since there are more women seeking careers today than ever before, and since many of these careers are in fields once thought to be the sole domain of men, it is necessary for the teacher to include books that portray women in such roles, among them *Maria Mitchell: Stargazer* by Katherine E. Wilkie, the biography of the first astronomy professor at Vassar College; *Challenge to Become a Doctor: The Story of Elizabeth Blackwell* by Leah Lurie Heyn; *What Can She Be? A Veterinarian* and *What Can She Be? A Lawyer* by Gloria and Esther Goldreich; *A Life for Israel: The Story of Golda Meir* by Arnold Dobrin; and *Oh Lizzie! The Life of Elizabeth Cady Stanton* by Doris Faber.

Traditionally, women have been portrayed in literature as mothers and homemakers. Although some persons claim that these are inferior roles, this is not so. It is not easy to be a good parent and homemaker, for these require a good deal of knowledge and skill. It is to be hoped that more books will be written that deal with the parental role in a perceptive way.

Common stereotypes about the sexes have generally been carried over into books. For example, when persons are asked to give masculine and feminine characteristics that are valued, the list on page 331 is often supplied.[8]

Studies have shown that parents' expectations of their children tend to be similar to the traits in this list. For example, parents tend to see boys as more aggressive and more physically vigorous, as more adventuresome, as more mechanically inclined, as more competitive, and as more noisy than girls, whereas girls are seen as softer and more cuddly, as more fragile, as more likely to be frightened, as more well-mannered, and as neater than boys.[9]

Yet many educators, psychologists, and sociologists are realizing that such "traits" are not necessarily biologically determined but may be learned. If females and males are conditioned to value certain traits, they will conduct themselves accordingly.

Interestingly, the reason that girls will read "boy books" but boys will not read "girl

---

[6]J. M. Stanchfield and Susan B. Fraim, "A Follow-up Study on the Reading Interests of Boys," *Journal of Reading* 22 (May 1979): 748–52.

[7]Jane Porter, "Research Report," *Elementary English* 49 (November 1972): 1028–29.

[8]P. S. Rosenkrantz et al., "Sex Role Stereotypes and Self-Concepts in College Students," *Journal of Consulting and Clinical Psychology* 32 (1968): 287–95.

[9]E. E. Maccoby and C. N. Jacklin, *The Psychology of Sex Differences* (Stanford, Cal.: Stanford University Press, 1974).

Male-Valued Traits	Female-Valued Traits
Aggressive	Does not use harsh
Independent	language
Unemotional; hides	Talkative
emotions	Tactful
Objective	Gentle
Easily influenced	Aware of feelings of
Dominant	others
Likes math and science	Religious
Not excitable in minor	Interested in own
crisis	appearance
Active	Neat in habits
Competitive	Quiet
Logical	Strong need for
Worldly	security
Skilled in business	Appreciates art and
Direct	literature
Knows the way of the	Expresses tender
world	feelings
Feelings not easily hurt	
Adventurous	
Makes decisions easily	
Never cries	
Acts as a leader	
Self-confident	
Not uncomfortable about being aggressive	
Ambitious	
Able to separate feelings from ideas	
Not dependent	
Not conceited about appearance	
Thinks men are superior to women	
Talks freely about sex with men	

books'' is probably that society seems to value ''masculinity'' more than ''femininity.'' Studies have shown that parents and teachers are usually not upset when girls engage in boy activities, but parents and teachers generally frown on boys' involvement in girl activities.[10]

Sex-role identity may be more ambiguous for the female who seeks a career. In order to succeed in a career, independence, initiative, aggressiveness to a degree, and competitiveness are needed. These are generally characterized as masculine traits, which some females may be loath to assume, and so a conflict arises. How can a female maintain her femininity, but also ''make it'' in a career? A similar case can be made with males, whose stereotype disallows tenderness, helping at home, and being sensitive to social relations.

Although resistance to departing from sex stereotyping exists, inroads are being made, and teachers are key persons in helping to make these inroads. Teachers who value nonsexist thinking can help their students to change their attitudes toward sexist views.[11]

Change in sex stereotyping of females in books started to become more evident in the early 1970s. For example, the 1973 Caldecott award went to *The Funny Little Woman* by Arlene Mosel, which concerns an inventive Japanese woman who outwits the gods. The Newbery award winner, *Julie of the Wolves,* by Jean George, concerns a thirteen-year-old Eskimo girl who, married to a simpleton, escapes and with resourcefulness is able to survive by making friends with a pack of wolves.

In these two books initiative and independence are shown as virtues in two females even though they are traits that are usually rewarded in males.

[10]Ibid.
[11]Cristina J. Simpson, ''Educational Materials and Children's Sex Role Concepts,'' *Language Arts* 55 (February 1978): 161–67.

Since the 1960s, science-fiction books, which are usually considered in the male domain, have tended to be oriented toward both sexes, where males and females play central roles. Some books in this category are: Madeleine L'Engle's *A Wrinkle in Time,* Robert O'Brien's *The Silver Crown,* Patricia Wrightson's *Down to Earth,* and H. M. Hoover's *Rains of Eridan* and *The Delikon.*

Although there seems to be a change in the role of females in sports, more needs to be done in this area. Significant sex differences in motor development have been found during children's early years.[12] By the time the children come to school, differences in sport skills appear, and the differences become more marked according to sex type as the children go through school. The marked differences may have been increased by cultural pressure and so teachers should provide books in which girls as well as boys excel in sports.

In the 1970s a number of journals devoted many articles to sexism in children's literature. There were also articles discussing the overuse of the male pronoun in writing, and ways in which to avoid this practice.

When children choose books, the teacher should not differentiate between male and female books. In fact, the teacher should not "push" any book on any child. Books at all interest levels should be made available to all children indiscriminately.

Criteria for Selecting Books

There are a number of factors which should be considered in selecting books for children. Criteria concerned with knowledge of children and what they enjoy in a book include:[13]

1. *Theme:* What the story is all about.
2. *Plot:* These grow out of good themes. Children like heroes and heroines who have obstacles to overcome, conflicts to settle, and difficult goals to win.
3. *Characterization:* As children mature in their reading tastes, they go from enjoyment of tales of action with stereotyped characters to enjoyment of characters who are individual, unique, and memorable.
4. *Style:* A difficult quality to define, but its absence is noticeable in books that are repetitious, boring, labored, and so on.
5. *Setting:* Concerns time and place of the story. It should enhance the plot, characters, and the theme of the story.
6. *Format:* Deals with the presentation of material, illustrations, quality of paper used, and binding. The illustrations should be attractive and pleasing to the eye as well as consistent with the story. The quality of the paper should not detract from the reading, and the print of the book should be appropriate for the reader.

CHILDREN'S LITERATURE AND CULTURALLY DIFFERENT CHILDREN

Should literary choice for children be based on the cultural groups from which they come or on the socioeconomic stratum of their families? Does the reading of good literature help to extend the reader's world?

A study on the reading preferences of inner-city children showed that they like to read about characters in middle-class settings, with positive self-concepts, and in positive group interaction.[14] This is contrary to the idea that they prefer to read stories of inner-city life.

All children, regardless of cultural backgrounds, enjoy "good" literature. For example, numerous research studies of the reading in-

[12]J. E. Garai and A. Scheinfeld, "Sex Differences in Mental and Behavioral Traits," *Genetic Psychology Monograph* 77 (1968): 203, 211.
[13]Huck, op. cit., pp. 6–14.

[14]Jerry L. Johns, "What Do Inner-city Children Prefer to Read?" *The Reading Teacher* 26 (February 1973): 462–67.

terests of children reveal that those from culturally different backgrounds do not vary considerably from others.[15] However, we all like to read books which depict characters from backgrounds similar to our own.

Reading about characters who have similar cultural backgrounds to theirs helps children to develop feelings of self-esteem and worth. It is important to recognize that the treatment of a character in literature may greatly influence individuals' perceptions of themselves. If children constantly see pictures and stories of persons similar to themselves in inferior roles, they may begin to think of themselves as inferior. Similarly, for example, if Caucasians constantly see other racial groups depicted in inferior roles, they may come to think of them in this way. Not only do children from diverse cultural backgrounds need to read about persons in similar cultural groups who have achieved, but it is good for all children to read about other groups of people in a positive way in order to develop better understanding.

If we were to think of all the different racial, religious, and ethnic groups that live in the United States—such as Indian, Mexican, Spanish, French, black, and so on—many children would be considered culturally different. It was only during the past fifteen years that fiction and nonfiction books began to be published especially for culturally different children.[16] In the *good* literature books, minorities are not portrayed in a stereotyped fashion. They are presented sympathetically and with sensitivity.

Between 1930 and 1968 only forty-nine books with black characters were on the recommended children's literature lists.[17] In the past few years many more books have been published with black protagonists in sympathetic roles (see the Selected Bibliography).

It is understood that the characteristics of "good" literature, which have been discussed previously for all children, are operative for children from divergent cultures as well. Regardless of the group to which children belong, the book they read must help them to feel good about themselves. It must help them to view themselves in a positive light, to achieve a better self-concept, and to gain a feeling of worth.

The importance of learning about other groups of people through literature is aptly expressed in the following:

> I never felt the world-wide importance of the children's heritage in literature more than on a day when I stood with Mrs. Ben Zvi, wife of the [then] President of Israel, in the midst of the book boxes she had filled for the centers in Jerusalem where refugee boys and girls were gathered for storytelling and reading of the world's great classics for children. "We want our boys and girls to be at home with the other children of the world," she said, "and I know of no better way than through mutual enjoyment of the world's great stories."[18]

THE BLACK CHILD AND BOOKS: A SPECIAL LOOK

Teachers must be especially perceptive to the needs, interests, and experiences of their black students. Literature is an area which can be effectively used by the knowledgeable teacher. It

[15]Patricia Jean Cianciolo, "A Recommended Reading Diet for Children and Youth of Different Cultures," *Elementary English* 48 (November 1971): 781.

[16]List compiled by Emerita Schroer Schulte, "Today's Literature for Today's Children," *Elementary English* 49 (March 1972): 355–63.

[17]Jane Bingham, "The Pictorial Treatment of Afro-Americans in Books for Young Children, 1930–1968," *Elementary English* 48 (November 1971): 880–85.

[18]Dora V. Smith, "Children's Literature Today," *Elementary English* 47 (October 1970): 778.

is important that the black child be given a sense of dignity, worth, and identity, and a feeling that being black is desirable.

> The better books depict black children as individuals whose identity includes name, home life, family, friends, toys, hobbies, etc. In addition, they are black, American, and first-class citizens. These books lead children naturally to the conclusion that differences—in personality, abilities, background—are desirable among people. Books of this sort which have already been published include the "interracial" *Gabrielle and Selena,* by Peter Desbarats, and *Hooray for Jasper,* by Betty Horvath. Charming and individualized black children are the central characters in the Ezra Jack Keats books, *The Snowy Day, Whistle for Willie, Peter's Chair,* and *A Letter to Amy,* as well as in the books *Sam* and *Big Cowboy Western,* by Ann Herbert Scott, and *What Mary Jo Wanted* and *What Mary Jo Shared,* by Janice May Udry. Books like these, on this level, should be so numerous that children will not be able to browse through a library shelf without finding one there.[19]

A book which hinders a child from finding his or her identity, which portrays the child in a stereotyped role, is a book that would be considered poor reading for all children.

When selecting books for a class library, teachers should try to put themselves in the position of the black child and ask, How would I feel if I read this book? Would this book make me come back for another one? Will this book interest me? Are these books on many readability levels? Does the book portray the black child as an individual? Are the adults portrayed in a nonchildlike manner? Are the characters supplied with traits and personalities that are posi-

tive? Would all children, regardless of color, want to read the book?

If the answers are "yes," the teacher should choose the book. But even one "no" answer should disqualify it.

The importance of providing children with books that convey hope and with which children can identify, because they mirror their lives, cannot be overemphasized. Another factor, which is as important, concerns the image that white children obtain when they read a book about black people. Since children are greatly influenced by what they read, the way that black persons are portrayed in books will have a profound effect on white children's perceptions of black people.

Good books can open doors through which can pass better understanding, mutual respect, trust, and the hope of people living together in harmony and peace.

BIBLIOTHERAPY

Bibliotherapy is a technique that can be used to interest children in books. If children see that books can help them, it may encourage them to read more.

If you have ever read a book in which the main character had a problem exactly like yours and if the book helped you to deal better with your problem, you were involved in bibliotherapy.

Reading guidance by teachers and librarians to help students with their personal problems is regarded as bibliotherapy. Bibliotherapy is the use of books to help individuals to cope better with their problems. The use of books (or bibliotherapy) to help persons is not a new phenomenon. As far back as 300 B.C. Greek libraries bore inscriptions such as "The Nourishment of the Soul" and "Medicine for the Mind." Alice Bryan, a noted librarian, in the late 1930s ad-

---

[19]Judith Thompson and Gloria Woodard, "Black Perspective in Books for Children," in *The Black American in Books for Children: Readings in Racism,* Donnarae MacCann and Gloria Woodard, eds. (Metuchen, N.J.: Scarecrow Press, 1972), p. 23.

vocated the use of books as a technique of guidance to help readers "to face their life problems more effectively and to gain greater freedom and happiness in their personal adjustment."[20] However, it probably was not until Russell and Shrodes published their articles on the "Contributions of Research in Bibliotherapy to the Language Arts Program" in 1950 that teachers attempted to bring bibliotherapy into the classroom. Russell and Shrodes discussed their belief that books could be used not simply to practice reading skills but also to influence total development. They defined bibliotherapy as "a process of dynamic interaction between the personality of the reader and literature—interaction which may be utilized for personality assessment, adjustment, and growth." They also say that this definition

> . . . is not a strange, esoteric activity but one that lies within the province of every teacher of literature in working with every child in a group. It does not assume that the teacher must be a skilled therapist, nor the child a seriously maladjusted individual needing clinical treatment. Rather, it conveys the idea that all teachers must be aware of the effects of reading upon children and must realize that, through literature, most children can be helped to solve the developmental problems of adjustment which they face.[21]

(For an understanding of the process of bibliotherapy, see references in the Selected Bibliography.)

The Uses of Bibliotherapy

Bibliotherapy can be used in both preventive and ameliorative ways. That is, some individuals, through reading specific books, may learn how to handle certain situations before they have taken place. Other persons may be helped to overcome some common developmental problem they are having at the time. For whatever purpose bibliotherapy is used, it will only be of value if teachers know *how* to use it in their classrooms.

In order to use bibliotherapy effectively, teachers should know about children's needs, interests, readiness levels, and developmental stages.

Bibliotherapy Themes

The kinds of problems that lend themselves to bibliotherapy are varied. For example, being the smallest child in the class or encountering the first day of school can be devastating to a child. Being an only child may cause difficulty for some children. A new baby may bring adjustment problems for some, and going to the hospital may be a frightening event for others. Moving to a new neighborhood or the simple dislike of a name can cause problems for a number of children. The death of a loved one, the fear of death, or the divorce of parents causes great anxieties to children, and just growing up can be confusing. These are just a few of the problems suitable for bibliotherapy.

The Teacher and Bibliotherapy

By reading books that deal with themes, such as those stated in the previous section, children can be helped to cope better with their emotions and problems. Perceptive teachers sensitive to their children's needs can help by providing books that deal with the same problems. However, since teachers are not clinicians, children who are having serious adjustment problems should be referred to the guidance counselor or school psychologist. Also, teachers must be

[20]Alice I. Bryan, "The Psychology of the Reader," *Library Journal* 64 (January 1939): 110.
[21]David Russell and Caroline Shrodes, "Contributions of Research in Bibliotherapy to the Language Arts Program, I," *The School Review* 58 (September 1950): 335.

careful not to give children who are anxious about a situation a book that would increase their anxiety. A teacher should also not single out a child in front of the class and give him or her a book which very obviously points out that child's defects. It would probably embarrass and upset the child more.

The school librarian and the special reading teacher may be excellent resources to help the teacher choose books for bibliotherapy. For best results, teachers should work very closely with them. Teachers should be familiar, also, with the *Elementary School Library Collection,* which is available in most libraries. This book is an invaluable aid because it has an annotated bibliography of children's books on all themes with both readability and interest levels indicated, as well as resource books for teachers.

After teachers use the *Elementary School Library Collection* or the aid of librarians to identify some possible books for bibliotherapy, they should peruse the books to determine whether they meet certain important criteria. Books for bibliotherapy should deal with problems that are significant and relevant to the students. The characters in these books should be "life-like" and presented in a believable and interesting manner. The characters' relationship to others in the book should be equally believable, and they should have motives for their actions. The author should present a logical and believable plot using vivid descriptive language, humor, adequate dialogue, and appropriate emotional tone. The situations presented should be such that minor problems can be separated from main problems. The episodes in the book should lend themselves to being extracted and discussed so that students can formulate alternate solutions. Also, the author should present enough data so that students can discern generalizations that relate to life situations. The book should also be written in such a manner that the readers' imaginations are so stirred that they can "enter the skin of another."

A good teacher, one who is perceptive to the needs of students and who recognizes the importance of individual differences, will be in a better position to determine when a problem lends itself to being presented to the whole class or when it should be handled on an individual basis. As was stated earlier, when a teacher wishes to give individual children books for bibliotherapy, the children should not be singled out lest they feel ostracized or humiliated. One chance to help the children choose books could occur during a school library period or a class library period. The teacher and/or school librarian could make a few suggestions to a child. The student could then decide by reading the first page of a few of the books that have been suggested.

Another way to interest individual students in books for bibliotherapy is to choose an episode from a book to read aloud to the class. The chosen episode should present the main character in a problem. Also, the protagonist should be one with whom the teacher feels a number of students can identify. After the episode is read, a discussion should take place on how the character resolves his or her problems. The author's solution should not be given. The book may then be offered to those individuals who would like to read it. The teacher should have a few copies of the book available because many of the students will want to read it.

Many times a teacher may find that a number of children in the class share a similar problem. Therefore, the teacher might want to introduce the problem in some way to the class and use a bibliotherapy technique to help the students cope with their problem. One technique to use is bibliotherapy and role playing.

The following is an example of how a teacher

can use bibliotherapy and role playing in an upper primary or lower intermediate grade-level class.

Scenario

The teacher overhears a number of children discussing their younger brothers and sisters in rather disparaging terms. Not only do many of the children seem to feel that their younger siblings get more love and attention, but they also seem to feel that the siblings "get away" with much more than they can. The teacher decides to use bibliotherapy and role playing to help the students adjust and cope better with their problem. After looking through a few books that deal with this theme, the teacher chooses Judy Blume's *Tales of a Fourth Grade Nothing* to read to the class. This book was chosen because it has most of the criteria discussed earlier and lends itself to being read aloud to the class; also the story will appeal to less mature as well as more mature students.

Introducing the Problem

The teacher asks the students to draw pictures of their families and pets, if they have any, and under each picture write one sentence that describes the member of the family or the pet. After the children have finished, a discussion concerning the pictures takes place. The teacher asks those children who have younger brothers or sisters to tell the class something about them. Those children who have no brothers or sisters should be called on to tell about their parents or pets. Some other questions the teacher might ask are

> How did you feel when your mother brought home your new baby brother or sister? If you have no younger brothers or sisters, how do you think you would feel if your mother brought home a younger brother or sister?

Bibliotherapy and Role Playing

The teacher reads aloud Blume's book *Tales of a Fourth Grade Nothing* to the whole class in a week's time. After the book is finished, the students discuss Peter's relationship to his younger brother, Fudge. Students are encouraged to share some of their experiences. After this, the students are told that they are going to do some role-playing. Each child who would like to will play the role of Fudge, Peter, the mother, or the father. A scene is set in which Fudge keeps interrupting Peter while Peter is trying to build a model plane. No dialogue is given. The children must spontaneously provide that on their own. After each role-playing scene, discuss with the class what took place, and ask for the role players to give their feelings about the parts. If time permits, have the children reverse roles. It is important that only those children who wish to role play should. No child should ever be forced to role play.

Bibliotherapy and Creative Problem-Solving

Another technique the teacher could use is bibliotherapy and creative problem-solving. In this method, almost the whole book is read aloud to the class. Before the ending, the students, using clues from the book, try to determine how the main character's problem is resolved. They are encouraged, also, to generate their own solutions. After the ending is read, the students are asked to compare their solutions with the author's. Then they can discuss which they liked better and why.

Bibliotherapy can be effective in helping students to better understand themselves and their feelings. When students realize that other persons have similar problems, they are able to cope better with their own. Bibliotherapy also encourages students to try to seek answers in a positive, intellectual, and logical manner.

Books as an Aid in Bibliotherapy

There are a number of excellent books which deal with some of the problems that children may encounter in today's world. Nan Hayden Agle's *Maple Street* is an enlightening story about a young black girl's desire to improve her street and come to terms with a prejudiced white girl. Mary Calhoun's book, *It's Getting Beautiful Now,* concerns a boy's emotional problems and drugs. Francine Chase's *A Visit to the Hospital* helps both parents and children in preparing for a stay in the hospital. Gladys Yessayan Cretan's *All Except Sammy* portrays a boy's attempts to win the respect of his musical family.

Perceptive teachers, alert to the needs of their students, should be able to aid them in choosing books which help them to cope more effectively with individual problems. As in all matters, the teacher should look for balance in the child's reading habits. A certain degree of escapism is fine, but the child must live in the real world and cannot be in a continuous state of fanciful thinking. (See the Selected Bibliography for annotated references that will help in selecting literature that portrays life as it is.) Table 17.2 consists of a good sampling of books for bibliotherapy organized by theme.

READABILITY AND INTEREST LEVELS IN CHOOSING BOOKS

There are usually one or two books that are very popular and make the rounds of almost all the children in the class. Although these books may be at the interest level of most of the children, they may not be at all of their reading ability levels. There are always a few children who feel left out because they can't read these books. They may take out the books and either walk around with them or make believe that they are reading them. By having the book in their possession they may feel they can gain the esteem they crave and need.

The teacher should not embarrass such students but should carefully choose books similar to the popular ones at their reading ability levels, and try to interest them in the substitutes. The teacher should speak individually to such a child and say, "I know how much you like books about heroes. Well, I was looking through this book the other day and I immediately thought of you. I just felt that you would enjoy this book." The teacher should then try to have the student read the first page. Once the child starts by reading the first page, the battle is almost won. The student will usually continue because the book is at both his or her reading ability and interest levels.

The teacher should have an ample supply of books at various readability and interest levels. To aid teachers in obtaining a proper selection, they can consult the *Elementary School Library Collection.* This reference work gives estimates of children's interest levels and reading difficulties for all the books listed. Having such books available is the essential first part. The other part is helping students choose books based on both their interest and reading ability levels. Unfortunately, as has been shown, a book may be at a child's interest level, but the child may be unable to read it independently. For example, *The Lion* by René DuBois would be of interest to preschool, kindergarten, and first-grade children. However, according to the Spache Readability formula for grades one to three, the book would be near the 3.5 grade level. This means it would have to be read to younger children. At the other end of the scale, there may be students in upper grades with difficulty in reading, who may be at a reading level as low as the preprimer. These students desperately need books at their interest levels. For-

Table 17.2

Title	Author	Level	Theme
Here's a Penny	Carolyn Haywood	Upper primary	Adoption
A Month of Sundays	Rose Blue	Upper primary/lower intermediate	Divorce
My Dad Lives in a Downtown Hotel	Peggy Mann	Upper primary/lower intermediate	Divorce
It's Not the End of the World	Judy Blume	Intermediate	Divorce
Elizabeth Gets Well	Alfons Weber	Primary	Illness (in a hospital)
A Girl Called Al	Constance Greene	Upper intermediate	A child who is different
Dinky Hocker Shoots Smack	M. E. Kerr	Upper intermediate	A child who is different
Maple Street	Nan Hayden Agle	Upper primary/intermediate	Prejudice
Shawn Goes to School	Petronella Breinberg	Preschool/early primary	The first day of school
Confessions of an Only Child	Norma Klein	Upper primary/intermediate	A new baby
Peter's Chair	Ezra Jack Keats	Preschool	A new baby
Weezie Goes to School	Sue Felt Kerr	Primary	Youngest child
Tales of a Fourth Grade Nothing	Judy Blume	Upper primary/lower intermediate	Dealing with a younger sibling
Nobody Asked Me if I Wanted a Baby Sister	Martha Alexander	Preschool	Dealing with a younger sibling
Sabrina	Martha Alexander	Preschool/early primary	Dislike of name
Then Again, Maybe I Won't	Judy Blume	Upper intermediate/young adult	The finding of self
Are You There God? It's Me, Margaret	Judy Blume	Intermediate	The finding of self
Nikki 108	Rose Blue	Upper intermediate	The finding of self
The Soul Brothers and Sister Lon	Kristin Hunter	Young adult	The finding of self
Run Softly, Go Fast	Barbara Wersba	Young adult	Death
The Dead Bird	Margaret Wise Brown	Preschool/kindergarten	Death
My Grandpa Died Today	Joan Fassler	Primary	Death
Charlotte's Web	E. B. White	Upper primary/intermediate	Death
Annie and the Old One	Miska Miles	Intermediate	Death
A Taste of Blackberries	Doris Buchanan Smith	Primary	Death
The Tenth Good Thing About Barney	Judith Viorst	Preschool/lower primary	Death

tunately, during the past decade, more books have been published which have the high interest but low readability levels required by such students.

Readability formulas are used to determine the reading difficulty of written material. Most readability formulas are based on both sentence length and syllabication; however, some may also use word lists. Readability formulas do not take other variables—such as experiential background of children, maturation, purpose of reading, and so on—into account. They also do not measure the abstractness of ideas nor the literary style nor quality of the written material. Readability formulas are not absolutely reliable, since different formulas on similar material may not produce the same scores. When a readability formula produces a score of grade four, it does not mean that all fourth-graders will be able to read the book. It merely means that a number of fourth-graders—approximately five to seven out of ten such readers—will have little trouble with the book.[22] Although readability formulas are imperfect tools, they do have value, for they give some idea of the difficulty of a book for specific groups of readers.

Regardless of which formula teachers use, they should be familiar with the methods for estimating readability. Teachers do not have to work out the exact estimates for each book, but by observing the sentence length and syllables, or sentence length and kinds of words—that is, the difficulty of the words used in a paragraph—they can estimate whether a book is at the proper level for their students to read independently. (See Appendix B for an example of a readability formula.)

Although it is difficult to ascertain completely what makes a book easy or hard, the following are "readability pluses" which parents, teachers, and librarians might look for in a book:[23]

Readability is excitement. A punchy beginning. Forceful and colorful language. Variety in style, including both long and short sentences. A subject that appeals to the reader. Interesting pictures and other illustrations.

Readability is familiarity. Plain talk and an informal style, especially for readers with difficulty in standard English. The words and expressions of ordinary speech. The familiar sentence patterns of spoken language. Material that deals with something the reader knows about and has experience with. Unfamiliar ideas explained in terms of familiar ideas.

Readability is clarity. A low percentage of abstract words. Difficult ideas explained and not clumped together. Paragraphs not too long or complicated. Ideas developed in logical order. Introductions and summaries where suitable.

Readability is visibility. Type large enough to read comfortably. Lines not so long that the eye has trouble finding the beginning of the next line. Paper and ink that let type stand out sharply— black ink on whitish nonglare paper is best. Plenty of light, without glare. Distance between eyes and print close enough for comfortable reading, but not too close.

Readability is a good book. It's the symmetry and warmth a poem transmits to you. It's a quality that computers find indigestible because it defies precise statistical analysis.

TELEVISION AND READING FOR APPRECIATION

Television is one of the competitors vying for children's time and attention. However, studies show that television can actually be a positive

---

[22]Allen M. Blair, "Everything You Always Wanted to Know About Readability but Were Afraid to Ask," *Elementary English* 48 (May 1971):442-43.

[23]Ibid., p. 443.

force in encouraging students to read rather than a negative one. Those programs that have peers modeling proreading behavior seem to encourage children to read because children imitate the behavior. A study found that a significant number of children who watched *Sesame Street* entered school with prolearning and proreading attitudes, even though the attainment of these attitudes was not the objective of the program.[24]

It has been hypothesized that since children like to watch other children on television, "peer role-modeling of reading behaviors could motivate and reinforce positive attitudes toward reading."[25] This substantiates what has been said earlier in this chapter regarding peer role-modeling and the need for the teacher to be a good role model by also reading while the children are reading.

Television can act as a positive force by portraying segments in which children choose to read rather than engage in another activity, by showing peers not disturbing other peers when they are reading, by having a child interest another in reading, and by showing situations in which everyone is engaged in reading.[26]

[24]Pamela M. Almeida, "Children's Television and the Modeling of Proreading Behaviors," in Chester M. Pierce, ed., *Television and Education.* (Beverly Hills, Cal.: Sage Publications 1978), pp. 56–61.

[25]Ibid., p. 59.
[26]Ibid., p. 60.

Student's Name: _____

Grade: _____

Teacher: _____

Diagnostic Checklist for Getting Children to Like Books

Part One

	Yes	No	Sometimes
1. The child voluntarily chooses to read.			
2. The child reads			
a. fairy tales and folktales.			
b. adventure stories.			
c. sports stories.			
d. biographies.			
e. autobiographies.			
f. nonfiction stories.			
g. mysteries.			
h. science fiction.			
i. poetry.			
j. books depicting various cultures.			
k. books to help him or her cope with an adjustment or emotional problem.			
l. other.			

Student's Name:_____

Grade:_____

Teacher:_____

Diagnostic Checklist for Getting Children to Like Books (Cont.)

Part Two

	Yes	No	Sometimes
1. The child usually finishes the book he or she chooses to read.			
2. The child asks for help in choosing a book.			
3. The child chooses books to read that are at his or her independent reading level.			
4. The child readily shares information about the book he or she reads with others or with the whole class.			
5. The child gives oral reports on books he or she has read.			
6. The child presents written reports to the class on books he or she has read.			
7. The child chooses to dramatize or role play some scenes or characters from books he or she has read.			
8. The child uses ideas gained from reading in his or her writings.			
9. The child asks to read to younger children.			
10. The child asks that the teacher read a story to the class.			
11. The child asks to tell a story to the class.			

Part Three

	Yes	No	Sometimes
1. State how many books the child claims he or she reads in a month.			
2. State how many books the child claims he or she attempts to read in a month but doesn't finish.			

SUMMARY

Chapter 17 provides teachers with the tools they will need to develop a reading for appreciation program in their classrooms. Teachers must recognize that they have to compete with other enjoyable activities that vie for their students' time and attention. In order to be able to compete effectively, teachers must provide time for children to read during the school day. They must also be enthusiastic about books, and they must establish a classroom environment that is conducive to reading. In choosing books for students, teachers must take into account sex differences and have a knowledge of the interests and needs of culturally different children. The teacher must also be especially perceptive to the black experience in literature.

Some knowledge of readability formulas, which are generally based on sentence length and the number of syllables in a word, should aid teachers in choosing books at their students' reading ability levels. A discussion of the use of books to help students to cope better with their developmental problems was presented, and it was suggested that this be used as a means to get students to read. A discussion on the use of television in the reading for appreciation program was also presented, as well as a diagnostic checklist for getting children to like books.

SUGGESTIONS FOR THOUGHT QUESTIONS AND ACTIVITIES

1. Choose a child who has had a reading problem or who still has one. Determine the child's reading ability and interests. Choose two books that you feel the child will enjoy.

2. Ask students in a class to state what they think a good book should have. List the criteria that they give. Ask them to choose a book and then to analyze it to see if it has the criteria that they have given.

3. You have a child in your class who does not like to read. What would you do to interest this child in books?

4. Choose and read a book that you feel primary-grade children will enjoy. Give your criteria for choosing the book. Explain how you would present this book to gain the attention and interest of your students. Do the same for the intermediate grades.

5. You teach an intermediate grade in an inner-city school with a large population of children who speak nonstandard English. What criteria would you use in choosing books for these children?

6. You have been appointed to a committee whose responsibility it is to determine the books that children like to read. How would you go about doing this?

7. Choose five library books. Determine their readability level.

8. You have been invited to speak on bibliotherapy. What books would you choose to discuss in your talk? Discuss why you chose these books.

SELECTED BIBLIOGRAPHY

General Books and Articles

Arbuthnot, May. *Arbuthnot Anthology of Children's Literature.* Glenville, Ill.: Scott, Foresman, 1976.

Bettelheim, Bruno. *The Uses of Enchantment: The Meaning and Importance of Fairy Tales.* New York: Knopf, 1976.

Gambrell, Linda B. "Getting Started with Sustained Silent Reading and Keeping It Going." *The Reading Teacher* 32 (December 1978): 328–31.

Hopkins, Lee Bennett. *The Best of Book Bonanza.* New York: Holt, Rinehart and Winston, 1980.

Huck, Charlotte. *Children's Literature in the Elementary School,* 3rd ed. updated. New York: Holt, Rinehart and Winston, 1979.

Lukens, Rebecca. *A Critical Handbook of Children's Literature.* Glenville, Ill.: Scott, Foresman, 1976.

McCracken, Robert A., and Marlene J. McCracken. "Modeling Is the Key to Sustained Silent Reading." *The Reading Teacher* 31 (January 1978): 406–408.

Root, Shelton L., ed. *Adventuring with Books: Twenty-four Hundred Titles for Preschool–Grade 8.* New York: Citation Press, 1973.

Rudman, Masha. *Children's Literature: An Issues Approach.* Lexington, Mass.: Heath, 1976.

Sadker, Myra P., and David M. Sadker. *Now Upon a Time: A Contemporary View of Children's Literature.* New York: Harper & Row, 1977.

Smith, Dora V. *Fifty Years of Children's Books: 1910-1960, Trends, Backgrounds, and Influences.* Urbana, Ill.: National Council of Teachers of English, 1963.

Sutherland, Zena, ed. *The Best in Children's Books.* Chicago: University of Chicago Press, 1973.

General References, Annotated

Gaver, Mary V., ed. *The Elementary School Library Collection: A Guide to Books and Other Media,* 12th ed. Newark, N.J.: Brodart, 1979. Classified book catalog listing titles considered to be a minimum collection for a K-6 school library. Also lists professional and audiovisual materials. Contains author, title, and subject indexes.

Haviland, Virginia. *Children's Literature: A Guide to Reference Sources.* Washington, D.C.: U.S. Government Printing Office, 1966. Annotated bibliography of references for children's literature.

White, Marion E., ed. *High Interest—Easy Reading.* Urbana, Ill.: National Council of Teachers of English, 1979. Annotated bibliography of books on contemporary themes for junior and senior high school students.

Wilson, H. W. *Children's Catalog,* 12th ed. New York: H. W. Wilson, 1971. Part 1—the "classified catalog"—is arranged according to the Dewey Decimal System and gives complete bibliographical data for each title; also recommended grade level and, often, evaluations from reviews. Part 2—the "alphabetical index"—gives author, title, subject, and analytical information.

Special Indexes, Annotated

American Library Association. *Subject and Title Index to Short Stories for Children.* Chicago: American Library Association, 1955. Index to about 5,000 short stories from 372 books for grades 3-9. Listed under subject with title.

American Library Association. *Subject Index to Poetry for Children and Young People.* Chicago: American Library Association, 1957. Subject index to poetry for grades K through high school.

Children's Books in Print. New York: Bowker, 1980-1981. A yearly updating of children's books in print with author, title, and illustrator indexes.

Eastman, Mary. *Index to Fairy Tales, Myths, and Legends, and Supplement 1937-52.* Boston: Faxon, 1926. Indexes to 1,500 folk and fairy tales by subject and title.

Sex Stereotyping in Children's Literature

Adell, Judith, and Hilary D. Klein, eds. *A Guide to Non-Sexist Children's Books.* Chicago: Academy Press, 1976.

Mitchell, E. "Learning of Sex Role through Toys and Books." *Young Children* 28 (April 1973): 226-31.

Nadesan, Ardell. "Mother Goose: Sexist." *Elementary English* 51 (March 1974): 375-78.

Sadker, Myra P. "Out of the Pumpkin Shell: The Image of Women in Children's Literature." In *Now Upon a Time: A Contemporary View of Children's Literature,* Myra P. Sadker and David M. Sadker, eds. New York: Harper & Row, 1977.

Stavn, Diane. "Reducing the 'Miss Muffet' Syndrome: An Annotated Bibliography." *School Library Journal* 97 (January 15, 1972): 32-35.

Weitzman, Lenore. "Sex Role Socialization in Picture Books for Preschool Children." *American Journal of Sociology* 77 (May 1972): 1125-50.

Culturally Different Children—Resource Books and Articles

Bresnahan, Mary. "Selecting Sensitive and Sensible Books About Blacks." *The Reading Teacher* 30 (October 1976): 16-20.

Keating, Charlotte Matthews. *Building Bridges of Understanding between Cultures.* Tucson, Ariz.: Palo Verde Publishing, 1971.

Long, Margo A. "The Interracial Family in Children's Literature." *The Reading Teacher* 31 (May 1978): 909-15.

Stoodt, Barbara D., and Sandra Ignizio. "The American Indian in Children's Literature." *Language Arts* 53 (January 1976): 17-21.

Sue, Paula Wee. "Promoting Understanding of Chinese-American Children." *Language Arts* 53 (March 1976): 262–66.

Tway, Eileen, ed. *Reading Ladders for Human Relations,* 6th ed. Washington, D.C.: American Council on Education, 1981.

Children and the Aged

Constant, Helen. "The Image of Grandparents in Children's Literature." *Language Arts* 54 (January 1977): 33–40.

Larrain, Virginia. *Timeless Voices: A Poetry Anthology Celebrating the Fulfillment of Age.* Millbrae, Cal.: Celestial Arts, 1978.

Sadker, Myra P., and David M. Sadker. "Growing Old in the Literature of the Young." In *Now Upon a Time: A Contemporary View of Children's Literature,* Myra P. Sadker and David M. Sadker, eds. New York: Harper & Row, 1977. (A bibliography is given.)

Children and the Handicapped

Greenbaum, Judith, Marilyn Varas, and Geraldine Markel. "Using Books About Handicapped Children." *The Reading Teacher* 33 (January 1980): 416–19.

Lass, Bonnie, and Marcia Bromfield. "Books About Children with Special Needs: An Annotated Bibliography." *The Reading Teacher* 34 (February 1981): 530–33.

Sadker, Myra P., and David M. Sadker. "Annotated Bibliography of Books Depicting the Handicapped." In *Now Upon a Time: A Contemporary View of Children's Literature,* Myra P. Sadker and David M. Sadker, eds. New York: Harper & Row, 1977.

Children and Death

Kingston, Carolyn T. *The Tragic Mode in Children's Literature.* New York: Teachers College Press, 1974.

Kübler-Ross, Elisabeth. *On Death and Dying.* New York: Macmillan, 1969.

_____. *Questions and Answers on Death and Dying.* New York: Macmillan, 1974.

Reed, Elizabeth. *Helping Children with the Mystery of Death.* Nashville, Tenn.: Abingdon Press, 1970.

"Theme: Learning About Death." (Special Topic) *Language Arts* 53 (September 1976): 673–87, 690–94.

Bibliotherapy

Brown, Eleanor F. *Bibliotherapy and Its Widening Applications.* Metuchen, N.J.: Scarecrow Press, 1975.

Moody, Mildred T., and Hilda K. Limper. *Bibliotherapy: Methods and Materials.* Chicago: American Library Association, 1971.

Rubin, Dorothy. "Bibliotherapy: Reading Toward Mental Health." *Children's House* 9 (September 1976): 6–9.

Rubin, Rhea Joyce. *Bibliotherapy: A Guide to Theory and Practice.* Phoenix, Ariz.: Oryx Press, 1978.

Teachers and Parents as Partners in the Diagnostic-Reading and Correction Program

INTRODUCTION

"Mommy, what's the name of this book?" asks Jennifer.

"The name of the book is *The Cat in the Hat*," replies her mother.

"Daddy, what does this say?" asks Johnny.

"It says 'Don't touch,' " replies his father.

"Mommy, what is this word on the cereal box?" asks Paul.

"The word is 'yummy,' " replies his mother.

"Mommy, what does the sign say?" asks Sharon.

"The sign says 'Stop,' " replies Sharon's mother.

"Daddy, what's this word in the book?" asks Carol.

"The word is 'happy,' " replies Carol's father.

And so it goes. Many young children are curious about words, and they see them all around. The persons they go to for help are the obvious ones—their parents. Parents are their first teachers. This is natural, and hardly anyone would question parents' rights to help their children satisfy their thirst for learning and desire to read; that is, hardly anyone would question what

these children's parents are doing today. However, it was just a short time ago that educators would have questioned parents' helping their children not only formally but also informally. Educators were very jealous of their rights when it came to teaching children, especially in reading. Strong outcries emanated from professionals' lips that parents didn't know what they were doing and that they should not attempt to teach their children to read before they came to school. Reasons given included such statements as "The parents don't know the proper methods" and "The children will be bored when they come to school." Many parents believed these statements. For example, in the 1950s Dolores Durkin, a noted reading authority, in her study of early readers reported more early readers coming from homes of blue-collar families than from those of professional parents. A possible reason for this result is that the prevailing view in the 1950s was that children should learn to read in school and not before. Professional parents were usually more aware of this view and subscribed to it, whereas parents of a lower socioeconomic status were less aware of this view and did not subscribe to it.[1] As a result, if a child asked a professional parent to tell him or her a word, the parent supposedly did not. In the early 1960s, according to Durkin, more early readers were found who came from upper-middle-class homes because it was no longer fashionable to discourage parents from teaching their children to read.[2] Many parents were beginning to take a more active role in their children's learning, and this trend has continued into the 1980s.

In this chapter we will be concerned with why this active involvement on the part of parents has continued and we will look at the role that parents are and should be playing in the reading program. After you finish reading this chapter, you should be able to answer the following questions:

1. What caused a change in educators' attitudes toward parental involvement?

2. What are educators' attitudes toward parental involvement?

3. What effect has Title I had on parental involvement?

4. What role do parents play in Title I programs?

5. What are some examples of parental involvement programs for preschoolers?

6. What are some examples of parental involvement programs not associated with federal funding?

7. What is the role of the parent-teacher conference?

8. What factors help to make a good parent-teacher conference?

---

[1]Dolores Durkin, *Children Who Read Early* (New York: Teachers College Press, 1966), pp. 46–48, 136.
[2]Ibid, pp. 90, 136.

PARENTAL INVOLVEMENT IN THE SCHOOLS

Parental involvement in the schools is not a new phenomenon. Parents sit on the boards of education; they are involved in parent-teacher associations, parent councils, and parent clubs. Parents help formulate school policy, have say in curriculum, and even help to choose textbooks. Parents definitely have a voice in school matters. However, until rather recently, parents have not been encouraged to take an active role in working with their own children, particularly in reading. Teaching was considered the sole domain of the educator, and parents who wanted to teach their children were usually looked upon as meddlers, troublemakers, and outsiders. At best they were looked upon as well-meaning but unknowledgeable, and as already stated, until the late 1950s parents were admonished not to teach their children to read at home. Today in many school districts across the country parents are seen as partners and potential resources rather than as unknowing meddlers. What has caused the pendulum to swing in the other direction?

Some Possible Causes for a Change in Attitude Toward Parental Involvement

A number of things have happened not only in changing educators' attitudes toward parental involvement in reading instruction but also in changing parents' attitudes. A strong factor that cannot be overlooked is that parents began to lose confidence in the schools because of the great number of reading failures found there. With this loss of confidence came the desire for more direct involvement.

Rudolf Flesch's book *Why Johnny Can't Read—And What You Can Do About It,* which was written in 1955, probably helped to raise the consciousness level of parents concerning the role they should be playing in helping their children learn to read. Flesch's book was addressed to parents, and it was written primarily to help parents help their children learn to read by using a phonic method. Whether one agrees with the views expressed in the book or not is not as important as the impact that the book made, and indeed it did make a great impact. Parents wanted to know more about what their children were doing in reading, and many wanted to be more directly involved.

The increase of reading problems in the schools probably helped to change educators' attitudes as well as parents' attitudes. The reading problem may have caused educators to take another look at this great potential resource—parents—because many began to feel that they could use all the help they could get.

However, the greatest impetus for parental involvement probably came from the influx of federal monies to fund certain programs related to the improvement of children's reading skills. Almost all these programs mandated parental involvement. Head Start, which was initiated in the summer of 1965, is one such program. Its target audience is young children, that is, preschoolers and kindergartners. Follow Through, which is another such program, was first initiated as a pilot project in 1967 and became nationwide in 1968. Its audience is the children who participated in the Head Start program. Probably the passage of Title I in 1966 had the most effect on parental involvement because its programs cover a much larger population of children than Head Start. Under Head Start, Follow Through, and Title I programs, parental involvement is mandatory.

It may be that parental involvement is more a matter of economics for some educators than a change of attitude. It is to be hoped that this is not so. It may also be that the parental involvement in these federally funded programs stimulated other parents to become more involved

and to take a more active role in their children's education. There is a definite trend toward more parental involvement in regular reading programs across the country, which seems to refute the belief that parental involvement is merely an economic factor for educators and to affirm the belief that parents and educators are interested in working together as partners in the education of children.

WHAT IS TITLE I?

A special short section is included on Title I programs because of the great impact they have had on parental involvement in reading programs across the country and because there is so much confusion about what Title I is itself.

Title I of the Elementary and Secondary Education Act (ESEA) was signed into law in 1965 to provide federal monies to state education agencies, which, in turn, suballocate the funds to local school districts.[3] The purpose of the law is to help educationally deprived children, ages five to seventeen, living in low-income areas. When Title I was first passed, local school districts had to have at least one hundred children or 3 percent of their local enrollment from low-income families in order to qualify. Numerous amendments have been passed through the years, and eligibility requirements have become more lenient. Although the state guidelines vary somewhat from state to state concerning the dissemination of monies and the eligibility of students in the program, the following is what generally happens: A local school district which has at least ten educationally deprived children aged five to seventeen who are receiving Aid to Families with Dependent Children (AFDC) or

[3]*History of Title I ESEA,* U.S. Department of Health, Education and Welfare DHEW Publication No. (OE) 72–75 (Washington, D.C.: U.S. Government Printing Office, 1972).

who come from homes that are below the poverty level can apply to the state education agency for Title I monies. Then the state disseminates the funds based on its particular formula. The school district must identify the school that these children are attending. Once the schools with the highest concentration have been identified, all educationally deprived children in that school, whether they come from low-income homes or not, are eligible for the Title I program.

Title I programs must be supplemental; that is, they must be in addition to the ongoing developmental reading, language arts, or mathematics program rather than replacements for it. The state education agency has the authority to approve local Title I projects, which must be designed to meet the special educational needs of the children being served.[4]

WHAT IS THE ROLE OF PARENTS IN TITLE I PROGRAMS?

As already stated, parental involvement is mandatory as of 1970 in Title I programs. In 1971 a more formal involvement of parents was ensured by a federal regulation mandating parent councils. In 1978, the federal guidelines again mandated the establishment of advisory councils by the local school district. To guarantee more than lip-service involvement, the federal regulations state that each local educational agency shall give each advisory council which it establishes "responsibility for advising it in planning for, and implementation and evaluation of, its programs and projects. . . ."[5]

[4]Carol Sue Fromboluti, *Title I Elementary and Secondary Education Act: Questions and Answers* (Washington, D.C.: U.S. Government Printing Office, 1979).

[5]Public Law 95-561, Title I—Amendment to Title I of the Elementary and Secondary Education Act of 1965 (November 1, 1978), p. 16.

Each local school district must set up a parent advisory council on both the district and the school level. All members must be selected by the parents who live in the school district or project area, and the majority of members must be parents of participating children. The local school system must help the council to function effectively in a number of ways. One way is to provide a program of training for the members of the council so that they will be able to carry out their responsibilities.

An Example of Parents as Teaching Partners in a Title I Program

The specifics of Title I programs are not mandated by the state or federal government, so programs may vary from school district to school district; the use of parents in the instructional aspects of the program usually varies since no mandate is given for their involvement in this component.

One program reported in the literature consists of a series of about five meetings on alternate weeks. The meetings are designed to make the parents feel "comfortable in school, to give them a sense of the potential importance of the role they can play with their children, and to give them specific materials and ideas for helping their children read at home."[6] In the program parents are given a taste of what it's like to learn to read; they are given books at their children's reading levels and asked to spend ten minutes a night helping their children read; and they play reading games that help reinforce skills children are learning and which can be played at home. In this program parents are encouraged to share their experiences with others at the meetings, which not only gives parents a feeling of security and calms fears but also pro-

[6]Annette Breiling, "Using Parents as Teaching Partners," *The Reading Teacher* 30 (November 1976):188.

vides helpful suggestions. The topics presented at the meetings vary, but each one seems to be concerned with helping parents learn more about the reading process and the methods and approaches teachers use. The program also includes student participation, which usually consists of a child reading for a few minutes while parents listen.

Parents' responses to the program have been very good, and they report noticeable improvement in the reading ability of their children.

PARENTAL INVOLVEMENT IN PRESCHOOL PROGRAMS

Many parents want help for their preschool children. Preschool help gained its greatest impetus from the federal funding of programs such as Head Start in the middle 1960s, which mandated parental involvement. Ira Gordon played a significant role in this development. All his programs used paraprofessionals who visited the home and served as parent educators to demonstrate specially designed home learning activities to the parent.[7]

The trend for preschool help and parental involvement has continued, as can be seen in Gallup's 1979 poll on parents' attitudes. In the poll, parents with children who have not yet started school or kindergarten were asked: "Do you think the school could help you in any way in preparing your child for school?"

Those respondents who have no children in school represent the group most eager to have preschool help for their children (see Table 18.1). When the parents who desired help were asked "what the school could do," the suggestion offered most often was the distribution of a

Table 18.1 (1979)

	Could School Help With Preschool Child?		
	Yes %	No %	Don't Know/ No Answer %
Parents who presently have no children in school	53	34	13
Parents with one or more children in public school	37	53	10
Parents with one or more children in parochial school	40	40	20

pamphlet or booklet telling in detail what parents should do to prepare the child for school. One parent is quoted as saying, "I should like to know exactly what they expect of the child, such as the ABCs, numbers, and other areas of learning." Another frequently made suggestion was to invite parents and their preschool children to visit the school to see what goes on in a typical day. Some parents thought that it would be a good idea to designate a day when a preschool child could actually sit in the kindergarten class with other children to see what it is like. Still other parents suggested that a regular preschool program, such as Head Start, be made part of the educational system. Many respondents said that such a preschool program already exists in their community.[8]

From the 1960s onward, we begin to see a number of programs in which parents are directly involved in teaching their young children some basic beginning reading skills. In some of the programs parents are taught certain skills

---

[7]Patricia P. Olmstead et al., *Parent Education: The Contributions of Ira J. Gordon* (Washington, D.C.: Association for Childhood Education International, 1980), p. 8.

[8]George Gallup, "The Eleventh Annual Gallup Poll of the Public's Attitudes Toward the Public Schools," *Phi Delta Kappan* 61 (September 1979):33–44.

that they then use to teach their children, and in some they work with preschool teachers and then provide supplementary instruction at home. An example of such a program is the Preschool Readiness Outreach Program (PROP), which states as its primary aim the desire "to share with parents of three to five year olds ideas on ways they could help their children develop beginning reading skills."[9] In the program parents had to attend twenty-six weekly three-hour workshops, which were held in local elementary schools. Each session focused on a basic skill such as oral expression, visual perception, and auditory discrimination; the primary aim of each session was for each parent to construct a game to develop one of the basic skills. At the beginning of each workshop, parents would share their experiences concerning the previous week's game; then the workshop leader would present the current week's game, explaining its uses and how to construct it. For the remainder of the workshop, parents constructed the games and participated in an informal discussion.[10]

PARENTAL INVOLVEMENT IN REGULAR SCHOOL READING PROGRAMS

There are many children who have reading problems who are not going to schools designated as Title I schools. What about the involvement of the parents of these children in reading programs. Also, what about the involvement of parents whose children have no reading difficulties? The trend does seem to be for more parental involvement for these two groups of

parents also; however, probably more parents participate whose children have some kind of reading problem.

The participation of parents in many school districts is usually dependent on how aggressive the educators and parents are in demanding such involvement. The involvement of the parents in the regular reading program seems to vary from district to district, and even in some school districts, from school to school. In one school system, you will find an organized program, and in another you will find that the program is up to the individual teacher in each individual class. The programs that do exist usually are similar in format in that they generally include workshops, instructional materials, and book suggestions. What is presented, however, will vary from district to district. The following is an example of a program that was developed in a local New Jersey school system to incorporate parental involvement in its regular reading program for all children in grades one through five. The program consists of instructional packets, book suggestions, and three workshops. At the first workshop, a reading specialist explains the reading program that is in use in the school system. The parents are acquainted with the basal reader series, and the terminology that is used is also explained. At the second workshop the parents witness a reading lesson from the basal reader series, which uses the Directed Reading Approach. The third session is entitled "A Book Talk." At this session books at different readability and interest levels are presented, and suggestions are made on how to involve children in reading them.

Another part of the program concerns instructional materials. For those children who have reading problems, parent packets are produced which consist of activities based on the skills that children are working on in class. Different parent packets are available for different

[9]Carol Vukelich, "Parents Are Teachers: A Beginning Reading Program," *The Reading Teacher* 31 (February 1978):524.
[10]Ibid., pp. 525–26.

grade levels. For those children who have no reading problems, materials are sent home which help parents to capitalize on their children's reading interests. A special packet which emphasizes more difficult books, especially the Newbery award winners, is sent home to the parents of children who have been identified as highly able or gifted.[11]

A program of special interest was developed in a school system for highly able readers in grades two through six, their teachers, and parents. The program, called the "Junior Great Books Program," began in 1979 and included twelve volunteer parents and twelve teachers. A parent and a teacher were paired off, and then they worked together as a team. The parents who volunteered had to take the two-day training session, which was conducted by a special person from the Great Books Foundation, located in Chicago. The sessions consisted primarily of helping parents learn about the kinds of questions they should ask, as well as how to conduct the discussions. The children who participated in the program were considered "top readers" by their teachers. The criteria that teachers used were teacher-made and standardized test results as well as a child's ability to assume responsibility. The parent-teacher team met every week to plan for the reading discussions, which took place in the regular classroom during the regularly scheduled reading period for forty-five minutes. Both the parent and the teacher helped to lead the discussion with a particular group of children.[12]

It's interesting to note that a number of the basal reader series are including suggestions for parental involvement in their teacher's editions. For example, *Reading Basic Plus* has suggestions for parents at the end of every lesson of each readiness teacher's edition. "These were designed to apprise parents of the major skills their children are learning in school. The suggestions include simple activities that parents might use at home to help reinforce their children's understanding of the skills. The publisher grants permission to teachers to reproduce the suggestions and send them home with the children."[13] The *Teacher's Resource Package for Reading Basic Plus* also includes a Suggestion for Parents section, which appears at the bottom of each page of the Collection Test and which is supposed to help parents reinforce skills taught in class. The producers of the reading series feel that these suggestions help the parents participate in their children's reading progress. An example of an activity from a Collection Test is on page 353.[14]

How Successful Are Parental Involvement Programs?

The success of any program that demands voluntary participation has to be based on turnout—not initial turnout, but continuous turnout. The programs reported in the literature and those surveyed by the author had excellent parent participation. Most of the reading coordinators claimed that parent turnout had grown and that verbal feedback had been very good. The parents in the programs claimed that since their involvement in the program their children were more interested in reading, and the parents of children who had reading difficulties claimed that their children's reading skills had improved as well as their attitude.

[11]Ewing Township Public Schools, Ewing, New Jersey.

[12]Hopewell Valley Regional School District, Hopewell Valley, New Jersey.
[13]*Go Read!* (Teachers Edition), *Reading Basic Plus* series (New York: Harper & Row, 1980), p. T7
[14]Copyright © 1980, 1976 by Harper & Row, Publishers, Inc.

NAME _____

Read the story. Draw a line under the words that answer each question.

One sunny day, Miguel went shopping with his father. They got on a bus and soon they were downtown. Miguel needed a new coat. They went to a big store that sold many different things. Miguel's father bought him a coat and a new sweater. Then his father bought a plant. Before they went home, they stopped to have something to eat.

1.   What did Miguel and his father do first?

    They bought a coat.   They got on a bus.

2.   What kinds of things did Miguel and his father buy?

    things you can put on   things you can play with

3.   What did Miguel and his father do before they went home?

    They bought a coat.   They had something to eat.

4.   How do you think Miguel and his father got home?

    They got into their car.   They took the bus.

5.   Which of the things that Miguel and his father bought can keep you warm?

    a new coat and sweater   a plant and something to eat

Skills: Conclusion, Sequence, Classification
Suggestion for Parents: Have your child read the page to you. Then take turns with your child naming other things that can keep a person warm.

Are Parental Involvement Programs a Passing Fad?

The movement for more rather than less parental involvement in reading programs should squelch the idea that parents will lose interest in their desire to be partners in teaching. The desire for more parental involvement can be seen in the responses to some questions on the *Gallup Polls of Attitudes Toward Education,* which began in

1969. In the 1971 and 1976 opinion polls, there were questions concerning courses for parents to help their children. The responses of both parents and those persons who had no children in the schools were overwhelmingly in favor of attending such courses[15] (see Tables 18.2 and 18.3).

A number of colleges have become sensitive to parents' need and desire for more knowledge about the reading act and what the schools are doing in teaching reading. As a result, some have instituted courses for parents and some have provided special workshops designed to involve parents in their children's reading instruction. For example, in one college a summer reading clinic started a summer parent group because the instructors felt that "parents should know what their children would experience in the clinic and how they could continue to help them when the clinic ended."[16] The parent coor-

dinator of the clinic claimed that parents were responsive and that they were eager to attend.[17]

In a number of schools parents are not involved in any formal reading program, but they volunteer to be tutors in the regular reading program. Usually, the parent volunteer works with a special reading teacher or coordinator or learning disability person. These persons usually help the parent volunteers so that they will be able to tutor effectively those students who have been identified as needing help.

The 1980 Gallup poll further substantiates the fact that parents definitely want to be involved as partners in the education of their children[18] (see Table 18.4). The trend toward parental involvement, particularly in the area of reading, is not a fad.

[15]Stanley M. Elam, ed., *A Decade of Gallup Polls of Attitudes Toward Education 1969–1978* (Bloomington, Ind.: Phi Delta Kappa, 1978), pp. 108, 272.

[16]Helen Feaga Esworthy, "Parents Attend Reading Clinic, Too," *The Reading Teacher* 32 (April 1979): 831.
[17]Ibid.
[18]George Gallup, "The Twelfth Annual Gallup Poll of the Public's Attitudes Toward the Public Schools," *Phi Delta Kappan* 62 (September 1980): 33–46.

Table 18.2 (1971)

A suggestion has been made that parents of school children attend one evening class a month to find out what they can do at home to improve their children's behavior and increase their interest in schoolwork. Is it a good idea or a poor idea?

	National Totals %	No Children in Schools %	Public School Parents %	Parochial School Parents %	High School Juniors and Seniors %
Good idea	81	82	80	81	75
Poor idea	13	11	16	15	21
No opinion	6	7	4	4	4
	100	100	100	100	100

Table 18.3 (1976)

As a regular part of the public school educational system, it has been suggested that courses be offered at convenient times to parents in order to help them help their children in school. Do you think this is a good idea or a poor idea?

	National Totals %	No Children in Schools %	Public School Parents %	Parochial School Parents %
Good idea	77	76	78	74
Poor idea	19	18	20	25
Don't know/ no answer	4	6	2	1

Table 18.4 (1980)

Question: In your opinion, should or should not parents be asked to meet with school personnel before each new school semester to examine the grades, test scores, and career goals for each child and to work out a program to be followed both in school and at home?

	National Totals %	No Children in Schools %	Public School Parents %	Parochial School Parents %
Yes, favor this plan	84	85	83	83
No, do not favor	11	9	14	14
Don't know	5	6	3	3

GRANDPARENTS SHOULD BE INVOLVED TOO

Why not involve the elderly in reading programs in which they could work directly with children as tutors and helpers? Why not have children read aloud to the elderly? Why not bring the grandparents into the mainstream? Why not, indeed?

Interestingly, we are living in an era when a person's life expectancy is the greatest that it has ever been, and as a result there are many more elderly people who are visible. Even though there is an increased interest in gerontology and in more benefits for the elderly, and the elderly have become more vocal, they are usually shunned, especially by young people. Moreover, with the advent of retirement communities and nursing homes, the elderly are probably more segregated from society today than ever before.

The treatment of the elderly in children's literature has probably been the most neglected and the most poorly portrayed of all other areas. Children are greatly influenced by the way elderly people are portrayed, especially in fairy tales. When children were asked how elderly people are shown in fairy tales, the children responded, "They are witches."[19] Obviously, these children have been greatly influenced by the portrayal of the old woman as a mean, cross, wicked hag or witch in such famous fairy tales as "Hansel and Gretel," "Sleeping Beauty," and "Snow White and the Seven Dwarfs."

As stated earlier, today the elderly are more visible, but not usually by children because of the burgeoning of senior communities. It is claimed that the more involved the elderly are, the happier they are, and the longer they live. It would seem to be a good idea, both for young people and the elderly, to have them work together. If young people can see that the elderly are not like the stereotypes portrayed in print, their attitudes toward the elderly could become more positive.

The elderly take part in some community programs developed to foster parental involvement, but their involvement is usually sporadic; that is, it's based more on chance than a concerted effort to get them involved. The programs that incorporate senior citizens as aides or tutors in reading are usually based in a particular school rather than in a districtwide program. For example, in Princeton, New Jersey, some schools have a program in which fifth-graders work in a cooperative effort with the elderly. The fifth-graders eat lunch with the elderly, and at the luncheon they act as the hosts and hostesses. After the luncheon, the senior citizens work with the children as tutors.

There is one community in northern Michigan making a concerted effort to integrate senior citizens into its daily school life. The school system of Harbor Springs has initiated a program in which senior citizens are encouraged to participate in all school activities, and the senior citizen center is housed in the school's old library, which was renovated to fit the needs of the elderly.[20] The project at Harbor Springs is believed to be the first of its kind, but it is to be hoped that it will be one of many.

PARENT-TEACHER CONFERENCES

In some schools the only parent-teacher involvement may be through the parent-teacher conference. This conference is an excellent opportunity for parents and teachers to learn to feel more comfortable with one another, as well as to exchange information. Also, the parent-teacher conference may be the only way for parents to learn about the reading program and the specifics of how individual children are doing.

Some teachers look with dread on parent-teacher conferences; therefore they structure them so that very little time is allowed for parent input or questioning. Unfortunately, such attitudes are usually conveyed to parents, and a free exchange is generally inhibited. For parent-teacher conferences to work, there must be a feeling of confidence on both sides. The more confidence a teacher has, the more comfortable he or she will feel with parents.

For parent-teacher conferences to be effective, teachers must be friendly, interested, and allow for an exchange of ideas. It is also important for teachers to recognize that although they have twenty-five or thirty students in the class, this particular child is the one who is important to the parents. Most importantly, since this conference is primarily an exchange of ideas,

---

[19]Myra P. Sadker and David M. Sadker, *Now Upon a Time: A Contemporary View of Children's Literature* (New York: Harper & Row, 1977), p. 77.

[20]Sara Gay Dammann, "New Older Students Join Younger Ones," *The Christian Science Monitor*, September 15, 1980.

teachers should encourage parents to give some insights into the children that would be helpful in teaching them. Remember, it is doubtful that anyone knows these children better than their parents. If the children need any special help, teachers should point this out to parents and explain precisely what they can do.

Parent-teacher conferences need not take place only during the reporting period. Whenever a need for a conference arises is the right time to call for one. However, teachers should remember that successful parent-teacher conferences require careful planning and effort.

SUMMARY

Chapter 18 is concerned with parental involvement in the schools' reading programs. In the 1950s many parents were discouraged from attempting to help their children learn to read; however, in the 1970s and the 1980s the trend is definitely toward more parental involvement. Parents are looked upon as partners in education, and as partners they are beginning to take a more active role. Parental involvement was triggered by a number of factors, two salient ones being loss of confidence in the schools and the input of federal funds mandating parental involvement. The reading programs that include parental involvement vary from school district to school district and even from school to school in the same school district; however, more and more school districts are developing programs that involve parents. Even the publishing companies are including special sections in their reading series specifically for parents and children to do together. Not only is there a trend for parental involvement in the reading program but there also seems to be a concerted effort in some communities to involve grandparents, too. The parent-teacher conference was discussed as an excellent means for parents and teachers to get to know more about each other and to exchange information about an individual child.

SUGGESTIONS FOR THOUGHT QUESTIONS AND ACTIVITIES

1. You have been put on a special committee in your school district to represent your school. The committee was formed to try to learn how parents can be more involved in the schools' reading programs. What suggestions would you make?

2. If you were asked to conduct an opinion poll concerning parents' attitudes about school and in particular about the reading program, what kinds of questions would you ask?

3. A suggestion was made at a meeting that the elderly become more involved in working directly with children in your school. How do you feel about this? In what way do you feel the elderly can help children in the reading program?

4. Survey a school district to determine the kinds of federally funded programs that it has. Then try to find out about the ways in which parents are involved.

5. Choose a school in your area. Try to set an appointment with an administrator to learn how that school involves parents in its reading programs.

SELECTED BIBLIOGRAPHY

Breiling, Annette. "Using Parents as Teaching Partners." *The Reading Teacher* 30 (November 1976): 187–92.

Cassidy, Jack. "Grey Power in the Reading Program—A Direction for the Eighties," *The Reading Teacher* 35 (December 1981): 287–291.

Grimmett, Sadie A., and Mae McCoy. "Effects of Parental Communication on Reading Performance of Third Grade Children." *The Reading Teacher* 34 (December 1980): 303–308.

Nicholson, Tom. "Why We Need to Talk to Parents About Reading." *The Reading Teacher* 34 (October 1980): 19–21.

Olmstead, Patricia P., et al. *Parent Education: The Contributions of Ira J. Gordon.* Washington, D.C.: Association for Childhood Education International, 1980.

Swaby, Barbara. "How Can Parents Foster Comprehension Growth in Children." *The Reading Teacher* 34 (December 1980): 280–83.

Vukelich, Carol. "Parents Are Teachers: A Beginning Reading Program." *The Reading Teacher* 31 (February 1978): 524–27.

Glossary

Accommodation. Child developing new categories rather than integrating them into existing ones—Piaget's cognitive development.

Affective domain. Concerned with the feelings and emotional learnings that students acquire.

Affixes. Prefixes (*which see**) that are added before the root word and suffixes (*which see*) that are added to the end of a root word.

Analogies. Relationships between words or ideas.

Analysis. Breaking down something into its component parts.

Anecdotal record. Recording observed behavior over a period of time.

Antonyms. Words opposite in meaning.

Appendix. A section of a book containing extra information that does not quite fit into the book but that the author feels is important enough to be presented separately.

Appraisal. Part of a diagnostic pattern—a student's reading performance in relation to his or her potential.

Appreciative reading. Reading for pleasure and enjoyment from books that fit some mood, feeling, or interest.

*Which see refers to the immediately preceding word that is defined elsewhere in the glossary.

Assimilation. A continuous process which helps the individual to integrate new incoming stimuli to existing concepts—Piaget's cognitive development.

Association. Pairing the real object with the sound of the word.

Auding. Highest level of listening, which involves listening with comprehension.

Audiometer. An instrument used for measuring hearing acuity.

Auditory discrimination. Ability to distinguish between sounds.

Aural. Refers to listening.

Basal reader approach. An approach involving a basal reader series. This approach is highly structured; it uses a controlled vocabulary, and skills are sequentially developed.

Base. Same as root (*which see*).

Beginning reading readiness. Those prerequisite activities directly related to reading that precede formal reading.

Behavioral objective. Statement which describes what students will be able to do after they have achieved their goal.

Bias. A mental leaning, a partiality, a prejudice, or a slanting of something.

Bibliotherapy. The use of books to help individuals to cope better with their emotional and adjustment problems.

Bilingual. Using or capable of using two languages.

Breve. The short vowel mark (˘).

Capacity level. See **Listening capacity level.**

Categorizing. A thinking skill involving the ability to classify items into general and specific categories.

Central idea. See **Main idea.**

Checklist. A means for systematically and quickly recording a student's behavior; it usually consists of a list of behaviors that the observer records as present or absent.

Classroom tests. Teacher-made tests; also called informal tests (*which see*).

Cloze procedure. A technique that helps teachers gain information about a variety of language facility and comprehension ability skills.

Cloze test. Reader must supply words which have been systematically deleted from a passage.

Clusters. Clusters represent a blend of sounds.

Cognitive development. Refers to development of thinking (*which see*).

Cognitive domain. Hierarchy of objectives ranging from simplistic thinking skills to the more complex ones.

Combining forms. Usually defined as roots (*which see*) borrowed from another language that join together or that join with a prefix (*which see*), a suffix (*which see*), or both to form a word, for example, *aqua/naut.*

Communication. Exchange of ideas.

Comparison. A demonstration of the similarities between persons, ideas, things, and so on.

Competency-based instruction. Embraces two essential characteristics: learning objectives, defined in behavioral terms, and accountability.

Compound word. Separate words that combine to form a new word, for example, *grandfather, stepdaughter, sunlight.*

Computer-aided instruction. Instruction using computers.

Concentration. Sustained attention. It is essential for both studying and listening to lectures.

Concepts. A group of stimuli with common characteristics.

Connotative meaning. Includes all emotional associations of the word.

Consonant blends. A combination of sounds blended together so that the identity of each sound is retained.

Consonant clusters. Same as consonant blends (*which see*).

Construct. Something which cannot be directly observed or directly measured—such as intelligence, attitudes, and motivation.

Context. The words surrounding a particular word that can shed light on its meaning.

Contrast. A demonstration of the differences between persons, ideas, things, and so on.

Corrective reading. Takes place within the regular classroom.

Creative reading. Uses divergent thinking skills to go beyond the literal comprehension, interpretation, and critical reading levels.

Criterion-referenced tests. Based on an extensive inventory of learning objectives in a specific curriculum area; they are not norm-based.

Critical reading. A high-level reading skill that involves evaluation and making a personal judgment on the accuracy, value, and truthfulness of what is read.

Crossed dominance. The dominant hand on one side and the dominant eye on the other.

Culturally different. Refers to those children whose parents have usually been born in another country and who speak a language other than English; it may also refer to a child who is born in the United States, but English is not the dominant language spoken in the child's home.

Deductive teaching. Students are given a generalization and must determine which examples fit the rule, going from general to specific.

Denotative meaning. The direct, specific meaning of the word.

Derivatives. Combinations of root words with either prefixes (*which see*) or suffixes (*which see*) or both; for example, prefix (*re*) plus root word (*play*) = *replay.*

Developmental reading. All those reading skills that are systematically and sequentially developed to help students become effective readers throughout their schooling.

Diagnosis. The act or art of identifying difficulties and strengths from their signs and symptoms, as well as the investigation or analysis of the cause or causes of a condition, situation, or problem.

Diagnostic-reading and correction program. Reading instruction interwoven with diagnosis and correction.

Diagnostic reading test. Provides subscores discrete enough so that specific information about a student's reading behavior can be obtained and used for instruction.

Dialect. A variation of language sufficiently different to be considered separate, but not different enough to be classified as a separate language.

Dictionary. A very important reference tool that supplies word meanings, pronunciations, and a great amount of other useful information.

Digit span. Refers to amount of words or numbers an individual can retain in his or her short-term memory.

Digraph. Usually consisting of either two consonants or two vowels which represent one speech sound, for example, *ch, ai.*

Diphthongs. Blends of vowel sounds beginning with the first and gliding to the second. The vowel blends are represented by two adjacent vowels, for example, *oi.* For syllabication purposes, diphthongs are considered to be one vowel sound.

Divergent thinking. The many different ways to solve problems or to look at things.

Educational factors. Those factors that come under the domain or control of the educational system and influence learning.

Environmental psychology. Focuses on behavior in relation to physical settings.

Equilibrium. According to Piaget, a balance between assimilation (*which see*) and accommodation (*which see*) in cognitive development (*which see*).

Evaluation. A process of appraisal involving specific values and the use of a variety of instruments in order to form a value judgment.

Exceptional children. Those children who deviate so much from the "average" that they require special attention.

Experience story. A basic teaching technique in reading founded on experiences of students.

Fact. Something that exists and can be proved true.

Finding inconsistencies. Finding statements that do not make sense.

Frustration reading level. The child reads with many word recognition and comprehension errors. It is the lowest reading level and one to be avoided.

Glossary. A listing of the meanings of specialized words or phrases.

Grapheme–phoneme relationship. Letter–sound relationship.

Graphemes. The written representation of phonemes (*which see*).

Graphemic base. A succession of graphemes that occurs with the same phonetic value in a number of words (*ight, ake, at, et,* and so on); same as phonogram (*which see*).

Group tests. Administered to a group of persons.

Halo effect. A response bias that contaminates an individual's perception in rating or evaluation.

Homographs. Words which are spelled the same but have different meanings.

Homonyms. Words which sound alike, are spelled differently, and have different meanings.

Homophones. Same as homonyms (*which see*).

Independent reading level. Child reads on his or her own without any difficulty.

Index. A list of topics discussed in a book and page numbers indicating where the topics are discussed.

Individualized instruction. Student works at own pace on material based on the needs, interests, and ability of the student.

Individual tests. Administered to one person at a time.

Inductive teaching. Students discover generalizations by being given numerous examples which portray patterns; going from specific to general.

Inference. Understanding that is not derived from a direct statement but from an indirect suggestion in what is stated.

Informal Reading Inventory (IRI). A valuable aid in helping teachers determine a student's reading problem(s). It usually consists of oral and silent reading passages selected from basal readers from the preprimer to the sixth- or eighth-grade levels.

Informal tests. Teacher-made tests (*which see*).

Instructional reading level. The teaching level.

Intake of language. Listening and reading.

Intelligence. Ability to reason abstractly.

Interpretation. A reading level that demands a higher level of thinking ability because the material it involves is not directly stated in the text but only suggested or implied.

IQ. Intelligence Quotient; mental age divided by chronological age multiplied by 100.

I.P.A. International Phonetic Alphabet.

Kinesics. Study of the gestures which may or may not accompany speech (message-related body movement).

Language. A learned, shared, and patterned arbitrary system of vocal sound symbols with which people in a given culture can communicate with one another.

Language arts. The major components are listening, speaking, reading, and writing.

Language-experience approach. A nonstructured emerging reading program based on students' experiences, which incorporates all aspects of the language arts into reading.

Laterality. Refers to sidedness.

Learning center. An integral part of the instructional program and vital to a good individualized program. An area is usually set aside in the classroom for instruction in a specific curriculum area.

Linguistics. The scientific study of language.

Listening capacity. To know the meaning of words when they are said aloud.

Listening capacity level. The highest level at which a learner can understand material when it is read aloud to him or her.

Listening capacity test. Given to determine a child's comprehension through listening.

Literal comprehension. The ability to obtain a low-level type of understanding by using only information that is explicitly stated.

Locator test. Used to determine at what level a student should begin testing.

Look-and-say. A word recognition technique in which a child's attention is directed to a word and then the word is said.

Macron. The long vowel mark (⁻).

Main idea. The central thought of a paragraph. The term *central idea* is usually used when referring to a group of paragraphs, an article, or a story. The procedure, however, for finding the main idea and the central idea is the same for both.

Mainstreaming. The placement of handicapped children in the least restrictive educational environment that will meet their needs.

Measurement. Part of the evaluative process; involves quantitative descriptions.

Memory span. The number of discrete elements grasped in a given moment of attention and organized into a unity for purposes of immediate reproduction or immediate use; synonym for digit span (*which see*).

Miscue. Unexpected response to print.

Miscue analysis. A process that helps researchers learn how readers get meaning from language.

Morpheme. The smallest individually meaningful element in the utterances of a language.

Morphology. Involves the construction of words and word parts.

Motivation. Internal impetus behind behavior and the direction behavior takes; drive.

Myopia. Nearsightedness.

Norm-referenced tests. Standardized tests with norms *(which see)* so that comparisons can be made.

Norms. Average scores for a given group of students, which allow comparisons to be made for different students or groups of students.

Notetaking. A useful study and paper-writing tool.

Objectivity. The same score must result regardless of who marks the test.

Observation. A technique that helps teachers collect data about students' behavior.

Open syllable. A syllable having a single vowel and ending in a vowel. The vowel is usually long, for example, *go*.

Opinions. Based on attitudes or feelings; they can vary from person to person, but cannot be conclusively proved right or wrong.

Oral. Refers to speaking.

Outgo of language. Speaking and writing.

Overlearning. Helps persons retain information over a long period of time; occurs when individuals continue to practice even afer they think they have learned the material.

Peer tutoring. A student helps another student gain needed skills.

Perception. A cumulative process based on an individual's background of experiences. It is defined as giving meaning to sensations or the ability to organize stimuli on a field.

Perceptual domain. Part of the reading process that depends on an individual's background of experiences and sensory receptors. (See **Perception.**)

Phoneme. Smallest unit of sound in a specific language system; a class of sounds.

Phonemics. Deals with the problem of discovering which phonemes are part of the conscious repertoire of sounds made by speakers of a language or dialect.

Phonetics. The study of the nature of speech sounds.

Phonics. The study of the relationships between letter symbols of a written language and the sounds they represent.

Phonogram. Same as graphemic base (*which see*).

Phonology. Branch of linguistics (*which see*) dealing with the analysis of sound systems of language.

Physical environment. Refers to any observable factors in the physical environment which could affect the behavior of an individual.

Preface. A short introduction to a book.

Prefix. An affix (*which see*); a letter or a sequence of letters added to the beginning of a root word which changes its meaning, for example, *re* plus *play* = *replay.*

Principle. Refers to rules or guides.

Projective technique. A method in which the individual tends to put himself or herself into the test.

Propaganda. Any systematic, widespread, deliberate indoctrination or plan for indoctrination.

Proxemics. Study of the effects of space or distance on human interaction; a form of nonverbal communication.

Proximodistal development. Muscular development from the midpoint of the body to the extremities.

Questions. A good way for students to gain a better insight into a subject; questioning also gives the instructor feedback and slows the instructor down if he or she is going too fast.

Readiness. An ongoing, dynamic process which teachers use to prepare students for various learning activities throughout the school day.

Reading. The getting of meaning from and the bringing of meaning to the written page.

Reading comprehension. A complex intellectual process involving a number of abilities. The two major abilities involve word meanings and reasoning with verbal concepts.

Reading expectancy formula. Helps teachers determine who needs special help; helps determine a student's reading potential.

Reading management system. Stresses individual differences and usually includes a set of instructional objectives for a skill area, precriterion- and postcriterion-reference tests, as well as other diagnostic tests, instructional materials, and a system for record-keeping.

Reading process. Concerned with the affective (*which see*), perceptual (*which see*), and cognitive (*which see*) domains.

Reading readiness. Preparing students for the reading lesson by taking into account their maturation, past experiences, and desire to learn.

Reading readiness tests. Supposed to predict those children who are ready to read.

Recall. The process of finding the answer to a question in one's memory without rereading the text or notes.

Reinforcement. Any stimulus, such as praise, which usually causes the individual to repeat a response.

Reliability. The extent to which a test instrument consistently produces similar results.

Remedial reading. Takes place outside the regular classroom and is handled by special personnel.

Role playing. A form of creative dramatics in which dialogue for a specific role is spontaneously developed.

Root. Smallest unit of a word that can exist and retain its basic meaning; a base, for example, *play.*

Schwa. The sound often found in the unstressed (unaccented) syllables of words with more than one syllable. The schwa sound is represented by an upside-down e (ə) in the phonetic (speech) alphabet. A syllable ending in *le* preceded by a consonant is usually the final syllable in a word and contains the schwa sound.

Self-fulfilling prophecy. Teacher assumptions about children become true, at least in part, because of the attitude of the teachers, which in turn becomes part of the children's self-concept.

Semantic clue. Meaning clue.

Semantic mapping. A graphic representation used to illustrate concepts and relationships among concepts such as classes, properties, and examples.

Silent consonants. Two adjacent consonants, one of which is silent, for example, *kn (know), pn (pneumonia).*

Silent e rule. In a word or syllable containing two vowels separated by one consonant, and having an *e* as the final vowel, the first vowel is usually long and the final *e* is usually silent, for example, *bake, note.*

Skimming. Reading rapidly to find or locate information.

Sociogram. A map or chart showing the interrelationships of children in a classroom and identifying those who are "stars" or "isolates."

SQ3R. A widely used study technique that involves five steps: survey, question, read, recite or recall, and review.

Standardized oral reading test. Individually administered test that helps teachers analyze the oral reading performance of students.

Standardized reading achievement test. Usually part of a test battery that includes other curriculum areas besides reading; measures general reading achievement.

Standardized survey reading test. Measures general reading achievement; similar to a reading achievement test.

Standardized tests. Tests that have been published by experts in the field and have precise instructions for administration and scoring.

Study, how to. (1) Build good habits, (2) devise a system that works for you, (3) keep at it, (4) maintain a certain degree of tension, and (5) concentrate.

Suffix. An affix (*which see*); a letter or a sequence of letters added to the end of a root word, which changes the grammatical form of the word and its meaning; for example, *prince* plus *ly = princely.*

Summary. A brief statement of the essential information in a longer piece. The main idea of an article and the important events should be stated in a summary, although not necessarily in the sequence presented in the article. The sequence should be followed if it is essential to understanding. A summary does not include the summarizer's opinions.

Supporting details. Additional information that supports, explains, or illustrates the main idea. Some of the ways that supporting details may be arranged are as cause and effect, examples, sequence of events, descriptions, definitions, comparisons, or contrasts.

Survey batteries. A group of tests in different content areas.

Sustained silent reading (SSR). Practice in independent silent reading.

Syllable. A vowel or a group of letters containing one vowel sound, for example, *blo.*

Synonyms. Words similar in meaning.

Syntax. Refers to word order or position of the word in a sentence.

Synthesis. Building up the parts of something, usually into a whole.

Table of contents. A listing of chapter titles, major headings, and page numbers at the beginning of a book.

Teacher-made tests. Tests prepared by the classroom teacher for a particular class and given by the classroom teacher under conditions of his or her own choosing.

T.E.S.L. (Teaching English as a Second Language). Concentrates on helping children who speak a language other than English or who speak non-standard English to learn English as a language.

Thinking. Covert manipulation of symbolic representations.

Topic sentence. States what the paragraph will be about by naming the topic.

Validity. The degree to which a test instrument measures what it claims to measure.

Visual discrimination. The ability to distinguish between written symbols.

Word recognition. A twofold process that includes both the recognition of printed symbols by some method so that the word can be pronounced and the association of meaning to the word after it has been properly pronounced.

Informal Reading Inventory[1]

Summary Sheet

Name _____   Age _____

Grade _____   Teacher _____

Level	Word Recognition in Isolation (No. of Errors)	Oral Reading W.R. No. of Errors/ Total No. Wds.	Oral Reading Comp. % Errors	Oral Reading Comp. % Correct	Silent Reading Comp. % Errors	Silent Reading Comp. % Correct	Listening Capacity % Errors	Listening Capacity % Correct
Preprimer								
Primer								
First								
2¹								
2²								
3¹								
3²								
4								
5								
6								
7								
8								

[1]Adapted from the Placement Inventory of the *Holt Basic Reading Series.*

Level at which Word Recognition Inventory
(WRI) was begun   _____

Level at which oral reading was begun   _____

Oral reading—word recognition
   Independent level   _____

   Instructional level   _____

   Frustration level   _____

Oral reading—comprehension
   Independent level   _____

   Instructional level   _____

   Frustration level   _____

Silent reading—comprehension
   Independent level   _____

   Instructional level   _____

   Frustration level   _____

Listening capacity level   _____

Word analysis
   Consonants—single
      initial   _____

      medial   _____

      final   _____

   Consonants—double
      blends   _____

      digraphs   _____

   Consonants—silent   _____

   Vowels—single
      short   _____

      long   _____

   Vowels—double
      digraphs   _____

      diphthongs   _____

Effect of final *e* on vowel   _____

Vowel controlled by *r*   _____

Structural analysis
   prefixes   _____

   suffixes   _____

   combining forms   _____

   inflectional endings   _____

Compound words   _____

Accent   _____

Special Notes on Strengths and Weaknesses

Comments on Behavior During the Testing

Recommendations

SPECIAL NOTES

Information on the following are given in the body of Chapter 9:

1. Code for marking oral reading errors (p. 118)
2. The scoring of oral reading errors (pp. 117–119)
3. Criteria for estimating the reading levels (pp. 112–114)
4. Administering the IRI (pp. 121–133)
5. Examples (pp. 124–133)

Partial credit may be given for comprehension questions if an answer consists of more than one part. For example, if the answer to a question consists of three names, and the student has named only one, the student should get one-third credit. If the answer to a question consists of two things, and the student gives one only, the student should receive half credit.

Do not count mispronunciations of difficult proper nouns in the oral reading passages as errors. You may pronounce these for the children if necessary.

Word Recognition Inventory (WRI)

	Preprimer		*Primer*		*First*
1.	apples _____	1.	looked _____	1.	room _____
2.	house _____	2.	afternoon _____	2.	part _____
3.	night _____	3.	ask _____	3.	school _____
4.	ran _____	4.	that _____	4.	apartment _____
5.	play _____	5.	now _____	5.	her _____
6.	said _____	6.	white _____	6.	bring _____
7.	make _____	7.	street _____	7.	family _____
8.	city _____	8.	then _____	8.	climb _____
9.	blue _____	9.	women _____	9.	thumb _____
10.	cow _____	10.	him _____	10.	middle _____
11.	jump _____	11.	save _____	11.	another _____
12.	asked _____	12.	morning _____	12.	winter _____
13.	again _____	13.	sleep _____	13.	heard _____
14.	mouse _____	14.	pick _____	14.	next _____
15.	game _____	15.	friends _____	15.	about _____
16.	went _____	16.	benches _____	16.	smell _____
17.	sheep _____	17.	wings _____	17.	own _____
18.	road _____	18.	mother _____	18.	forget _____
19.	stop _____	19.	home _____	19.	beautiful _____
20.	store _____	20.	small _____	20.	special _____

Word Recognition Inventory (WRI) (*Cont.*)

	2¹			2²			3¹	
1.	ready	____	1.	island	____	1.	aside	____
2.	afraid	____	2.	planned	____	2.	afford	____
3.	behind	____	3.	spears	____	3.	leather	____
4.	moved	____	4.	leaving	____	4.	detective	____
5.	under	____	5.	dries	____	5.	front	____
6.	until	____	6.	empty	____	6.	exactly	____
7.	straw	____	7.	speech	____	7.	pajamas	____
8.	idea	____	8.	beside	____	8.	body	____
9.	giant	____	9.	feathers	____	9.	lobster	____
10.	mountain	____	10.	hair	____	10.	tomatoes	____
11.	daughter	____	11.	contest	____	11.	careful	____
12.	birthday	____	12.	forest	____	12.	beginning	____
13.	minutes	____	13.	learn	____	13.	flour	____
14.	chair	____	14.	repairs	____	14.	early	____
15.	horrible	____	15.	distant	____	15.	aluminum	____
16.	drop	____	16.	believe	____	16.	shirt	____
17.	telephone	____	17.	garden	____	17.	gentlemen	____
18.	party	____	18.	change	____	18.	parade	____
19.	horse	____	19.	village	____	19.	jealous	____
20.	answer	____	20.	course	____	20.	president	____
						21.	ground	____
						22.	control	____
						23.	soldier	____
						24.	package	____
						25.	umbrella	____

Word Recognition Inventory (WRI) (*Cont.*)

	3^2		4		5
1.	pictures _____	1.	magnificent _____	1.	irresistible _____
2.	energy _____	2.	arithmetic _____	2.	contribution _____
3.	sharpen _____	3.	circuit _____	3.	impossible _____
4.	crawls _____	4.	history _____	4.	noticing _____
5.	haunted _____	5.	gypsy _____	5.	tattered _____
6.	curly _____	6.	flutter _____	6.	lagoon _____
7.	hoofprints _____	7.	laughter _____	7.	pressure _____
8.	oxygen _____	8.	earthworm _____	8.	pinnacle _____
9.	empty _____	9.	frighten _____	9.	grumbling _____
10.	neighbors _____	10.	homework _____	10.	building _____
11.	color _____	11.	important _____	11.	attention _____
12.	costume _____	12.	tumble _____	12.	bluegrass _____
13.	drown _____	13.	thought _____	13.	innocent _____
14.	closet _____	14.	perfectly _____	14.	resemble _____
15.	least _____	15.	surface _____	15.	lacquer _____
16.	nature _____	16.	buried _____	16.	vanilla _____
17.	officer _____	17.	valuable _____	17.	storekeeper _____
18.	motorcycle _____	18.	kitchen _____	18.	biscuit _____
19.	rich _____	19.	moment _____	19.	muzzle _____
20.	ribbon _____	20.	superior _____	20.	version _____
21.	sunshine _____	21.	reflection _____	21.	architect _____
22.	blanket _____	22.	popular _____	22.	triumph _____
23.	favorite _____	23.	century _____	23.	foundation _____
24.	suppose _____	24.	heave _____	24.	enormous _____
25.	clues _____	25.	amazement _____	25.	hatchet _____

Word Recognition Inventory (WRI) (*Cont.*)

	6		7		8
1.	counselor _____	1.	fundamental _____	1.	demolition _____
2.	medium _____	2.	notations _____	2.	hierarchy _____
3.	initiation _____	3.	hibernating _____	3.	equilibrium _____
4.	rustling _____	4.	oddities _____	4.	metropolitan _____
5.	propel _____	5.	adamant _____	5.	bilateral _____
6.	dolphin _____	6.	repercussions _____	6.	nickered _____
7.	geology _____	7.	ideological _____	7.	expedition _____
8.	glacial _____	8.	silhouettes _____	8.	obsessively _____
9.	communicate _____	9.	kilometers _____	9.	lactic _____
10.	linguistic _____	10.	paraphrase _____	10.	radiance _____
11.	computer _____	11.	text _____	11.	commandant _____
12.	stowaway _____	12.	cadence _____	12.	vagabonds _____
13.	accomplish _____	13.	peerless _____	13.	passionate _____
14.	veranda _____	14.	millenium _____	14.	sacrilegious _____
15.	primitive _____	15.	usurpations _____	15.	taboo _____
16.	association _____	16.	deliberate _____	16.	fuming _____
17.	mascot _____	17.	vouch _____	17.	impulsively _____
18.	tabulator _____	18.	jaded _____	18.	quarries _____
19.	lateral _____	19.	nitrates _____	19.	crisis _____
20.	wrought _____	20.	laudable _____	20.	jeopardize _____
21.	censorship _____	21.	reincarnation _____	21.	facsimile _____
22.	glower _____	22.	unique _____	22.	waterlogged _____
23.	ponder _____	23.	liable _____	23.	agony _____
24.	disbelief _____	24.	bankruptcy _____	24.	unalterable _____
25.	hesitate _____	25.	sedan _____	25.	intercoms _____

Preprimer

ORAL READING (50 WORDS)[2]

Introduction: You will be reading a story about a cat. Then I will ask you questions about the story.

"I want to play," said the cat.
"The little boy likes to play.
He will play with me."

The cat ran to the little boy.
"No, no, cat," said the little boy.
"I do not want to play with you.
I want to play my game."

The cat ran out.

Comprehension Questions

		Points
(fact)	1. Who said, "I want to play"? (Cat.)	20
(fact)	2. What does the cat think the little boy likes to do? (Play.)	20
(fact)	3. What did the boy want to do? (Play with his game.)	20
(inference)	4. What does the cat usually do to show it wants to play with the little boy? (The cat runs to the little boy.)	20
(fact)	5. What did the cat do when the boy said that he did not want to play with it? (Ran out.)	20

Scoring Scale

Levels	Word Recognition Errors	Comprehension Errors
Independent	0–1	0–10 pts.
Instructional	2–3	11–25 pts.
Frustration	5 or more	50 pts. or more

[2]Level 6, "Can You Imagine?" *The Holt Basic Reading Series*, pp. 44–45.

SILENT READING[3]

Introduction: Read this story about a cat. I will be asking you some questions after you finish reading it. Read it carefully.

"The little girl likes to play,"
said the cat.
"She will play with me."

The cat ran up to the girl.

"No, no, cat," said the little girl.
"I do not want to play with you.
I want to read my book."

"Mouse, mouse," said the cat.
"Come on out."
"Come out and play with me."

"No," said the mouse.
"I will not play with a cat."

Comprehension Questions

			Points
(fact)	1.	What does the cat want to do? (Play.)	20
(fact)	2.	Whom does the cat ask to play with him? (The little girl and the mouse.)	20
(fact)	3.	Why doesn't the little girl want to play with the cat? (She wants to read a book.)	20
(fact)	4.	What does the mouse tell the cat? ("I will not play with a cat.")	20
(inference)	5.	Why do you suppose the mouse said, "I will not play with a cat"? (Cats kill/chase mice.)	20

Scoring Scale

Levels	*Comprehension Errors*
Independent	0–10 pts.
Instructional	11–25 pts.
Frustration	50 pts. or more

[3]Ibid., pp. 46–47.

Primer

ORAL READING (66 WORDS)[4]

Introduction: You will be reading a story about Amy. Then I will ask you questions about the story.

On Amy's street there were three houses.
And one was Amy's.

There were places to play.
And there were boys and girls to play with.
But Amy was lonely.

The boys on the street were too big.
They didn't want to play with Amy.
And the girls on the street were too little.
Amy didn't want to play with them.
What Amy wanted was a friend.

Comprehension Questions

			Points
(fact)	1.	What could you find on Amy's street? (Places to play, boys, girls, three houses.)	20
(fact)	2.	How did Amy feel? (Lonely.)	20
(fact)	3.	Why didn't Amy play with the boys on her street? (They were too big, they didn't want to play with her.)	20
(fact)	4.	Why didn't Amy play with the girls on the street? (They were too little, she didn't want to play with them.)	20
(inference)	5.	Why was Amy lonely? (She had no one her age to play with.)	20

Scoring Scale

Levels	Word Recognition Errors	Comprehension Errors
Independent	0–1	0–10 pts.
Instructional	2–3	11–25 pts.
Frustration	7 or more	50 pts. or more

[4]Level 7, "A Place for Me," *The Holt Basic Reading Series,* adapted from pp. 86–88.

SILENT READING[5]

Introduction: Read the story about a young girl and some puppies. I will be asking you some questions after you finish reading it. Read it carefully.

Amy went to see the puppies again.
She liked all of them.
But she loved the little one.
And the little puppy loved Amy.
He ran to Amy when she came in.
When she went home,
he wanted to go, too.
One day Amy went
to see the puppies.
They were not there!

''Where are the puppies?''
she asked Brad.

''The puppies are gone,'' he said.
''The house is too small.
It's too small for all the puppies.
Daddy had to find homes for them.''

Comprehension Questions

		Points
(fact)	1. What did Amy go to see? (Puppies.)	10
(fact)	2. How did Amy feel toward the puppies? (She liked all of them.)	10
(fact)	3. Which puppy did Amy like best? (The little one.)	10
(inference)	4. How did the puppy show that he liked Amy? (He ran to her when she came in. He wanted to go with her when she went home.)	10
(inference)	5. Has Amy seen the puppies before? (Yes. The word *again* is used.)	10
(fact)	6. What happened one afternoon when Amy went to see the puppies? (She couldn't find them. They were gone.)	10
(fact)	7. What had the boy's father done with the puppies? (He had found homes for them.)	10
(fact)	8. Why had Brad's father found homes for the puppies? (The house was too little for all the puppies.)	10

[5]Ibid., pp. 95–96.

(word meaning)   9. What word in the story means "liked very much"? (Love.)   10

(word meaning)   10. What word in the story means "little"? (Small.)   10

Scoring Scale

Levels	*Comprehension Errors*
Independent	0–10 pts.
Instructional	11–25 pts.
Frustration	50 pts. or more

First

ORAL READING (85 WORDS)[6]

Introduction: You will be reading a story about Belinda. THen I will ask you questions about the story.

It was spring.
Birds were singing.
Flowers were everywhere.
All the people had on new spring hats.

''I would like a new spring hat, too,''
Belinda said to her mother and father.

''You would?'' asked Mother.
''We'll get one for you.''

''When?'' asked Belinda.

''Soon,'' said Mother.
''But we can't get one for you now.
You will have to wait.''

Belinda waited.
All the time she was playing
and going to school, she waited.

''One day Belinda said,
''I'll have to find my own hat.''

Comprehension Questions

		Points
(fact)	1. What season of the year was it? (Spring.)	10
(fact)	2. What signs of spring does the story tell about? (Birds were singing, flowers were everywhere, and people had on new spring hats.) (Student should give two for complete credit.)	10
(fact)	3. What did Belinda want? (A new spring hat.)	10
(fact)	4. Who would get a new hat for Belinda? (Belinda's mother and father.)	10

[6]Level 8, ''A Time for Friends,'' *The Holt Basic Reader Series*, pp. 108–10.

(fact)	5. Who said, "We'll get one for you"? (Mother.)	10
(fact)	6. When did Belinda's mother say they would get Belinda a new hat? (Soon.)	10
(fact)	7. What was Belinda doing while she was waiting for her hat? (She was playing and going to school.)	10
(fact)	8. What did Belinda decide to do? (To find her own hat.)	10
(inference)	9. Why did Belinda decide to find her own hat? (She became impatient from waiting so long.)	10
(inference)	10. Does *soon* mean the "next day" to Belinda's mother? Explain. (No. In the story it says that Belinda went to school and played—time is going by. Also, it says *one day* to show time has gone by.)	10

Scoring Scale

Levels	Word Recognition Errors	Comprehension Errors
Independent	0–1	0–10 pts.
Instructional	2–4	11–25 pts.
Frustration	9 or more	50 pts. or more

SILENT READING[7]

Introduction: Read the story about Belinda and her new spring hat. I will be asking you some questions after you finish reading it. Read it carefully.

Belinda found another hat.
She liked this one very much.
She put it on and went to show Grandma.

"Belinda," said Grandma,
"What is that on your head?"

"It's my new spring hat,"
said Belinda.
"I found it.
Do you like it?"

"I do," said Grandma.
"But it looks a little like the box
the cat sleeps in."

[7]Ibid., pp. 115–16.

Belinda looked in the mirror.

"You are right, Grandma," she said.
"I can't wear this."

Belinda put the box back on the floor,
and the cat got into it.

Comprehension Questions

		Points
(fact)	1. What did Belinda find? (Another hat.)	10
(fact)	2. How did she feel about the hat? (She liked it very much.)	10
(fact)	3. Whom did she show the hat to? (Grandma.)	10
(fact)	4. What did Grandma say the hat looks like? (The box the cat sleeps in.)	10
(fact)	5. Did Belinda agree with her Grandma? (Yes.)	10
(inference)	6. Why did Belinda decide not to wear the hat? (She realized it was the cat's box.)	10
(inference)	7. Why did the cat get into Belinda's hat? (It was the cat's box.)	10
(main idea)	8. What is the main idea of the story? (Belinda finds a hat, which is the cat's box.)	10
(inference)	9. Where had Belinda found the hat? (On the floor.)	10
(inference)	10. What kind of person is Grandma? Explain. (A kind person; a nice person—she doesn't laugh at Belinda's new hat.)	10

Scoring Scale

Levels	*Comprehension Errors*
Independent	0–10 pts.
Instructional	11–25 pts.
Frustration	50 pts. or more

2¹

ORAL READING (99 WORDS)⁸

Introduction: You will be reading a story about a lake. Then I will ask you questions about the story.

Jill, Ellen, Bob, and Edward lived near a lake. They were good friends. And they thought they were lucky to live so near the water. They could go for a swim every day.

A man named Mr. Brown lived near the lake, too. Sometimes Mr. Brown went swimming with the children.

One day the children went to Mr. Brown's house. They asked him to go for a swim with them. Mr. Brown said, ''We can't go for a swim. We may never swim in the lake again.''

''Why not?'' asked Edward.

''Because the lake is polluted,'' said Mr. Brown.

Comprehension Questions

		Points
(fact)	1. Where did the children live? (Near a lake.)	10
(fact)	2. What could the children do every day? (Go for a swim.)	10
(fact)	3. Why did the children think they were lucky? (They lived near the water.)	10
(fact)	4. Who was Mr. Brown? (A man who lived near the lake.)	10
(fact)	5. Why did the children go to Mr. Brown's house? (To ask him to go swimming with them.)	10
(fact)	6. Did Mr. Brown go swimming with the children every day? (No, he only went sometimes.)	10
(fact)	7. What happened to the water in the lake? (It became polluted.)	10
(word meaning)	8. What does *polluted* mean? (It means to make unclean or impure.)	10
(inference)	9. How do we know the children like one another? (It says that they were good friends.)	10
(inference)	10. How do we know that the children like Mr. Brown? (They asked him to go swimming with them.)	10

Scoring Scale

Levels	Word Recognition Errors	Comprehension Errors
Independent	0–1	0–10 pts.
Instructional	2–5	11–25 pts.
Frustration	10 or more	50 pts. or more

⁸Level 9, ''People Need People,'' *The Holt Basic Reading Series*, pp. 104-105.

SILENT READING[9]

Introduction: Read this story about children who live near a lake. I will be asking you some questions after you finish reading it. Read it carefully.

"What is making the lake polluted?" asked Jill.

"It could be a lot of things," said Mr. Brown. "Let's go down to the lake and look at it."

Mr. Brown and the children went to the lake. They looked into the water. It wasn't clean. They walked around the lake. And they saw why it wasn't clean.

"Look at that garbage in the water," said Jill. That's what's polluting the lake."

"They walked on. Edward saw oil on the water. "Look at that oil," said Edward. "That oil pollutes the water, too. It comes from boats on the lake."

"Come here," said Ellen. "Take a look at this. Here are tires in the lake!"

"Why would people throw tires into a lake?" asked Bob.

"They just don't stop to think" said Mr. Brown. "But they are not the only ones who pollute the lake. The people who own that factory pollute the water, too."

Comprehension Questions

			Points
(fact)	1.	Who asked, "What is making the lake polluted?" (Jill.)	10
(fact)	2.	Why does Mr. Brown suggest that they go look at the lake? (To see why the lake is polluted.)	10
(fact)	3.	What did Jill see that is polluting the lake? (Garbage floating in the water.)	10
(fact)	4.	What other things did the children see that were polluting the lake? (Oil and tires.)	10
(fact)	5.	Where did the oil on the lake come from? (Boats.)	10
(fact)	6.	What other people did Mr. Brown say were polluting the lake? (The people who owned the factory.)	10
(fact)	7.	Bob asked why people threw tires into the lake. What was Mr. Brown's answer? (He said that people didn't stop to think.)	10
(word meaning)	8.	What is a factory? (A factory is a place where things are made.)	10
(main idea)	9.	What is the main idea of the story? (Children discover what makes a lake polluted.)	10
(inference)	10.	What kind of a person is Mr. Brown? Explain. (A nice person because he spends time with the children, and he explains things to them.)	10

[9]Ibid., pp. 105–107.

Scoring Scale

Levels	Comprehension Errors
Independent	0–10 pts.
Instructional	11–25 pts.
Frustration	50 pts. or more

2²

ORAL READING (148 WORDS)[10]

Introduction: You will be reading a story about Abu. Then I will ask you questions about the story.

Most of the time Abu was happy. Mornings he liked to watch the sun come up. It came right out of the sand like a ball. And at night he liked to hear the sounds of his mother and father as they talked.

Some nights the sides of the tent were up to let in the air. Then Abu would look at the stars in the sky. And he would pretend that each star was a sheep. He would watch the sheep until he fell asleep. Then Mother would come and cover him up.

Other times Abu would pretend that each star was a drop of water. "If we had all that water," he would say, "we would never have to move again. Our tent would be a real home. Mother wouldn't have to keep packing our things. And Father could have a real chair to sit on."

Comprehension Questions

			Points
(fact)	1.	What did Abu do in the morning? (He liked to watch the sun come up.)	10
(fact)	2.	What did Abu like to do in the evening? (He liked to hear the sound of his mother and father talking.)	10
(fact)	3.	How is the rising sun described? (It came out of the sand like a ball.)	10
(fact)	4.	How did Abu feel most of the time? (Happy.)	10
(fact)	5.	Why would the sides of the tent be put up? (To let air in.)	10
(fact)	6.	What two things did Abu pretend that the stars were? (He pretended that they were sheep and that they were drops of water.)	10
(fact)	7.	What reasons did Abu give for wishing that the stars really were water? (He and his family would have a real home, and they would never have to move again.)	10
(word meaning)	8.	What does the word *pretend* mean? (It means "make believe.")	10
(inference)	9.	Why did Abu and his family move a lot? (They moved because there wasn't enough water.)	10
(inference)	10.	How do we know that Abu's mother did not go to sleep at the same time as Abu? (She would cover him after he fell asleep.)	10

[10]Level 10, "The Way of the World," *The Holt Basic Reading Series*, pp. 150–51.

Scoring Scale

Levels	Word Recognition Errors	Comprehension Errors
Independent	0–2	0–10 pts.
Instructional	3–7	11–25 pts.
Frustration	15 or more	50 pts. or more

SILENT READING[11]

Introduction: Read the story about Abu. I will be asking you some questions after you finish reading the story. Read it carefully.

Abu began digging. He dug so much that he couldn't see out of the hole. To carry the dirt out he had to climb up little stairs he had made in the side of the hole. At last he fell asleep, and his father had to carry him into the tent. As he put Abu to bed, he smiled. "The child has dreams, and sometimes dreams hurt. But dreams, like water and food, make boys grow into men."

The next day the camels were packed. Abu went to take a last look at the hole he had made. He looked at his rock wall. Then his eyes went down the stairs he had made. At last he was looking at the bottom of the hole. At the bottom the sand was darker than it had been. He took off his shoes and started down the stairs.

Deeper and deeper he went until he reached the bottom of the hole, and his feet could feel wet sand. He got down on his knees to feel it with his hands. It was wet. It was really wet!

Comprehension Questions

		Points
(fact)	1. What was Abu digging? (A hole.)	10
(fact)	2. What did he make in the side of the hole? (Stairs.)	10
(inference)	3. How do we know the hole is deep? (Abu had to make stairs to go down it.)	10
(fact)	4. What did Abu's father say about dreams? (They make boys grow into men.)	10
(fact)	5. What does Abu's father compare dreams to? (Water and food.)	10
(inference)	6. What was Abu looking for? (Water.)	10
(inference)	7. Why was the sand in the hole wet? (Because he had struck water.)	10
(main idea)	8. What is the main idea of the story? (Abu digs a deep hole to find water.)	10

[11]Ibid., pp. 157–58.

(inference) 9. Where does Abu live? (In a desert.) 10

(inference) 10. What kind of person is Abu? (A hard-working person; a patient
person; someone who doesn't give up; a hopeful person.) 10

Scoring Scale

Levels	*Comprehension Errors*
Independent	0–10 pts.
Instructional	11–25 pts.
Frustration	50 pts. or more

3¹

ORAL READING (212 WORDS)¹²

> **Introduction: You will be reading a story about children cleaning out an attic. Then I will ask you questions about the story.**

The houses on the old man's block were big and tall. But the biggest of all was the house of Mr. M. B. Pendleton. The children had seen it, but they had never been inside it.

"Here we are," said the old man. He took out his big key ring and let them into the house. He led them up to the attic.

All over the attic were old tables, lamps, and piles of newspapers. There were boxes with writing on them that said Books, Mary's Wedding Dress, Peter's Football. There was even a small box marked Rags. Kevin picked it up and thought it was very heavy for a box of rags.

The children went up and down the stairs like ants, carrying bundles and putting them on the sidewalk. In less than three hours, the job was done.

"That makes me feel much better. How much do I owe you?" asked Mr. Pendleton.

"We started at one o'clock," Jack said. "Now it's five minutes to four."

"Let's call it three hours," the old gentleman said. "At twenty cents an hour for three of you, that's sixty cents for each hour. Three hours is a dollar and eighty cents. I'll make it two dollars even." He gave the children the money.

Comprehension Questions

		Points
(fact)	1. Describe the houses on Mr. Pentleton's block (Big and tall.)	10
(fact)	2. Had the children ever been in Mr. Pendleton's house before? (No.)	10
(fact)	3. Where did Mr. Pendleton take the children? (The attic.)	10
(fact)	4. State two things that were in the attic. (Old tables, lamps, piles of newspaper, and so on.)	10
(fact)	5. What was peculiar about the box of rags? (It was heavy.)	10
(fact)	6. How much did Mr. Pendleton pay the children? (Two dollars.)	10
(fact)	7. How long did the children work? (A little less than three hours.)	10
(main idea)	8. What is the main idea of the story? (Children work hard to clean out an attic.)	10
(inference)	9. How do we know that the children worked hard? (It said that they went up and down the stairs like ants.)	10
(inference)	10. How do we know that there were lots of things in the attic? (It took three children almost three hours to clean it out.)	10

¹²Level 11, "Never Give Up," *The Holt Basic Reading Series*, pp. 233–34.

Scoring Scale

Levels	Word Recognition Errors	Comprehension Errors
Independent	0–2	0–10 pts.
Instructional	3–11	11–25 pts.
Frustration	21 or more	50 pts. or more

SILENT READING[13]

Introduction: Read this story about some children and a box of rags. I will be asking you some questions after you finish reading it. Read it carefully.

"Listen," said Kevin. "Remember how heavy that little box was that was marked Rags?"
"Yes," said Jack.
"I'm going to look inside it," Kevin said. The children watched as Kevin opened the box.
"Those are rags, all right," Jack said.
"Rags can't be that heavy," Kevin said. He reached in and pulled out some rags. Under them was a leather box. Kevin lifted the lid.
"It's nothing but some old silver," said Kevin.
"I thought it might be worth something," said Ruth.
"Kevin lifted out a silver spoon. It was a beautiful shape. "Maybe if we shine the silver, it might be worth a lot of money," he said. "We could sell it."
"We can't sell it. It belongs to Mr. Pendleton," Ruth said.
"He told us to take it away," said Kevin. "It's just like we found it. Finders, keepers! The garbage truck would have come and taken the box."

Comprehension Questions

		Points
(fact)	1. Why did Kevin want to look inside the box marked Rags? (The box was heavy and he knew that rags weren't that heavy.)	10
(fact)	2. In addition to rags, what was in the box? (A leather box with some silver in it.)	10
(fact)	3. What did Kevin suggest they do with the silver? (Shine it up and try to sell it.)	10
(fact)	4. What did Ruth think of Kevin's idea? (She said that they couldn't sell it because it belonged to Mr. Pendleton.)	10
(fact)	5. Why did Kevin think they could sell the silver? (He said that finders were keepers and that the garbage truck would have taken the box away.)	10

[13]Ibid., pp. 234–35.

(inference) 6. What didn't Mr. Pendleton know about the box? (That it contained silver.) 10

(main idea) 7. What is the main idea of the story? (Some children discover silver in a box marked Rags.) 10

(inference) 8. Why did Mr. Pendleton give away the box? (He thought it just contained rags and was therefore worthless.) 10

(inference) 9. What kind of person is Kevin? (Curious; a good thinker because he realized that rags shouldn't weight so much; a little greedy.) 10

Scoring Scale

Levels	*Comprehension Errors*
Independent	0–10 pts.
Instructional	11–25 pts.
Frustration	50 pts. or more

3²

ORAL READING (180 WORDS)[14]

Introduction: You will be reading a story about a bird named Kiya. Then I will ask you questions about the story.

Kiya was a free bird. From dawn to sundown he would sweep the sky, the sand, and the sea looking for food. He kept a close eye on the harbor to pick up after fishermen. On the beach he watched the children and ate sandwiches they couldn't finish. Like all sea gulls, he was willing to eat almost anything.

Kiya began the day at dawn. He left the little island where he lived and went right to the harbor. He wanted to be there when the fishermen came in to clean their fish.

This morning no fishermen were in, but the sea had left on the rock a bundle of seaweed, crabs, and snails—all tangled in wire.

Kiya flew around the bundle. When he had found it quite safe, he went to work. He had to pick out the seaweed to reach the snails and crabs. But the wire kept getting in his way.

Kiya had to tug at the wire until one end came free. Then he put his head in the opening and pulled out the seaweed.

Comprehension Questions

			Points
(fact)	1.	What kind of bird was Kiya? (A sea gull *or* a free bird.)	10
(fact)	2.	What was Kiya willing to eat? (Almost anything.)	10
(fact)	3.	When did Kiya look for food? (From dawn to sundown.)	10
(fact)	4.	Where did Kiya go first? (The harbor.)	10
(fact)	5.	Why did Kiya go to the harbor? (The fishermen cleaned fish there.)	10
(fact)	6.	What had the sea left? (A bundle of seaweed, crabs, and snails all tangled in wire.)	10
(inference)	7.	How do we know Kiya is a careful bird? (He flew around the bundle first to make sure it was safe.)	10
(inference)	8.	How does the sea leave such things as the bundle on the beach? (The tide carries them in and they are left on the beach as the tides goes out.)	10
(main idea)	9.	What is the main idea of the story? (Kiya, a sea gull, spends his days looking for food.)	10
(inference)	10.	Why was Kiya interested in the bundle? (He wanted to eat the snails and crabs.)	10

[14]Level 12, "Special Happenings," *The Holt Basic Reading Series*, pp. 96–97.

Scoring Scale

Levels	Word Recognition Errors	Comprehension Errors
Independent	0–2	0–10 pts.
Instructional	3–9	11–25 pts.
Frustration	18 or more	50 pts. or more

SILENT READING[15]

Introduction: Read this story about a bird named Kiya. I will be asking you some questions after you finish reading it. Read it carefully.

Kiya was stuck. The harder he tried to free himself, the tighter the wire pulled. At last he freed his wings, but a loop of wire bound his back and one leg so tightly that he could not move it.

A boy was sitting in his boat watching the gulls. When he saw Kiya's trouble, he got out and ran toward the bird. The frightened Kiya flapped his wings and rose out of reach, even though the wire cut into his back and leg.

The bird glided over to the sandy beach and made a clumsy landing on one foot. He hopped along the cool hard sand near the water, dragging part of the wire that bound him.

People were already gathering on the beach for a day in the sun.

"Look at the sea gull!" someone called. "He's all tangled up in something."

People ran toward Kiya. Hands reached out for him. Beating his wings, Kiya managed to raise himself again.

He flew to the high dune where the sea gulls perch at noon. The other gulls were still away looking for their morning meal. Hungry as Kiya was, it hurt him too much to fly. He wanted only to be left in peace.

Comprehension Questions

		Points
(fact)	1. What happened when Kiya tried to free himself? (The wire got tighter around his back and leg; it cut him.)	10
(fact)	2. What did the boy do when he saw that Kiya was in trouble? (He got out of his boat and ran toward the gull.)	10
(fact)	3. How did the wire change the way Kiya moved? (It made him land clumsily, hop on one foot, and beat his wings harder to take off.)	10
(fact)	4. Why did Kiya fly away from the boy? (He was frightened.)	10
(fact)	5. Why didn't Kiya look for food with the other gulls? (It hurt him too much to fly. He wanted to be left in peace.)	10

[15]Ibid., pp. 98–99.

(fact)	6. Why were people gathering on the beach? (For a day in the sun.)	10
(inference)	7. How do we know that Kiya does not trust people? (Kiya flew away from them, even though he was in great pain.)	10
(inference)	8. How do we know that it was difficult for Kiya to fly? (Kiya had to beat his wings before he managed to raise himself.)	10
(word meaning)	9. What does the word *beating* mean in the phrase *beating his wings*? (Flapping repeatedly.)	10
(main idea)	10. What is the main idea of the story? (Kiya, trapped in the wire and in pain, flies away from the people.)	10

Scoring Scale

Levels	*Comprehension Errors*
Independent	0–10 pts.
Instructional	11–25 pts.
Frustration	50 pts. or more

4

ORAL READING (153 WORDS)[16]

Introduction: You will be reading a story about girls and baseball. Then I will ask you questions about the story.

Miss Kirby's room went wild. They had won!

Susan was waiting for Jamie at the edge of the playground. They were going to walk home together as they always did. "You really were great," Nick was saying to Jamie as the team came to the gate. "And don't forget," he said to Scott, "you made as many funny jokes as anybody when I picked Jamie to be our catcher."

"I know," Scott said. "But you've got to agree, it looks pretty funny. We're the only baseball team in the whole school with a girl for a catcher!"

Jamie's face got red. She ducked her head the funny way she always did when she felt embarrassed. But Susan could tell she was pleased with what the boys were saying. In fact, Jamie was very popular with the boys in school. But except for Susan, she didn't have any really close friends among the girls.

Comprehension Questions

		Points
(fact)	1. What position did Jamie play on the team? (Catcher.)	10
(fact)	2. Why were the children in the story happy and excited? (They had won the game.)	10
(fact)	3. Why had some of the boys on the team made jokes about Jamie being the catcher? (She was the only girl on the team. Their team was the only one in the school with a girl on it.)	10
(fact)	4. How did the boys on the team really feel about Jamie? (They liked her and thought she was a good player. She was popular with the boys.)	10
(fact)	5. Who picked Jamie to be the catcher? (Nick.)	10
(fact)	6. Who is Jamie's close girlfriend? (Susan.)	10
(fact)	7. What did Jamie do whenever she got embarrassed? (She ducked her head, her face got red.)	10
(inference)	8. How do we know Nick isn't prejudiced? (He chose a girl to be the catcher on the team.)	10
(inference)	9. Why did Jamie feel embarassed when the boys were talking about her? (She was being singled out and complimented.)	10

[16]Level 13, "Time to Wonder," *The Holt Basic Reading Series*, pp. 66–67.

(main idea) 10. What is the main idea of the story? (Jamie, the only girl on the
baseball team, helps her class win the game.)   10

Scoring Scale

Levels	Word Recognition Errors	Comprehension Errors
Independent	0–2	0–10 pts.
Instructional	3–8	11–25 pts.
Frustration	15 or more	50 pts. or more

SILENT READING[17]

Introduction: Read this story about Miss Kirby's room. I will be asking you some questions after you finish reading it. Read it carefully.

The next morning Susan waited and waited for Jamie to walk to school with her. Finally at a quarter after eight, she gave up. Susan ran down the street to meet Pam. By running almost the whole way, the two girls got to school on time. Jamie wasn't there. But then just as the last bell rang, Jamie rushed into the room and slid into her seat. It wasn't until recess that Susan had a chance to ask Jamie why she had been so late.

"I forgot my baseball glove," Jamie said "and I had to go all the way back home to get it. We only have four more days to practice before our big game with Mr. Shock's room."

Pam joined them. "Why did you have to go home for your glove, Jamie? Why couldn't you borrow somebody else's when it's your turn to catch?"

"I'm the only one on the team that's left-handed," Jamie said. "I have to have my own glove. But it's getting so worn out. It isn't much good anymore. I wish I could get a new one."

After lunch Miss Kirby sat down quietly at the desk and began marking papers. Susan raised her hand, but Miss Kirby didn't see it. Then she cleared her throat, shuffled her feet, and waved her hand wildly. Miss Kirby looked up. "Yes, Susan, what is it?" she said.

Comprehension Questions

			Points
(fact)	1.	Why did Pam and Susan run all the way to school? (They didn't want to be late.)	10
(fact)	2.	Who was Susan waiting for? (Jamie.)	10
(fact)	3.	At what time did Susan give up? (A quarter after eight.)	10
(fact)	4.	Why was Jamie almost late? (She forgot her baseball glove, so she had to go back home to get it.)	10

[17]Ibid., pp. 72–73.

(fact)	5. Why did Jamie have to use her own baseball glove? (She is left-handed.)	10
(fact)	6. Whom were Miss Kirby's children going to play against? (Mr. Shock's room.)	10
(word meaning)	7. What does *recess* mean? (A stopping of work for rest or relaxation.)	10
(inference)	8. Has Jamie had her glove for a long time? How do you know this? (Yes. It's worn out.)	10
(inference)	9. Does Jamie take the baseball game seriously? Explain. (Yes. She went home to get her glove; she is concerned about only four days to practice.)	10
(main idea)	10. What is the main idea of the story? (Susan and Pam are almost late to school because they were waiting for Jamie, who forgot her baseball glove.)	10

Scoring Scale

Levels	Word Recognition Errors	Comprehension Errors
Independent		0–10 pts.
Instructional		11–25 pts.
Frustration		50 pts. or more

5

ORAL READING (278 WORDS)[18]

Introduction: You will be reading a story about a rocket. Then I will ask you questions about the story.

The rocket nicknamed Nell had to be moved from the shop to the launching tower, which was nineteen kilometers (12 miles) away. It was wrapped in blankets and lifted like a piece of delicate china. Then it was set on a smaller trailer and tied in place. A truck carefully pulled the trailer over the trail to the launching site.

The flight tower, which would guide the rocket in its takeoff, could be seen in the distance. At first glance it looked much like the steel tower of a windmill. But no turning wheel could be seen. The tower was open at the top to let the rocket escape. The four steel supports were firmly anchored in concrete.

The rocket, looking like a giant dart, was about three meters (11 feet) long. That is twice the height of the average person. It was twenty-two centimeters (11 inches) around, about that of a lunch plate. Its nose was a smooth, shiny cone, shaped to pierce the atmosphere easily. At the other end were balancing vanes, formed like the tail of a fish. These vanes were to keep the rocket on its course. They must hold firm and not be swished about as a fish's tail is flipped.

Inside the cylinder were many delicate parts. There were pipes, small tanks to hold gasoline and liquid oxygen, and a powerful motor. The weight was less than 23 kilograms (50 pounds).

Near the base of the tower was a dugout with a heavy trapdoor. From this safe place, Albert Kisk could touch off the flight. Farther away was a shelter of sheet iron. Dr. Robert Goddard and two crew members would wait there.

Comprehension Questions

			Points
(fact)	1.	What was the rocket nicknamed? (Nell.)	10
(fact)	2.	Where was the rocket moved? (To the launching tower.)	10
(fact)	3.	What did the rocket look like? (A giant dart.)	10
(inference)	4.	How do we know that the rocket was handled carefully? (It was wrapped in a blanket and treated like delicate china.)	10
(fact)	5.	Why was the rocket's nose shaped like a cone? (To pierce the atmosphere easily.)	10
(fact)	6.	How was the rocket to be kept on course? (By balancing vanes.)	10
(fact)	7.	What were the balancing vanes formed like? (The tail of a fish.)	10
(fact)	8.	Where would Dr. Goddard and two crew members wait? (In a shelter of sheet iron.)	10

[18]Level 14, "Freedom's Ground," *The Holt Basic Reading Series*, pp. 264–65.

(inference) 9. How do we know that the men who built the rocket had a special feeling for it? (They gave it a nickname.)   10

(main idea) 10. What is the main idea of this story? (A rocket nicknamed Nell and its movement to the launching tower are described.)   10

Scoring Scale

Levels	Word Recognition Errors	Comprehension Errors
Independent	0–3	0–10 pts.
Instructional	4–14	11–25 pts.
Frustration	27 or more	50 pts. or more

SILENT READING[19]

Introduction: Read this story about a rocket. I will be asking you some questions after you finish reading it. Read it carefully.

All members of the crew were busy putting the rocket into perfect shape in the tower. Early in the afternoon, Mrs. Goddard drove out in her car. As the photographer, she was ready with her camera. Larry Mansur, with telescope and stopwatch, was at a safe distance to measure time and distance.

The valves and containers for gasoline and liquid oxygen were given a final check. Then the igniter was fired. (Think of a big man weighing 74.6 kilograms [200 pounds] resting all his weight on one leg of a chair.) The rocket was allowed to rise 5 centimeters (two inches). The pressure rose to 84 kilograms (225 pounds). Then Dr. Robert Goddard gave the signal. And Albert Kisk, from the dugout, released the rocket.

With a mighty roar the rocket moved up through the 18.3 meter (sixty-foot) tower. Up it went, faster and faster, shrieking as it rose. In seven seconds, it was 122 meters (four hundred feet) above the tower. According to Larry Mansur's measurements, it reached a height of 610 meters (two thousand feet). An important part of Dr. Goddard's dream had come true. He had used liquid fuel to shoot a rocket into the air.

Many years slipped by. Test after test was made. Some experiments failed and others succeeded. Goddard's test rockets soared fewer than 610 meters into space, but his genius, experiments, and dreams provided the principles on which the mighty program of space rocketry is founded today.

Comprehension Questions

                                                                            Points

(fact) 1. What was Mrs. Goddard's job? (Photography—she took pictures.)   10

[19]Ibid., pp. 265–66.

(fact)	2. What was Larry Mansur's job in the rocket experiment? (To measure the time and distance of the rocket's flight.)	10
(fact)	3. What instruments did Larry Mansur use in his work? (A telescope and a stopwatch.)	10
(word meaning)	4. What is a telescope? (An instrument for viewing distant objects.)	10
(fact)	5. What part of Dr. Goddard's dream came true with this rocket test? (He was able to use liquid fuel to shoot a rocket in the air.)	10
(fact)	6. What height did Dr. Goddard's rocket reach? (610 meters or two thousand feet.)	10
(fact)	7. What did Dr. Goddard's rock experiments provide? (They provided the basic principles for our present space program.)	10
(inference)	8. Why can we call Dr. Goddard a pioneer? (He was the first person to do scientific rocket experiments.)	10
(main idea)	9. What is the main idea of the story? (Dr. Goddard's dream of launching a rocket using liquid fuel was realized.)	10
(word meaning)	10. What does *launch* mean? (To set in motion, to release or send off.)	10

Scoring Scale

Levels	*Comprehension Errors*
Independent	0–10 pts.
Instructional	11–25 pts.
Frustration	50 pts. or more

6

ORAL READING (276 WORDS)[20]

Introduction: You will be reading a story about archaeology. Then I will ask you questions about the story.

Almost with the first spade that was thrust into the earth, Arthur Evans shot back ten thousand years. When he realized that there was such wealth to be found in the earth, he gathered together a skilled team. The team changed often with the passing years, but there were always people with special knowledge of geology, art, architecture, and other fields to work with him.

A series of test pits were dug at different places on the site of the mound. The layers of earth in these pits could be read like a book by trained geologists. They would slowly be able to figure out how the layers were formed, why they differed from each other, and what natural and human events accounted for the changes.

The test pits told an astounding story. They showed immediately that the mound Evans had observed was artificial. The pits led Evans to believe that the site of Knossos, capital of Minos, had been continuously occupied for at least ten thousand years! The task at hand would not be to dig into the earth, but to peel back layers that had been built up by people for thousands of years.

The top layers of the pits, at a few feet below the surface, revealed objects of brilliant workmanship. Going on down the pit, other layers gave up pottery and utensils belonging to earlier periods. The items resembled objects painted on the walls of tombs and temples in Egypt. Since the ancient Egyptians left many dates and records, an approximate date for the pottery unearthed at Knossos could be found by comparing it with the pottery in the Egyptian wall paintings.

Comprehension Questions

		Points
(fact)	1. How far back in time was Arthur Evans thrust with his first spade into the earth? (Ten thousand years.)	10
(fact)	2. What kind of special knowledge did the team Arthur Evans gathered together have? (Geology, art, architecture, and other fields.)	10
(fact)	3. What were dug at different places? (A series of test pits.)	10
(fact)	4. What did the test pits show? (That the mound Evans had observed was artificial.)	10
(fact)	5. What was the task at hand? (To peel back layers of earth that had been build up by people for thousands of years.)	10
(main idea)	6. What is the main idea of the selection? (The test pits revealed evidence that the site of Knossos may have been occupied for ten thousand years.)	10

[20]Level 15, "Riders on the Earth," *The Holt Basic Reading Series*, pp. 468–69.

(word meaning) 7. Arthur Evans was an archaeologist. What is an archaeologist? (A person who studies past human life through objects from the past.)   10

(word meaning) 8. What does the word *astounding* mean? (Amazing.)   10

(inference) 9. What can we infer about Arthur Evans; that is, what kind of man was he? (Patient—he spent many years working at the site; knowledgeable—almost with the first spade, he realized that there was such wealth to be found in the earth.)   10

(word meaning) 10. What does *geology* mean? (The study of the earth's physical history and makeup.)

Scoring Scale

Levels	Word Recognition Errors	Comprehension Errors
Independent	0–3	0–10 pts.
Instructional	4–14	11–25 pts.
Frustration	28 or more	50 pts. or more

SILENT READING[21]

Introduction: Read this story about something that the archaeologists found. I will be asking you some questions after you finish reading it. Read it carefully.

Year after year of digging revealed a form of architecture which had never been seen before. Wood played an important part in the palace's construction. Once, in the dim past, Crete must have been well wooded. There was no doubt that the palace had been built upon the foundations of earlier structures, because changes from many periods had been made. The materials and techniques of these changes gave important clues to the time they occurred.

As each level was cleared and floors and ceilings propped up, an astounding building of at least five stories was revealed. Great light wells brought illuminaton to the lower levels. These light wells, centrally placed in the building, served to keep out the strong winds of winter.

An incredibly modern way of life became evident. Pushing on, the diggers found that the palace had a servants' quarter, a throne room, storage rooms, and places for worship and bathing. Several altars were discovered, some with traces of offerings and the figurines of gods and goddesses on them. The symbol of the double ax seemed to mark royal property.

When the throne room was being excavated, traces of the outline of a wooden throne was found in what must have been its original position. A copy was made. The throne room in its restored magnificence is breathtaking. A short, crooked corridor leads off this room. It is believed

[21]Ibid., pp. 471–72.

to have led to the queen's apartments. Objects found in this section of the palace suggest that the queen lived in great style and cleanliness.

Comprehension Questions

		Points
(fact)	1. What had the palace been built upon? (The foundations of earlier structures.)	10
(fact)	2. How many stories did the building that was revealed have? (At least five stories.)	10
(fact)	3. How were the archaeologists able to tell the period of time when changes were made in the structure of the palace? (The materials and the techniques gave important clues to the time in which they occurred.)	10
(fact)	4. For what two purposes did the builders of the palace construct great light wells? (To light up the lower levels of the palace and to keep out the strong winter winds.)	10
(fact)	5. What symbol seemed to mark the royal property? (A double ax.)	10
(inference)	6. What led the archaeologists to believe that there were many trees on Crete at the time the palace was built? (Wood was used in the construction of the palace. The throne was made of wood.)	10
(inference)	7. What did the archaeologists find that showed that the people of ancient Crete were very religious? (Altars were discovered. Traces of offerings and figurines of gods and goddesses were found.)	10
(fact)	8. What conclusion did the archaelogists reach about the way of life during that time? (It was amazingly modern.)	10
(word meaning)	9. What is the meaning of *illumination*? (The act of lighting up.)	10
(main idea)	10. What is the main idea of the selection? (Years of digging revealed a modern palace.)	10

Scoring Scale

Levels	*Comprehension Errors*
Independent	0–10 pts.
Instructional	11–25 pts.
Frustration	50 pts. or more

7

ORAL READING (238 WORDS)[22]

Introduction: You will be reading a story about a special convention. Then I will ask you questions about the story.

Seneca Falls was buzzing with excitement. For the next five days the main topic of the villagers' conversation was the woman's rights convention. Why was this happening in sleepy Seneca Falls, they wanted to know, and not in Syracuse or Rochester, or New York, where many conventions were taking place? Their excitement would have been even greater had it occurred to them that Seneca Falls was about to make history—that this was to be the first woman's rights convention ever to be held, not only in the United States but anywhere in the world.

Since the call was unsigned, they wondered who was behind all this, who the women were who organized it. Of one thing they were certain, whoever they might be, their neighbor Elizabeth Cady Stanton was one of them. Everyone in Seneca Falls knew Mrs. Stanton, knew that she held radical views on slavery and other issues. In the last several years she had been agitating for the Married Woman's Property Bill which had been passed in April of that year. Yes, she was probably the ringleader of it all.

The villagers guessed right. Elizabeth Cady Stanton was the primer mover of the forthcoming convention, but she was not the only mover. There was the well-known Quaker Lucretia Mott, and her sister, Martha C. Wright, and Mary Ann McClintock, and a woman named Jane Hunt, all busily working to make this convention a success.

Comprehension Questions

Points

(fact)   1. What caused the excitement in the village of Seneca Falls? (The prospect of the woman's rights convention.)   10

(fact)   2. Does the author feel that Seneca Falls was a likely place to hold the convention? Find details in the selection to support your answer. (No. The author describes Seneca Falls as "sleepy"—a quiet, unassuming place unlike the cities of Syracuse, Rochester, and New York which were more usual sites for conventions.)   10

(inference)   3. To what animal sound does the author compare the talk about the convention? (A bee buzzing.)   10

(inference)   4. What does the sound of a buzzing bee signify? (The sound of a buzzing bee gives the impression of much activity and animated talk.)   10

(inference)   5. Why did the villagers suspect that Elizabeth Stanton was one of the convention's organizers? (They knew she held radical

[22]Level 16, "To See Ourselves," *The Holt Basic Reading Series,* p. 544–45.

views on many issues and had worked for other women's causes.)   10

(fact)   6. Who besides Elizabeth Stanton were involved in organizing the convention? (Lucretia Mott, Martha Wright, Mary Ann Mc-Clintock, and Jane Hunt.)   10

(fact)   7. How many woman's rights conventions had preceded the one at Seneca Falls? Use the selection to support your answer. (None. This was the first woman's rights convention ever to be held not only in the United States but anywhere in the world.)   10

(word meaning)   8. What does *radical* mean? (Extreme, departing from the traditional.)   10

(main idea)   9. What is the main idea of the selection? (The first woman's rights convention was held in Seneca Falls.)   10

(word meaning)   10. What is a *prime mover*? (The person responsible for organizing something.)   10

Scoring Scale

Levels	Word Recognition Errors	Comprehension Errors
Independent	0–2	0–10 pts.
Instructional	3–12	11–25 pts.
Frustration	24 or more	50 pts. or more

SILENT READING[23]

Introduction: Read this story about a special convention. I will be asking you some questions after you finish reading it. Read it carefully.

When the women delegates presented their credentials at Freemason's Hall, the convention leaders refused to honor them on the grounds of their sex. The American male delegates protested. So did the women, of course. But the leaders were adamant. This precipitated a stormy debate in the hall. It was so stormy that one eyewitness described it in this way. "The excitement and vehemence of protest and denunciation could not have been greater if the news had come that the French were about to invade England."

The debate took up a lot of the convention's time, and when the question was finally put to a vote, the overwhelming majority voted against seating the women. They could remain at the convention, but only as spectators. They were obliged to take their seats in the gallery, "behind a bar and a curtain." Lucretia Mott and Elizabeth Cady Stanton sat next to each other.

William Lloyd Garrison was delayed in transit and arrived late at Freemason's Hall. When he saw what had happened to the women delegates, he refused to participate in the convention. To

[23]Ibid., pp. 546.

make his protest even more dramatic, he joined the women in the gallery. This was very embarrassing to the convention. After all, Mr. Garrison was the foremost American abolitionist and he was to have delivered a major address at this world gathering. Yet there he was, sitting up in the gallery, a silent spectator. The leaders sent up messengers to the gallery, pleading with him to come down. Every time his name was mentioned the entire convention rose to its feet and applauded. But Garrison would not come down. As long as the convention refused to seat the women properly, he would remain with them in the gallery.

Comprehension Questions

		Points
(fact)	1. Why were the women delegates refused entrance? (Because of their sex.)	10
(fact)	2. What was the reaction to the refusal to let women take part in the convention proceedings? (American male and female delegates protested.)	10
(fact)	3. Why did William Lloyd Garrison sit in the gallery with the women? (To make his protest more dramatic because he wanted the women to be properly seated.)	10
(word meaning)	4. What does *adamant* mean? (Firm and unyielding to pressure.)	10
(word meaning)	5. What does *precipitated* mean? (Caused or produced.)	10
(main idea)	6. What is the main idea of the selection? (Convention leaders refused to allow women delegates to participate actively in the convention.)	10
(inference)	7. What can we infer about the status of women from reading this selection? (They were not treated as first-class citizens.)	10
(word meaning)	8. What does *gallery* mean? (The highest balcony in a theater usually having the cheapest seats.)	10
(fact)	9. What was William Lloyd Garrison known as? (The foremost American abolitionist.)	10
(word meaning)	10. What is an *abolitionist*? (One who favors the doing away of slavery.)	10

Scoring Scale

Levels	*Comprehension Errors*
Independent	0–10 pts.
Instructional	11–25 pts.
Frustration	50 pts. or more

8

ORAL READING (248 WORDS)[24]

Introduction: You will be reading a story about a special whale expedition. Than I will ask you questions about the story.

In 1973, an expedition from the Fisheries Research Board of Canada, led by Dr. Michael Biggs and Dr. Ian McCaskie, conducted a thorough, month-long,* study of the population, following pods of whales around all day, every day, sometimes both day and night, taking thousands of photographs and getting a good idea of the daily routine of the whales. They used two sailboats to track the whales, and occasionally an aircraft to observe them from the air.

A second expedition, by Jim Hunter and Grahme Ellis, with still photography as its prime purpose, used a rubber boat to follow pods of whales around. They established a whale-watching post on Parson's Island.

Like the whales, they spent a good deal of time fishing for salmon, successfully! They had the experience of gradually being allowed to approach closer and closer to pods in their motor-powered craft, until eventually they were admitted to their midst, making delightful contact with the whales, taking thousands of photographs, and making many useful observations. Entering the water in the proximity of the group of whales called Stubb's pod, Grahme Ellis had an incredible experience as a young male swam in a tight circle around him, close enough so that Grahme could determine the sex of the whale and see the shape of his white head patch. The following day the same whale made a close approach to a rowboat Grahme was in, circling it several times. Grahme was literally shining after these experiences!

Comprehension Questions

		Points
(fact)	1. The expedition from Canada's Fisheries Research Board led by Drs. Biggs and McCaskie lasted for how long? (One month.)	10
(fact)	2. What was one of the goals of the expedition? (To get a good idea of the daily routine of whales.)	10
(fact)	3. In what year did Drs. Biggs and McCaskie lead their expedition? (1973.)	10
(fact)	4. For what purpose did the expedition use sailboats and aircraft? (To track the whales.)	10
(fact)	5. What was the purpose of the Hunter-Ellis expedition? (Taking still photographs.)	10
(fact)	6. What was the reaction of the whales to the presence of the men? Were they hostile, or totally accepting? Support your	

[24]Level 17, "Great Waves Breaking," *The Holt Basic Reading Series*, pp. 128–29.
* Hyphenated words in this passage are counted as two words.

answer with details from the selection. (The men were gradually allowed to approach closer and closer to pods until they were admitted to their midst.) 10

(inference) 7. How do we know Ellis behaved as a scientist when a young male whale swam in a tight circle around him? (He used the encounters to make first-hand observations about the whale; that is, he reacted as a scientist would.) 10

(fact) 8. What did the whales and the expedition by Jim Hunter and Grahme Ellis have in common? (They both spent time fishing for salmon successfully.) 10

(word meaning) 9. What does *proximity* mean? (Closeness.) 10

(main idea) 10. What is the main idea of the selection? (An expedition conducted a thorough study of whales through observation.) 10

Scoring Scale

Levels	Word Recognition Errors	Comprehension Errors
Independent	0–3	0–10 pts.
Instructional	4–13	11–25 pts.
Frustration	25 or more	50 pts. or more

SILENT READING[25]

Introduction: Read this story about an expedition. I will be asking you some questions after you finish reading it.

The most outstanding and interesting whale-watching activity of the summer of 1973 was an expedition called Project Apex. It was undertaken by Ocean Life Systems of Victoria, British Columbia. Project Apex was a filmmaking expedition and an experiment in interspecies communication. It succeeded marvelously. It was beyond my expectations. The expedition crew used an engineless sailboat, *The Four Winds*. It was equipped with electronic systems that permitted listening to the whales and projecting sound at them. The crew had an electronic synthesizer that generated imitations of orca sounds. This group of young adventurers sailed from Victoria to the Johnstone Strait early in July, and immediately made contact with orcas. Their work is detailed in a 16mm film called *Orca*. The film is a wonderful statement, the closest glimpse we have yet gained of these creatures. In it is documented the first ever unquestioned communicative exchange between free orcas and humans.

Soon after *The Four Winds* arrived in the Johnstone Strait, a lone adult male orca approached the vessel and emitted a single clearly audible vocalization, which was recorded. Sound-

[25]Ibid., pp. 129–30.

man–musician Erich Hoyt practiced imitating the sound on the synthesizer until he managed an imperfect but adequate imitation. The following day, the same whales were sighted. Erich sent out his imitation orca sound. Immediately, with a latency of only about two seconds, three orcas replied with an exact replication of Erich's imperfect imitation of one of their sounds! It was a remarkable moment! Of course, it was just a glimpse, but nonetheless full of promise.

Comprehension Questions

		Points
(fact)	1. What is the name of the organization that sponsored Project Apex? (Ocean Life Systems.)	10
(fact)	2. Where was the organization located? (Victoria, British Columbia.)	10
(fact)	3. What year did Project Apex take place? (1973.)	10
(fact)	4. What is Project Apex? (A filmmaking expedition and an experiment in interspecies communication.)	10
(fact)	5. What was the outcome of Project Apex? (It succeeded marvelously.)	10
(word meaning)	6. What does *replication* mean? (The act of producing a copy or duplicate.)	10
(fact)	7. What did the film *Orca* show? (Unquestioned communicative exchange between free orcas and humans.)	10
(fact)	8. How did the expedition crew imitate orca sounds? (They used an electronic synthesizer.)	10
(inference)	9. Why did the whale-watching expedition use an engineless sailboat? (The whales or orcas would be frightened by the sound of a motor.)	10
(main idea)	10. What is the main idea of the selection? (A whale-watching expedition is successful in communicating with whales.)	10

Scoring Scale

Levels	*Comprehension Errors*
Independent	0–10 pts.
Instructional	11–25 pts.
Frustration	50 pts. or more

APPENDIX B: The Fry Readability Formula

The Fry Readability Formula is simple and fast to compute. It can be used at the primary grades as well as other grade levels.

Average number of syllables per 100 words

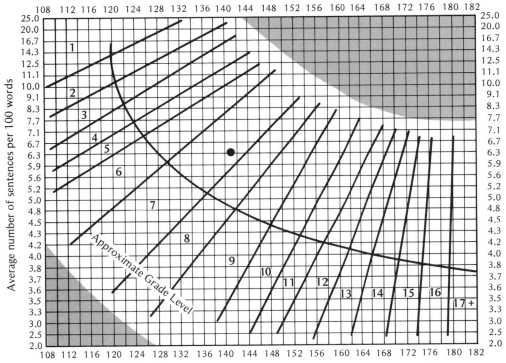

DIRECTIONS: Randomly select 3 one hundred word passages from a book or an article. Plot average number of syllables and average number of sentences per 100 words on graph to determine the grade level of the material. Choose more passages per book if great variability is observed, and conclude that the book has uneven readability. Few books will fall in gray area, but when they do, grade level scores are invalid.

Count proper nouns, numerals, and initializations as words. Count a syllable for each symbol. For example, "1945" is 1 word and 4 syllables and "IRA" is 1 word and 3 syllables.

EXAMPLE:

	SYLLABLES	SENTENCES
1st Hundred Words	124	6.6
2nd Hundred Words	141	5.5
3rd Hundred Words	158	6.8
AVERAGE	141	6.3

READABILITY 7th GRADE (see dot plotted on graph)

Index

Accent, 200–202
Accommodation (Piaget), 36–37
Achievement tests. *See* Tests
Adaptive behavior, 313
Affective domain, 8
   objectives for, 158–159
Affix, 253
American Association on Mental Deficiency (AAMD)
   classification scheme for mental retardation, 313–314
   definition of mental retardation, 313
Analogies
   correction techniques for, 246–247, 248–249
   criterion-referenced tests of, 244–246, 248
   explanation of, 244
   picture relationships and, 244–245
Analysis, 182
Anecdotal records. *See* Observation
Appraisal. *See* Diagnostic pattern
Appreciative reading, 318–319
   definition of, 318
   environment for, 320
   interesting children in, 320–321
   peer role-modeling, 321–322
   television and, 340–341
   time for, 319
   See also Children's literature; Sustained silent reading
Assimilation (Piaget), 36–37
Auding, 64, 65–66
   See also Listening
Audiometer, 64
Auditory acuity, 64
   teacher observation of, 64–65

Auditory discrimination, 62–63, 71–72, 151–153, 191–192
Auditory fatigue, 65
Auditory memory. *See* Memory span
Auditory perception. *See* Listening
"Average" children. *See* Individual differences

Base. *See* Root
Beginning reading readiness, 104
Behavioral objectives, 157–159
Betts, Emmett A., 112
Betts Reading Levels, 112–114
Bibliotherapy, 334–338, 339
Bilingualism, 49
Binaural considerations, 65
Birth order, 48
Bloom, B. S., 157–158
Bond and Tinker. *See* Reading expectancy formulas
Book selection. *See* Children's literature
Borderline children. *See* Individual differences
Botel Reading Inventory, 146, 147
Breve, 201
Brown-Carlsen Listening Comprehension Test, 73
Buros, Oscar. *See Mental Measurements Yearbooks*

California Achievement Tests, 100, 101, 104
California Short-Form Test of Mental Maturity, 86
Categorizing
   correction techniques for, 239–240, 242–243
   criterion-referenced tests of, 238–239, 241–242
   explanation of, 237–238
   See also Outlining; Semantic mapping; Sets and
      outlining

Central idea of a group of paragraphs
    correction techniques for, 231
    criterion-referenced tests of, 227–228, 229–230
    explanation of, 226
    See also Main idea
Children's literature
    black children and, 333–334
    child development and, 322, 323–329
    children's interest and, 322
    criteria for book selection, 332
    culturally different children and, 332–333
    diagnostic checklist for, 341–342
    readability and interest levels in, 338, 340
    sex differences and, 322, 330–332
    See also Appreciative reading; Bibliotherapy
CIRCUS, 73, 105
Classification. *See* Categorizing; Outlining
Closed syllable. *See* Syllable
Cloze procedure, 159–163
    reading levels scale for, 160
Clymer-Barrett Prereading Battery, 105
Cognitive Abilities Test, 86–87
Cognitive development, 9–10
    concepts and, 36–37
    See also Reading comprehension
Cognitive domain, 9–10
    objectives in, 158, 159
Combining forms, 253
    instruction in, 253–255
    list of, 255
Communication, 5
Comparison/contrasts, 219–220
Compound words, 253
Comprehension. *See* Reading comprehension
Comprehensive Tests of Basic Skills, 101, 104
Computer-aided instruction
    reading and, 303–304
Concentration. *See* Listening; Studying
Concept
    defining, 35–36
Concept development, 33–35
    educationally disadvantaged child and, 44
    informal inventory of, 40–43
    instruction and, 37–38
    language development and, 34
    outlining and, 38–39
    Piaget and, 36–37
    in primary grades, 39–40
    See also Semantic mapping
Configuration, 185–186

Consonant blends (clusters), 191, 193–194
Consonant clusters (blends), 191, 193
Consonant digraphs, 191, 194
Consonants, 191, 192–193
Content areas
    diagnosis and correction in, 136, 249
    vocabulary expansion and, 256, 259–260
Context clues, 182–183, 184
    correction techniques for, 221–222, 224–225
    criterion-referenced tests of, 220–221, 222–224
    explanation of, 219–220
    See also Homographs
Corrective reading, 6
Creative problem-solving, 64, 337
Creative reading. *See* Reading comprehension
Criterion-referenced tests, 25–26
    behavioral objectives and, 157–159
    examples of, 149–151
    norm-referenced tests and, 102
    standardized, 149
    teacher-made, 157
Critical listening, 64, 209
Critical reading. *See* Reading comprehension
Crossed dominance, 56–57
Culturally different children. *See* Children's literature

Decoding, 62, 67, 186
Derivatives, 253
Detroit Tests of Learning Aptitude, 73
    Oral Directions Test, 74–76
Developmental reading, 6–7
Diacritical marks, 201
Diagnosis
    defining, 10–11
    principles of, 11
    relation to definition of reading, 11
Diagnostic pattern, 81–82
    appraisal in a, 82
        formula for, 93–94
    diagnosis in a, 82
    identification in a, 82, 100
Diagnostic-reading and correction program
    defining, 6
    scenarios in, 292–300
    teacher's role in, 14
    See also Teacher
Diagnostic reading tests
    defining, 109
Dialect, 49
Dictionary, 183, 185, 280

Digit span, 63
  scale, 269
  tests, 154–156
  See also Memory span
Digraphs. *See* Consonant digraphs; Vowel
Diphthongs, 197
Disabled reader, 82
Divergent thinking, 209, 210
*Doren Diagnostic Reading Test of Word Recognition
    Skills,* 147
Durkin, Dolores, 209
Durrell Analysis of Reading Difficulties, 73, 147
  Checklist of Instructional Needs, 148
Durrell Listening-Reading Series, 73

Educable mentally retarded, 314–315
Educational factors, 58
  defining, 47
Educationally disadvantaged children, 44
  See also Title I
Elementary School Library Collection, 336, 338
English as a Second Language. *See* Teaching English as a
    Second Language
Evaluation, 20–21
Exceptional children, 313–314

Facts and opinion, 209
Family composition, 48
Final *e* rule, 196, 197, 198
Flesch, Rudolf, 347–348
Following directions. *See* Studying
Fry, Edward. *See* Readability formula
Frustration reading level, 112, 113

Gallup Poll
  reading and, 350, 354–355
Gates-MacGinitie Readiness Skills Test, 103, 105
Gates-MacGinitie Reading Tests, 101
Gates/McKillop/Horowitz Reading Diagnostic Tests,
    146–147
Gifted children. *See* Individual differences
Gilmore Oral Reading Test, 145–146
Goodman, Kenneth, 138
Grapheme-phoneme relationship (correspondence), 67,
    182, 186
Graphemic base. *See* Phonogram
Gray Oral Reading Tests, 146
Great Books Foundation, 352
Group tests. *See* Tests

Harris and Sipay. *See* Reading expectancy formulas
Hearing, 64
Henmon-Nelson Tests of Mental Ability, 87
Home environment, 48
Homographs
  accenting and, 201
  correction techniques for, 215–216, 217–219
  criterion-referenced tests of, 214–215, 216–217
  explanation of, 213, 214
  See also Context clues
Homonyms (homophones), 213–214

Independent reading level, 112–113
Individual differences
  "average" children, 308
  borderline (slow-learning) children, 308–309
    reading and, 309–310
  gifted children, 310–311
    reading and, 311–312
  mental age comparison, 89
  mental age span, 87, 89
  See also Exceptional children; Learning disabilities;
    Mainstreaming; Mental age
Individual Pupil Monitoring System—Reading, 149, 150
Individualizing instruction, 300
  commercially produced programs, 301
  common characteristics of, 301
  common sense about, 301
  teacher-made programs, 300–301
  See also Computer-aided instruction; Learning centers;
    Reading management systems
Inference
  correction techniques for, 234–235, 237
  criterion-referenced tests of, 232–234, 235–237
  explanation of, 231–232
Informal interviews, 171
Informal reading inventory
  administering, 121–133
  buffer zone of, 114
  candidates for, 93–94, 130, 134–135, 292–293, 296–297
  cautions about, 138–141
  commercially produced, 130
  constructing, 114–117
  diagnostic checklist for, 120–121
  example of, 367–408
  graded passages, 115–117
  graded word lists, 114–115
    sample size for, 115
  modified, 135–136
  overview of, 111–112

Informal reading inventory (*cont.*)
  reading levels of, 112–114, 139–140
  scoring
    comprehension, 141
    oral reading, 117–118, 140–141
      formulas for, 119–120
  See also Miscue analysis; Word lists
Instructional reading level, 112, 113
Instructional time, 16
  See also Reading comprehension
Intelligence, 82–83
  defining, 83
  language development and, 34–35
  nature-nurture controversy, 83
  reading and, 50–51
  See also Individual differences; IQ tests; Mental age
IQ tests, 83, 170
  group, 84
    examples of, 86–87
  individual, 84
    examples of, 84–86
Interest inventories, 171–174
Iowa Silent Reading Tests, 100
Iowa Tests of Basic Skills, 101
IOX Objectives-Based Tests Collection: Reading, 151

Jabberwocky, 62
Judge Joiner, 49
Junior Great Books Program, 352

Keystone Visual Survey Tests, 54
Kuhlmann-Anderson Intelligence Test, 87

Language arts, 61
Language development, 34–35
Language differences, 49–50
  See also Culturally different children; Nonstandard English
Laterality and reading, 56–57
Learning centers, 301–302
  designing, 302–303
  multimedia in, 303
Learning disabilities, 315
Left-handed children and reading, 56–57
Left-right orientation, 56–57
Library, school, 278
  See also Reference books
Library skills, 279–280
Listening
  comprehension, 65–66, 94

Listening (*cont.*)
  concentration, 65
  as decoding, 62, 67
  development of, 68–69
  diagnostic checklist of, 77–78
  levels of, 64–66
  reading and, 66–68
  nonstandard English and, 69–72
  teacher assessment of, 72–73
  standardized tests of, 73–76
  See also Auding; Auditory discrimination; Studying
Listening capacity, 64, 72–73, 124, 192
Listening capacity level, 112, 113–114
Listening capacity test, 94, 124–125
Locator tests, 102
Look-and-say method. *See* Whole-word method
Lorge-Thorndike Intelligence Tests, 87

Macron, 201
Main idea of a paragraph
  correction techniques for, 228–229, 231, 295–296
  criterion-referenced tests of, 227, 229
  explanation of, 225–226
  See also Central idea of a group of paragraphs; Studying; Summaries
Mainstreaming, 312–313
Management systems, reading, 304–305
Masking, 65
Measurement, 21
Memory span, 63
Mental age, 87, 89
Mental age span, 87, 89
Mental Measurements Yearbooks (Buros), 24–25
Mental retardation, 313–314
  adaptive behavior and, 313
Metropolitan Achievement Tests, 100, 101–102
Metropolitan Readiness Tests, 103, 105
Miscue analysis, 137–138
Mixed dominance, 56–57
Modified informal reading inventory approaches, 135–136
Morpheme, 62
Motivation, 83
Multiple meanings. *See* Homographs
Murphy-Durrell Reading Readiness Analysis, 103, 105

Noneducational factors
  defining, 47
Nonstandard English, 49–50
  attitudes toward, 49–50
  auditory discrimination and, 71–72

Nonstandard English (*cont.*)
  defining, 49
  listening and, 69
  oral language program and, 72
  reading and, 70
  speech and, 69–70
  spelling and, 70
  See also Teaching English as a Second Language
Norm-referenced tests, 23, 102
Notetaking. *See* Studying
Nutrition and learning, 57–58

Observation
  anecdotal records and, 166–168
  checklists and, 168–170
  uses of, 166
Open syllable. *See* Syllable
Oral language. *See* Nonstandard English
Oral reading, 110
  See also Informal reading inventory
Oral reading tests, 145
  examples of, 145–146
  See also Informal reading inventory
Ortho-Rater, 54–55
Otis-Lennon Mental Ability Test, 87
Outlining, 271–274
Overlearning, 265, 309

Parental involvement, 346–347
  basal reader series and, 352–353
  grandparents and, 355–356
  preschool programs and, 350–351
  regular reading program and, 351–352
  schools and, 347–348
  success of, 353–355
  See also Gallup Poll; Parent-teacher conference; Title I
Parent-teacher conference, 356–357
Peer instruction, 305–306
Peer role-modeling, 321–322
  television and, 340–341
Perceptual domain, 8–9
Perceptual factors, 54
  See also Auditory perception; Visual perception; Laterality and reading
Phonemes, 62
Phonic analysis and synthesis, 182, 186–187
Phonics
  defining, 186
  developmental sequence of, 187, 191–202

Phonics (*cont.*)
  learning skills of, 186–190
  See also Syllabication
Phonogram (graphemic base), 199
Physical health and reading, 57–58
Piaget, 36–37, 68
Picture relationships, 244–245
Practice tests, 102
Prefix, 253, 255
PRI Reading Systems, 73, 149
  Individual Diagnostic Map, 150
Projective techniques, 170, 174–175
Propaganda, 209
Proximodistal development, 56
Psycholinguistics, 138
Public Law 94–142, 307, 312
Published tests. *See* Standardized tests

Questioning techniques. *See* Reading comprehension; Studying

Readability and interest levels, 338, 340
Readability formula (Fry), 409
Readers' Guide to Periodical Literature, 280
Reading
  decoding and, 7–8, 67, 186
  defining, 7–10
  early years and, 13, 34–35
  process, 8–10
    affective domain, 8
    cognitive domain, 9–10
    perceptual domain, 8–9
Reading autobiography, 175–177
Reading comprehension
  acquiring skills in, 209–211
  categorizing
    creative, 209
    critical, 208–209
    interpretive, 208
    literal, 208
  defining, 207
  diagnosis and correction in, 212–249
  diagnostic checklist of, 250
  questioning and, 211–212
  skills, 207
  time spent in, 209
  See also Content areas; Vocabulary expansion
Reading expectancy formulas, 82, 89–93
Reading expectancy quotient, 93–94
Reading management systems. *See* Management systems

Reading readiness. *See* Beginning reading readiness
Reading readiness tests, 103–105
Record-keeping, 293–294
Reference books, 279–280
Reliability, 21, 22–23
Remedial reading, 6
Reversals, 56–57
Roget's Thesaurus of English Words and Phrases, 280
Role playing, 337
Root (base), 253
Russell, David, 335

Scenarios, 1–2, 256, 259–260, 292–300
   See also Teacher
Schwa, 199, 200, 201
Self-fulfilling prophecy, 16
Semantic clues, 184, 213
Semantic mapping, 38
Sequential Tests of Educational Progress, 73, 102
Sesame Street, 341
Sets and outlining, 38–39, 271–272
Sex differences, 51–54
   reading and, 52–54
   See also Children's literature
Shrodes, Carolyn, 335
Sight method. *See* Whole-word method
Silent consonants, 194
Skimming, 271
Slow learner. *See* Individual differences
Socioeconomic status and reading, 48
Sociogram, 305
Special letters and sounds, 198–199
Special reading teacher, 6
SQ3R. *See* Studying
SRA Achievement Series, 102
Standard English, 49
Standardized tests, 23–24
   achievement, 100, 101–102
   classification of, 24
   teacher selection of, 24–25
   See also IQ tests; Listening; Oral reading tests; Tests
Stanford Achievement Tests, 100, 102
Stanford-Binet Intelligence Scale, 85–86
Stanford Diagnostic Reading Test, 147, 149
Structural analysis, 183, 184–185
   See also Word parts
Student previews, 102–103
Studying
   building good habits in, 264–265
   concentration and, 267–269

Studying (*cont.*)
   diagnostic checklist for, 280–286
   following directions and, 269–271
   main idea and, 267, 274
   notetaking and, 276–277
   procedures for, 264
   question asking and, 275–276
   SQ3R and, 266–267
   summaries and, 274
   textbook reading and, 266–267, 274–275
   See also Outlining; Reference books; Skimming; Test-taking
Suffix, 253, 255
Summaries. *See* Studying
Survey battery, 24
Survey reading tests, 100
Sustained silent reading, 319
Syllabication, 199
   accenting and, 200–202
   phonics and, 200
   rules, 199–200
Syllable
   closed, 200
   defining, 199
   open, 200
   unaccented, 200, 201
Syntactic clues, 184, 213
Synthesis, 182

Teacher
   characteristics, 15–16, 20
   as classroom manager, 17–18
   expectancy, 16
   key person, 14–15
   planning, 16–17
   scenarios, 17–18
   See also Diagnostic-reading and correction program
Teacher-made tests. *See* Tests
Teaching English as a Second Language, 69–72
Tests
   achievement, 100, 170
   criteria for, 21–22
   group, 26, 28
   individual, 26, 28
   teacher-made, 25, 151–157
   tree diagram of, 27
   See also Reading readiness tests; Standardized tests
Test-taking, 277–278
   See also Studying
Textbook reading. *See* Studying

Through the Looking Glass, 5, 62
Title I, 348–349
  parental involvement in, 349–350

Underachiever, 82

Validity, 21, 22
Vision, symptoms of problems, 55
Visual discrimination
  defining, 55
  tests, 55–56, 153–154, 192
Visual perception, 54
Vocabulary and literature, 251
Vocabulary consciousness, 252
Vocabulary expansion, 249–260
  intermediate-grade level, 252–256
    diagnostic checklist for, 258
    dictionary skills, 255–256
  primary-grade level, 251–252
    diagnostic checklist for, 256–257
    dictionary skills, 252

Vowel
  controlled by *r*, 197
  digraphs, 197
  generalizations, 197
  sounds, 194–197

*Wechsler Intelligence Scale for Children, Revised
  (WISC-R),* 63, 84–85
Wepman Auditory Discrimination Test, 63
Whole-word method, 182
Woodcock Reading Mastery Tests, 151
Word analysis tests, 156–157
Word lists, 136
  examples of, 136–137
Word parts, 253–255
Work recognition
  defining, 181
  diagnostic checklist for, 202–204
  pronunciation strategies, 182–183
  word meaning strategies, 184–186
  See also Context clues; Decoding; Phonics
Word relationships. *See* Analogies